HANGERS AND FASTENERS

TYPE	CHARACTERISTICS
Plastic anchors 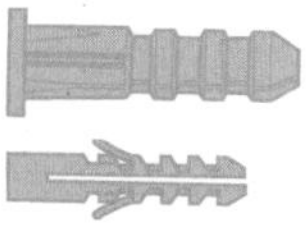	These are good for holding moderate loads on drywall and plaster. They also work well for ceramic tile and masonry. Drill a pilot hole to install.
Plastic anchors (hammer-driven type) 	These are good for holding light loads on drywall and plaster, and also suited for holding very light loads on ceilings. They are used with screws. Tap into wall with hammer.
Fiber anchors or shields 	These are good for holding light loads on drywall and plaster, and also moderate loads on masonry and ceramic tile. They are used with screws. Remains permanently installed in wall.
Lead or alloy anchors or shields 	These are sized to match the diameter of a lag bolt or screw; they are designed to support heavy loads on masonry and concrete surfaces.
Expansion anchors (sleeve type) 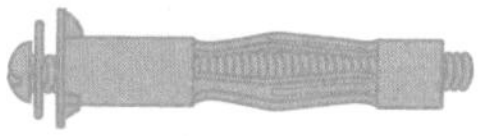	These are good for holding moderate loads on drywall, plaster, ceramic tile and concrete block. They are available in four sizes for different thicknesses of wall: ¼ in., ⅛ to ⅝ in., ⅝ to 1¼ in., and 1¼ to 1¾ in. Sleeve remains in wall once screw is removed.
Expansion anchors (sleeveless type) 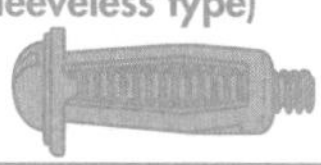	These are good for holding light loads on drywall, plaster, ceramic tile and concrete block. They are available in four sizes for different thicknesses of wall: ¼ in., 1⅛ to ⅝ in., ⅝ to 1¼ in., and 1¼ to 1¾ in. They must penetrate hollow cavity.
Expansion anchors (hammer-driven type) 	These come with a sleeve in four common sizes for different sizes ranging from 1¼ to 1¾ in. They are ideal for holding light loads on drywall and plaster, as well as for holding light loads on a ceiling.

SCREWS

TYPE	CHARACTERISTICS
Lag bolt (lag screw) 	Usually available in lengths from 1 in. to 12 in.; diameters from ¼ to ¾ in. Most common head shapes: hex; square. Thick, threaded shank provides greater strength and holding power than wood or masonry screw.
Drywall screw 	Usually available in diameter (gauge) ranges: No. 6 in lengths from 1 in. to 2¼ in.; No. 8 in lengths of 2½ or 3 in.; No. 10 in lengths of 3¾ in. Head flat; bugle-shaped.
Type A sheet metal screw 	Usually available in lengths from ¼ in. to 3 in; diameters from No. 2 to No. 14 (gauges) and of ⁵⁄₁₆ and ⅜ in. Most common head shapes: flat; pan; round; hex.
Type F sheet metal screw 	Usually available in lengths from ³⁄₁₆ inch to 3 inches; diameters from No. 4 to No. 10 (gauges) and of ¼, ⁵⁄₁₆ and ⅜ inch. Most common head shapes: flat; pan; round; hex.
Masonry screw 	Usually available in lengths from 1¼ to 4 in.; diameters No. 12 and No. 14 (gauges) (³⁄₁₆ and ¼ in.). Most common head shapes: flat for countersinking and concealing; hex-washer for easy removal.
One-way high-security screw 	Usually available in lengths from ½ in. to 3 in.; diameters from No. 4 to No. 14 (gauges) (⅛ to ¼ in.). Head design permits screw to be tightened, not removed.

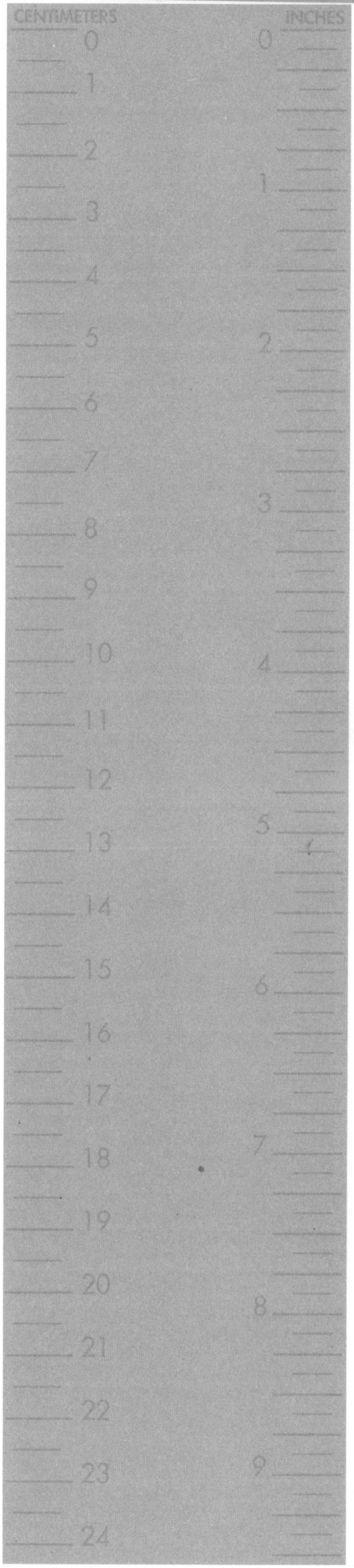

HOME
ANSWER
BOOK

Popular Mechanics

HOME ANSWER BOOK

Edited by
Steven Willson

Foreword by
Joe Oldham

HEARST BOOKS
NEW YORK

POPULAR MECHANICS HOME ANSWER BOOK

Library of Congress Cataloging-in-Publications Data
Popular mechanics: home answer book
p. cm.
ISBN 0-688-10854-7
1. Dwellings—Maintenance and repair—Amateurs' manuals.
I. Popular mechanics magazine
TH4817.3.P65 1991
643' .7—dc20 91-6938
CIP

Printed in the United States of America

First Edition

1 2 3 4 5 6 7 8 9 10

POPULAR MECHANICS

Editor-in-Chief
Joe Oldham
Home Improvement Editor
Steven Willson
Illustrator
George Retseck
Additional Illustrations
Don Mannes

Produced by ST. REMY PRESS

Publisher
Kenneth Winchester
President
Pierre Léveillé
Editor
Michael Mouland
Art Director
Francine Lemieux

NOTE

Care has been taken to ensure the accuracy of the information of this book. However, because of the changing codes, building regulations and by-laws, the publishers advise that you seek professional advice when undertaking repairs described in this book. The publishers cannot assume any responsibility for loss or damage resulting from reliance solely on the information contained herein.

FOREWORD

For 90 years, readers have turned to *Popular Mechanics* for advice on making their homes more comfortable and for solving some of the problems that arise in the course of home ownership. And every year the editors at *Popular Mechanics* sit down to reflect on what's worked and what hasn't. A large part of our evaluation centers on reader response to the articles and features that appear in the magazine. Our readers are quick to tell us when we do something they like, and judging by the letters that arrive from every corner of the country, we seem to be pleasing a lot of people. So came the idea to compile a "greatest hits" collection of home improvement articles that have appeared recently in the magazine.

Part and parcel of owning a home or, for that matter, renting an apartment is maintaining and enhancing it. And, while some people prefer to hire professionals, many others opt to save time and money by doing the work themselves. This book was created in this spirit. From installing a patio door to replacing an aging water heater, this volume covers a broad range of projects that are of particular interest to our readers. Whether the book inspires you to add extra storage space, or rescues you from a frozen pipe on a holiday weekend when plumbers are hard to come by, you'll find it an indispensable reference packed with easy-to-follow, step-by-step instructions that take the mystery out of home improvement. Should you choose to turn to a professional, the following pages will also decipher the language of contractors, carpenters, plumbers and electricians, while saving you money on the repairs you choose to do yourself. Either way, our goal is to help increase the value of your home while making it a better place in which to live.

Joe Oldham,
Editor-in-Chief
Popular Mechanics

How to invest in YOUR HOME

If a white-knuckle roller-coaster ride in the stock market isn't your idea of sane investing, maybe you should consider putting your money into a solid, familiar investment you can keep track of every day—your home.

Whether you're remodeling a dingy kitchen or bath, adding an extra bedroom or boosting the "curb appeal" of your house by installing attractive new siding and replacement doors and windows, you can often increase the market value of your home by the full amount or more than you spend on a home improvement. And, unlike stocks or bonds, renovating your home pays a valuable extra dividend—the sheer pleasure you and your family get from living in a comfortable house whose decor reflects your personal style. While a recent stock-market meltdown may have increased home remodeling's appeal as an investment, any crash should also warn you to give long and serious thought to what you're planning before embarking on a major improvement project.

More often than not, stock market turmoil of any significant magnitude signals a coming period of economic stagnation or recession—which means you could be affected by Wall Street even if you live on Main Street and don't own a single share of stock.

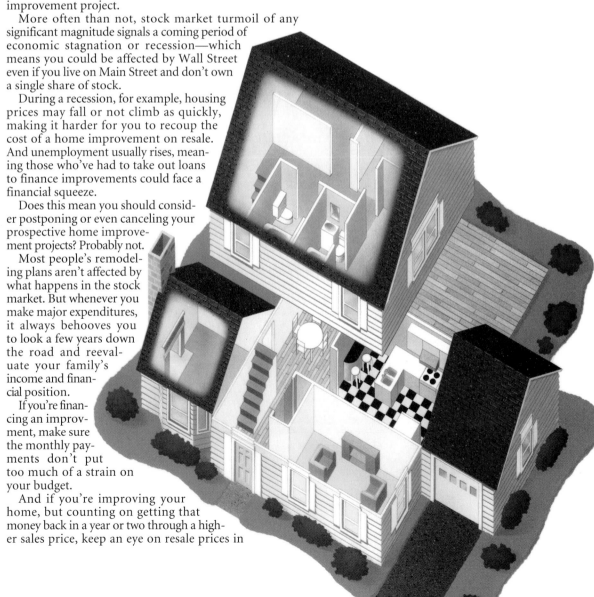

During a recession, for example, housing prices may fall or not climb as quickly, making it harder for you to recoup the cost of a home improvement on resale. And unemployment usually rises, meaning those who've had to take out loans to finance improvements could face a financial squeeze.

Does this mean you should consider postponing or even canceling your prospective home improvement projects? Probably not.

Most people's remodeling plans aren't affected by what happens in the stock market. But whenever you make major expenditures, it always behooves you to look a few years down the road and reevaluate your family's income and financial position.

If you're financing an improvement, make sure the monthly payments don't put too much of a strain on your budget.

And if you're improving your home, but counting on getting that money back in a year or two through a higher sales price, keep an eye on resale prices in your neighborhood. If they're flat or, worse yet, heading south, you might consider scaling down a planned improvement.

Instead of refurbishing your kitchen from ceiling to floorboards, you might settle for less costly touches such as new surfaces on cabinets and countertops, inexpensive flooring and a fresh coat of paint.

Be careful not to confuse improvements with basic maintenance, which includes interior and exterior painting, patching leaks, cleaning gutters and replastering. While these things do not add value to your house, a clean, well-kept house is easier to sell. Realtors estimate that 95 percent of prospective home buyers don't bother to go inside a house that doesn't have curb appeal.

In general, the higher the quality of the materials and workmanship, the higher your return will be. Although exact figures differ somewhat from house to house, neighborhood to neighborhood and region to region, there are definite cost-to-value relationships.

In short, now more than ever it pays to examine the financial side of home remodeling. Otherwise, the rules and guidelines which can help you balance the aesthetic considerations in home remodeling with the economic ones remain pretty much the same. Most important: Don't overimprove.

If you're remodeling for your own comfort and enjoyment, you don't have to worry about what you spend. But if you're doing it as an investment, you want to make sure you don't outprice other houses in your neighborhood.

For example, if you own a house worth $90,000 in a neighborhood where the top houses sell for $100,000 and you sink $50,000 into an elaborate renovation, your chances of getting $140,000 at resale are remote at best. People looking for $140,000 houses don't buy in $100,000 neighborhoods. Make sure the current market value of your house plus planned improvements do not exceed the value of the better houses in your area by 20 percent. That would mean limiting the renovation on a $90,000 house above to about $30,000—tops.

Timing plays an important role, too. People think they'll get their money back immediately. But that's not always true. Sometimes it takes a few years. In general, the longer you stay in your home after remodeling, the better your chances of recovering an improvement's cost.

Unless real estate prices in your town are booming or you've picked up your house at a bargain price, you should be wary of doing a major renovation if you plan to move within 2 years. You'll have little time to enjoy the remodeling yourself and you run the risk that the next buyer won't value the improvement enough to increase his or her bid for the house.

If you think you'll sell your house within 2 years, stick to cosmetic fixups, such as fresh paint inside and out, replacing floor coverings with new but inexpensive ones, and repairing cracked siding and crumbling window sash putty.

Improvements that bring your house up to par with the rest of the neighborhood should earn better returns than those that put you above the crowd. Adding a second bath to a one-bath house almost always returns 100 percent or more of its cost—as does expanding a two-bedroom house to three bedrooms if that's the norm for the neighborhood. But add a third bath or a fourth bedroom and you might recoup only 70 percent or less of your investment.

A local real estate agent should be able to tell you whether your planned improvement is too ritzy for your neighborhood. An agent can also tell you which remodeling projects excite today's home buyers enough to raise their bids and which provoke an ambivalent or even negative reaction to a house.

There's also a new emphasis on architectural design in home renovation. Aesthetics and good design are more important to today's 35- to 40-year-old home buyers. Not only must the individual project be well thought out and executed, but it should also fit in with the rest of the house.

This is especially important in exterior renovations of post-WWII suburban houses. Many such houses were erected quickly without much regard for architectural appeal and now they are being given a contemporary look with new siding, roofs, higher-impact entries and better landscaping. Thus, if you're a bit weak on design skill, it may pay to hire an architect or designer to help plan a major addition.

The quality of work also determines how much value the next buyer places on any improvement—or, in the case of a shoddily done job, how much the buyer actually detracts from his or her bid for the house.

If you don't have the skills of a professional craftsman, hire one. Keeping these guidelines in mind, here's a look at some new trends in the most popular remodeling projects and a run-down on the kinds of returns you can expect to get:

Replacement doors and windows

Replacing weather-beaten doors and windows remains the most popular residential remodeling project. And today's emphasis on high-quality wood or steel doors, unique window designs—such as round-tops, box, bays and clerestories, and technological innovations such as low-emissivity window coatings that increase energy efficiency—seem to be paying off in higher returns. You can expect to recoup as much as 57 percent of this investment now, versus just 40 percent 5 years ago. But the higher quality comes with a heftier price tag: Replacing all exterior doors and windows on a modest house can run from $7000 to $18,000.

Replacing windows and doors with new ones can add a visual appeal while saving on heating costs.

New siding

Installing new siding with insulating board is far less expensive—just over $6000 on average—and can boost your home's resale price by 75 percent to 100 percent of the project's cost. Higher energy efficiency accounts for some of this project's value, but more important is the enhanced curb appeal it gives your home. This makes your house easier to sell and helps it fetch a better price than less attractive houses on the same block.

Vinyl and vinyl-coated aluminum siding remain most popular because they require little maintenance, but owners of more expensive houses may be better off going with natural wood. It's more expensive and, if painted, more difficult to maintain, but it is generally preferred by home buyers at the upper end of the market. When renovating your house's exterior, pay special attention to creating a dramatic entry—for example, a landscaped brick path leading to a carved door flanked by fluted pilasters and topped by a classical pediment. This feature alone can help swing sales negotiations in your favor.

Room addition

Building a 15 x 25-ft. room addition is costly—close to $30,000 on average—and has a relatively modest recovery rate—about 70 percent if you sell within 2 years. But if you like your present location and simply need more space, you're often better off adding a room or even an entire second floor than buying a larger house. To get the best return on resale, make sure the addition blends in with the layout and architectural character of the house. Also, a multipurpose room addition that can be used as a family room, den or guest bedroom, for instance, will do better than one whose use is restricted to a single purpose such as a gym or workshop.

You should try to anticipate not just your own needs, but those of a typical buyer. Popular features now being found in room additions include fireplaces, skylights, cathedral ceilings with exposed beams, and built-in cabinetry for home entertainment centers designed to hold video and audio equipment.

Remodeled kitchen

The kitchen can have more impact on the market value of your house than any other single room. If the kitchen is new and well done, you may hear a sigh of relief from prospective buyers. But if it's in bad shape or has been remodeled on the cheap, you will probably hear them subtracting the cost of redoing it from their bid.

The trend today is toward opening up the kitchen to the living areas and bringing in natural light via skylights, greenhouse or clerestory windows. Sleek, Eurostyle cabinetry—made of either natural wood or high-quality laminates—are still all the rage, as are countertops of granite, marble or durable man-made marble look-alikes such as Colian and Avonite.

The kitchen can have more impact on the market value of your house than any other single room. If a remodeled kitchen is new and well done, potential buyers will be more willing to accept your asking price.

Many renovators are also going to the top of the line in appliances, with refrigerators featuring doors that accommodate panels to match your cabinets and ovens that feature range-top broiling with down-draft exhaust systems.

All this has raised the cost or kitchen renovation to $19,500 on average, while some contractors report doing kitchen makeovers for what a complete house sells for—$100,000 and up. While the returns on this investment are high—75 percent to 90 percent of the project's cost—you're better off from an investing standpoint opting for a medium-cost renovation than an ultra-expensive one. But if a state-of-the-art kitchen is your goal and you're planning to stay in your home for quite a few years, this is definitely the room to enjoy a splurge.

Remodeled bath

With a one-bath house a hard-sell in today's housing market, adding a second full bathroom to a house that has just one is among the best remodeling investments you can make. Getting all your money back at resale is almost guaranteed and you can often recoup as much as 85 percent of the cost—typically between $5600 and $12,900. Remodeling an existing bathroom is comparable in cost—$4500 to $11,500—but doesn't pay off quite as well, recouping about 73 percent of your investment. Opulence is the catchword in bath remodeling today. Whirlpool tubs, separate tubs and shower stalls, skylights and huge windows, imported ceramic tile on walls and floor, color-coordinated fixtures—all have become practically commonplace in the American bathroom during the past 5 years and, as a consequence, have driven up the cost of the average remodeled bath 80 percent.

If your bathroom is small or you think you'll sell your house within the next 2 years, opt for good-quality standard items instead of expensive whirlpools and Italian marble tiles.

If, however, you plan on remaining in your house or enjoy indulging yourself, then feel free to turn your '50s bathroom into an '80s sybaritic pleasure chamber.

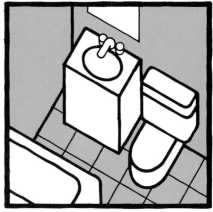

A house with one bathroom is difficult to sell in today's market. Adding a second one is a good investment.

Wood deck

While lumber price increases as high as 30 percent have boosted the cost of a 320-sq.-ft. pressure-treated pine deck to $5300 on average, the entertainment and leisure value of wood decks makes them favorites all over the country. Even in cold climates you can expect to recover 75 percent to 80 percent of your costs on resale and in warmer climates—where the absence of a deck is a minus—decks get even higher returns. New trends include decks with several levels, planks arranged in patterns, privacy walls on one or two sides and use of decks in place of concrete porches. If you want a redwood or cedar deck, you can expect the cost to jump 15 percent to 20 percent.

Fireplace

Its low cost—$2600 to $4000—and high recovery—as much as 140 percent—make a fireplace the best home remodeling investment you can make. The returns on fireplaces are also high in warmer regions like the South and Southwest because people like the notion of the warmth and coziness fireplaces evoke. Many people now put fireplaces in corners to conserve space, while others still prefer a free-standing fireplace in the center of a room.

To allow more flexibility in choosing a place for yours, stick to a "zero clearance" model. The top, sides and bottom remain cool while a fire turns inside, allowing you to install it against any surface.

To avoid air leaks and to ensure your fireplace meets all building and safety codes, proper installation is key. You may want to turn this project over to an experienced building contractor.

Energy savers

Unlike most remodeling projects, energy improvements can begin paying off from the day of installation by lowering fuel bills. Start with the simplest, and cheapest, tasks such as weather stripping around doors and windows, replacing any broken window panes and caulking around window frames.

While you may recoup your investment in warmer climates and in neighborhoods where having a swimming pool is considered almost essential, as an investment pools don't hold much water.

Next, make sure you have adequate insulation in the attic and in crawl spaces. The cost: about $500 to $700, depending on how many square feet you must cover and the necessary R-value, which is a measure of resistance to heat loss in winter and heat gain in summer. Generally, you'll need anywhere from R-22 to R-38. Installing insulation in your home's walls is relatively expensive and may not lower your energy bills enough to justify the cost. Recovery on energy improvements, however, is very difficult to gauge. Home buyers don't get as excited about less visible and unglamorous projects such as new insulation. But keeping receipts showing lower fuel bills might help boost the return on this improvement when it comes time to sell.

Swimming pool

New automatic maintenance equipment has eliminated some of the hassles in owning a pool, but returns are still notoriously low on this investment—30 to 35 percent in cooler climates. Meanwhile, the costs remain high—$19,500 on average, and elaborate pools can cost over $30,000. You might recoup more in warmer climates and in posh neighborhoods where a pool may almost be a necessity for resale. A swimming pool may be a worthy personal indulgence. But viewed as an investment, this project doesn't really hold much water.

Financing home improvements

Finding a loan to finance a remodeling project is relatively easy. Most banks, savings and loan associations and credit unions are willing—make that eager—to lend anywhere from $30,000 to $50,000 for a gut rehab of your kitchen, or to pass out just a few thousand dollars to put a new face on your cabinets.

This chart gives you an idea of the returns you can hope to gain on various projects. Doing some of the work yourself can decrease initial expenditures.

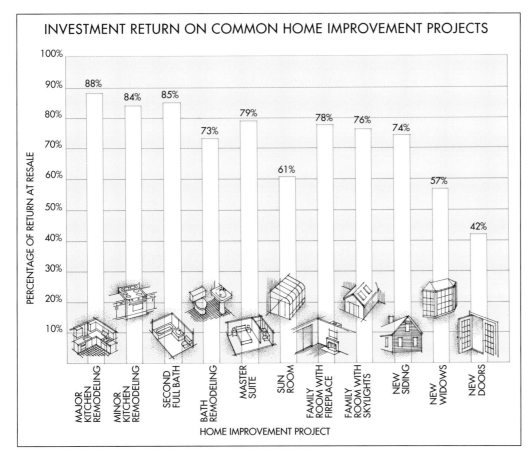

INVESTMENT RETURN ON COMMON HOME IMPROVEMENT PROJECTS

PERCENTAGE OF RETURN AT RESALE

- MAJOR KITCHEN REMODELING — 88%
- MINOR KITCHEN REMODELING — 84%
- SECOND FULL BATH — 85%
- BATH REMODELING — 73%
- MASTER SUITE — 79%
- SUN ROOM — 61%
- FAMILY ROOM WITH FIREPLACE — 78%
- FAMILY ROOM WITH SKYLIGHTS — 76%
- NEW SIDING — 74%
- NEW WIDOWS — 57%
- NEW DOORS — 42%

HOME IMPROVEMENT PROJECT

What's hard, however, is sifting through a lender's ever-growing menu of options—home equity lines of credit, home improvement loans, second mortgages and personal loans—to find what works best for you. You can start narrowing down your choices by examining the tax status of different loans. Under the new tax laws, consumer debt is no longer tax deductible. You can save that valuable tax deduction, though, by sticking to loans such as home equity lines, second mortgages and home improvement loans that are secured by your home. Interest on such loans remains fully deductible provided the total amount of debt on your house doesn't exceed $1 million—not likely to be a problem unless you are Leona Helmsley.

This tax-deductible feature can save you substantial bucks on a large project. During the first year of a $20,000 loan at 12 percent, for example, you will pay $2400 in interest. But if those payments are tax deductible and you're in the 28 percent tax bracket, the after-tax cost of that loan is $1728—a savings of $672, or $56 a month. Your actual savings will probably be greater since tax-advantaged loans typically have lower interest rates than other loans even before taking tax deductions into account.

Of course, you will also want to factor in other considerations, such as ease of getting the loan—does the lender require a detailed financial history from you, how long does it take from application to advancing the funds—and the length of time you have to pay it back. The longer the repayment term, the lower your monthly payments will be, but the interest you pay will be higher.

Even if you have enough money stashed away in savings, you may still want to finance an improvement rather than ante up cash. One reason is that you should always have enough readily available money in savings accounts, certificates of deposit or money-market accounts to carry you through an emergency, such as unexpected medical bills, major car repairs, or an episode of unemployment. Once you spend savings on a home improvement, you can only get that money back by selling your home or borrowing against it.

Here's a quick rundown on the best options for financing home remodeling projects, large and small:

Home equity line of credit
This type of loan has become increasingly popular in recent years for all kinds of borrowing because it offers the best combination of low interest rates, flexible repayment schedules and tax-advantaged status. Though there are an unnerving number of variations, once you cut through the flash and dash, the underlying principle is the same: The lender establishes a line of credit against the equity in your home, and you borrow against it as you need it. To figure out how large a line you qualify for, the lender appraises your house to establish its market value, takes up to 80 percent of that amount and then subtracts your home mortgage. Thus, if your house is worth $200,000, and you have a $60,000 first mortgage, you may very well qualify for a line of credit as high as $100,000.

You can usually draw on the loan by writing a check or, in some cases, by using a credit card linked to your home equity loan account. The ease of tapping into the line makes it ideal for improvement projects that may involve many payments to suppliers and contractors over a period of several months. Many lenders offer the option of paying interest only for the first 5 years of the loan. After that, you pay off the remaining balance over a period of 10 to 15 years. If you choose, you can pay off the entire balance at any time.

Most home equity lines carry an adjustable interest rate, usually pegged 1 or 2 percentage points above the prime rate. With prime recently at 10 percent, the going rate on these loans is currently 11 percent to 12 percent. You've got to look beyond the interest rate, though, to figure the true cost of your line. Since a home equity line is actually a second mortgage on your home, you must also pay many of the closing costs associated with first mortgages. Such charges—loan origination points, appraisal and application fees, a title search—can add anywhere from several hundred to several thousand dollars to the cost of your loan. Some lenders offer home equity lines with either no or low closing costs—$150 to $300—but they may charge a higher rate—prime plus 2 or 3 percent. If you plan on using your home equity line sparingly, however, you may be better off opting for a line with low initial costs and a slightly higher rate than one where you shell out thousands up-front and save 1 percentage point a year on the rate.

Second mortgage

Like a home equity line, a second mortgage loan is made against the equity in your home—that is, the market value of your house minus your first mortgage. But instead of allowing you to borrow against a line of credit, a second mortgage gives you all your money at once. This means you will be paying interest on the full amount of the loan even if you aren't actually ready to put all the money to work in your remodeling project. Second mortgages come with either a fixed rate or an adjustable rate. Whichever you choose, you will probably pay 2 to 4 percentage points or more above the going rate on a first mortgage—more if you get a second from a consumer finance company rather than a bank. You should expect to pay roughly 13 to 16 percent for a second mortgage. You will also incur the regular closing costs associated with a first mortgage, which can add a few hundred to a few thousand dollars to the cost of the loan. Lenders are less likely to drop or reduce the closing costs with a second mortgage. Repayment terms vary widely, but typically lenders give you 10 to 20 years to pay back a second mortgage.

Home improvement loan

Since the advent of home equity lines, home improvement loans are relegated to small improvement projects—usually under $25,000. But they do have one big advantage: speed. Most lenders can approve them within 2 days and have the money available for you within 2 weeks. Since home equity lines and second mortgages involve title searches and other red tape, it may be 4 to 6 weeks before you can actually tap your loan. Some lenders might want to take a look at the plans for your project before they okay the loan; others will approve the loan with the stipulation that the funds are used only for home improvement. Generally, the rate on a home improvement loan is about the same as that for a second mortgage, but the repayment term is usually shorter, 5 to 10 years—which means the monthly payments are higher. You can borrow up to $15,000 and comfortably spread the payments over 15 years, however, by dealing with a lender who offers home improvement loans insured by the Federal Housing Administration's Title I program. Since these loans are guaranteed by the United States Government, lenders consider them less risky and, therefore, you stand a chance of getting a better rate than with a regular home improvement loan. One caveat: Not all home improvement loans are actually secured by your home. The interest payments are fully tax deductible only if the lender has actually recorded a lien against your house.

Take a close look at the tax status for the type of financing you choose when remodeling. Some options are better than others.

Personal loans

Like home improvement loans, personal loans offered by banks, savings and loan associations and credit unions are a quick way to drum up cash. With sufficient income and a solid credit rating, you can get a loan of $5000 to $25,000 within a week or so. But personal loans have several disadvantages; none of the interest is tax deductible. Repayment terms are a short 3 years or so, which makes for high monthly payments. Also, unless you have a savings account or certificate of deposit to offer as collateral, you will usually pay a much higher rate than for home improvement loans, second mortgages and home equity lines. Today, lenders often charge 16 percent or more for unsecured personal loans. Given these shortcomings, you should only turn to this option if you need the money right away, plan to pay it off very quickly or you need cash not just for home improvements, but for other purposes as well.

Credit cards

For low-cost projects—say, $2000 or less—you can opt for the sheer convenience of plastic. By charging building materials to your credit card, or paying for them with a cash advance against your card, you get instant cash without the hassle of loan applications. And you have the option of paying the balance off all at once—or stringing it out over several years by making the minimum monthly payment. Convenience does have its price: None of the interest you pay on credit-card debt is tax deductible and the average interest rate on credit cards is a near usurious 19 percent. Unless you enjoy fattening lenders' coffers, avoid this expensive option for all but the smallest of home improvement projects.

Once set on a project, you must decide whether you are going to do it yourself or hire a professional. Naturally, the more work you can do yourself, the more you'll save on labor costs and the better the return will be on your financial investment. If you don't have the tools or know-how, then you'll have to hire someone to do the work for you. Of course, we at *Popular Mechanics* hope you'll be doing as much of the work as possible, not only to get a good return on your investment, in the form of sweat equity in your home, but in personal satisfaction as well.

PLUMBING, HEATING & VENTILATION 1

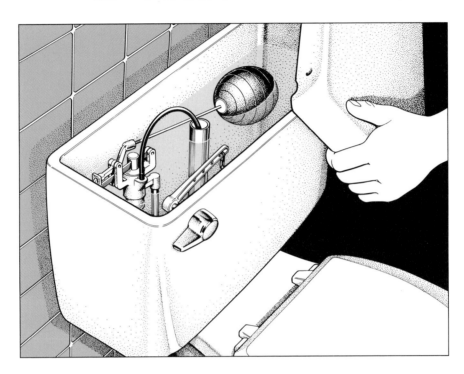

How to clear clogged DRAINS

Degree of difficulty: Easy   **Estimated time:** 45 minutes   **Average cost of materials:** N/A

A clogged or sluggish drain is not a major catastrophe, but it can be a real nuisance. Luckily, correcting a troublesome drain is a simple matter, requiring only the most basic of tools.

As always, gaining access is half the battle. Because trap clogs are easier to clear than line clogs, and generally do not require trap or drain disassembly, you'll want to start with a plunger. To avoid losing the force of the plunger through secondary passageways, always plug the sink's other compartment opening.

Also, try for a good seal around the plunger cup on both the up and down strokes. A little petroleum jelly or liquid soap on the rim of the cup will improve the seal.

Secondly, try plunging with a little water in the basin. The water will help force the trap and will indicate when you've broken through. And finally, follow any drain-cleaning procedure by running very hot water down the drain for about 5 minutes.

If plunging does not clear the blockage, you'll need to free the line with an inexpensive hand snake. While some sources suggest snaking through the fixture drain, this is rarely a workable solution. Instead, take the time to disconnect the sink trap and snake through the open line at wall or floor level. To remove a trap, use adjustable pliers or a pipe wrench to loosen the slip nuts on the trap. Remember that the trap will contain water, and additional water may be backed up in the

The first step in clearing any clogged drain is to try using a plunger—in most instances, clogs are dislodged easily using this method. For best results, always be sure to plug any secondary passageways—such as this tub overflow opening.

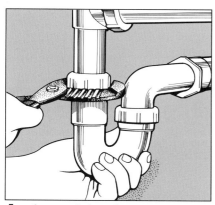

1 *To free a sink drain, first remove trap in waste line with pliers. Be sure to place bucket under trap to catch waste water.*

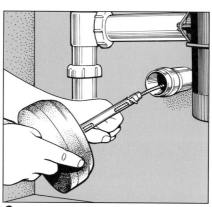

2 *Once trap is removed, push snake cable into waste line and turn handle in a clockwise direction until line is clear.*

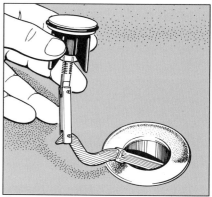

3 *To remove hair, or plunge a tub with a pop-up tripwaste mechanism, gain access to drain line by lifting out pop-up arm.*

4 *To remove hair, or plunge a tub with a plunger-type tripwaste, gain access to drain line by removing cover screen.*

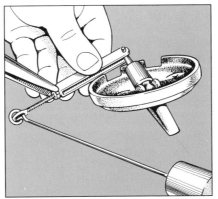

5 *To adjust plunger-type tripwaste, first remove it from overflow opening, then tighten or loosen locknut to move lift rod.*

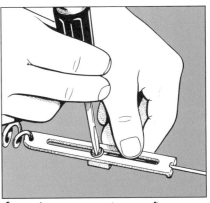

6 *To adjust a pop-up tripwaste, first remove it from overflow opening, then loosen setscrew to free lift rod. Move rod as needed.*

line, so keep a bucket underneath the trap. Then loosen the nut that secures the trap arm to the drainage-line fitting (Fig. 1).

With the trap off, feed the cable into the line and crank clockwise (Fig. 2). If you find brief, stubborn resistance, the cable will have encountered a local clog, usually near a bend in the pipe. Crank back and forth through the clog several times before retrieving the cable. If you find steady resistance throughout the length of the line, move the cable back and forth—a foot or two at a time—until you've reached the stack connection.

With the cable retrieved, reassemble the trap and flush the line with plenty of hot water. Often a snaked line will clog again when loosened debris collects at a bend in the line. If the water drains briefly, then backs up again, use a plunger to force the debris. Keep plunging until the water flows freely.

Clearing bathtub drains

Before assuming a clogged drain line on a tub, look to the tripwaste mechanism. Quite often, the mechanism will attract a hair clog or simply need adjustment.

Hair clogs are a given on pop-up-style drains. Begin by turning the control lever to the open position and grasping the plug. Slowly pull the plug and its trip lever out of the drain shoe (Fig. 3). If hair accumulation on the pop-up lever is the problem, you'll see it immediately. Simply remove the hair. Then turn the control to the closed position and feed the pop-up lever and plug back into the drain.

Plunger-style tripwastes seldom collect hair, but if yours is plugged, simply remove the cover plate screw (Fig. 4), lift off the plate, and remove the debris.

A more likely problem is that the tripwaste mechanisms—on both plunger and pop-up styles—may need adjustment. In a plunger-style tripwaste, the rod will need to be shortened to increase flow. With a pop-up style mechanism, the opposite is true. In any case, you'll usually find one of two rod configurations: a locknut and threaded rod setup (Fig. 5), or a slotted strap and setscrew arrangement (Fig. 6). You'll simply loosen the locking device and adjust the rod up or down, as needed. As a little adjustment goes a long way, make your changes in ⅛-in. increments.

If the problem is not in the tripwaste, expect it either in the trap connected to the drain or in the waste line connected to that trap. As a trap clog is likely, plunging the drain is the simplest approach. Again, you'll have to keep the pressure from escaping through the overflow. With luck, you may be able to plug the overflow slots in the cover plate. If not, remove the cover plate (Fig. 7) and pull out the tripwaste mechanism (Fig. 8). Then, stuff a wet rag into the opening.

If plunging the drain offers no solution, you'll probably need to use a snake to clear away the obstruction. Unlike sink traps, most tub traps are inaccessible and cannot be taken apart, so you'll have to work the cable from inside the tub. Don't try working through the drain; the snake won't go past the drain-shoe tee. Instead, remove the cover plate and tripwaste and insert the cable through the overflow tube (Fig. 9).

Within 2 ft. of the overflow opening, you'll feel resistance at the trap. Slowly work the cable through the trap and crank into the drain line. Then, work it just as you would in a sink line.

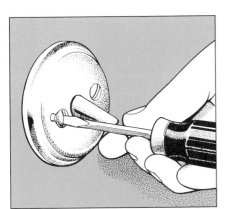

7 *If drain requires plunging or snaking, remove cover plate on overflow opening. Plate is usually attached with two screws.*

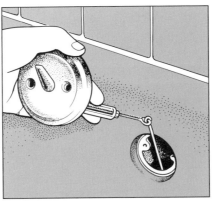

8 *With cover plate free, lift out tripwaste mechanism. If plunging, cover overflow opening with damp rag, then work plunger.*

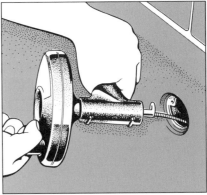

9 *If snaking is required, slide cable into overflow opening and turn handle clockwise. Advance cable as necessary.*

How to repair
A BATHTUB DRAIN

Degree of difficulty: Easy Estimated time: 1 hour Average cost of materials: N/A

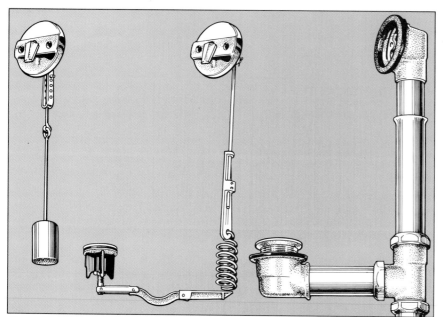

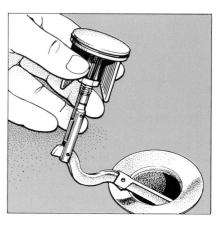

1 *Two basic tripwastes are internal plunger (left) and pop model (middle). Both fit standard drain system (right) with vertical overflow and horizontal drain-opening tubes.*

2 *To clean plunger type, just remove screen. For pop-up (shown above) just pull mechanism from drain opening.*

Repairing a poorly working tub drain is one of those intimidating tasks for most people. All the important parts seem to be hidden under the tub or inside an adjacent partition wall. In practice, however, nothing could be further from the truth, because the working parts can all be removed, cleaned, adjusted and reinstalled from the outside. All you need to know is what type of drain you have.

Tub drains, usually called tripwastes by plumbers, come in two basic styles with the same purpose, namely to close off the tub opening so the water does not drain until you want it to. The one on the left is called an internal plunger (Fig. 1). When you flip the trip lever below the faucets, the plunger slides past a drain baffle in the overflow tube and prevents the water from passing into the drain sys-

tem. This type of tripwaste calls for a simple screen which covers the drain opening at the bottom of the tub.

The second type is called a pop-up tripwaste. When you operate its trip lever, it allows a drain stopper—positioned in the drain opening—to fall into the opening, closing it off and thus preventing any water drainage.

In most cases, the tripwaste just needs to be cleaned and sometimes adjusted (Figs. 3 through 5). Accumulations of hair and soap are the usual culprits. Don't force the trip lever when it's stuck; you can distort the mechanism's adjustment, which will have to be repaired as well.

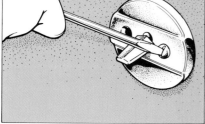

3 *To remove plunger tripwaste—or vertical seal of pop-up—unscrew overflow cover plate. It's attached to overflow tube.*

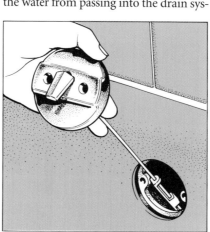

4 *Pull mechanism from overflow tube and clean thoroughly. Apply heat-proof grease, then reinstall and check operation.*

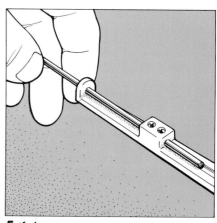

5 *If plunger or spring arm needs adjustment, move connecting rod on fitting and retighten. Reinstall and check.*

How to repair
FROZEN PIPES

Degree of difficulty: Medium   **Estimated time:** 2 hours   **Average cost of materials:** $20

Winter is the season of frozen pipes. While there are a few things you can do to keep pipes from freezing, once a freeze occurs, you'll need to fix it immediately to avoid water damage. Most freezes occur in crawl spaces, in floors cantilevered over the foundation or areas where cold air enters through cracks in walls, roof or foundation. The room temperature is often well above freezing, but exposure to a thin stream of cold air is all that's required to freeze a pipe.

When freezes occur within interior walls, look to the upper reaches of your home for an air leak. It's quite common, for example, for an entire bath group to freeze when cold air is driven down a flue or chimney chase, especially when the chase is framed in wood instead of built with masonry. Be sure to check the flashing at the top of the chimney chase for a leak. Caulk gaps in flashing or nail it down if it's loose.

If a freeze occurs within a plumbing wall that joins an exterior wall, look for a poorly nailed lap in vertical siding. Also, check for a broken putty seal around gas pipes or air-conditioning lines that pass through the exterior wall.

Insulation is the best prevention. Spaces between sills and block walls should be packed with batt insulation. Pipes in a crawl space or cantilevered floor joists should be insulated, too. Foundation cracks should be pointed with mortar or caulked to block air seepage.

To minimize damage after frozen pipes have thawed, waterproof areas around and below pipes with drop cloths and remove furnishings that may suffer from water damage. Also arm yourself with pails and mops—a wet/dry shop vacuum is useful for conquering floods.

Contrary to popular belief, hot water pipes will freeze. All things being equal, hot water pipes freeze before cold water pipes. A likely reason for this seemingly illogical occurrence is that heated water contains fewer dissolved mineral salts. These salts are cooked out and remain as scale in heaters and boilers. Just as salt added to water produces a higher boiling temperature and lower freezing temperature, salt removed has the reverse effect. When temperatures are at the freezing

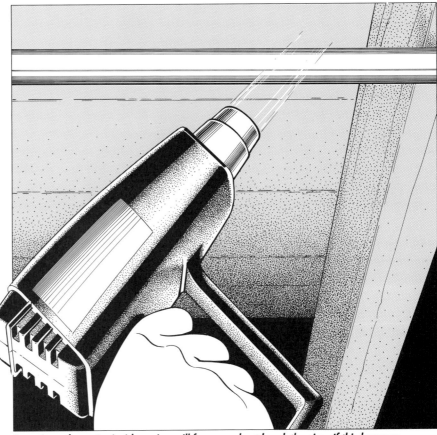

Sometimes the water inside a pipe will freeze and not break the pipe. If this happens, the fix is easy: Just heat the frozen section with a heat gun or soldering torch.

margin, the hot side will freeze while the cold side may not. The lesson here is that both cold and hot water pipes should be insulated in questionable areas.

Another common freeze point is the drainage chamber of a frost-proof exterior garden faucet, also called a sill cock. These outside faucets rupture in cold weather when hoses are left attached and an air lock prevents the water in them from draining. Their water flow is stopped ahead of their drainage chamber, so a leak won't be detected until the sill cock is used in the spring.

Making repairs
Begin by shutting off the water supply at the meter or where it enters the house from the well. Then open all faucets.

To get at a ruptured pipe, you may need to cut away some drywall or plaster.

But make any holes as small as possible to minimize repair work later. Follow the directions on Page 111 for instructions on how to repair holes in drywall.

Next, thaw the frozen pipe with a heat gun or torch. If using the latter, put a doubled-up piece of sheet metal behind the pipe to prevent burning adjacent framing members. Keep an appropriately rated fire extinguisher handy just in case.

The repair approach you take will depend on the type of piping material you have. Splits in copper piping are better removed (Fig. 1) and a new section of copper pipe spliced in place (Fig. 2).

Freezes in steel piping (commonly called iron piping) occur along the pipe's rolled seam. Quite often, if you can get at the seam, you'll be able to tap it closed with a ball-peen hammer and install a repair clamp over the split (Fig. 3). Of course, completely removing the split section (Fig. 4) and replacing it with a threaded union and new length of pipe is a better alternative (Figs. 5 and 6).

As plastic water pipes will nearly always split with a freeze, you'll have to cut out the damaged section (Fig. 7) and replace it. In most cases, you'll simply splice a

new section in place using solvent-cement couplings. All you'll need is a tubing cutter or hacksaw, couplings, cement and a stub of pipe.

If the split is small, however, you may be able to cut out only an inch or so and join the two ends with a push-fit plastic coupling. Lubricate the pipe with dish-

washing detergent, push on the fitting and tighten (Fig. 8). Its O-ring seals are virtually leak-proof.

Frozen frost-proof sill cocks are better replaced with models having built-in vacuum breakers. These are called freeze-proof sill cocks. For more information on how to install a freeze-proof sill cock,

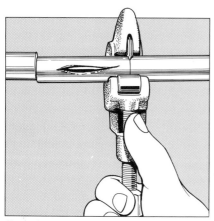

1 *Cut out ruptured section of copper pipe using tubing cutter. Make the cuts at least ½ in. from the split.*

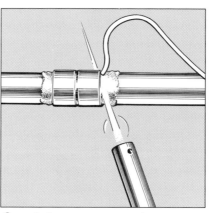

2 *Apply flux to new section of pipe and install with sweat couplings. Hold solder above and heat it from below.*

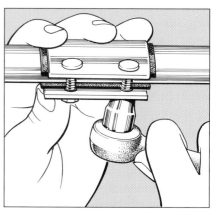

3 *Steel pipe often ruptures along its seam. Often you can tap seam shut with ball-peen hammer, then install repair clamp.*

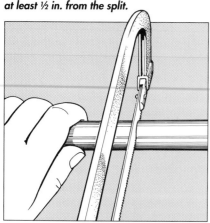

4 *Cut iron pipe with hacksaw a few inches beyond split. Use wrench to unthread damaged pipe from nearest fitting.*

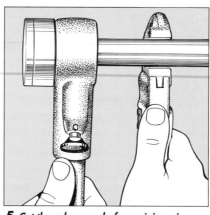

5 *Cut threads on end of remaining pipe with a die. Hold pipe securely with pipe wrench while cutting new threads.*

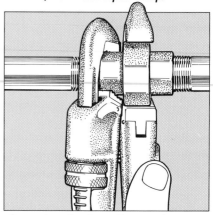

6 *Cut, thread and install new replacement pipe. Join pipe ends with pipe joint compound and union fitting.*

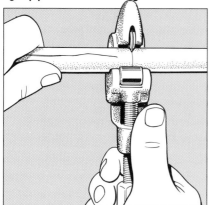

7 *Cut out ruptured plastic pipe with tubing cutter. Make sure to remove all damage. Splits can be hard to detect.*

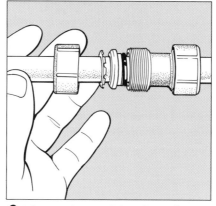

8 *Join new pipe to existing pipe with couplings and cement. Or, for small splits, use push-fit coupling (above).*

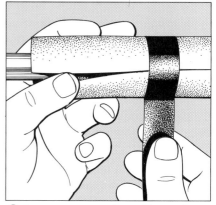

9 *Cover pipes exposed to cold air with foam-rubber insulation, split to wrap over pipe. Tape insulation every 12 in.*

How to repair your TOILET

Degree of difficulty: Easy   Estimated time: 3 hours   Average cost of materials: $25

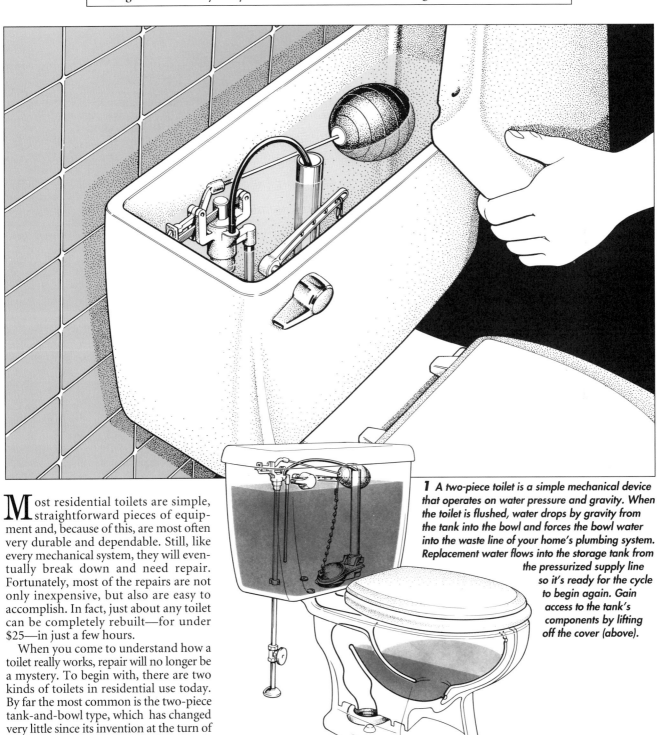

M ost residential toilets are simple, straightforward pieces of equipment and, because of this, are most often very durable and dependable. Still, like every mechanical system, they will eventually break down and need repair. Fortunately, most of the repairs are not only inexpensive, but also are easy to accomplish. In fact, just about any toilet can be completely rebuilt—for under $25—in just a few hours.

When you come to understand how a toilet really works, repair will no longer be a mystery. To begin with, there are two kinds of toilets in residential use today. By far the most common is the two-piece tank-and-bowl type, which has changed very little since its invention at the turn of the century. These toilets flush primarily by the weight of the water held in their tanks. This weight, also known as head

1 A two-piece toilet is a simple mechanical device that operates on water pressure and gravity. When the toilet is flushed, water drops by gravity from the tank into the bowl and forces the bowl water into the waste line of your home's plumbing system. Replacement water flows into the storage tank from the pressurized supply line so it's ready for the cycle to begin again. Gain access to the tank's components by lifting off the cover (above).

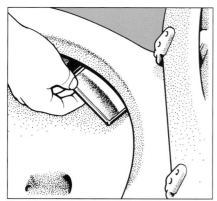

2 *A dirty bowl usually means poor water flow from rim openings. To check clogged openings, hold mirror under rim.*

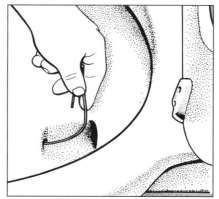

3 *If the bowl flushes sluggishly, check for a bacteria-clogged siphon hole. Bend a coat hanger and use it to clear the hole.*

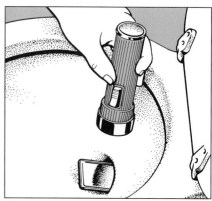

4 *To check for a partial blockage at the top of the trap, shine a flashlight onto a mirror placed in the bottom of the bowl.*

pressure, allows the unit to operate with very few mechanical parts.

The other type differs in that it is made in one piece. These toilets are offered by a variety of companies, but are generally known as silent-flush models. Aside from appearance, the main difference is that silent-flush toilets rely less on gravity and more on control valves. Silent-flush toilets are complicated enough to require a detailed discussion on their own, so only two-piece toilets will be discussed here.

How a two-piece toilet works

When you press down on your toilet's flush lever, it pulls up a chain, or wire, connected to a rubber stopper that is shaped like a ball or a flapper. This lifts the stopper off of its flush valve seat, which connects the tank and the bowl. Basically, this pulls the plug on the stored water and sends it into the bowl. The stopper is hollow and has a trapped bubble of air inside. This air bubble holds up the stopper until the receding water level carries it back down onto its seat.

When the water level drops, a hollow float ball attached to a brass rod drops with it. The other end of the rod controls a stopper inside a water inlet valve, called a ballcock. The rod acts as a lever. When the ball goes down it pulls this stopper up, allowing water from your supply system to rush through the valve and into the tank. As the tank begins to fill, the weight of the water presses on the seated flush valve stopper and forces a seal preventing the water from leaving the tank. As the rising water level carries the float ball up, the inlet valve stopper is forced back into the ballcock and the water is shut off.

The bowl on the other hand, has no mechanical parts. In terms of design, it is little more than a vitreous china water trap, not unlike the P-trap under your kitchen sink. The water you see standing

in the bowl is the water held by the trap. This water serves two important functions. It keeps the bowl clean and seals off the sewer gas that is always present in your drainage pipes. Without this trapped water, every toilet would need a mechanical seal, similar to those found in airplane toilets.

When the flush valve is opened, the water rushes into the hollow rim of the bowl by force of gravity. The rim has a dozen or so small, slanted openings and one larger opening. The smaller openings are visible under the rim and send water coursing down the sides of the bowl in a diagonal pattern. The larger opening, about ½-in. dia., dumps a forceful jet of water into a channel inside the bowl. Though this channel is concealed, its opening is directly across from the drain opening in the toilet.

A toilet is then flushed by water sent from two directions. Water from the rim openings cleans the bowl and starts the trapped water in its spiral up through the trap. The water from the larger opening sends a jet of water into the drain and forces the trap.

As soon as water spills over the trap, a siphoning action pulls the rest of the water in the bowl with it. When not enough water is left to fill the narrow passage at the top of the trap, the siphon is broken and all the water pulled to the top of the trap slips back into the bowl. Aside from the small amount of water added through the overflow tube, the water left standing in the bowl after a flush is the water that didn't make it over the trap.

That's how a toilet is meant to work, but let one component fail and you'll be left with an often confusing array of symptoms. The good news is that these symptoms are your quickest route to effective repairs.

■ Symptom No. 1: Your toilet flushes normally but is sluggish and often needs more than one flush to clear the bowl. The sides of the bowl are also stained and need frequent cleaning.

Toilets that flush sluggishly do so for one of three reasons. If the toilet has never flushed properly, you can count on a flawed trap or an inadequate vent in the waste line. As these conditions are rare,

8 *Once the collar is cut off, simply hook the flapper eyelets over the side pegs and connect the lift chain to the flush lever.*

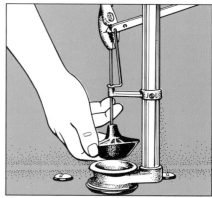

9 *To remove a defective tank ball, hold the lift wire with pliers and unthread the ball. Old, brittle rubber will often tear.*

5 *To clear congested rim holes, pour a 50/50 mixture of warm water and vinegar into the flush valve. Ream holes with wire.*

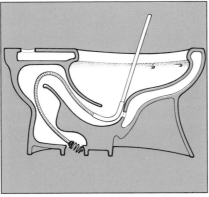

6 *Use closet auger to clear large obstructions. Auger's cable is long enough to reach the soil pipe below the bowl.*

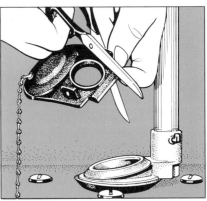

7 *If replacing flapper on a flush valve that has no side pegs, slip collar over the tube. If pegs are present, cut off collar.*

save investigating them for last. More probably the trouble is a bacteria-clogged siphon hole or partial clog at top of trap.

Bubbles are a sure sign of a partially blocked trap. Flush the toilet and watch for air bubbles between ⅛ and ¼ in. in dia. They will rise out of the trap opening halfway through the flush. As the water goes down, the bubbles will come up. Items that can cause a partial blockage are toothpaste caps, cotton swabs and hair pins. A partial blockage usually means that some such obstruction rests against the side of the top of the trap.

To locate the blockage, dip the water out of the bowl with a paper cup. Then hold a pocket mirror at an angle facing into the drain opening. Shine a flashlight into the mirror so that the beam is bounced toward the top of the trap. This will allow you to see the obstruction. When you learn its shape and location, fashion a hook from a piece of wire and snag the blockage. Then, flush the toilet several times to clear the passageway.

If you see no obvious bubbles, assume a bacteria-clogged siphon hole and mineral-clogged rim openings. You will usu-

ally be able to see a buildup in the siphon hole. To clear the opening, ream it with a piece of wire. The clog should fall forward into the bowl as you work.

If your toilet seems to need cleaning more and more frequently, flush the toilet and watch the action of the water as it spills from the rim openings. It should course down the sides of the bowl diagonally. If the water slides straight down the sides of the bowl, the rim openings are partially clogged with calcified minerals and bacteria.

To correct this problem, shut the water off and empty the tank. Then, while holding the flush valve stopper up, pour a 50/50 mixture of warm water and white vinegar into the flush valve opening. Much of it will drain into the bowl, but some will be trapped at the clogged openings. Let it stand for half an hour. Then ream each opening with a wire. If the openings are really clogged, start with a rigid wire—a coat hanger is ideal—and work up in size to a small screwdriver. To keep the problem from recurring, install a chlorine tank treatment and use lime-dissolving bowl cleaner.

As for improper venting or a flawed bowl trap, check the venting first. Each toilet in your home must have its own 2-in. vent or be within 6 ft. of a full-size vertical stack. This evaluation may require a plumber. If you are sure your bathroom is properly vented, assume a flawed toilet.

■ Symptom No. 2: Your toilet clogs and overflows, or passes only water.

A toilet that does not flush at all is likely to have a larger blockage at the top of its trap. Such a blockage may be caused by too much paper, but is more likely the result of a foreign object and paper combination. Occasionally, you will be able to retrieve a full blockage with the mirror-and-wire method or a plunger, but a closet auger is often a better alternative.

To use a closet auger, pull the cable back through the handle so that only the pilot spring shows at the bend. Then insert the bend into the drain opening of the toilet and push the cable through the housing until it stops against the top of the trap. When you feel the resistance of the trap bend, crank the cable in a clockwise direction. If you feel a snag, continue to crank in the same direction while retrieving the cable.

If you can't feel a snag, continue cranking through the drain until you run out of cable. Then retrieve the cable and repeat the process several times more. Finally, flush the toilet repeatedly and watch for bubbles that indicate a partial blockage.

■ Symptom No. 3: Your toilet continues to run until you wiggle the flush handle.

This is a common problem that is almost always a quick fix. It is either caused by a lift chain that is too long or by a lift-wire guide that is poorly aligned. Which one depends upon the design of the flush valve. Start by shutting off the water and flushing the toilet. If your flush valve has a rubber flapper, look for too

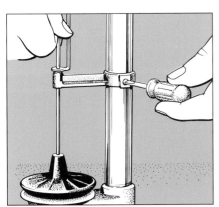

10 *If the tank ball drifts to one side as it falls, loosen screw in lift-wire guide, then rotate guide until wire falls properly.*

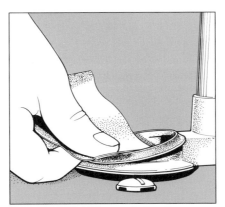

11 *Before installing new ball or flapper, sand valve seat flush with fine sandpaper. To avoid damage, use a light touch.*

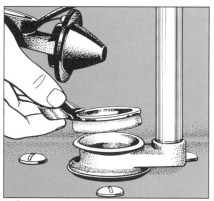

12 *If seat is damaged beyond repair, it must be replaced or retrofitted with new seat as shown. Epoxy bonds it to old seat.*

13 *If you find a broken overflow tube, pull old tube out, pry threads from the flush valve, and thread a new tube in place.*

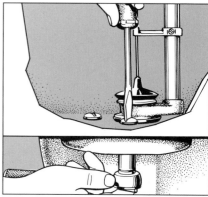

14 *To separate a tank from a bowl, first unscrew the tank bolts. Hold one end with a screwdriver—use a socket on the other.*

much play in its lift chain. To make the adjustment, unhook the chain at tank lever and reconnect it in a lower link. Try for an adjustment that leaves no more than ½ in. of slack in the chain.

If your toilet has a flush valve with a lift wire and a tank ball (some are ball-shaped and some are wedge-shaped), start by removing the tank lid and watching the action of the lift wire and tank ball through several flushes. This should give you a fairly good idea as to where the ball is landing and how the guide should be moved.

Use one hand to steady the flush valve's overflow tube and another to loosen the setscrew in the guide. With the setscrew loosened, move the guide only slightly in the desired direction. Then tighten the screw and turn the water back on.

■ Symptom No. 4: The water mysteriously comes on in your toilet tank automatically every half hour or so, runs for a minute, then shuts off.

This phantom operation stumps a lot of home owners, and is especially annoying in the middle of the night. In most cases, all that is required here is a new flapper ball or tank ball. If your toilet has a flapper, buy a universal replacement. A universal flapper has an eyelet on each side—where it hinges—and a center collar made to fit over an overflow tube. You will need to use one or the other, but not both. If your flush valve has side pegs for the eyelets, cut the collar from the flapper.

In any case, empty the tank and slip the old flapper from its eyelets, or cut through its collar with a utility knife or scissors. Before installing the new flapper, run a finger around the flush valve seat. Through years of use, dissolved mineral salts in the water can calcify on the flush valve and keep the flapper from seating properly. Rub a finger over the seat. If

the seat feels rough or gritty, sand it lightly with grit cloth or sandpaper.

If your toilet has a tank ball instead of a flapper, repair will differ slightly. Start by shutting off the water and draining the tank. Then hold the lower lift wire steady with a pair of pliers and unthread the ball from the wire. Rubber tank balls deteriorate with age, so don't be surprised if the ball strips away from its threaded brass insert. If this happens, simply hold the insert with one plier and thread the lift wire from it with another. With the old ball removed, sand the flush valve seat, and thread the new tank ball onto the lower lift wire.

■ Symptom No. 5: Your toilet continues to come on at regular intervals, even though the tank ball or flush valve has been replaced and the flush valve seat has been sanded.

This symptom means that your flush valve seat has a factory defect or is simply worn out. The best solution, of course, is to replace the valve, but replacement will require that you separate the tank from the bowl. If your stool has a wall-

mounted tank with a fragile chrome flush valve connecting the bowl, or if breaking your toilet in half sounds like more than you want to tackle right now, try an epoxy seat replacement kit.

Start by shutting off the water and flushing the toilet. Follow by sponging the remaining water from the tank and drying the flush valve seat. With the seat dry, sand it lightly until it feels smooth. Remove the epoxy from the kit and press it onto the bottom of the replacement seat. Then press the replacement seat firmly onto the flush valve and connect the lift chain to the flush lever.

Replacing a flush valve

A better and more reliable solution is simply to replace the flush valve. You'll find both plastic and brass versions at your local hardware store. Brass will last longer and will be less likely to cause problems later. Replacing a flush valve is not that difficult, but expect it to take an hour or so. Begin by shutting the water off and flushing the toilet. Then sponge all remaining water from the tank and disconnect the water supply tube from the

18 *Ballcock seals differ by manufacturer. This one features a plastic plunger with an O-ring and a separate seat seal.*

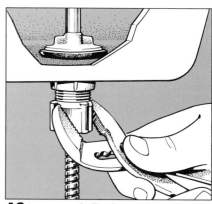

19 *To remove ballcock, start by unthreading nut under tank that holds water-supply tube to ballcock shank.*

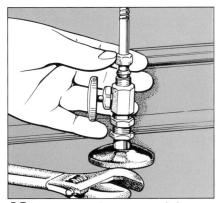

15 *Next, remove the water supply line. This can be done at ballcock connection under the tank or at the shutoff valve.*

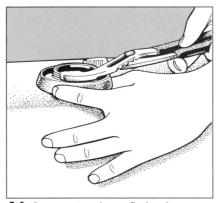

16 *If you must replace a flush valve, separate the tank and bowl, then turn the tank over. Remove the washer and nut.*

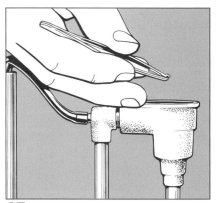

17 *Sediment causes ballcock to perform poorly. To check, take off diaphragm cover and remove particles with tweezers.*

ballcock. With the tank empty, remove the tank bolt nuts, lift the tank from the bowl, and set it upside down on the floor.

To remove the flush valve, pry the washer from the valve spud and undo the large spud nut. You'll then be able to pull the valve out from the inside.

Before installing the new valve, sand the area around the tank opening. Then coat the tank washer with pipe-joint compound or petroleum jelly and insert the valve spud through the tank. Turn the spud nut onto the spud and tighten until snug, plus about three complete turns. Finally, slide the new spud washer onto the spud and set the tank back in place.

If your toilet is more than a few years old, buy new tank bolts and washers. Corroded bolts and brittle washers are usually more trouble than they are worth.

In any case, slide a rubber washer onto each tank bolt. Drop the tank bolts through the tank holes and through the corresponding holes in the bowl. Then start a rubber washer, a metal washer and nut onto each bolt from below and tighten the nuts. When tightening tank bolts, remember that vitreous china can break

under too much pressure. Don't tighten any one bolt all the way down. Rather, move from bolt to bolt, tightening each only a few rounds before moving to the next. Keep in mind that with most brands, the tank does not actually touch the bowl, but is suspended by the spud washer. Stop tightening the tank bolts as soon as you feel firm resistance. Then reconnect the toilet supply tube, connect the flapper chain to the tank lever, and turn on the water.

■ Symptom No. 6: Your toilet does not shut off completely after flushing, but trickles a small stream of water into the bowl. You will also hear a slight but prolonged hissing sound.

These symptoms invariably signal trouble at the ballcock. In most cases, the ballcock needs a new seal or needs to be replaced entirely. In a few cases, the problem may only be some sediment in the diaphragm. In any case, shut the water off and remove the diaphragm screws from the top of the ballcock. Then lift the float, float arm and diaphragm cover off the ballcock.

If the trouble is sediment, you'll be able to see it in the diaphragm. Use tweezers to pick it out. If you don't find sediment, assume a faulty seat or diaphragm seal. As for repair, you'll have two choices. You can either replace the seal or replace the entire ballcock assembly. The factors influencing your decision will be the condition of the diaphragm seat and the material of the ballcock.

Because imperfections in plastic ballcocks are difficult to see or feel, you will often be better off replacing a troublesome plastic model. If your ballcock is made of brass, and if the seat shows no signs of wear, a diaphragm seal kit will save you time.

Ballcock diaphragm designs are proprietary, so your best bet is to purchase a kit made especially made by your toilet's manufacturer.

Replacing a ballcock
Replacing a ballcock is not hard. You'll have to drain the tank, but you won't need to disturb the tank-to-bowl connection. Loosen the compression nut that holds the supply tube to the shank of the ballcock. Next, loosen the jamb nut holding the ballcock in place. With the nut removed, the entire assembly should lift right out.

Before installing your new ballcock, apply pipe-joint compound to the rubber washer. Insert the shank through the tank opening, tighten the jamb nut and reconnect the supply tube. You'll probably have to adjust the float level on the ballcock. Bend the rod for large adjustments. For minor corrections, use the adjustment screw at the top of the diaphragm. Try and get the water level about an inch below the top of the overflow tube.

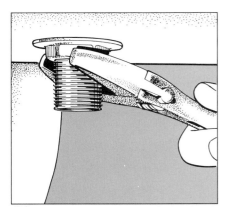

20 *Next, loosen and remove the hex-head jam nut that actually holds the ballcock to the tank. Hold the ballcock from inside.*

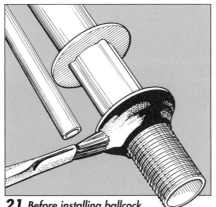

21 *Before installing ballcock, clean opening. Coat ballcock washer with pipe-joint compound or petroleum jelly.*

■ Symptom No. 7: The tank handle falls out or is loose.

22 *If sediment is a problem, install a replacement designed to cope with it; the replacement should come apart easily.*

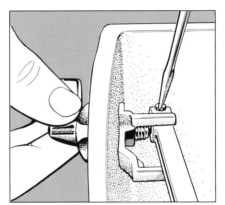

23 *To replace two-piece flush lever, loosen screw and remove handle. One-piece levers have nuts with left-hand threads.*

24 *Wax ring gasket forms seal between bowl and waste line. Gaskets also come in rubber and wax-covered rubber.*

The only trick to replacing a flush lever is in remembering that it has left-hand threads. Armed with this information, the rest is a matter of loosening the retaining nut and pulling the lever out by the handle. The replacement handle will go in the same way, only in reverse order. If your toilet's flush lever is made in two pieces, loosen the setscrew in the lever before undoing the nut.

■ Symptom No. 8: Water appears around the base of the toilet. The toilet may also rock side-to-side slightly when used.

Water around a toilet is a sure sign that the seal between the bowl and toilet flange has been broken.

Bowl gaskets come in three forms: rubber, beeswax and a newer rubber covered by wax. Each has its advantages and disadvantages. Wax gaskets are by far the most popular, primarily because one size fits nearly every installation and because they are inexpensive, costing about $1. Rubber gaskets, on the other hand, seldom leak once installed, are reusable and are less problematic when the right thickness of gasket is used. The disadvantage is

that the right thickness must be determined in advance, which is not always easy. Rubber gaskets are also more expensive, $3 to $6. New, wax-covered rubber gaskets ($3 to $4) are a compromise between the two. They provide the strong seal associated with rubber units and also afford the minor gap-filling capabilities of the wax gaskets.

In determining which gasket to use, consider the use the toilet will get and the kind of floor supporting it. If the toilet will be used by a very heavy or handicapped person, or if the floor level has been raised by subflooring or quarry tile, rubber gaskets are a better choice. Wax gaskets generally hold up well in most other situations.

To reset a toilet, drain the tank and dip all water out of the bowl. Then undo the supply tube connection, either at the ballcock or at the shutoff valve. Once this is done, pry the caps from the closet bolts at the base of the bowl and undo the nuts from the bolts. Then straddle the bowl, grasp it on each side near the seat hinges and pull up. Set the toilet down on a few sheets of newspaper and gently lay it over

on its side. (If the floor is especially hard, use more newspaper to pad the bowl against damage.) This will expose the horn, or drain opening of the toilet.

Use a putty knife to completely scrape off all remaining wax from around the horn of the bowl and from the bowl flange on the floor. Next, slide the old closet bolts from the flange and replace with new bolts. Press a new gasket onto the flange so it's centered between the bolts. Then pick the bowl up and walk it over to the flange. Align the bowl so that you can see the closet bolts through holes in the base. Then settle bowl down onto the gasket.

Before tightening the closet bolt nuts, make sure the back of the tank sits square with the wall. Then tighten the bolts, each a little at a time. Draw the nuts down only until you feel firm resistance. Then sit or stand on the toilet to compress the gasket further. This should allow you to draw the bolts down another two rounds.

Finally, turn the water back on. After a few days of use, tighten the closet bolts again until they feel snug. Then, snap the caps over the bolts to complete the job.

25 *When moving a toilet with the tank attached, you'll get the best balance point if you hold the bowl near the seat hinges.*

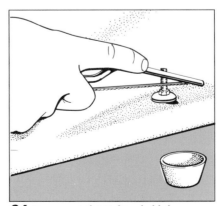

26 *To secure toilet, tighten hold-down nuts until bowl doesn't rock. Then cut off bolt tops and snap caps in place.*

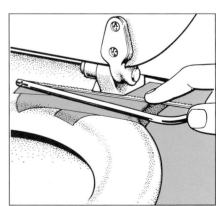

27 *To replace broken seat, hinge bolts must be removed. If rusted, cover bowl rim with tape and cut bolts with hacksaw.*

How to install
A WASTE DISPOSER

Degree of difficulty: Medium   **Estimated time:** 6 hours   **Average cost of materials:** $325

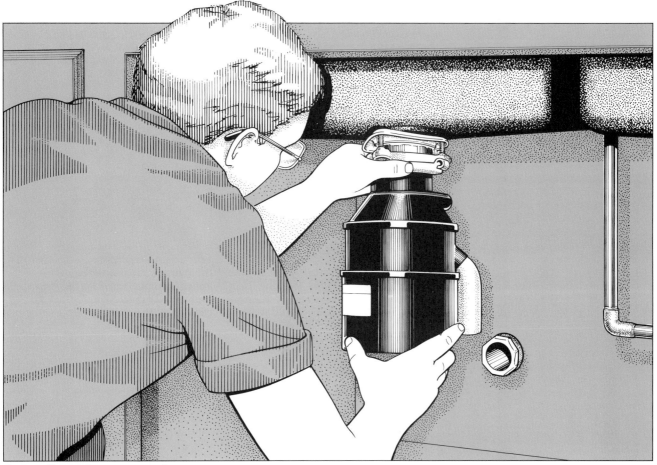

A waste disposer is a great convenience. And installing one yourself can save on the cost of having it done professionally. There are two main types to choose from: a continuous feed model and a batch feed model.

A garbage disposer, or food waste grinder as some manufacturers call it, is an appliance whose popularity has grown substantially in the last 25 years or so, and with good reason. These units provide for efficient and sanitary disposal of waste food within the kitchen where the waste is generated. This reduces the amount of refuse that must be stored until collection day, and at the same time eliminates many of the unpleasant odors caused by decaying food. These sturdy appliances can provide years of trouble-free service for a relatively small initial investment, especially if you do the installation yourself.

There are two basic kinds of disposers: batch feed and continuous feed. Both are mounted under the sink and grind waste in the same way. Both require a constant flow of cold water during use. The dif-

ference is in how they are operated. The batch feed models are activated only when a stopper, or cover, is placed in the throat of the disposer. It functions as a switch that turns on the motor. To dispose of the waste, the stopper is removed, the waste dropped in, then the stopper is inserted and the material is ground up and washed down the drain.

Continuous feed models are activated by a remote switch that's mounted on the unit itself, inside the cabinet, or on the wall above or beside the sink. The disposer throat remains open when the unit is operating and waste can be fed continuously without inserting a stopper switch. Continuous units can handle a larger volume of waste quickly, but the batch models have the safety advantage, which should be a consideration if you have small children.

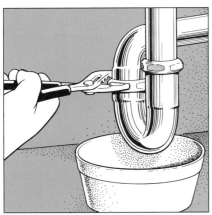

1 *Begin by removing the existing waste line. Loosen the P-trap nuts with pliers or a pipe wrench and let the water drain from the trap into a bowl or pail.*

How disposers work

Most disposers have two basic parts: the lower housing that contains the motor and the upper grinding chamber that contains a flywheel—equipped with fly-weights, or hammers—and a shredder ring. The flywheel is connected directly to the motor shaft. As the waste parti-cles are fed into the unit, they are struck by the flyweights and thrown out against the shredder ring. This ring is perforat-ed with a series of sharp-edged holes that cut the particles into small pieces. When sufficiently reduced, the waste passes through the shredder ring, washes down below the flywheel and out the drainpipe. Larger deposits are thrown repeatedly against the shredder until they are ground to the appropriate size.

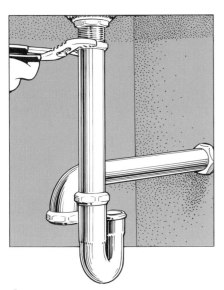

2 *Loosen the slip nut that joins the tailpiece to the threaded sink sleeve and pull the tail-piece from the fitting. Empty the remaining water from the trap.*

All disposers are designed to operate with a heavy stream of cold water running at all times. The water not only flushes away the waste, it also lubricates the seal around the motor shaft. If the unit is operated without water, the seal will be destroyed, allowing moisture to reach and ruin the motor. Cold water also congeals grease and fat particles, which permits them to be shredded. Run the water for 15 to 20 seconds after the dis-poser is switched off to be certain the drain lines are flushed clean.

All disposers are equipped with some form of overload switch that protects the

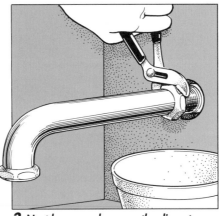

3 *Next loosen and remove the slip nut that joins the drainpipe to the plumbing stack within the wall. Keep all fittings and gaskets for later use.*

motor by shutting off the power if the flywheel becomes jammed. Some have automatic or manual reversing switches that allow the shaft to turn in the oppo-site direction to free any obstruction. Other models are equipped with a red reset button. If these units jam, the obstruction must be removed manually and then the button pushed in before the unit will operate again.

Most disposers also have a connecting fixture for mounting the waste line from a dishwasher. The unit shown here is equipped with such a fixture, but it was not used for this installation.

But before buying anything, check your local building codes to determine if a dis-poser installation is permissible. Some municipalities do not allow their use, and others have such convoluted require-ments that installing a disposer becomes financially impractical.

According to the National Standard Plumbing Code, your waste disposer installation must conform to the follow-ing minimum requirements: First, the sink waste hole must have a 3½ in. dia. Second, the drainpipe must be no small-er than 1½ in. in inside dia. And third, if

installed in a double sink (like the one shown here), each basin must drain into a separate trap.

Preparation

Begin work by removing the cabinet doors for easy access. Then disassemble the existing drain trap using a pipe wrench or wide-mouth pliers. Keep in mind that the trap is filled with water to prevent sewer odors from coming up through the drain hole, so put a bowl or pail under it to catch the water.

Next, remove the tailpiece from the bottom of the sink strainer and the drain-

4 *To remove the sink strainer, unthread the locknut, then pull off the bell-shaped washer and its rubber gasket. Push the strainer up into the sink bowl.*

pipe that enters the wall. Then remove the locknut, washer and gasket that secures the strainer to the sink bowl and push the strainer up. If it doesn't move at first, you might have to tap it lightly with a hammer. Keep in mind that the strainer is not threaded into the sink; it is merely imbedded in plumber's putty. But over time this putty can harden and the strainer will seem like it's attached. When it's free, remove all the old putty from the sink depression using a putty knife and scour the flange with an abrasive household cleanser.

5 *Begin the disposer installation by applying a generous bead of plumber's putty to the underside of the sink sleeve lip. Be sure the entire lip is covered.*

6 *Thoroughly clean the sink opening to remove the old putty and then press the new sink sleeve into place. Wiggle the sleeve back and forth for a uniform seal.*

Take the sink sleeve that comes with the disposer and apply a generous amount of plumber's putty to the underside of its flange, as shown in Fig. 5. Then, insert the sleeve into the sink waste hole and push down with your thumbs until some of the putty squeezes up around the sleeve.

From below, slide the disposer mounting assembly in place over the sleeve. This assembly has a fiber gasket, a backer ring and a mounting ring with three setscrews. Slide these in place, then attach the snap ring underneath and begin tightening the screws. Tighten each only a few turns before moving on to the next. This prevents the backer ring from becoming distorted, which would cause a poor seal.

7 *Once the sink sleeve is seated in the drain hole, install the mounting assembly parts in the following order: fiber gasket, backer ring, mounting ring and snap ring.*

At this point, it's a good idea to install the electrical power cable in the underside of the disposer unit. Once the unit is mounted, this connection is much more difficult. Determine where you want to place the remote switch, then cut a suitable length of cable. Be sure to use the proper gauge cable specified for your unit.

Remove the protector plate on the bottom of the disposer and pull out the black and white electrical leads. Install a cable connector in the hole provided on the base of the unit, then push one

end of the switch cable through it and tighten the cable in place. Strip off the outer insulation from the cable and the last ½ in. of insulation from the black and white wires. Join the white (neutral) wires together and the black (hot) wires together using wire nuts of the appropriate size. (For added safety and a more secure connections, wrap electrical tape around wire nuts whenever you make these connections.) Next, peel back any insulation that may be around the ground wire, then bend the end of the ground wire around the green-colored grounding screw in the unit's base and tighten the screw secure-

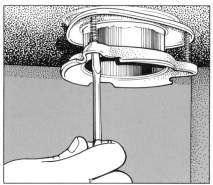

8 *Secure the sleeve and mounting assembly by tightening the setscrews on the mounting ring. Work progressively, driving each screw a few turns at a time.*

ly. (Whenever making screw connections, make sure to wrap wires clockwise around screws for safe and secure electrical work.) Push the wires back into the cavity and replace the cover.

Next, install the drain tailpiece and gasket that comes with the disposer. On this unit, the rubber gasket fits within a depression on the housing and then the tailpiece slides over the gasket. A separate mounting plate is screwed into the housing to secure the whole assembly.

Mounting the unit
Mount the disposer by lifting it up against the mounting ring and hand-turning the lug ring—on the disposer—in a clockwise direction. Finish tightening the lug ring using the small wrench supplied with the unit.

Next, install a tailpiece extender onto the tailpiece with a slip-nut gasket. Then, install the P-trap and hand-tighten its slip nut. Measure the distance from the open end of the trap to the wall nipple at the stack opening, and cut the drainpipe to length using a hacksaw fitted with a sharp blade. (The drainpipe usually extends into the nipple approximately 1½ in.) Make all of the connections and securely tighten all nuts with a wrench or pliers.

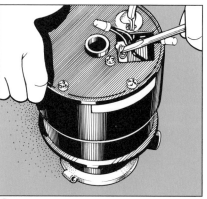

9 *Install the electrical cable by removing the cover plate and joining the white wires together, the black wires together and the ground wire to the green screw.*

Attach a utility switch box to a convenient place, either inside the cabinet or above the sink on the wall. The in-wall installation is much more involved because it requires cutting a hole in the plaster or drywall, attaching a box through the hole, and fishing the wire into the box—all without damaging the wall finish beyond the point where it will be covered by the switch cover plate. Unless you feel up to the challenge or want to hire an electrician to make the installation, the in-cabinet switch is the better idea. Merely screw it to the cabinet partition and make the electrical connections described below.

Begin by removing two of the knockout plates on the box and installing cable connectors in the holes so that their threaded ends are inside the box. Then insert the disposer cable into one of the connectors and tighten the screw clamp. Make sure the cable extends at least 6 in. into the box.

Fishing wire
Next, bore a 1-in.-dia. hole in the back of the sink cabinet for the new feeder

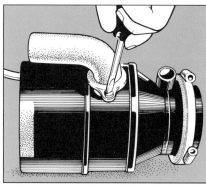

10 *To install the tailpiece, insert the gasket between the tailpiece and disposer housing, then slide the tightening plate into position and attach with screws.*

11 *Lift the disposer into place, then turn the lug ring by hand until all lugs catch. Finish tightening the lugs with the angled wrench supplied with the unit.*

cable from your fuse or breaker box. You'll have to fish new cable up through the floor and into this cabinet hole, which is the most difficult part of the whole disposer installation. It requires boring a hole up through the floor from the basement.

To do this, first determine where the hole should be by measuring from some common reference point that would apply to both the kitchen and the basement, such as the juncture of two outside walls. Then find the corresponding point in the basement and bore up from there. You must be extremely careful when boring into any enclosed area. There may be other electrical cables, hidden from view. Bore slowly and do not push so hard that the bit jumps through when the hole has been bored.

A straightened coat hanger is one of the best fishing tools you can use. Simply push one end into a hole and move the hanger around until it finds the other

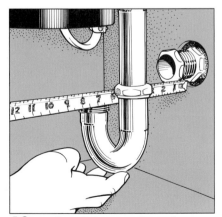

12 *Install a tailpiece extender and a P-trap, hand-tightening the slip nut for each. Position trap to align with stack opening and measure the length between them.*

hole. If you get someone to help by looking in the second hole with a flashlight you can speed up the whole process and avoid a good deal of aggravation. Once the hanger slides through the second hole, loop the end of your cable onto it, then carefully pull both through the openings.

The other end of this cable must be installed in the house service panel, a connection that is a job for a licensed electrician. But if you have managed to mount the switch box, fish the wire from the panel to the box, and have made all the appropriate connections, then the charge will be minimal. Keep in mind that the disposer must be placed on its own circuit, not ganged with another appliance or receptacle.

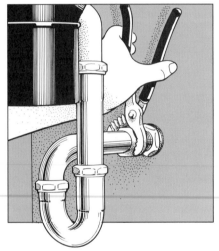

13 *Install the drainpipe, making sure that it's pitched slightly toward the stack opening. When satisfied with the fit, finish tightening all nuts with pliers.*

Once the new cable is through the cabinet hole—but before it's attached to the service panel—install it in the switch box. Leave 6 in. of cable inside just as before and strip the wire in the same way. Join the white wires together with a wire nut. Then cut a 5-in.-long grounding pigtail from some extra wire and join to the other two ground wires with a wire nut as shown. Take this pigtail, bend a loop in the end and wind it around a green-colored grounding screw at the back of the box. Tighten the screw securely.

Next, bend a short loop in the end of each black wire and attach the wires to the corresponding switch screws. Push all the wires back into the box and screw the switch unit into the threaded holes on the top and bottom of the box. Make certain that when the switch lever is pointing down, it reads OFF. Install the covering plate. Finally, attach the loose cable to the cabinet partition using electrical cable sta-

ples spaced approximately 10 in. apart. Be especially careful not to puncture the cable insulation.

Freeing a jammed disposer
Once the waste disposer installation is completed, objects may cause the disposer to jam. If the disposer jams, turn off the power remove any obstructions that caused the jam, wait 15 minutes and then press the reset button on the unit's motor casing. Turn on the unit and try it again. If this doesn't solve the problem, you'll have to take another course of action.

Turn off the power again and position a broomstick in the disposer opening so one end rests on the impeller. Use the broomstick to rotate the flywheel coun-

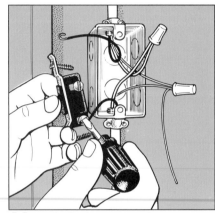

14 *Join both white wires with a wire nut, and both ground wires and a grounding pigtail with a wire nut. Attach each black wire to a switch screw as shown.*

terclockwise; try the disposer again. If your unit has a hex-head hole at the bottom of the motor unit, turn off the power and turn a hex wrench back and forth to free the flywheel.

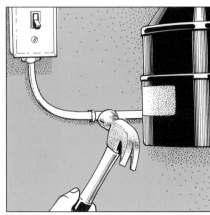

15 *Attach the electrical cable to the cabinet side with cable staples driven about 10 in. apart. Be careful not to cut the insulation with a staple point.*

How to repair
A DISHWASHER

Degree of difficulty: Medium   **Estimated time:** 4 hours   **Average cost of materials:** $30

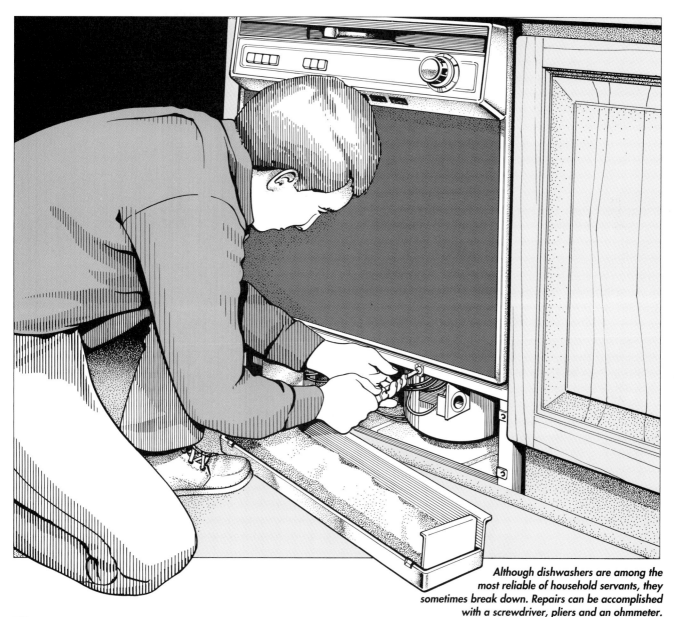

Although dishwashers are among the most reliable of household servants, they sometimes break down. Repairs can be accomplished with a screwdriver, pliers and an ohmmeter.

Looks are often deceiving. Take a built-in dishwasher. When a breakdown occurs, you may think you have to unbolt the unit and pull it out from under the counter. But in reality, there are only two failures (and they rare ones at that) which may require this much trouble. You can probably fix every other failure yourself with comparative ease, a minimum of tools and very little previous experience fixing major appliances.

Three big ones

The three most common dishwasher repairs are a leaking pump, lack of water fill into the dishwasher, and failure of water to drain properly.

Although all dishwashers work similarly, there are some differences in components from model to model. For example, most models have drain valves. Some don't. Those without drain valves have motors that reverse direction of rotation to pump water out of the machine. If you encounter a variation that stumps you, you can get help at an appliance parts store. In addition to the advice which most sales people can provide, parts stores sell do-it-yourself repair manuals that are published by appliance manufacturers. Follow the detailed directions in these manuals to deal with major problems.

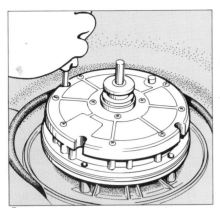

1 To gain access to pump, begin by removing spray arm. Then unscrew top of the wash cycle pump housing. Set screws aside.

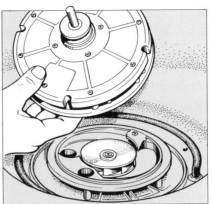

2 Lift off the top of the housing and set it aside. With top off, the wash cycle impeller is exposed. Check impeller for cracks.

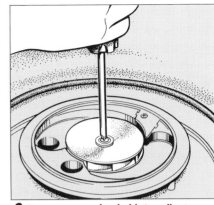

3 Remove screw that holds impeller In place. Then lift impeller off pump shaft and set it aside so it won't be damaged.

Leaking pump

Don't dismiss a trace of water on the floor as a minor leak: It could be a sign that the motor is about to be ruined. To check this out, unscrew the bottom access panel and see if there is water under the pump. If there is, check to see if the water inlet or drain hose has split, or if the overfill switch has failed. If these all look fine, then you'll have to replace the seals in the pump, especially if the pump and motor are an integrated assembly, as they are in most dishwashers.

The pump sits on top of the motor and is also driven by the motor. A damaged seal, therefore, may allow water to seep in and short out the motor. Instead of $10 or $15 for a kit containing new seals, you could end up spending over $200 for a new motor if a bad seal isn't replaced quickly. You can buy a seal kit for your model from an appliance parts store. Before you begin to work, turn off the water and the power to the dishwasher at the circuit breaker or fuse box. Post a note on the fuse box or breaker panel informing others that you are working.

To begin the task, open the door, remove the bottom rack, and pull off the lower spray arm. If the lower spray arm is held in place by a cap, unscrew the cap. In many models, including the dishwasher illustrated here, there are two filters. They are a coarse strainer for catching large particles and a self-cleaning, fine-mesh strainer to catch smaller particles. Remove both of them.

From here on, there are quite a number of parts and screws that have to be removed before reaching the seals. As you take them off, lay out the parts in order. Keep their fasteners with them. Doing so will help you avoid misplacing a component and will make reassembly easier.

Two-pump system

The pump in most dishwashers is actually two pumps in one. One, the wash cycle pump, circulates water to the lower and upper spray arms during the washing cycle. The second, the drain cycle pump, pumps water from the dishwasher at the end of the washing cycle. In order to get at the seals (in the unit illustrated

here, there are three seals that have to be replaced), unscrew and then remove the top of the wash-cycle pump housing (Figs. 1 and 2). Then, unscrew and remove the wash cycle impeller and set it aside (Figs. 3 and 4).

Be sure to inspect the wash cycle impeller for damage. If you are ever faced with a problem of dishes not coming clean and have checked on the most likely reasons—water temperature not being hot enough, dishwasher detergent that has been stored too long and has lost potency, and improper stacking of dishes—a cracked wash cycle impeller should be next on the list of possible causes.

To continue disassembly, lift off the bottom of the wash cycle pump and unscrew the part under it, which performs two jobs. It serves as a seat for the self-cleaning, fine-mesh strainer, and it separates the wash cycle pump from the drain cycle pump (Fig. 5).

Sealing the pump

Note: The procedure outlined here will help as a general guide to aid you in

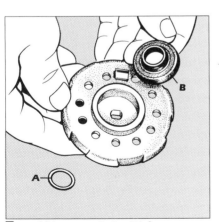

7 In addition to an O-ring (A) that goes around the motor shaft, this impeller has a rubberized seal that must be replaced.

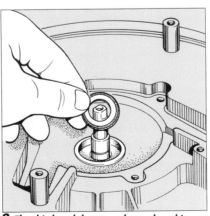

8 The third seal that must be replaced is a ceramic seal at the bottom of the pump housing. Press the new seal in place.

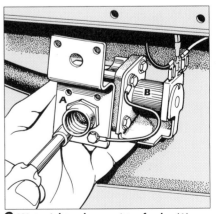

9 Water-inlet valve consists of valve (A) and solenoid (B). To check the filter inside the valve, remove the mounting bolts.

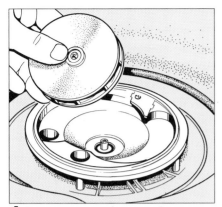

4 *As you remove each part, make sure to check exactly how it was installed so that your reassembly later will be mistake-free.*

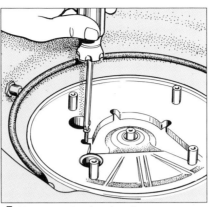

5 *Next, unscrew the plate that separates the wash cycle and drain cycle pumps. Then lift it off to expose the drain cycle impeller.*

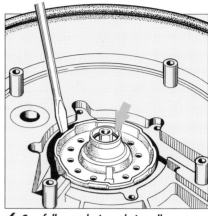

6 *Carefully pry drain cycle impeller out of pump housing using a flat-blade screwdriver. Note the O-ring location (arrow).*

resealing a pump. The seals in your pump may not be positioned exactly as they are in the pump shown in this example.

The seals are located in the drain cycle pump housing. To reach them, pry the drain cycle impeller off the motor shaft (Fig. 6). Do this gently to avoid damaging the part. When this has been done, the three seals which have to be replaced can be removed.

To differentiate between these three seals, let's refer to them as a ceramic seal, a rubberized seal and an O-ring. The ceramic seal is pressed into the pump housing cavity on which the drain cycle impeller sits. The rubberized seal is positioned in the hollow on the bottom of the drain cycle impeller (Fig. 7). The O-ring is positioned around the motor shaft inside the top of the drain cycle impeller.

As the drain cycle impeller is removed, the rubberized seal and O-ring can be picked up with your fingers. Use a small screwdriver to pry the ceramic seal from the drain pump housing cavity (Fig. 8). Don't let the screwdriver slip and damage the pump housing or motor shaft.

To complete the resealing operation, dip the new ceramic seal in water and press it into the drain pump housing cavity with your fingers. Push the new rubberized seal into the hollow on the bottom of the impeller and reinstall the impeller. Then, install the new O-ring around the motor shaft and press it securely into place.

Faulty water fill

If you have insufficient supply of water, or a complete lack of water, going into the dishwasher, the most likely reasons for this are an open circuit in the water-inlet valve solenoid, a bad overfill switch, and a faulty timer.

Work on the water-inlet valve solenoid first. Begin by unscrewing the bottom access panel. The water-inlet valve with the attached solenoid will be in plain view (Fig. 9). In many dishwashers, the water-inlet valve is held by a bracket that is bolted to the chassis. Disconnect the water supply line from the valve. Remove the clamp from the hose on the valve outlet and pull off the hose. Unscrew the brack-

et from the chassis and disconnect the pull-off, push-on electrical connectors from the solenoid terminals. Important: Wires must be reconnected to their respective terminals; as you remove each connector, label it using masking tape.

See if there's a little cone-shaped, metal filter screen inside the valve intake nozzle. If this filter clogs, the supply of water needed by the dishwasher to get dishes clean will be reduced or cut off altogether. Pry the screen out of the nozzle and wash it under a water faucet using a toothbrush to remove particles (Fig. 10). A mild acidic solution, such as vinegar, helps to clean any stubborn particles from the screen.

Testing the solenoid

Set an ohmmeter on the RX100 scale and attach the leads of the meter to the terminals of the solenoid to check continuity (Fig. 11). A reading between 500 and 2000 ohms indicates that the solenoid is operating properly. However, if the ohmmeter shows a reading of infinity (∞), the solenoid is bad. Refer to the directions

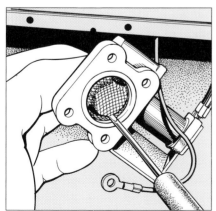

10 *Carefully remove the filter screen from the valve by prying with a small screwdriver. Gently brush any debris from the screen.*

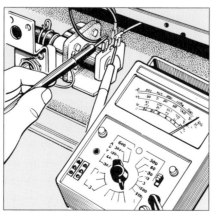

11 *To check continuity of solenoid, turn off power, then set ohmmeter to the RX100 scale and touch probes to terminals.*

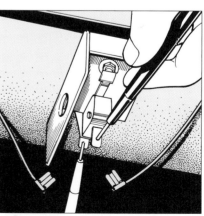

12 *Also check the continuity of the overfill switch by holding the meter to the wire terminals on the switch.*

13 *To get inside console where the timer is located, unscrew console panel. Then carefully pull it away and let it dangle.*

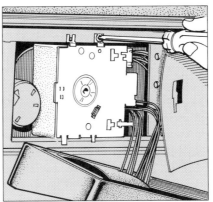

14 *If the timer must be replaced, check for all attaching screws and remove them. Lift out timer and disconnect the wires.*

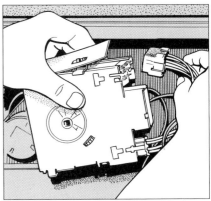

15 *Install a new timer by first attaching the wires, then sliding it back into the console. Tighten mounting screws securely.*

on Page 66 for using an ohmmeter or VOM to make electrical tests on appliance components.

A solenoid winding opens when it's warm and closes when cold, because the winding expands and contracts according to temperature. The valve, therefore, may operate on one occasion, but not on another. Therefore, a continuity test made when a valve is cold could indicate that it's okay when it isn't.

Make another test after running hot water over the solenoid for a few minutes. If you get an acceptable ohmmeter reading, then chances are that the lack of water going into the dishwasher lies with a burned-out overfill switch or with a faulty timer.

Testing the overfill switch

In most dishwashers, the overfill switch is part of a float assembly. This assembly, which is wired in series with the water-inlet valve and is positioned under the machine near the valve, turns off water intake if the water-inlet valve or timer fails. If this didn't happen, water could

feasibly overflow the tub and cause a messy flood.

The overfill switch, however, can fail in a way that results in a reverse reaction. A bad switch can keep the float in a raised position, which will prevent a perfectly good water-inlet valve from opening to allow water into the tub. So can an object wedged under the float. Therefore, before proceeding, check beneath the float to make sure a spoon or some other object isn't lying there. Then, use the float as a guide—it's inside the dishwasher, usually in the left- or right-front corner—to find the overfill switch, which will be bolted under the tub in line with the float.

To test the overfill switch, reach up and disconnect wires from the switch terminals. Be sure to label each wire for the terminal to which it attaches. Then, hold or attach ohmmeter leads to the terminals (Fig. 12). With the float in its normal position and no water in the dishwasher, the switch should show continuity (0 ohms). With the float raised, it should show an open circuit (infinity). Anything else requires replacing the overfill switch.

Working with the timer

Testing to see if the timer has failed necessitates that you connect the water-intake hose and wires to the solenoid, turn on the water, connect an ohmmeter and turn on the current. Although it isn't difficult, you will be working with live circuits and water, which is very dangerous. We strongly suggest that you leave this job to a qualified service person.

You could try a different approach. After all other tests have failed, take a gamble that the problem is being caused by a bad timer and just replace the part (Figs. 13 through 15).

Failure to drain

As mentioned before, many dishwashers have drain valves that are controlled by the timer to open at the end of the washing cycle. This permits waste water to be pumped out of the machine. When you take off the lower access panel, a drain valve, if there is one, will be visible. Unscrew it from the chassis and disconnect the drain hose.

A drain valve is controlled by a solenoid (Fig. 16). If water does not drain from the dishwasher at the completion of the washing cycle, test the drain valve solenoid for continuity with an ohmmeter in the same way that the water-inlet valve and overfill switch are tested for continuity. If an infinity reading is shown by the meter, replace the drain valve.

In and out

Suppose instead of no draining, water comes into the machine, but it drains right out again. This fairly common occurrence is caused by debris, usually a toothpick, pit or bone that has gotten past filters and worked its way inside the valve. It can cause the valve to jam (Fig. 17). Remove the valve and inspect it for any obstruction. Use needle-nose pliers to clear it out.

16 *To remove drain valve, disconnect wires from solenoid (A), unscrew valve (B) from chassis, and disconnect drain hose (C).*

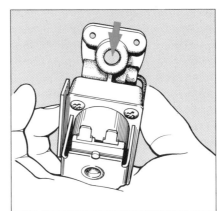

17 *Carefully inspect nozzle (arrow) of drain valve to see if something is jamming the opening. If so, remove obstruction.*

How to replace
A WATER HEATER

Degree of difficulty: Medium   **Estimated time:** 6 hours   **Average cost of materials:** $300

Whether you own an electric or gas water heater, chances are that it will one day wear out and need to be replaced—a relatively inexpensive job if you do the work yourself.

Like all things mechanical, water heaters do break down. And, when it's time to have yours replaced, you can expect the installation charge to equal, or exceed the cost of the heater itself. The good news is you can remove your old heater and install the new one yourself.

Garden-variety water heaters with 5-year warranties can cost as little as $125. A permit to do the job and an inspection may be required in your area, but don't let that intimidate you. Just keep in mind the $120 to $160 you'll be saving by doing it yourself.

When to replace a heater
Strictly speaking, a water heater need not be replaced until its tank begins to leak. An inoperative heater with a sound tank can be repaired. However, if your unit is several years past its warranty, it's probably unwise to invest more than $50 in repairs. There's no way of knowing how long the tank will last and you'd probably be better off replacing the entire unit. Remember, if the manufacturer loses faith in the heater after 5 years, there's probably a good reason to do so yourself.

Regardless of the age of your heater, if the tank develops a leak, replace it soon to avoid major water damage.

Choosing the right heater
As you shop for a new water heater, you'll find a confusing array of brand names, efficiency ratings and warranties. There are many more brand names on the market than water heater manufacturers. This

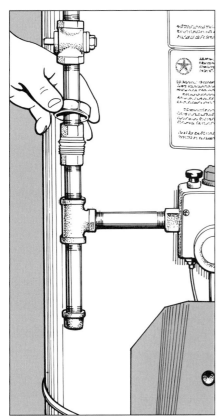

1 After turning off gas valve, loosen the union below the valve and disassemble the piping that connects to control valve.

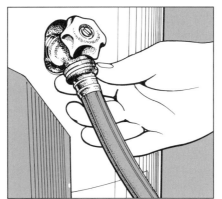

2 Attach a garden hose to the drain valve. Open the T & P valve or the hot-water taps in your house and drain the tank.

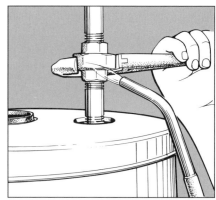

3 Disconnect iron water pipes by loosening unions with pipe wrench. Stubborn unions may require heating with torch.

means that more than one brand name is being manufactured by the same company. If you're looking for a standard heater with a 5-year warranty in the $125 to $175 price range, then you'd probably do best to ignore the brand and simply shop for the best price.

The real differences occur when shopping for extended-life and high-efficiency heaters. Extended-life heaters may feature dual anode rods. These are magnesium rods that retard tank corrosion by acting as electrolytic sacrifices. Instead of your tank corroding, the anode rods corrode. While all heaters have at least one anode rod, having two can greatly increase the time before tank corrosion creates a serious problem. Extended-life units may also feature fill tubes designed to keep any sediment from collecting on the bottom of the tank and, if your choice is electric, they may have heavier heating elements.

Other extended-life water heaters with 10-year warranties are virtually the same as ordinary units warranted for 5 years. In this case, you're simply betting with the manufacturer that the heater will actually last 10 years. It's at least a $70 wager that will likely pay off.

High-efficiency heaters have foam insulation instead of fiberglass. The extra R-factor involved is particularly valuable if you use your hot water only a few hours a day, as do most working couples. They may also have two anode rods, an antisediment fill tube, and a modified burner assembly.

Base your decision on as much technical information as you can get and pay close attention to the estimated energy cost printed on the sticker on the heater. You can expect to spend over $400 for the best of these models.

Removing the old heater

If you have an electric heater, shut off its circuit breaker or remove its fuse at the main panel. Remove the cover plate near the conduit entrance on the heater cabinet. Remove the wire nuts and disconnect the wires and ground connection. Undo the box connector that secures the conduit to the cabinet and pull out the wires. When working around electricity and water, always take appropriate measures to prevent electric shock. Ensure that the floor around the water heater is dry and always double-check that the power to the water heater has indeed been turned off.

If you have a gas heater, shut the gas valve by turning it to its cross-line position. Most codes require this valve to be within 3 ft. of the heater's control valve. Loosen the union below the valve and disassemble the piping that connects to the heater (Fig. 1).

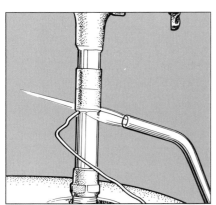

7 After soldering length of copper pipe into adapter and threading into tank, use sweat coupling to join to existing pipe.

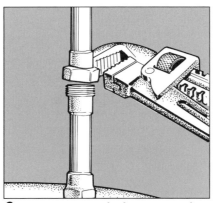

8 Copper pipes can also be reconnected with a brass union. Solder the bottom half to the stub before threading into heater.

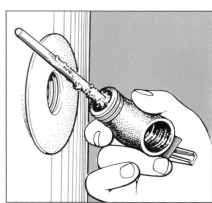

9 A clogged T & P valve means that the one you install should be checked periodically by lifting the manual release lever.

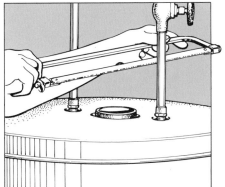

4 *Copper pipes can simply be cut with a hacksaw. Leave pipe stubs in place for use as handles when carrying the tank away.*

5 *If the new tank is installed on a sloping floor, level the heater by shimming under the legs with wood shingles.*

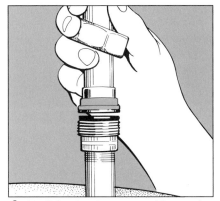

6 *This dielectric union uses a rubber washer and a plastic insert to keep the brass upper half from contacting the iron half.*

With the energy supply disconnected, shut off the water inlet valve and attach a garden hose to the heater's drain valve (Fig. 2). Then open the T & P (temperature and pressure) valve at the top of the heater and drain the water into the nearest floor drain. If yours is an older model with no T & P valve, open the hot-water faucets in your home.

If your heater is not electric, then the next step is to disconnect the exhaust flue. In most cases, the flue will be fastened to the flue hat with sheet-metal screws. Simply remove the screws and lift off the flue piping.

Removing the water pipes
If your heater is supplied by iron pipes or you have copper pipes that are connected by unions, loosen the unions to disconnect the pipes (Fig. 3). You can also simply cut copper pipes with a hacksaw or wheeled pipe cutter (Fig. 4). Leave the pipe stubs connected to the heater to use as handles when carrying the old heater out of the house.

After the water heater is completely disconnected from its energy source, piping and flue, grasp the pipe stubs and rock it in a side-to-side motion to move it. Enlist the aid of helper if the tank is too heavy to lift on your own.

Connecting the new heater
If the floor is level, simply slide the new heater under the water pipes and align it properly. If it's to be positioned near a floor drain, as many are, then you'll need to shim one side of the heater to compensate for the sloping floor. Use short pieces of cedar shingles or strap iron to shim the legs so the unit is plumb and secure (Fig. 5).

When connecting the water inlet and outlet pipes, it's generally okay to duplicate the type and configuration of fittings that existed on your old heater. If, however, you live in an area that has prolonged high humidity or your water has a high concentration of dissolved mineral salts, and your pipes are copper, it's advisable to connect the heater with dielectric unions.

Because the fittings on the heater are made of iron, a direct copper-to-iron connection under these conditions can significantly increase the rate at which the iron corrodes.

A dielectric union consists of a threaded iron half, a brass half and a threaded iron collar (Fig. 6). Separating the two halves is a rubber washer. A plastic insert separates the iron collar from the brass. With this union you can join copper to iron without any direct contact between the metals. If you're unsure as to whether this union is necessary in your area, check with your local building code authorities or a plumber.

If no dielectric unions are required, then the connection is a relatively simple job. Measure between the existing pipes and the heater fittings and cut two pieces of copper pipe to length, taking into account the shoulder depth of the adapters. Then, flux an end of each pipe stub and insert them in the adapters. Solder them on a fireproof surface. Remember, never solder an adapter after threading it into the cold-water inlet, as you may melt the plastic fill tube.

When the adapters have cooled, wrap three layers of Teflon tape clockwise around the threads of the male adapters.

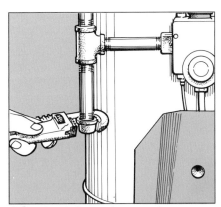

10 *Before lighting pilot on gas heaters, loosen bottom cap to remove trapped air. Then allow gas in the room to dissipate.*

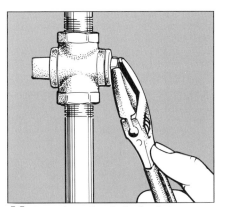

11 *Gas valves often leak after being operated. After gas is turned on, tighten stem nut on the back of the valve a half turn.*

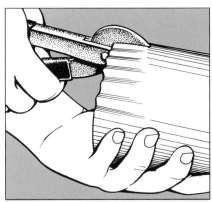

12 *If you end up with two female ends on flue pipe, crimp one end with a crimping tool, or with needle-nose pliers.*

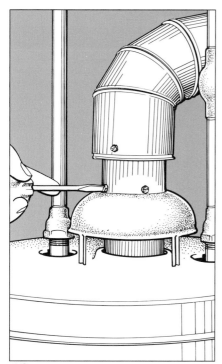

13 If necessary, use a vent increaser to connect the heater's 3-in. flue hat to a 4-in. vent. Secure joints with sheet-metal screws.

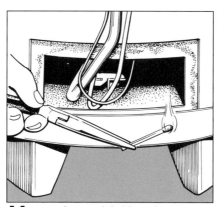

14 A wooden match held in a long pair of pliers is best for lighting the pilot. Press pilot button and slide match into heater.

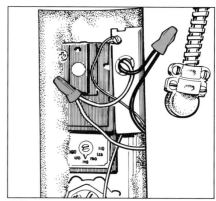

15 On electric units, secure conduit with an approved box connector. Connect wires with wire nuts and then secure ground wire.

Thread them into the heater fittings and tighten. Then, clean and flux the remaining pipe ends and join them with copper sweat couplings (Fig. 7).

If you can't raise the existing pipes high enough to slide the couplings in place, use slip couplings which have no center stops. Slide the slip couplings over the pipe stubs before threading the adapters in place. As an alternative, you can use brass unions in place of the sweat couplings (Fig. 8).

If you live in an older home with galvanized iron pipes, simply thread an appropriately sized galvanized nipple into each fitting and join the nipples to the existing pipes with galvanized unions. Apply some pipe compound to the threads of each connection. Avoid any temptation to use black iron nipples or fittings, as they'll rust in a short period of time.

Installing a T & P valve

Today, every heater must be equipped with an approved temperature and pressure relief valve. Should the control mechanism on a heater stick in the ON position, this valve will bleed off the excess steam pressure. Check the T & P valve on your old unit for sediment buildup. If it's clogged, then make a point of checking your new valve periodically to ensure safe operation (Fig. 9). The critical thing to look for when buying a T & P valve is its

psi rating. Check the rating on your new heater first, and purchase an appropriate valve.

To install the valve, simply coat the threads with pipe compound and thread the valve into the heater opening. You may find the heater opening on the side or the top. Most codes require that you install a drainpipe that extends from the valve to within 3 in. of the floor. Consult your local municipality or a plumber regarding special requirements.

Connecting the gas

Make sure you use only black iron pipe for the gas line. Compounds in the gas can cause the zinc coating on galvanized pipe to flake away and enter the control valve. In many cases you'll be able to use the nipple/fitting arrangement from the old heater. If not, thread an appropriately sized nipple into the control valve and thread a ½-in. tee to it. Thread a second nipple into the top of the tee and attach the bottom half of the union. Then, thread a short nipple into the bottom of the tee and install an iron cap on the open end. Finally, tighten the union. Typically, pipe compound is used on all gas joints. However, Teflon tape does the job and ensures that no compound particles work their way into the control valve.

Turn the gas on and check for leaks by brushing a solution of warm water and liquid dish detergent on all the joints. If bubbles appear, turn off the gas, take the piping apart, and start over. When all the joints are tight and the gas is on, slightly loosen the cap on the nipple below the tee to bleed air out of the line. Then retighten (Fig. 10). Because gas valves can leak after they've been used, tighten the stem nut on the back of the valve a half turn (Fig. 11).

Next, install the flue pipe. Most new heaters have 3-in.-dia. flue hats, but many codes require 4-in.-dia. pipes; consult

your local authorities about what applies in your area. If you do need to use 4-in.-dia. pipes, install a step-up adapter on the flue hat to accommodate the larger pipe. Join all connections with sheet-metal screws (Fig. 13).

If your old flue pipe is sound, you can simply reinstall it. New pipe usually comes with its snap seam apart. Simply cut it to length with tin snips. Use a hacksaw to cut pipe with a closed seam. If you end up with two female ends, form a male end with a flue pipe crimping tool or needle-nose pliers (Fig. 12). Take care not to cut yourself on any sharp metal pipe edges.

Connecting the electricity

Chances are, the existing electrical wires can be reconnected just as you found them in the old heater. Your old wiring will need to be replaced, however, if it doesn't meet your local electrical code. The wires leading from the ceiling or wall must be encased in flexible or rigid conduit and fastened to the heater with an approved box connector. You may find that a separate disconnect box may be required in your area. Since connecting a new disconnect box requires that you work inside the main service panel, this job is better left to a licensed electrician.

Fish the wires into the cabinet and secure the cable with the box connector. Join the black wire to the black lead and the white wire to the white lead with approved wire nuts. Then screw the ground wire to the green terminal in the cabinet (Fig. 15). Finally, make sure that the heater thermostat is covered with insulation and replace the cover plate.

Before turning the power on, fill the tank with water and bleed all air through the hot and cold faucets in your home. Never energize a dry heating element in an electric tank. It will burn up in a matter of seconds.

How to install
A FREEZE-PROOF FAUCET

Degree of difficulty: Medium   **Estimated time:** 3 hours   **Average cost of materials:** $24

Outdoor faucets, also known as sill cocks or hose bibs, have come a long way in recent years. They have evolved into a freeze-proof design that eliminates the need to drain them in the fall when the temperature dips below freezing.

Virtually everyone in northern climes is familiar with the fall ritual of shutting off water to the house's sill cock, then draining them. This prevents the water in the sill cocks from freezing and breaking it. Freeze-proof sill cocks eliminate this ritual because they are self-draining.

Freeze-proof sill cocks can replace standard sill cock without major retrofitting. Because of this, they can be installed by someone with modest plumbing skills and a modest tool kit. Seek additional advice from plumbing professionals where you purchase the sill cock.

Sill cock evolution
In most homes built prior to the 1960s, sill cocks were little more than surface-mounted shutoff valves. Water flow to them was controlled by a shutoff valve installed well inside the house, to reduce the danger of it freezing.

Those who were busy with other fall activities, however, forgot to drain the sill cock. To remedy the situation, the plumbing hardware industry introduced the frost-proof sill cock. These are equipped with extra-long stems. The end of the stem reaches far enough inside the house so water is shut off well away from where it could freeze. Often, those who thought they were safe with a frost-

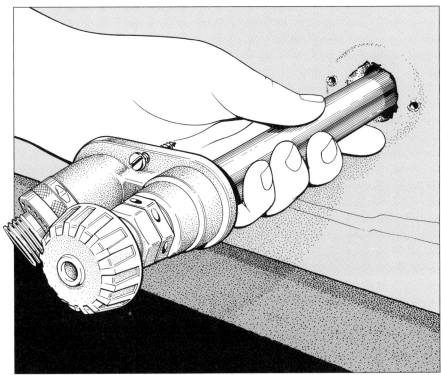

A freeze-proof exterior garden faucet, or sill cock, eliminates the need to drain water from these outdoor fixtures in the fall when temperatures plunge. To protect the garden hoses attached to the sill cock, however, bring them indoors at the first sign of cold weather.

proof sill cock have left garden hoses attached to them only to have the sill cock burst during a cold snap. A vacuum may form from leaving the hose attached, preventing the sill cock from draining. This led to the development of the first freeze-proof sill cock. Freeze-proof sill cocks let air into the faucet through an opening called a vacuum breaker. This ensures the sill cock drains regardless of whether a hose is attached. Some also have a drain hole separate from the nozzle.

Freeze-proof sill cocks have stems from 6 to 30 in. long. The latter is for installations where the sill cock is placed on a wall cantilevered over the foundation. A typical 10-in. freeze-proof sill cock costs about $24.

Installation
You may find the original sill cock was installed with iron or copper pipe. The former is slightly more difficult to remove and replace than the latter. Since copper is the more common of the two types of pipe, it's the one shown in this example. Also, once iron pipe is removed and the fittings are installed to connect copper pipe to it, the installation is the same for the two pipe varieties.

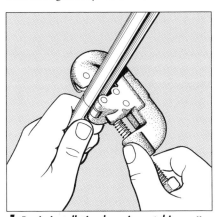

1 *Begin installation by using a tubing cutter to cut supply line to the old sill cock.*

2 *Remove the old sill cock from outside by unscrewing two flange screws from siding.*

3 *With water line cut simply pull out old sill cock and length of pipe attached to it.*

4 *Prepare supply line for soldering by polishing away tarnish with steel wool.*

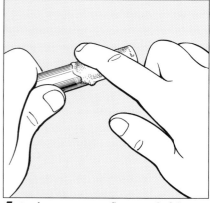

5 *Apply noncorrosive flux to end of the cut tubing and end of the new sill cock.*

In either case, shut off water at a point before the valve that controls the water flow to the sill cock. If you just shut the valve that feeds the sill cock, you won't be able to remove the valve. Open the sill cock, and drain that section of pipe.

With copper pipe, cut the supply line before the valve with a tubing cutter (Fig. 1). Remove the screws holding the sill cock to the house's siding. Pull out the sill cock.

To remove a sill cock installed with iron pipe, remove the screws holding the sill cock to the house's siding. Then, using two pipe wrenches, remove the interior valve and connecting pipe. Fasten one wrench to the pipe connecting the valve to the sill cock. Fasten the second wrench to the valve, and slowly turn the pipe out of the valve. Keep one wrench on the valve and move the second wrench to the pipe on the other side of the valve. Carefully turn the valve off the end of the pipe.

With iron pipe, thread an iron coupling to the supply line and thread a copper adapter into that. Wrap the threads on both fittings with Teflon tape to ensure a leak-proof joint. In areas with high min-

eral content in the water, use a dielectric union to connect the iron supply line to a length of copper tubing that will receive the sill cock. Such a union will prevent electrolytic corrosion caused by joining dissimilar metals.

Now the procedure is the same for both copper and iron pipe. Push the sill cock in from the outside of the house, but don't screw it in place. Measure the distance from the adapter or the cut end of the copper tubing to the sill cock. Cut a connector piece of copper pipe to suit. If the sill cock is long enough, all that may be necessary is to fit the end of the sill cock over the supply line (this will depend on the sill cock and the hardware you use to connect to the feed line).

Clean all connecting surfaces with steel wool (Fig. 4) or emery cloth, and apply flux to the ends to be soldered (Fig. 5). Push the joints together. Before sweating the joints, check that the run of pipe leading to the sill cock slopes slightly downhill. If not, lift the run of pipe using pipe hanger strap. Nail the strap into a floor joist, wrap it around the pipe and fasten it with a small nut and bolt. You may have to nail a scrap piece of wooden block

between the floor joists to position the pipe hanger strap.

Next, level the sill cock if the nozzle is mounted next to the handle (Fig. 7) and plumb it by eye if the nozzle is below the handle. Screw it to the siding. Back off the sill cock's handle so the washer on the stem's end won't get burned when you solder the joints.

Back inside, hold the solder above the joint, and heat the joint from below until the solder flows into the joint (Fig. 8). Quickly wipe the joint with a dry cloth to remove any solder globs and to ensure a clean, bright joint. Turn on the water, check for leaks, and you're done.

Garden hoses

To ensure that the hoses you connect to the sill cock have long lives, reel them in at the first sign of cold weather. Garden hoses are available in three different materials: plastic, reinforced plastic, or rubber. Plain plastic is the cheapest and the least durable of the three, but all types have the potential to get damaged if they are allowed to freeze. Consult the instructions on Page 202 for ways to repair your garden hoses.

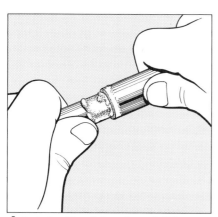

6 *Push the sill cock into the end of the cut tubing. No coupling is necessary for joint.*

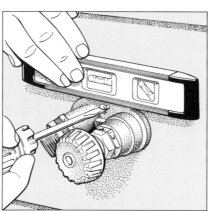

7 *Level freeze-proof sill cock. Attach to siding by driving in flange screws.*

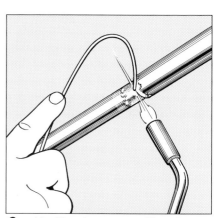

8 *Hold solder above joint and heat from below until solder melts and fills joint.*

How to troubleshoot
A WATER WELL

Degree of difficulty: Medium   **Estimated time:** 3 hours   **Average cost of materials:** $20

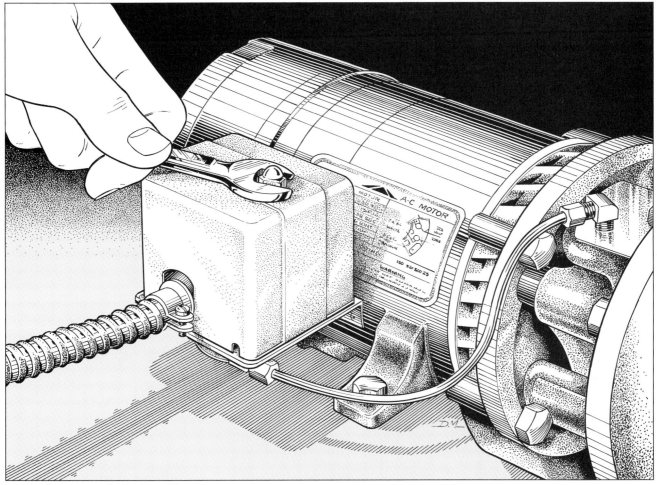

City-dwellers may not be familiar with water wells, but in millions of homes nationwide, water wells are the main components in plumbing systems.

There are roughly 13 million domestic water wells at work in the U.S. today. And while these systems are generally dependable, they can act up periodically. It's just in the nature of the beast. When a major component does fail, it's a good idea to hire a professional to make the repair. But most well system problems are minor and can cost little or almost nothing to fix. Learning how to approach the problems symptomatically is the trick, and not a complicated trick, once you gain a general understanding of the way water wells work.

To begin, there are four basic well types in use today. Three are fairly modern and one is a holdover from earlier times. They are most easily separated by their pumping mechanisms: piston pumps, single-drop and double-drop pipe jet pumps, and submersible pumps. Piston pumps can be located either at the surface or inside the well casing, jet pumps are always at the surface and submersible pumps—as their name implies—are always positioned inside the well casing, suspended within the water table.

Piston pumps

Because few piston pumps have been installed since the 1950s, we'll focus on the other types. But a few words on these great old pumps is in order. A piston pump is nothing more than a suction pump. Water is drawn into the pump cylinder by means of a moving piston that is fitted with leather seals which bear against the cylinder walls. In the old days,

41

and today as well, many of these pumps were driven by windmills. The piston is connected to a rod that extends up through the well casing and is attached to the shaft driven by the wind against the windmill's characteristic paddles. A check valve within the piston holds the water in place while another stroke pulls more water into the cylinder and up the riser pipe. With each stroke more water is raised until it finally spills from the riser at the surface. In this application the piston cylinder is submerged within the water well casing.

Piston pumps can also be located at the surface, either in the form of a classic hand-operated pitcher pump or in an electric version that features a cast-iron flywheel. These surface models work in the same basic way as the submersible piston pumps.

Jet pumps

As mentioned earlier, jet pumps come in two basic types: single-drop pipe and double-drop pipe. Both are located on the surface and operate by suction, so they are capable of lifting water only from shallower wells. They also need a continuous prime to work, which means the drop pipe or pipes plus the pump cavity have to be full of water in order to pull up more water. This prime is held by a foot valve as shown in the comparative drawings on Page 43.

When the pump is turned on, the prime water is pushed through the pump by impellers and new water is pulled up behind the prime water. The suction of a jet pump is further enhanced by an ejector. On single-drop systems, this ejector is located in the pump. Viewed simply, the ejector is nothing more than a restriction that boosts the velocity of the water passing through the pump. This creates a continuous vacuum that increases the lifting power of the pump.

On double-drop systems, the ejector is located at the bottom of the well and connects the two drop pipes. Water is drawn up through one pipe and once it gets to the pump, a portion is diverted into the second pipe. As the return water drops down this pipe, it passes through the ejec-

tor which creates even more pressure and greater lift in the suction pipe.

Because jet pumps are surface mounted, they must always fight the opposing forces of head pressure—the relative weight of a column of water—and atmospheric pressure. As such, their lifting power varies geographically. A single-drop pump may be able to lift water only from a 20-ft.-deep well in the mountains, but could lift up to 30 ft. of water on the plains. A two-drop system does substantially better, with many being able to lift water from 100 to 120 ft. deep. The design of the ejector is another variable with jet pumps; the smaller its restriction, the greater its lift.

Submersible pumps

In these systems, the pump is suspended directly in the aquifer. The pump itself contains an impeller that is powered by a sealed electrical motor. When the pump turns on, it simply forces water up the drop pipe and into your home. A submersible pump is generally considered the most trouble-free. But it does have

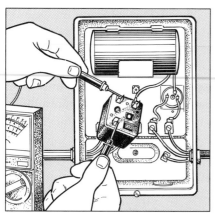
1 To test relay switch, set ohmmeter on RX1 scale and touch probes to terminals. No movement of arrow means a bad switch.

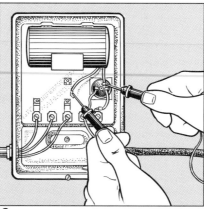
2 To test capacitor, leave ohmmeter on same setting and touch probes to terminals. No arrow movement means it's bad.

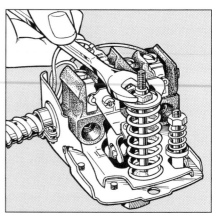
3 Remove cover and tighten nut on top of cut-in spring to increase pressure at which well pump turns on.

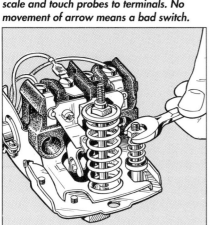
4 Adjust nut on cut-out spring the same way. Then turn on, run pump through full cycle, and note pressure readings.

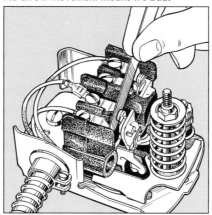
5 Clean both sets of points with small file or matchbook cover. Remove any filings, then re-gap points to proper specification.

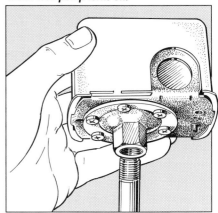
6 If you have to replace pressure switch, remove old switch and install new one of same rating. Attach wires accordingly.

SINGLE-DROP JET PUMP SYSTEM

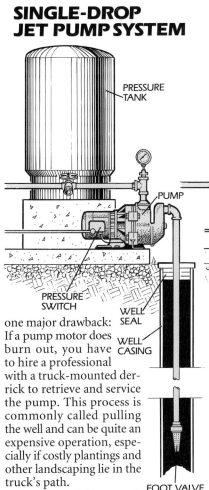

PRESSURE TANK

PUMP

PRESSURE SWITCH

WELL SEAL

WELL CASING

FOOT VALVE

DOUBLE-DROP JET PUMP SYSTEM

PRESSURE TANK

PUMP

PRESSURE SWITCH

WELL SEAL

WELL CASING

EJECTOR

FOOT VALVE

SUBMERSIBLE PUMP SYSTEM

PRESSURE TANK

DISCONNECT PANEL

CONTROL BOX

WELL CAP

PRESSURE SWITCH

PITLESS ADAPTER

WELL CASING

TORQUE ARRESTOR

PUMP

DM

TECHNICAL ASSISTANCE: GOULD PUMPS, INC.

one major drawback: If a pump motor does burn out, you have to hire a professional with a truck-mounted derrick to retrieve and service the pump. This process is commonly called pulling the well and can be quite an expensive operation, especially if costly plantings and other landscaping lie in the truck's path.

As you might expect, submersible pumps tend to be found in geographic clusters depending on the depth of the regional aquifer. For example, in the Southwest and some mountainous areas, the water is commonly several hundred feet deep. Neither piston pumps nor jet pumps can work in these areas.

Pressure tank and switch

The pump may well deliver the water but it's the pressure tank and pressure switch that make the system work in your home. These two components are common to just about every well system and they account for most of the performance problems that well owners encounter. Before going into pressure-related service problems, let's first take a brief look at how this end of the system works.

A pressure tank is often just a galvanized steel tank with an air-injection valve at its top or bottom. Threaded into the side of the tank, near the bottom, is a brass tee that has several ports. The two ends of the tee connect the well piping and the house piping to the tank. A pressure switch, pressure gauge and drain valve are often threaded into this tee as well. Though in many cases, one or all of

these are located elsewhere. Their individual positions make little difference in their performance.

When the system is newly installed, the air inside the tank is compressed against the top of the tank by the water pumped in from the well. The contents of the tank, then, consist of two layers: one liquid and the other compressed air. When an amount of water is drawn through a faucet, the air in the tank expands to displace the departed water. Because of this, the pump is not activated each time water is used but only after a substantial drop in tank pressure. This reduces wear and tear on the pump.

Tank pressure is indicated by the pressure gauge and monitored by the pressure switch. Pressure switches are calibrated to turn on the pump at one pressure and to turn it off at another. A 20/40 switch, for example, starts the pump when tank pressure drops to 20 psi and turns it off again when the pressure reaches 40 psi.

Electrical problems

If you have water one day and don't have it the next, remember the obvious. As any well specialist will tell you, a good share of service calls amount to little more than blown fuses or tripped breakers. The reason for this is simple: Electric motors require up to eight times more amperage to start than to keep running. Because of this increase in demand, a momentary start-up overload will occasionally trip your breaker or blow your fuse.

The only pumps not plagued by start-up overloads are those with capacitors built into their wiring systems. A capacitor will build up and store amperage and release it during motor start-up, thus preventing the fuses or breakers from blowing. You'll know a capacitor system if you have a separate control box near the pressure tank. If this type of system repeatedly trips breakers, then test across the relay switch with an ohmmeter (Fig. 1). Also test across the capacitor (Fig. 2). With the needle set to the RX1 scale—for both tests—the needle should jump forward and then settle back when you touch the terminals. If the needle doesn't respond, assume a defective component and replace the relay switch, capacitor or both as required. Caution: Avoid touching the capicitor terminals; capacitors have the potential to hold a considerable electrical charge and can cause electric shock. Also take adequate precautions when working with electricity; double-check that power is turned off when it needs to be. For information on how to use an ohmmeter, consult the directions given on Page 66.

Pressure switch problems

The two most common pressure switch problems are drift and fouled contact points. In the first instance, as a pressure

43

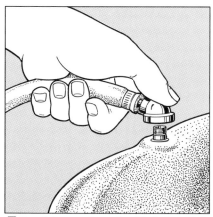

7 If tank is waterlogged, add air through snifter valve. Use compressed air or bicycle pump, or drain the tank and refill.

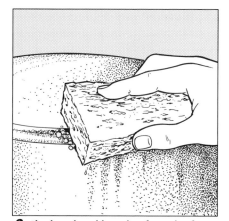

8 Check tank welds and snifter valve for air leaks by covering surface with soapy water and checking for air bubbles.

switch ages, its springs can weaken, allowing the pressure range to drift upward. When this happens, you may need to adjust the cut-in or cut-out settings on the switch. Remove the switch cover and look for two spring-loaded nuts, one large and one small. The larger spring and nut control the cut-in pressure.

To increase the pressure at which the well pump is turned on, tighten the nut on the larger spring (Fig. 3). To increase the pressure at which the pump shuts off, tighten the nut on the smaller spring (Fig. 4). Loosening these nuts, of course, will decrease the pump's cut-in and cut-out pressures. Although the potential range of adjustment is considerable, exceeding the stated limits of the switch can stress the pump motor. A 20/40 switch, therefore, should be adjusted only within 20- and 40-lb. extremes. The switch cover should have the recommended high- and low-pressure ratings on the manufacturer's label.

The second most common switch problem is simply one of maintenance.

The switch contains contact points similar to those found in the distributors of older cars. When these points become fouled, resistance is created, which creates heat, which in turn trips the breaker.

To solve this problem, shut off the power, remove the switch cover and file the closed points behind both springs with a small point-gapping file or the striking surface on a matchbook (Fig. 5). Wipe away any filings and other dirt that fall from the points. Then turn on the power and check the pressure ratings through a complete pumping cycle. To get the proper ratings, you may have to adjust the gap somewhat.

If the switch fails to operate properly after the spring and points adjustments, it's time to replace it with one of the same pressure and voltage ratings (Fig. 6). To do this, simply shut off the power, drain the tank, undo the wires and unthread the old switch; then install the new one. Then turn on the power, check the pressure gauge through a complete cycle and adjust the springs if necessary. Again, take

extra care when working with electricity and double-check your work.

Waterlogged tanks

As mentioned earlier, your pump doesn't come on every time you draw a glass of water because part of the tank contains compressed air. Eventually, however, some of this air will be carried out with the water. Also, in some cases, a pinhole leak in the tank will allow the air to escape. When the air is reduced or gone, the tank is referred to as "waterlogged." This causes the pump to turn on often and shut off early which shortens pump life. If your tank has an air-injection or snifter valve, simply add more air to the tank using compressed air or even a bicycle pump (Fig. 7). As a rule of thumb, the pressure of the air you add should be 2 to 3 lbs. less than the cut-in pressure of your switch.

If you don't have a snifter valve, simply drain the tank, which will allow more air to come in. Then refill the tank with water and you should be back in business. If a waterlogged tank is a frequent problem, however, suspect a tank leak, either at the snifter valve or on the surface, particularly where the tank has been welded. To test for a leak, add more air, then sponge a rich mixture of liquid dishwashing soap and warm water onto the tank. If you see bubbles coming from the snifter valve, replace it. If you see bubbles on the tank, you'll want to replace the whole tank.

Repriming

As mentioned before, most of your well troubles will be associated with the electrical or pressure systems. This is particularly true if you have a submersible pump which is generally trouble-free. Jet pumps, on the other hand, can go out of prime. When this happens, the pump will run continuously but deliver little or no water.

Luckily, repriming a jet pump is a quick fix. You'll find a prime nut on the pump and usually another one on the drop pipe—or one of the drop pipes—at the top of the well casing. Unthread these nuts and then simply pour pure water down the well until both openings overflow. Because the drop-pipe opening—if you have one—will be lower than that of the pump, fill the drop pipe first (Fig. 9), cap it off and move to the pump (Fig. 10). When the pump opening overflows, cap it off and restart the system. If the pump once again loses its prime soon after starting, assume that there's a clog in the foot valve. In this case, the drop pipe—or pipes—need to be pulled and the foot valve cleared or replaced.

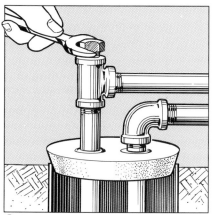

9 If your jet pump system has priming nut above well cap, remove nut and fill pipe with water. Then reinstall plug.

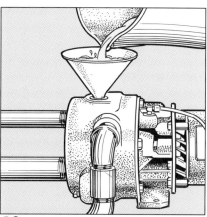

10 Remove priming plug on top of pump and pour water into cavity until it overflows. Reinstall plug and tighten securely.

How to choose
A WATER FILTER

Water that flows into our homes must sometimes be treated to bring it within tolerable purity levels.

1 One of the most common types of filters uses a replaceable activated-charcoal cartridge (inset). This unit mounts to spout and can be bypassed when filtered water is unnecessary.

Water has long been a symbol of cleanliness, purity and health. But today's modern world of technology has changed this. The practice of dumping industrial wastes into convenient nearby streams is probably as old as industry itself. Until the last century, though, there just wasn't enough industry to have a noticeable effect on the quality of the nation's water. Over time, increased industrialization and a boom in population combined to challenge the assumption that there was plenty of good water for everyone.

A recent Environmental Protection Agency study found that 30 percent of the water systems serving communities with populations of 10,000 or more were contaminated with industrial chemicals—an astounding figure considering that there are over 60,000 public water supply systems in the United States. To add insult to injury, a Cornell University study concluded that 66 percent of the households that were researched had substandard water.

The solution?

Ultimately, the problem must be dealt with at the source by joint efforts of government and industry, since over the years hundreds of millions of pounds of toxic chemicals are dumped into the nation's rivers, streams and lakes in the form of agricultural pesticides, sewage, heavy metals, radioactive substances, gas and industrial waste. Many concerned home owners, however, are not prepared to wait until something is done by government and industry to solve this enormous water pollution problem. Instead, they are directing their attention to immediate

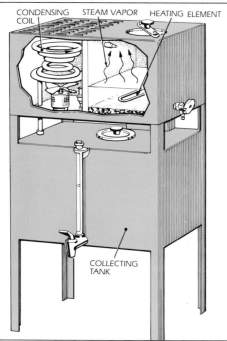

2 *Distillation condenses clean water vapor and leaves impurities behind. Storage tank collects water to be gravity fed.*

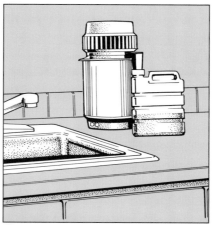

3 *Smaller capacity distillation units are available for countertop use. In about 7 hours, 1 to 1½ gallons can be produced.*

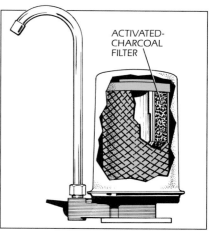

4 *Countertop charcoal filters are connected to a cold-water pipe. Replace elements as recommended by manufacturer.*

ways to treat the water in their homes used to drink and cook with. This is a highly complex task. The scope of the problem demands a variety of filtering systems—each suited for specific contaminants, depending on the water problem in a particular region.

The pollutants

To date, over 70,000 different water contaminants have been identified. These contaminants can be divided into five general classes: biological impurities (largely bacteria, but may include viruses and other microscopic parasites), dissolved organic compounds (including PCBs and other halogenated compounds), heavy metal salts (such as lead and mercury), dissolved gasses (primarily radon, which usually only appears in private wells) and suspended solid particles (such as asbestos fibers).

One obvious solution for clean drinking water is to buy bottled water. However, bottled water typically costs about 70 cents per gallon. And, it's certainly not as convenient as drawing water from your kitchen tap. Treating your own water is not only cheaper but offers you the assurance that the job is indeed being done properly.

Any attempt to treat a water supply must begin with an investigation into what contaminants are actually present. (See the information source list on Page 48 for places where you can get your water

tested, and for more details on water quality). Choosing a water treatment system designed to remove bacterial contamination, for instance, would be useless and unnecessary if your water is free of bacteria but contains other industrial wastes. (See the chart, below.)

Basic treatments

Perhaps the simplest filtering system is one that screens out suspended particles in the water such as asbestos. Sediment filters are graded as to the size of particle they will allow through and can range

from 5 to 25 microns. Many filtering systems use a sediment filter as a prefilter to remove large particles that may damage another part of the system.

Chemical treatment for eliminating bacteria, such as the addition of chlorine, is usually performed at the municipal water supply. Chlorination is done to prevent contamination of the water as it travels through the network of water pipes underground and reaches the home.

The most recent water-pollution problem to hit the headlines is radon, a naturally occurring radioactive gas which

Water Treatment Chart*	Reverse-osmosis	Distillation	UV radiation	Activated Charcoal	Ion-exchange	Aeration	Sediment filter	Chemical treatement
Bacteria[1]			●					●
Lead	●	●						
Mercury	●	●						
Arsenic	●	●						
Nitrates/Nitrites	●	●						
Sodium (salt)	●	●						
Organic chemicals				●				
Pesticides	●			●				
Radon				●		●		
Hard water					●			
Iron					●	●[2]		●
Odor				●		●		
Asbestos							●	
Cloudiness							●	

* Chart list some common contaminants and methods of treatment.
1. Activated-charcoal absorption may be require after UV or chemical treatment.
2. Ion-exange plus aeration.

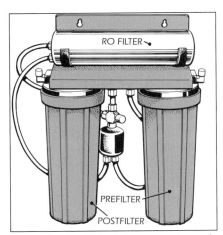

5 *Combination RO unit features a charcoal postfilter and sediment prefilter in separate canisters for simplified servicing.*

6 *Small tap-mounted RO filter can be used at home or on the road. It's capable of producing up to 12 gallons of water per day.*

became known largely as a result of its effect on the quality of air inside the home. The presence of radon gas in a home more often points to problems with a house's foundation, rather than with the water supply. But because radon is soluble in water, it has emerged as yet another cause for concern. When water containing radon leaves the tap or shower head, the radon dissipates into the air creating an unexpected air pollution problem. For this reason, treating for radon contamination means not only treating the drinking water, but treating the entire water supply for the home. One way of dealing with water containing radon is through outdoor-mounted aerators that allow the radon to dissipate harmlessly into the atmosphere. Radon contamination, like bacteria, is handled at the municipal level.

Charcoal filters
The most common type of water treatment uses an activated-charcoal filter to remove such contaminants as pesticides and organic chemicals, or to eliminate odors in water.

Activated-charcoal filters are also effective in removing radon and other dissolved gasses.

Activated-charcoal has the ability to adsorb, or bond strongly to, the impurities rather than simply absorbing them like a sponge.

After a period of time, a charcoal element will become loaded with contaminants and must be changed.

Because most contaminants can't be easily perceived in the water, you'll have to set up a schedule for filter replacement to ensure that your water is always clean. Base this on the manufacturer's instructions. Some units are equipped with automatic metering devices that gauge the

amount of water that has passed through the filter.

Charcoal filters are not effective against biological contaminants. In fact, these units can act as incubators for bacteria when left unused. Because of this, it's a good idea to let the water run through a charcoal filter for a few minutes after a long weekend or vacation.

Activated-charcoal filters come in a variety of sizes ranging from those that connect directly to the tap (Fig. 1), to those that are connected to the pipes that supply drinking water (Figs. 4 and 8). Prices can range from about $25 for the smaller units to $300 for large-capacity in-line models. The large units generally require less frequent filter changes.

Distillation systems
Traditionally, one of the most reliable methods for removing impurities in water is distillation. First, an electric heating element boils the water. Then, the steam is condensed and collected in a storage tank (Fig. 2). Metal salts and suspended solids don't vaporize and are removed. However, the distillation process will also remove desirable additions to the water such as fluoride. Distillation units give mixed results with dissolved organic compounds. Chemicals with high boiling points may be left behind when the water vaporizes, but others may boil off with the water and remain in the condensed product.

Distillation is a slow process that consumes a considerable amount of energy. A typical home-sized unit with a storage capacity of 3 to 25 gallons can take 2 to 3 hours to produce 1 gallon of distilled water. Small countertop models collect distilled water in a separate container and can take 7 hours to produce a gallon (Fig. 3). The cost to pro-

duce a gallon of distilled water can range from about 20 to 30 cents.

These units are independent of the house plumbing and are generally placed where the water is needed. Because the water is not under pressure, the unit must be high enough for convenient gravity-fed operation. Water stored for an extended length of time can become recontaminated with airborne bacteria. If the still's out of use for a while, drain and clean the storage tank before using it for drinking water.

Distillation units are also fairly expensive to buy, ranging in price from $200 to $600 depending on the capacity of the unit and features.

Ultraviolet irradiation
Ultraviolet irradiation (UV) water purifiers are quite effective against bacterial contamination. They are not, however, useful for any of the other types of pollution. They operate on the principle that exposure to intense ultraviolet light will destroy most microorganisms. These units are of particular value where water is obtained from a well. Homes serviced by a municipal water supply usually receive water already treated for biological contamination. UV purifiers are

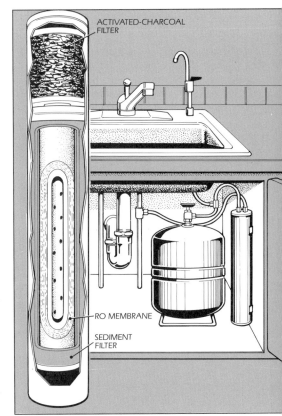

7 *RO units often use a pressurized tank to hold water until it's needed. This unit combines charcoal, sediment and RO filters.*

Maintaining an RO filter may include periodic replacement of the membrane. Some water filter manufacturers claim that adequate cleaning of their products is accomplished through an automatic back-flush cycle.

An RO unit is typically connected directly to the plumbing system and is often set up to service several taps. Because some of the water entering the filter becomes a waste stream for carrying the contaminants away, RO units usually make use of a storage tank to keep an ample supply of clean water on supply. While operating costs are low, average size units may range from $500 to $1000 in price. Small, tap-mounted units (Fig. 6) are also available.

Dealing with hard water

Aside from the contaminants that should be removed for health reasons, there are an assortment of chemicals that can make life somewhat difficult. Hard water contains sulfates and bicarbonates of calcium and magnesium. These calcium and magnesium bicarbonates can break down when the water is heated, leaving scaly deposits inside boilers, pots, coffee makers and irons. And, hard water can also interfere with the sudsing action of soap.

While it can help to replace soaps with synthetic detergents and to use cleansing products that contain softening additives, the most direct way of handling the problem is by treating the water with a water-softening unit that uses ion-exchange resins.

These resins are in the form of small beads. When hard water passes through the unit, the calcium and magnesium bond to the resins. After a certain period of time, the resins become saturated.

A salt-water solution is then flushed over the beads, removing the calcium and magnesium and replacing them with sodium. When the regeneration process is complete, the unit is ready to go to work again.

Depending on the type and make of the unit, the saturated resins may be replaced periodically by a qualified service company.

Other machines are self-regenerating and vary in the degree to which they're automatic (Fig. 9).

Be aware that because an ion-exchange unit replaces the chemicals that cause hard water with sodium, it's not advisable for those on sodium-restricted diets to drink water from this unit. Also remember that if you do need a softener, make sure you isolate your main cold water drinking faucets from your outdoor ones. Softened water is not suitable for feeding lawns and gardens.

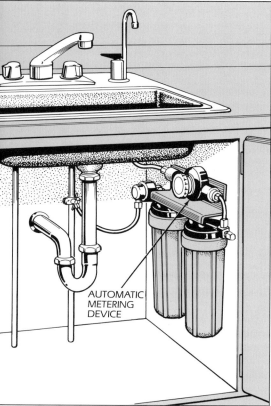

8 *Combination charcoal and sediment filter is connected to cold-water line. Unit has a metering device to signal filter changes.*

usually installed in combination with other filter types.

Reverse-osmosis units

Reverse-osmosis (RO) units employ a cellophane-like membrane as a filter. When water is forced against the membrane, a portion of it passes through, leaving the impurities behind to be carried away by a waste stream. These filters can be effective in dealing with dissolved salts, suspended solids and dissolved chemicals. RO units are commonly paired with an activated-charcoal filter to handle dissolved gases and assist in the removal of organic compounds. A sediment prefilter is commonly included to remove suspended particles before the water reaches the RO membrane (Figs. 5 and 7).

When shopping for an RO unit, take note that two types of membrane are available. One is designed to be used with chlorinated water where any bacteria has been eliminated. Because the bacteria can damage this type of membrane, it's important to make sure that you choose the right kind. Therefore, those who have unchlorinated tap water should use the membrane designated for that purpose—it's not bothered by bacteria, but will be damaged by the chlorine.

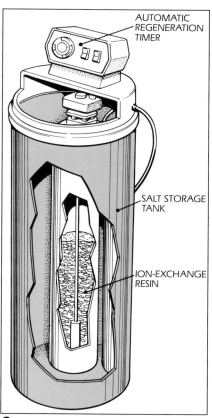

9 *Regenerating water softener has central canister containing ion-exchange resins. Salt-water cleans the resins.*

Lead pipes

If the results of your water tests reveal a high level of lead (typically above 0.05 mg/l), your copper water pipes may be joined with lead solder or the pipes themselves may be made of lead. Inspect the pipes for either lead-soldered joints or for lead pipes, which have a dull finish and can be scratched easily. Have a qualified plumber replace lead pipes, or resolder copper pipes with low-lead or silver solder, if present.

Water testing information sources

Several organizations, including retailers, offer information on water filters and testing. For a more comprehensive list of contaminants and water purity levels contact:

■ Water Quality Assocn., 4151 Napierville Rd., Lisle, IL 60532, (708) 505-0160.

■ Department of Public Affairs, EPA, A-107, Washington, DC 20460.

■ Water Test Corp., 33 S. Commercial St., Manchester, NH 03101, (800) 426-8378.

■ Sears offers free water-testing kits. Call (800) 426-9345.

How to maintain
A GAS-FIRED FURNACE

Degree of difficulty: Easy   **Estimated time:** 1 hour   **Average cost of materials:** $10

You've read and heard the yearly ads offering a routine tune-up of your gas furnace, but what exactly will you get for your money? In most cases, the entire job consists of cleaning and lubricating the blower unit and cleaning and adjusting the burner assembly. Rarely are new parts required.

Still, such simple maintenance is a worthwhile investment (even if you decide to pay for it) in the battle against the twin threats to furnace life and efficiency: dust and rust. A well-maintained furnace will last longer.

The value will be even greater when you handle the job yourself. This is a project that takes less than an hour and saves a service charge and scheduling hassles. As long as you stay clear of the control valve and limit switches, and put back everything as you find it, there's little chance of a serious blunder.

We should emphasize that we're assuming that yours is an older furnace that operates safely and predictably. We'll also limit our discussion to the simplest components within the furnace cabinet. We'll leave control valves, relays, thermostats and heat exchangers in the hands of professionals. We'll also assume that you change furnace filters regularly.

Reading the signs
When working properly, each burner in the cabinet should yield a continuous, steady blue flame. The ignition start

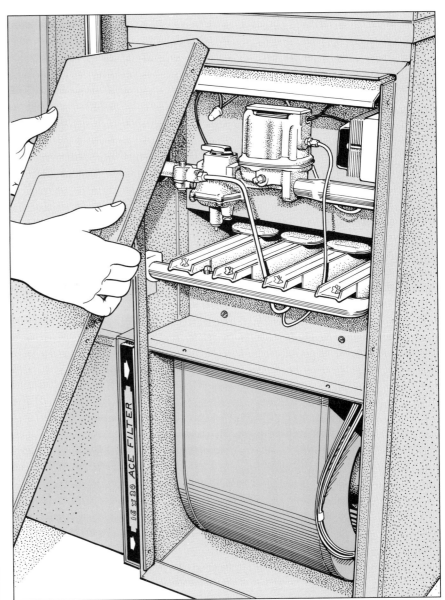

Turn off power to the furnace at the unit's disconnect switch or at the main service panel. Gain access to the blower and burners by lifting off the front panel.

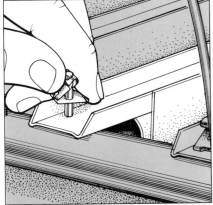

1 *After freeing the furnace's front panel, free burners from their supply-feed piping by removing fastening clips.*

should progress from one burner to the next evenly and without hesitation or a late flash.

A dirty, improperly adjusted burner assembly will display a variety of symptoms, all of which are visible through a given heating cycle. All you'll need to do is pull up a chair, remove the access panel, and observe. A standard gas furnace will have two, three or four burners, each with some sort of ignition crossover device. Study these components in both their start-up and continuous stages.

If you see a burner-to-burner start-up ignition that displays a noticeable puff and small flash, gas is not moving through the crossover pieces that ignite each burner in sequence. In all likelihood, one of

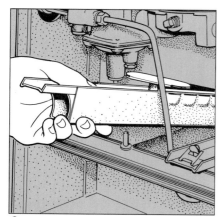

2 Tip the burner up and slide it out where you can work on it. Burners are often clogged on the inside by rust particles.

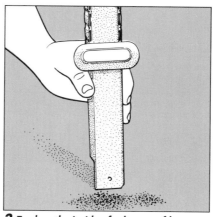

3 To clear the inside of a burner of loose rust particles, tap it firmly on the floor and vacuum up any debris.

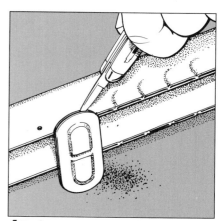

4 To clear a crossover member of rust particles or dirt, slide a knife blade, stiff wire or similar tool through it.

these crossover members is clogged with dirt or rust.

If you see a burner that does not ignite at all or only puffs on and off sporadically, it's a fairly good bet that the gas jet feeding that burner is partially plugged with dirt or rust.

On the other hand, a burner that shows flame gaps along its length during operation suggests that some of its gas ports are clogged. If you see a burner whose flame lift off its ports, you can bet that the air mixture on that burner is too rich. Conversely, if you see a flame that burns orange and "lazy" (wavering from side-to-side) assume too little air in the mix.

Cleaning the burner assembly
To begin, shut off the electrical disconnect so that the furnace cannot come on while it's being serviced. If your furnace does not have a dedicated disconnect, usually mounted on the side of the cabinet, shut off the circuit controlling the furnace at the main service panel or turn the gas control from ON to PILOT.

Once the panel is removed, vacuum the inside of the cabinet to remove all dust and cobwebs that could cause trouble later. This done, check the burner type and mounting mechanism. Conventional burners fall into two general categories. One is the "ribbon type" burner trough, shown here. The other assembly is made of cast iron and has two rows of round ports at the top of each burner. The differences between them is not important for our discussion. (If you find a third type, consisting of several steel burner tubes welded together, we suggest you call a service technician. This type must be disconnected from the control valve and pulled out in one piece.)

In most cases, each burner is attached to a gas feed pipe and is served by a removable gas jet. Each burner will also have some manner of air adjustment at its outer end.

Begin by removing the clip securing one of the burners (Fig. 1). Carefully lift the burner up and slide it out of its seat below the heat exchanger cell. Once

removed, up-end it, so that the open end faces down, and tap the burner repeatedly on the floor or some other hard surface (Figs. 2 and 3). This will dislodge the rust particles inside the burner.

If you've noticed gaps in the row of flames on that burner, poke a thin wire or small Allen wrench into each of the burner openings as well. Then tap the entire burner on the floor again. Finally, clean the openings in the crossover member with a thin-blade knife, and vacuum the entire burner thoroughly (Fig. 4).

To replace the burner, simply slide it back into position and replace the clip that holds it to the feed pipe. Then, remove each subsequent burner and repeat the process.

If one of the burners was not working, or flashed on only occasionally, you'll also want to clean the gas jet serving that burner. This is more easily accomplished while the burner is still out. It's usually best to back the entire jet from its threads in the feed pipe and clean it where you can see what you're doing. Again, a thin wire or

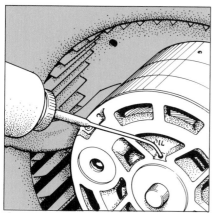

8 After uncapping, squirt several drops of turbine oil into the first shaft bearing port. Recap the port when done.

9 The long stem on a can of turbine oil will allow you to reach rear-shaft bearings without removing the motor.

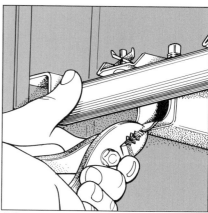

10 One type of air adjustment has an internal slide and open-end air intake. Pushing or pulling slide adjusts the air/gas mixture.

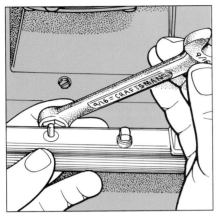

5 To remove a gas jet, use a box-end wrench. Because it is made of brass, the jet will break free with relative ease.

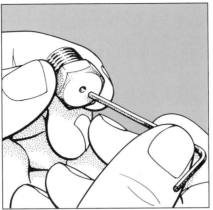

6 With the gas jet removed, use a stiff wire or Allen wrench to clear any dirt accumulation from a clogged gas jet.

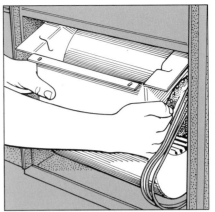

7 Most blower units are designed to be removed for servicing. Loosen the fastening screws and slide the blower out.

small Allen wrench works well in poking dirt or rust accumulations from the orifice (Figs. 5 and 6). Once you've cleared the orifice, thread the jet back into its opening and tighten it with a wrench until it feels snug. No joint compound is needed.

Servicing the blower unit

Servicing a furnace blower is easier than you might think, partly because manufacturers have designed them for easy access. Some blower housings are mounted on sliding tracks, while others tip down and out. At most, you'll need to undo a couple of hex-head screws and the electrical connection.

Begin by removing the blower compartment access panel. Remove the retaining screws and pull the fan housing out into your work space (Fig. 7). The unit's electrical connection will likely be in the form of a simple, two-prong plug. Unplug it to give yourself enough room to maneuver.

Pulling the unit will reveal a good deal of greasy dust on the motor's bell-hous-

ing and on the louvers of the fan. Both accumulations are potentially troublesome, as they cause the motor to run hot and the fan to move less air.

The best approach is to brush the dust loose with an old toothbrush, and then vacuum the entire assembly with a bristle attachment. It's also possible to remove the squirrel cage and hose it down with water, but this is seldom necessary.

With the blower unit cleaned up, check for oil ports on the bell housing, at each end of the shaft. These may be obvious, as when flip-cap ports are provided, or they may be merely rubber plugs, which are harder to find. A third possibility may be sealed bearings, which don't need lubrication. Check closely in any case.

If all you find are two rubber plugs, pry them out with a screwdriver or knife, and give each opening an ample squirt of turbine oil (Figs. 8 and 9). Turbine oil is more heat-resistant than other light lubricants and can be found at most appliance outlets. Finally, replace the two plugs and slide the blower unit back in place. Plug

the electrical connection back in and replace the hex-head screws. Finally, replace the lower access panel and restore power to the furnace.

Adjusting the burners

Air adjustments for gas burners come in several shapes (Figs. 10 through 13). You'll either find some form of sliding sleeve, which is open-ended, or rotating end caps. By sliding the sleeves or rotating the caps, you'll align their openings, to greater or lesser degree, with those of the burner.

To adjust the air mixture, turn the thermostat up so that the furnace kicks on. With the burners in operation, check for abnormal flames. If the flames burn blue but lift off of the burner, reduce the amount of air intake until the flames settle down. If you see an orange, lazy flame increase the amount of air intake. Continue to adjust each burner until you see a steady blue ribbon of flame above each. Finally, replace the access panel and settle in for a comfortable winter.

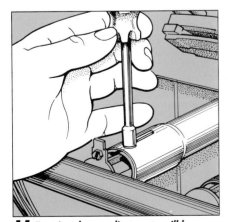

11 Exterior-sleeve adjustments will have setscrews which lock the adjustment in place. Loosen setscrews with a nut driver.

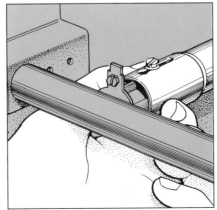

12 With the setscrew loosened, slide the sleeve forward, or back, to adjust for the proper amount of air.

13 A final air-adjustment mechanism features a rotating cap, which aligns its opening with those of the burner.

How to maintain
RADIATORS

Degree of difficulty: Easy Estimated time: 1 hour Average cost of materials: $15

There are still a good many steam and hot water radiant heat systems in service today, and many still cycle through iron radiators. Keeping these systems (many of which are over 50 years old) working smoothly can be a challenge. While the boiler end of a steam or hot water system should probably be left to the pros, servicing radiators is well within the reach of most do-it-yourselfers.

Types of systems
The degree of difficulty and the amount of service required will depend, to a great degree, on which type of system you own. While the earliest systems were steam-driven, and many still are, many others have since been converted to hot water. These conversions make energy sense, as it takes fewer BTUs to create hot water than it does steam. In fact, you'll find three or four different types of radiant heat boiler systems today. The most recent installations will have fin-tube baseboard heaters or even in-floor radiant piping, often controlled by several zone switches located throughout the home. The radiating parts of these systems are pretty much maintenance-free.

With older systems, you'll find several variations. You might see a steam-heat/radiator system, a hot water radiator system or a steam system converted to hot water. The latter two are probably most common.

Of the two types, hot water systems, both original and converted, are the easiest to service. In fact, air lock is about the only problem in hot water radiators. If you find a single, cold radiator, you can bet there's air trapped in a few of its cells. To solve this problem, you'll just need to release the air through a brass bleeder valve located high on the outlet side of the radiator (Fig. 1). These valves will vary in configuration, but most can be opened with a hex-head key or a screwdriver. Just turn the key or screw counterclockwise until air and water begins to sputter through the bleeder. As soon as water alone sprays through, close the valve.

Servicing steam radiators
With steam radiators, you'll find two likely trouble spots. Both have to do with trapped water. If the radiator does not

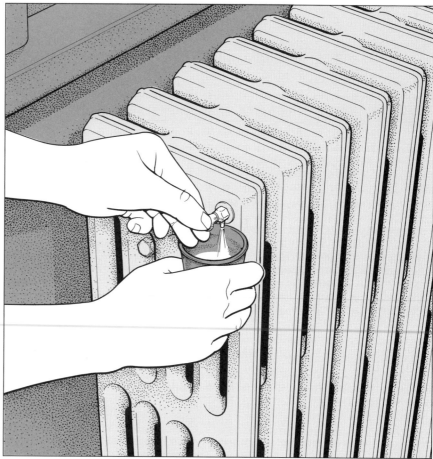

Bleeding a hot-water radiator at the beginning of each heating season is a mundane but necessary ritual. In homes equipped with older steam radiators, new steam vents must often be installed when the old vents fail. Neither task, however, is very difficult.

heat, chances are the steam vent (a small blow-by valve located high on the last cell of the radiator), may be clogged. This happens over time, as water released through the vent meets room temperature air and calcifies around the opening.

You might try scraping away these mineral salts, but replacing the vent is a cheaper and more certain long-term solution. As the threaded fittings of these vents are made of brass, they can usually be freed fairly easily, often without the help of a wrench (Fig. 2).

Start by isolating the radiator from the rest of the system by closing the inlet valve. This will allow you to work on that radiator without shutting down the boiler. Then, thread the old vent out and

thread the new one in until it feels snug and the vent opening faces straight up. To facilitate easy removal next time, lightly coat the threads with an anti-seize compound (Fig. 3). Finally, turn the radiator back on.

If a radiator does not heat consistently and emits a pounding noise, assume that the bellows in the steam trap has failed. A steam trap may take several shapes, depending on the manufacturer, but you'll find it spliced between the radiator outlet and the condensate return pipe, at floor level. A steam trap collects water that condenses from the steam and routes it back to a condensate collection tank near the boiler. The thermal bellows within the trap is heat sensitive and allows

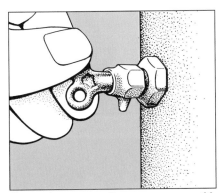

1 *On a hot-water radiator, use a compatible key or screwdriver to open the bleeder-valve and release trapped air.*

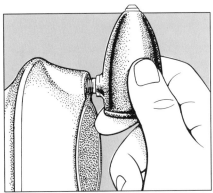

2 *Shut off inlet valve and unscrew steam vent from its threaded opening. This can usually be done easily.*

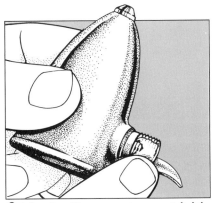

3 *Before installing a new steam vent, lightly coat its threads with anti-seize compound to ease removal in the future.*

only the relatively cool water to escape. The steam is thereby trapped and held within the radiator.

When a bellows fails, steam is allowed past it, draining heat from the radiator cells and producing a pounding noise. The simplest approach is to open the trap and replace the bellows, and possibly, the trap seat. Both are relatively inexpensive. As seats are often fused to the trap through years of oxidation, they can be very difficult to remove. Unless a seat is clearly pitted, it is better left in place.

The access cap of the trap may also be stuck in place, so start by tapping lightly around the female threads of the trap with a hammer. To undo the cap, use a 12-in. pipe wrench and apply steady pressure (Fig. 4).

With the cap removed, use channel-joint pliers or a small wrench to unthread the old bellows from it (Fig. 6). Then, take the bellows with you to a well-stocked heat-and-air service company for a compatible replacement. (The new bellows may not look like the old one.) Finally, thread the new bellows into the cap, coat the cap threads with anti-seize compound, and thread the cap back into the

bowl of the trap (Fig. 7). When you recharge the radiator, it should be its old self again.

Maintaining radiators

Because heating can be the highest monthly expense during the winter, it's a wise idea to follow some simple steps to obtain the most heat from your radiators. Begin by periodically vacuuming

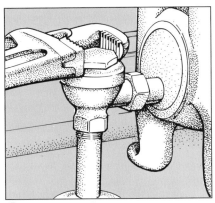

4 *To remove a defective steam-trap bellows, apply steady pressure with a 12-in. pipe wrench to loosen the cap.*

dust and debris that may have collected between the heating cells. Move furniture away from the fronts and sides of radiators. Also, a reflective metal plate placed behind a radiator can help to optimize the amount of heat generated. Avoid painting radiators; paint buildup can significantly decrease the heat produced by a radiator.

Saving on heating costs

Since the cost of energy skyrocketed, home owners have been advised to lower their thermostats—particularly at night. And drawing curtains at night can help prevent heat from escaping. Whether your heating system is gas-fired or runs on oil, you can reduce the heating part of your energy bill by sealing cracks and crevices around windows and doors with weather stripping or caulk. Follow the directions on Page 164 to install a storm door, if necessary. Some utility companies offer free energy audits and provide tips on how to save on energy costs. In some instances, they will provide gaskets to install behind socket plates and switch plates if an audit reveals that heat is escaping into the walls at these points.

5 *A thermal steam-trap bellows is flexible, allowing it to expand and close the trap against escaping steam.*

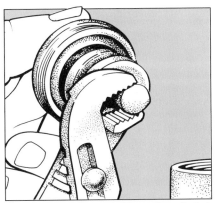

6 *Even if no defect is visible, replace the bellows with a new one. To remove it, thread it from its cap with pliers or a wrench.*

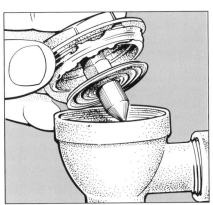

7 *After threading a new thermal bellows into the cap, coat the cap threads with compound and tighten the cap in place.*

How to choose
AN AIR CONDITIONER

Selecting an air conditioner depends on the size of the area to be cooled and energy efficiency factors.

Home air conditioning, over the relatively brief span of a Baby Boomer's lifetime, has erupted from an almost unheard-of luxury to a virtual necessity. In 1948, despite a multimillion-dollar promotional campaign, there was so little interest in home air conditioning that the Carrier Corp. was considering chucking the whole idea. By the mid-'80s about 85 percent of the new homes built came with air conditioners. In many areas, air conditioning has become the largest single user of electric power. As a nation, we now spend about $10 billion dollars a year—more than the entire gross national product of many Third World nations—to keep cool and dry.

Modern air conditioning really started about 1900, when Willis Carrier conducted his pioneering investigations into the relationships between air temperature and humidity that led to the world's first air conditioner installation. It took another quarter-century before air conditioning was used just to make people comfortable, and then it was still enough of a novelty to draw crowds at movie theaters. Signs outside proudly proclaimed "20 degrees cooler inside!" But it wasn't until the early '50s that air conditioner sales took off. Since then, areas of the country that had been thought of as just too hot became prime real estate for sun-belt living.

What they do
An air conditioner does two different, though quite related, jobs: cooling indoor air and removing unwanted moisture from that air. Both tasks require taking energy from inside and dumping it outside. It's easy to see that if an air conditioner pulls energy (in the form of heat) out of the air, the air's temperature will drop. How it removes moisture is a little less obvious.

The basic point to keep in mind is that the warmer air gets, the more moisture it can hold. If air—at any temperature—is holding all the water vapor it can, it's said to be saturated, or to have a relative humidity (RH) of 100 percent. If it contains, say, half that amount, its RH will be 50 percent. If you lower the temperature of the air without adding or removing any moisture, its capacity for holding water vapor would drop, and its RH would rise. Drop the temperature low enough, and the air can no longer hold all its moisture: that's why air conditioners sometimes drip water. If the cool air is reheated by mixing with the warmer air in the room, the air will have a lower RH due to the water removed when the air was cold.

How they work
Many people think air conditioners are mysterious gadgets. They're really not. Although they are more complicated than, say, electric fans or space heaters, they do their job by making use of only a couple of basic principles. First, when a gas is compressed, it gets hot—think of how a bicycle pump heats up when you inflate a tire—and when a liquid evaporates, it gets cold—think of an alcohol rub-down. Secondly, a hot material gives off heat to its surroundings and a cold one absorbs heat.

The essential components of an air conditioner, heat pump and refrigerator are a compressor, a condenser, an evaporator and a working fluid. The fluid liquifies when compressed and evaporates when the pressure is released. Nowadays this fluid is a fluorocarbon, such as DuPont's Freon compounds. In times past, sulphur dioxide and ammonia were used widely.

In an air conditioner, the evaporator is located indoors while the compressor and condenser are located outdoors where the room's heat is to be dumped. The working fluid is cycled back and forth between them. Here's an idea of how the air-conditioning cycle works:

In the evaporator, liquid refrigerant is allowed to evaporate by releasing the pressure applied to it. Its temperature drops sharply, and the cold gas absorbs heat from the room, via the fins on the evap-

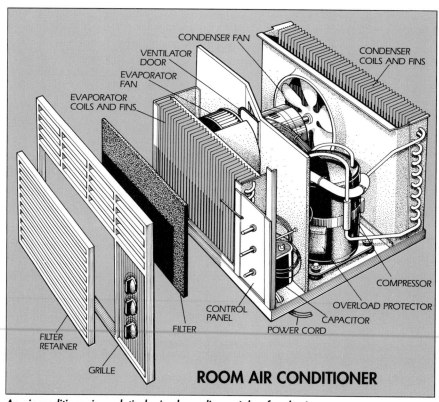

CONDENSER FAN
VENTILATOR DOOR
EVAPORATOR FAN
EVAPORATOR COILS AND FINS
CONDENSER COILS AND FINS
FILTER RETAINER
GRILLE
FILTER
CONTROL PANEL
POWER CORD
CAPACITOR
OVERLOAD PROTECTOR
COMPRESSOR

ROOM AIR CONDITIONER

An air conditioner is a relatively simple appliance. It has four basic parts: an evaporator that absorbs heat from a room, a condenser that expels this heat outside, a working fluid that changes from gas to liquid as it circulates between the two coils, and a compressor.

orator's coils. The gas, somewhat warmed now, is then pumped to the compressor. There, the gas is compressed until it liquefies, becoming quite warm (about 200° F.) in the process. The hot liquid then goes to the compressor's condenser coils where it loses heat to the outside air. The cooled liquid is then pumped to the evaporator, where the entire cycle starts again. The net result? Heat from the indoors absorbed by the evaporator's coils is "dumped" outside the house.

Just about all air conditioners used in the home work this way, but there are some major variations in design. Probably the most popular kind of home air conditioner is the room, or unitary, type. Unitary models are so called because the entire assembly is built in a single unit, designed to be mounted in a window or in a specially made cavity in the exterior of a wall.

The next most popular type is the central air conditioner. This is a single unit that services a number of rooms, or a whole house. Typically, the evaporator is located in a furnace duct that supplies air to many rooms of a house. The condenser and compressor are separated from the evaporator, and are mounted outdoors. Insulated tubing connects them all.

The third, and newest, type of air conditioner is the so-called split model. Introduced a few years ago by the Japanese, split air conditioners use a single condenser and compressor, much like central units.

But, instead of using a single duct-mounted evaporator, the split models have multiple point-of-use evaporators—one for each room that requires cooling. Instead of circulating cooled air, like the central units, the split units circulate refrigerant to the various locations being cooled throughout the house.

Advantages and disadvantages

Each type has its advantages and disadvantages. Unitary air conditioners have the lowest installed cost—their packaged design makes for a "plug-in" installation. All that is needed is a wall or window that separates indoors from outdoors and an adequately sized electric line. Everything—compressor, condenser, evaporator and air-circulation fan—is built into the package. Unitary air conditioners only cool the area in which they're installed. But if you want to cool several rooms, you're stuck with purchasing several units.

Also, because a unitary model has its condenser and evaporator located fairly close together, it's hard to avoid heat from the hot side leaking over to the cool side, and thus lowering the air conditioner's efficiency. The proximity of the compressor to the inside of the house also makes for potentially noisy operation.

Central air conditioners, on the other hand, are more demanding in terms of installation and, as a result, have higher installation costs. However, central models do tend to have higher efficiencies than unitary ones and can be designed to filter air better than the unitary type. The remote compressor also helps keep noise levels low.

The split types, as you might guess, are a sort of compromise between the other two. Installation problems are similar to those of central air conditioners. In homes without existing heating ductwork, the split models are considerably simpler to install than central units. But if the ductwork is in place, installation costs of split units are apt to be higher. Splits share the central models' quiet operation. They also offer the advantage of easy zoning, which central models lack. Efficiencies of split type air conditioners are typically high, in part because they tend to make the most of the latest technology. Since splits don't use a common air-circulating duct, they're not suited for whole-house filtered air supplies.

How to buy

Moving heat from one place to another isn't cheap. In fact, over the last 10 years or so, most of the research and development on air conditioners has focused on reducing the operation costs. While this effort has paid off in models with improved energy efficiencies, the units tend to cost more, in a way offsetting the savings in energy use, at least for the first several years of operation. It takes a bit

of calculation to see which air conditioner is best for you.

To begin with, you'll have to determine the cooling requirements of your home. If you are planning to purchase a central or split system, it's best to have a cooling contractor come to your house and do a cooling audit. He or she will measure the volume of air in each room; the number of windows; the area they occupy and their orientation toward north, south, east and west; the type and amount of insulation present in the walls and ceiling; and many other aspects of the estimating business.

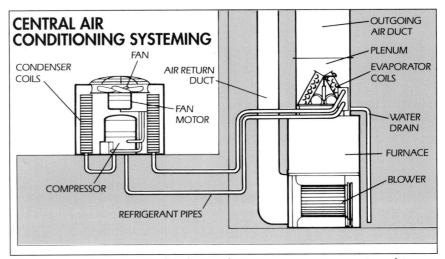

A central air-conditioning system has the same basic components as a room air conditioner but they are positioned differently. In the central system, the compressor and condenser coils are located outside the house, the evaporator coils are located inside your home's furnace, and the working fluid passes between the two locations in insulated pipes.

It's important to realize that any air conditioning system must be sized properly to the cooling load; otherwise the high efficiencies of the equipment will be lost. While it is possible to do this audit yourself, it's a better idea to have at least three different contractors do it for you. Get written estimates from each one and make sure the specifications are for the same equipment.

If, however, you are looking for a room air conditioner that you plan to install yourself, you'll have to do the audit. For a thorough job, the best source is a booklet called *The Consumer Selection Guide For Room Air Conditioners*, published by the Association of Home Appliance Manufacturers. It costs $1 from AHAM, 20 North Wacker Dr., Chicago, IL 60606.

The result of this audit will be the required cooling load expressed in BTU/hr. This is how the units are sold. If you don't have time to do the full-scale audit, a ballpark figure can be determined by multiplying the square footage in your room by 27 to get the estimated BTU/hr.

But do keep in mind that this represents the roughest of estimates. The audit is by far the best way to go.

Efficiency ratings

After you've determined the number of BTU/hr. you need, shop for the unit that meets your load requirements. The two key numbers are the purchase price and the Energy Efficiency Rating. The EER is simply a measure of how much electricity an air conditioner consumes per unit of heat removed from the room. It's expressed in BTUs per watt. The higher the EER, the more energy efficient the air conditioner will be.

The EER is like a car's EPA rating. It's a useful number for comparing air con-ditioners, but it's less useful for estimating just what an air conditioner will cost over a cooling season's actual operation. That's because EERs are measured under a carefully controlled set of circumstances. They can't reflect the machine's perfor-mance under the different conditions.

The EER number appears on a bright yellow label, marked *Energy Guide*, that all air conditioners must carry. The label also carries the unit's BTU/hr. cooling load rating and shows where the particular unit falls in comparison to other mod-els of the same capacity. The label also gives the estimated costs for running the unit for a year in the area of the country in which you live. (For more on estimat-ing your yearly costs, see the box on this page.) Low efficiency models generally have EERs around 6. High efficiency units sport EERs around 9, although newer models can be found with EERs as high as 10. Keep in mind that split and central units have higher EERs than room mod-els, often between 10 and 15.

Another number you may find listed on some air conditioner specifications is the dehumidification capacity, generally in terms of pints per hour.

Unfortunately, there is no generally accepted test procedure for this charac-teristic. Therefore, it's not clear what these numbers mean or how much to rely on them when comparing different units.

With all this information on hand, your choice should be based on a reasonable estimate of how much the unit will cost to operate for your cooling season. As men-tioned before, the high efficiency models often have the higher price tags, but their increased efficiency can spell out lower operating costs that could pay for the higher price within a few years. This is why your home cooling audit and intel-ligent shopping with the *Energy Guide* label are so important.

Warranty and repair

Before you make your final decision, be sure to factor in the type of manufactur-er warranty and whether the retailer has a service department with a good local reputation. Generally, room air condi-tioners perform remarkably well, but when they don't, you need a local repair facility. While some retailers offer extend-ed warranties, they tend to be expensive. If you can, use a credit card that offers extended warranties on purchases.

Finally, how you run your air condi-tioner can make as much difference to your electric bill as which model you buy. First and foremost, don't run it unless you need it. Once outdoor temperatures drop to about 80° F, you can often do just as well by opening a window. Also, try raising the temperature setting a little bit. It's hard to predict exactly what this will save in any particular situation, but some studies have shown that raising the set-ting 2° or 3° can provide between 10 and 25 percent savings in operating costs.

Also, keep windows closed during the day when you are not air conditioning because most houses take a relatively long time to heat up if they are sealed. Keep shades or blinds closed particularly on windows that face east and west because, in the summer, heat gains from these two directions are greater than from windows that face south. Finally, keep the filter clean and whenever possible, run the unit in the recirculating mode, rather than its ventilating mode.

What Are The Savings Of High Efficiency?

A high-efficiency air conditioner will definitely cost less to run than its lower-efficiency counterpart. It will also generally have a higher price tag. The chart and map below should help you decide which unit is the best buy.

To fill in the chart, you'll need to find out—or estimate—a few num-bers. The first is the number of hours during the year that the unit will be operating. The map below shows the average number of hours for the var-ious regions of the United States. This is a rough but serviceable number.

Next, you need the BTU/hr. rating. This depends on the size and other characteristics of the room you want to cool. To determine this, see the explanation on Page 55. Then you need the EER rating for the unit you want to buy. This appears on the bright yellow *Energy Guide* label attached to every unit. The last piece of information you need is the rate you pay for electricity. You can obtain this either from an old electric bill or by calling your local utility. The .001 column is simply to convert your answer into dollars per year.

In the sample below, we are com-paring the estimated yearly operating costs of a low-efficiency room air con-ditioner (EER 6) and one with a high rating (EER 9.5). As you can see, the higher EER unit would save more than $26 a year in operating costs.

Hours of Operation (from map)		Air Con-ditioner Rating (BTU/hr.)		EER (from label)		Electric Rate ($/KWH)		Conversion Factor		Yearly Operating Cost
600	×	8000	÷	6	×	.09	×	.001	=	$72.00
600	×	8000	÷	9.5	×	.09	×	.001	=	$45.47

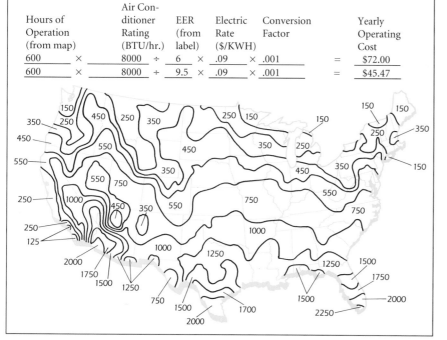

How to install
A VENTILATOR

Degree of difficulty: Medium   **Estimated time:** 5 hours   **Average cost of materials:** $50

Ventilators can solve humidity problems in bathrooms. Depending on the model, a ventilator can be combined with a lighting fixture. Make sure to shut off power to the circuit and test that power is indeed off before working.

Ever since the energy crunch of the mid-1970s, home owners have been busy sealing drafts and adding insulation to combat energy loss—both heating and cooling. However, while these conservation measures are effective in saving energy, in many cases they create a new problem: inadequate ventilation. Many good-intentioned people have buttoned up their houses so tightly that stale room air and moisture have no way to escape. Proper ventilation is especially important in the bathroom where excessive moisture can ruin paint, wallpaper and, eventually, the wall itself along with the insulation behind it. Most bathrooms have a window for ventilation. But, it's inconvenient to open and close the window every time someone uses the bathroom, showers or shaves. And in the winter, the window is seldom opened.

An effective way to end moisture problems in any bathroom—with or without a window—is to install a ventilator unit. A ventilator is simply a ceiling-mounted exhaust fan that draws out moist, stale room air and vents it through a duct to the outdoors. If your bathroom is located on the top floor, it is easiest to vent the unit through the roof. For bathrooms situated below another floor, you'll need to vent it through the house wall. We show how to handle both types of installations here.

Ventilators are available in a wide variety of styles and sizes to suit your needs

57

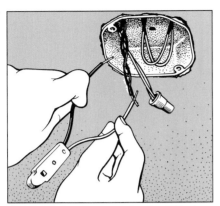

1 *Hold probe of tester on hot lead (black wires) and touch other probe to metal box. Power is off if the tester doesn't light up.*

2 *Hold the ventilator housing upside down against the ceiling and trace around its flange with a pencil to mark the cutout.*

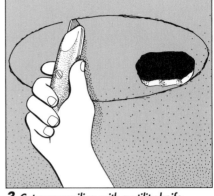

3 *Cut away ceiling with a utility knife. An off-center cutout positions electrical box on ventilator nearest to the power cable.*

and decor. They're sold at home centers and kitchen and bath showrooms. The ventilator installed here is a combination exhaust fan and light.

Ventilators are rated according to the cubic feet of air they exhaust per minute (cfm) and by their operating noise level, which is measured in sones.

One sone, for example, is equivalent to the sound made by a modern refrigerator. A typical ventilator operates at about 3 to 4 sones.

To determine the volume of your bathroom, multiply: length x width x height. An 8 x 10-ft. room with an 8-ft.-high ceiling contains 640 cu. ft. Therefore, a 100-cfm ventilator will exchange the room air in about 6½ minutes and more than nine times per hour. When selecting your ventilator, keep in mind that the minimum recommended air exchange rate for bathrooms is eight changes per hour. Also, some ventilators can be placed directly over a tub or shower stall. For this type of installation, though, you must use a ground-fault circuit interrupter (GFCI) as an added safety precaution against electrical shock. Consult Chapter 6 for information on GFCIs and where they should be installed.

In addition to the ventilator, you'll also need a length of round duct, either flexible or metal; a vent cap for mounting to the roof or side wall; and, if any rewiring is necessary, some nonmetallic sheathed electrical cable.

Installation procedures
The installation shown is the most common and easiest: replacing an existing ceiling-mounted light fixture with a fan-light ventilator. For other installations, you'll have to tap into a nearby circuit and run an electrical cable to the ventilator's location. If you are inexperienced with electrical installations, you may want to hire a licensed electrician to do the

wiring. You will still save money, however, if you install the ventilator yourself following the directions here.

Shutting off the power
Begin by shutting off the power to the light fixture at the fuse box or circuit breaker panel and post a note nearby advising others that you are working on the circuit and that it should remain off. Remove the light fixture to expose the electrical box. Next, use an electrical circuit tester to check that power to the circuit is indeed off. Place one probe of the tester on the hot lead (black wires) and hold the other probe on the metal box (Fig. 1). Just to be safe, check the other lead, too.

When the tester verifies that the power is indeed off, then it's safe to proceed. The box will be wired either at the end of an electrical run or, more likely, in the middle of a circuit. In either case, remove the existing electrical box. All the electrical connections will be made later in the junction box on the ventilator unit itself.

Notice that the box on the ventilator is usually positioned off to one side—it isn't

mounted in the center of the unit. Therefore, it's important to position the ventilator so that its box is closest to the wires in the ceiling. Otherwise, the wires may not be able to reach into the box and it would be impossible to make the necessary connections.

Next, hold the ventilator upside down against the ceiling and trace around its housing with a pencil (Fig. 2). Using the pencil line as a guide, cut out the ceiling with a compass saw or a sharp utility knife (Fig. 3).

Notice that the hole from the old electrical box is located off-center, near the edge of the cutout. This will position the electrical box on the ventilator nearest to the existing wires.

Then, nail or screw wood blocks to the joists to provide solid support for mounting the ventilator (Fig. 4). You may need to double up the blocks in order to center the ventilator in the ceiling cutout. Test-fit the ventilator in the cutout to be sure that it sits flush with the finished ceiling. This is important since the grille and lens assembly won't fit properly if the housing isn't installed correctly. Now

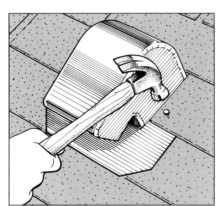

7 *Fasten vent cap with roofing nails fitted with rubber washers. Nail through flashing and apply roof cement to nail heads.*

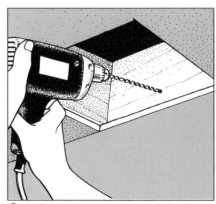

8 *To install a wall-mounted vent cap, first cut away the ceiling and bore a pilot hole through the header joist to the outside.*

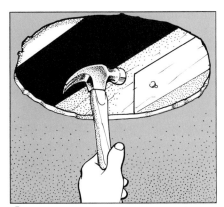

4 Nail wood-block supports to joists for mounting the ventilator. If possible, work from above in the attic or crawl space.

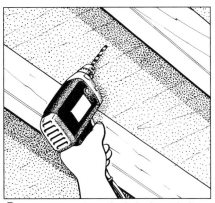

5 Bore a ⅜-in.-dia. pilot hole through the roof, between two rafters, to establish the center of the roof-mounted vent cap.

6 After sawing the vent-cap hole, apply roof cement to cap's bottom surface and slide it under the upper course of shingles.

decide where to run the duct—either up through the roof or out through the side of the house.

Roof-mounted vent

From inside of the attic, mark the desired vent-cap location on the roof between two rafters. Choose a spot near the ventilator to avoid a long duct-run with lots of bends. The straighter the duct-run is, the more efficiently the ventilator will work. Bore a ⅜-in.-dia. hole through the roof to establish the center of the vent cap (Fig. 5). Push a brightly colored wire through the hole to make it easy to spot from outside.

Now, working from the outside of the house, use the ⅜-in.-dia. center hole as a reference point to lay out and cut the vent-cap hole. Make the cutout in the roof with a saber saw or compass saw.

Next, carefully pull out the nails from the shingles directly above the cutout. Then, slide the vent cap into place so that its flashing is under the upper course of shingles and over the lower course (Fig. 6). Trim the shingles, if necessary, to cover the maximum amount of flash-

ing. Remove the vent cap and spread roof cement on the underside of the flashing to prevent water leakage.

Slide the vent cap back into place and nail through the shingles and flashing using aluminum roofing nails with rubber washers (Fig. 7). Cover each exposed nail head with roofing cement. Now go inside and attach the duct to the vent cap and run it to the ventilator location. Save the final connections until the ventilator has been installed.

Wall-mounted vent

When it isn't possible to vent through the roof, you'll have to run the duct above the ceiling and have it vent out through the side of the house.

Start by peeking up into the ceiling cutout to determine which direction the joists run. The duct will run between the joists and out the wall. It's easiest to vent out the nearest wall.

However, if the nearest wall is the front of the house, you may want to vent the duct in the opposite direction out the back where the vent cap will be less noticeable. Running perpendicular to the

ceiling joists, at the outside wall, is the header joist. Note that it's necessary to bore a pilot hole through the header joist to the outside to indicate the center of the vent cap.

In the best of situations, you'll be able to reach the header from the ventilator cutout in the ceiling. But more than likely, the wall will be too far away to reach. In this case, it's necessary to cut an access hole in the ceiling, where it meets the wall, to expose the header. Measure about 12 in. from the wall and cut out a section of ceiling from the center of one joist to the center of the next. If you remove the ceiling section carefully, it can be replaced and patched.

Now, with the access hole cut, bore a ⅜-in.-dia. pilot hole through the header, sheathing and siding (Fig. 8). Then, move outside and, using the pilot hole as a guide, lay out the wall vent-cap hole.

Next, cut the vent-cap hole with a saber saw (Fig. 9). Slide the vent cap into the hole and hold it against the siding. Scribe a pencil line around the cap's flange onto the siding.

Then, pull away the vent cap, apply caulk inside of the lines (Fig. 10), and slide the cap back in place. Secure the vent cap by screwing through its flange with aluminum or stainless-steel pan-head wood screws (Fig. 11).

From the inside, slip the stabilizer ring over the vent-cap pipe and nail it to the header joist with 1-in. roofing nails (Fig. 12). Next, attach the duct end to the vent-cap pipe with duct tape. Then, feed the duct between the joists until the free end has reached the ceiling cutout that was made for the ventilator.

Wiring procedures

The easiest way to make the electrical connections is from above in an attic. However, you can also fish the wires through the ventilator's box and make

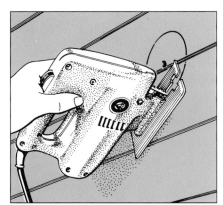

9 Using the pilot hole as a guide, cut out the vent-cap hole with a saber saw. Most vent caps accept 3-in. or 4-in.-dia. ducting.

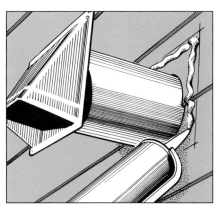

10 Hold vent cap against siding and mark its outline. Then, apply caulk inside of the pencil lines all around the vent-cap cutout.

11 *Push the vent cap tight against siding and fasten with pan-head wood screws. Clean off any caulking that squeezes out.*

12 *From the inside, slip the stabilizer ring over the end of vent-cap pipe. Attach ring to the header with 1-in. roofing nails.*

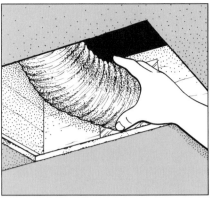

13 *Attach the duct to vent-cap pipe with duct tape or use a nylon cable tie. Use flexible duct, as shown, or round metal duct.*

the connections from below, if you are working on the first floor.

First, attach a cable connector to the electrical cable. Be sure that the threaded, male portion of the connector is facing toward the end of the cable. Secure a 12-in. length of scrap wire to the cable end. This scrap-wire leader makes it easy to fish the cable into the box from below. Next, remove a circular knockout plug from the side of the box. Then, while holding the ventilator near the ceiling, make the final connections to attach the duct to the housing. Secure the duct with duct tape. Also, fish the scrap-wire leader through the knockout hole. Pull the leader and cable into the box from below as you push the ventilator up into the ceiling. Fasten the ventilator to the ceiling with 1-in. No. 6 pan-head screws. Slip the locknut of the cable connector over the end of the leader wire and cable and thread it onto the connector. Tighten the nut to secure the connector and cable to the box. Cable connectors are required by code. Check your local electrical code for other requirements. Now remove the scrap-wire leader from the cable end.

The ventilator is wired with two separate sets of leads so that the light and exhaust fan can be controlled by separate electrical switches.

To operate them individually, you'll need to run a separate switch leg to the ventilator to handle the second switch. To operate the light and fan with one switch, simply connect the black wires in the housing to the black, hot lead of the cable. Then, connect the white wires to the white, neutral cable lead. Secure connections with wire nuts. Fasten ground lead to the grounding screw in the box.

With the wiring completed and the housing secured to the ceiling, the next step is to install the light fixture and the fan assembly. The housing's two receptacles provide easy, plug-in installation. First, install the fan by inserting its two tabs into the housing and securing it with a single sheet-metal screw (Fig. 15). Plug the fan into the receptacle. Next, plug the light fixture into the remaining receptacle and fasten it to the fan assembly with a wing nut (Fig. 16). Although this is a typical installation, be sure to read the

more detailed instructions accompanying your particular ventilator before you begin working.

Now, install the grille and lens assembly. The assembly attaches to the housing with two spring-wire clips. Squeeze the clips together and insert them into slots cut in the housing. This system makes it easy to lower the lens to change the light bulb.

Install a light bulb and push the grille right up to the ceiling to be sure that the clips hold it securely in place. Finally, turn the power back on and flip on the wall switch. You've just completed the first step toward ending your bathroom moisture problems.

Mildewcide paint additives
Another method of discouraging mildew buildup in a bathroom is to paint the walls with specially treated paint. A mildewcide is added to paint before it is applied to walls. In combination with a bathroom ventilator, this can be an effective way of eliminating bathroom mildew growth. Follow label directions for correct use.

14 *After making electrical and duct connections, fasten the ventilator's housing to the wood-block supports with screws.*

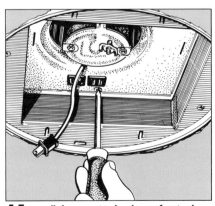

15 *Install the prewired exhaust fan in the housing and secure it with a sheet-metal screw. Plug the fan into the receptacle.*

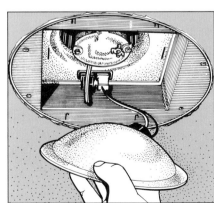

16 *Then, plug the light fixture into the remaining receptacle and fasten it to the fan assembly with the provided wing nut.*

How to check your INDOOR AIR

Here are some guidelines to follow in assessing the quality of air in your home.

Stories about indoor air pollution are getting a lot of play these days. We see them popping up in local newspapers, on national TV newscasts, and just about everywhere in between. Many of these problems are the result of new products being introduced into the home environment. Other harmful products have been with us for a long time, though we may not have realized that they were dangerous. Take for instance chemical paint removers. Some are made with volatile solvents such as xylene, toluene and acetone. Most brands are highly flammable and their vapors cause headaches and nerve damage after long periods of use. As well, the fumes from the highly effective and nonflammable solvent strippers made with methylene chloride have been shown to cause cancer, kidney disease, irregular heart beats and even heart attacks. To prevent accidental direct exposure to these chemicals it is necessary to wear a respirator and neoprene work gloves, as well as other protective clothing.

But what about avoiding exposure to other chemicals we don't know about?

The issue is cause for even greater concern when these substances surface in our homes—where we spend so much of our time. While the root cause of the danger changes with the substance, all are exacerbated by something most of us did in the 1970s and '80s: namely, weatherizing our homes in response to the energy crisis. We increased our insulation, tried to caulk everything in sight, and weather-stripped windows and doors so they could function like air locks in a submarine. These measures reduced air infiltration, which was the whole point. But at the same time, they reduced ventilation, and in the process trapped air in the house for longer periods of time. Naturally, this resulted in much higher concentrations of a variety of harmful gases and other substances.

Until recently, laying the blame for indoor air pollution on the doorstep of weatherization was common practice. And there's a good bit of wisdom in this point of view. But current research suggests that even the most conscientious weather-stripper only cuts air infiltration by about 25 percent. There's still a lot of air moving through our homes and,

because of this, more attention is being paid these days to trying to eliminate the sources of pollution, instead of relying on ventilation to solve the problem.

We do bring some dangerous substances into our homes ourselves, such as various cleaning agents and solvents—not to mention home repair and improvement products that have been proven, in some cases, to be the most toxic of all. We also have some habits that harm indoor air quality, such as reducing the concentration of oxygen—and increasing the carbon monoxide—by using open flame space heaters without proper ventilation. Yet, once we realize the dangers of these practices, we can stop quickly. There are, however, some things over which we have little control, namely radon, asbestos and formaldehyde. These three substances are essentially "built-in" to our homes, and as such, require special attention.

Radon

Radon is a problem and a product of nature. Uranium gives off this odorless, colorless gas during its natural decaying process. The gas, which is found in the soil, tends to penetrate the house through cracks in the foundation, and around plumbing and electrical openings. Once inside, the gas decays again into particles that attach to dust. If the particles are inhaled, they can lodge in the lungs and can eventually cause lung cancer. According to the Environ-mental Protection Agency, radon exposure is responsible for a tremendous number of lung cancer deaths every year—as many as 5,000 to 20,000 cases. The reason radon gets into our homes in

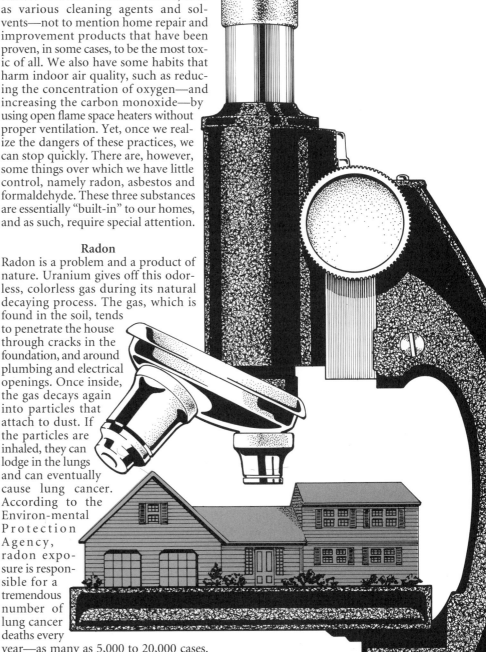

the first place is because of the difference in air pressure between the ground and the inside of the house. Generally, the lower pressure in the home—caused by a variety of factors, including the use of indoor air by furnaces, stoves, clothes dryers and other appliances—draws the gas into the living area.

Radon is not a problem in all homes. Certain geographic areas are known to have higher uranium deposits than others. One such example is the Reading Prong, a swatch of real estate that extends from eastern Pennsylvania, across western New Jersey and into New York. Nationwide, radon may be a problem in 12 million homes. But because we can't sense radon, we need help to find out if it is entering our home, and at what concentration.

Testing services and labs

"People should call the environmental Radiation Office in their state," says Melissa Wing, problem assessment specialist for the EPA office in New York. "We want the state to serve this function because there are too many variables that create a hazardous environment. Five houses on a block may have high levels of radon, yet another five may not. And houses on the other side of the state may share the problem. The individual states have a better idea of the areas that have problems right now."

The state Radiation Office will put you in contact with a laboratory that tests for radon. The EPA has developed a special measurement proficiency program that tests selected independent laboratories for their ability to correctly measure radon levels.

These labs aren't accredited, but they do meet the criteria for doing the necessary analysis.

The labs can provide a variety of radon detectors. The detectors and the analysis range in cost from $10 to $10,000. Some are as simple to use as opening a package and placing the detector on a shelf, while others require a trained operator

The EPA recommends that home owners screen their homes with one of the less expensive models if they suspect a problem. You can send for one of two types of detectors—charcoal canister or Alpha track. These are placed in your home according to the manufacturer's instructions and, after a relatively short period of time, are sent back to the lab for results.

There are disadvantages to any detection method. The charcoal canister is sensitive to temperature and humidity and the Alpha track must be in place for three months. But either is a logical first step in determining air quality.

Generally, you should place the screening device you choose in the lowest livable part of the house since the lowest area is usually the entry point for radon. Close doors and windows for 12 hours before the test, and keep them closed as much as possible throughout the test period. The results will tell you if there is a potential radon problem. Additional measurements will determine the severity of the problem.

Depending on the type of detector used, results are reported in one of two ways: Working levels (WL) measure radon decay products, and picocuries per liter (pCi/l) measure the concentration of radon gas. The EPA considers 0.02 WL

Because radon is odorless and colorless, special commercially available test equipment

or 4 pCi/l an average measurement for homes. Anything above these levels requires attention. The higher the radon reading, the higher your risk. Based on studies of uranium miners, a reading of 1 WL or 200 pCi/l exposes those in the house to the same risk as someone who smokes four packs of cigarettes a day.

Keep in mind that estimating actual risk is a tricky business. The EPA calculations assume a person will spend 75 percent of his or her time in the house for 70 years—something very few people actually do. The scientific community

simply uses the available data to estimate the statistical risk, just as they can give us statistical odds on being in a car accident every time we turn the ignition key.

A number of techniques will reduce radon levels. Basically, they are divided into two categories: Those that remove radon, and those that prevent radon from entering the home.

Ventilating radon

You can ventilate by installing a window fan or an air-to-air heat exchanger. Both can cut radon levels by 90 percent. The fans are inexpensive and could cost about $100 a year to run.

But besides exhausting radon, a fan also expels the heated or cooled air from the room. Even if you tried to isolate the basement from the rest of the house by insulating the basement ceiling, you'd still have to face the prospect of freezing pipes in colder regions during the winter.

An air-to-air heat exchanger runs between $500 and $1500 and an additional $100 a year in electricity costs, but you save about 70 percent of the heat in the area. The exchanger pulls air from inside the house and air from the outside into a single, divided unit. As both air streams pass, the warm air from the house heats the cool air from outside, thus reducing your heat loss as you gain fresh air and expel radon-laden air to the outside. The installation for whole-house units requires duct work and proper sizing. Window-mounted units for individual rooms may help for low concentrations of radon but usually won't work for houses with densities above 0.2 WL or 40 pCi/l.

Other techniques prevent the radon from coming into the house. They vary from sealing cracks in the foundation to surrounding the house with drain tiles and connecting the tiles to a pipe equipped with a fan. The fan exhausts the radon before it enters the building.

Sealing cracks used to be the prescribed radon treatment, and many more complicated methods require this first step. But, "sealing cracks is probably the least successful technique," says David Grimsurd, program leader for the Indoor Environment Program at the Lawrence Berkeley Laboratory. "Our experience with energy conservation methods shows that sealing all the cracks is extremely difficult. The concentrations of radon are so small that you must seal everything to be effective."

Lawrence Berkeley Laboratory studied a variety of techniques in 15 houses with radon problems in the Pacific Northwest. Grimsurd says that slab ventilation and overpressurizing the basement rank as the best techniques from this study. Each of these methods reduced radon levels by 95 to 99 percent.

In slab ventilation, pipes are installed vertically through the slab into the ground below. (LBL tested this system only on houses that rested on aggregate or highly permeable soil.) The pipes are then connected to an outside vent equipped with a fan that draws the radon from the aggregate or soil below the house before it can enter the living area. This system costs between $1000 to $2000 to install, plus electricity to run the fan all year.

LBL also experimented with overpressurizing the basement in 4 of the 15 houses it studied. Researchers found that since radon enters a building because the air pressure is usually lower in the house than it is outside, if they increase basement pressure they can keep out radon. This method calls for completely sealing off the basement from the rest of the house and then delivering air from the upper floors to the basement. It was used only on houses with forced-air heating systems. Researchers sealed off the basement cold-air return and installed a fan in the cold-air return coming from the rest of the house. The forced cold air, part of which was diverted to the basement on its way to the heating system, increased the air pressure in the basement area. A small increase in pressure does the trick. This is one of the newer ideas, but it worked for this series of tests.

All of the techniques available have drawbacks. In some cases, you will be trading clean air for higher heating bills. There can also be problems with freezing pipes, noise from fans and condensation. The solution you choose will depend on the location and severity of the problem.

For more information on radon in homes, contact your state Radiation Protection Office or the EPA regional office nearest you. They offer the following free booklets: *A Citizen's Guide To Radon: What It Is And What To Do About It*, *Radon Reduction Methods: A Homeowner's Guide*, and *Radon Reduction Techniques for Detached Houses*. The last booklet is also available from the U. S. EPA Center for Environmental Research Information, 26 West St. Clair St., Cincinnati, OH 45268. Specify publication EPA-625-586-019.

Asbestos

Asbestos is another product of nature that found its way into about 3,000 different home products, including pipe insulation, roofing, siding, flooring and all kinds of appliances. The material is durable and very heat resistant. In the '60s and '70s, problems experienced by people who manufactured the product—and some who installed it—began to surface. The result was a series of highly publicized court cases and a proposed ban on all products containing asbestos.

If breathed in and lodged on lung tissue, asbestos can cause lung cancer and mesothelioma, a cancer of the chest and abdominal lining. The EPA attributes 3,000 to 12,000 cancer cases a year to the material. What makes matters worse is that an asbestos-caused disease can take as long as 40 years to develop.

In January 1986, the EPA proposed an immediate ban on the manufacturing, processing and importing of some asbestos-containing products, as well as a

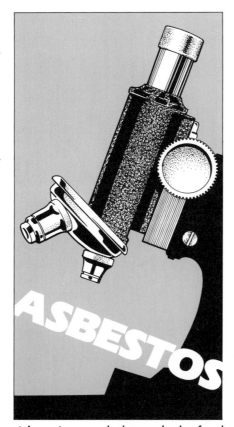

Asbestos is a natural substance that has found its way into over 3,000 different home products, from ceiling and floor tiles to insulation around pipes and ductwork.

10-year phase-out of the rest. But even with the ban, and the fact that the use of asbestos has declined in recent years, there are still places where it can be found in homes, especially older homes. The dangerous situations are where the asbestos is exposed and friable—where it can be crumbled into dust.

When asbestos is crumbled, microscopic fibers are released into the air and become breathable. However, most asbestos-containing products found in the home have the fibers encapsulated, so there is no danger unless the capsule is broken. An asbestos floor tile in good condition is not a threat, but sawing or sanding it—thus releasing the fibers into the air—is definitely a problem.

Identifying asbestos in your home

It is a good idea to identify the asbestos-containing products in your home and check their condition. The most typical examples are around hot water or steam pipes, and around furnace duct work. In these cases, the substance was used for insulation and often looks like white corrugated paper. A plumber or heating contractor should be able to spot asbestos-containing insulation by looking at it. The EPA recommends that you contact your state health authorities for the name of a laboratory that will analyze a sample. The analysis will not cost a great deal, and the lab will explain how to obtain and package the sample. If you find asbestos, don't try to remove it. Tampering with it could release the fibers.

You may, however, be able to encapsulate the material. But, in most cases, a qualified asbestos-abatement contractor should deal with the material either to seal it or remove it. Some states have asbestos contractor certification programs. To remove the material, these contractors wear special clothing and respirators. First, they seal off the area containing the asbestos from the rest of the house, then they spray the area with a fine mist of water to keep the dust down. They remove the asbestos and dispose of it according to guidelines established by local health officials. The area is then cleaned with wet mops, sponges or rags. A typical home vacuum cleaner is never used because the fibers are so small they could pass through the cleaner and be blown into the air. Some contractors do, however, use specially designed vacuums for cleanup. The cost of asbestos removal depends on the amount of the material and how it was installed.

Formaldehyde

Formaldehyde is a resin used in products which account for about 8 percent of the U.S. Gross National Product. Some of these products include urea formaldehyde insulation, hardwood plywood used in wall paneling, particleboard used as an underlayment, and medium density fiberboard used in furniture, countertops and cabinets. Problems with this insulation ultimately led the Consumer Product Safety Commission to ban it. The ban was later overturned in court, although by the time this happened, the insulation business had essentially died due to the bad name given to formaldehyde.

Experiences with formaldehyde show that some people are sensitive to the fumes emitted from the material. These fumes can cause burning eyes and irritation of the mucous membranes. Formaldehyde has also been shown to cause cancer in laboratory test animals, and recently, the EPA determined that it was a probable cause of cancer in human beings.

The emissions quandary

Several years ago, the Consumer Federation of America petitioned the CPSC to regulate the formaldehyde emission rates of structural products used in homes. The commission looked at construction techniques: where the boards are used, how they are installed, and how much formaldehyde escapes into the air.

"We found that in conventional housing, using conventional construction techniques, there is no great risk from formaldehyde," says Ron Medford, project manager, Household Structural Products, CPSC. The products are changing and, "there has been a declining use of particleboard among builders. Many are going to single-floor systems that require exterior-grade plywood, which has a different resin in it." These studies have, however, prompted many manufacturers to use less formaldehyde in their products. The National Particle Board Assocn. and an organization called the Hardwood Plywood Manufacturers Assocn. developed voluntary standards to reduce the substance in their products. The amount of formaldehyde released depends on the surface area containing formaldehyde and the volume of the house. Smaller houses and mobile homes, which contain a lot of these boards, have a likelihood of higher emission rates. Formaldehyde emission rates do lessen over time. This, coupled with the fact that many products adhere to some guidelines, means even recently built houses should not pose a serious problem.

But if someone in your family is sensitive, you can ventilate the area and paint the surface of the formaldehyde-containing material with any paint that acts as a vapor retarder.

This is especially important in the case of medium-density fiberboard. This particular material is the highest emitter of formaldehyde and is not governed by voluntary standards.

For your home improvement projects, be sure to look for particleboard and hardwood plywood that conforms to the standards of the associations mentioned

above. Or use products that follow the Housing and Urban Development standards for mobile homes. Some manufacturers print a warning label on the boards. But again, this is a voluntary step.

"The problem is a consumer may see the label on one board, go to another and not see the label and assume there is no formaldehyde in it. We don't want that," says Medford.

The CPSC has not acted on its study. Medford says the commission will probably work in conjunction with manufacturers in setting voluntary guidelines for the manufacture of fiberboard, rather than developing mandatory emission standards. The CPSC considers a level of

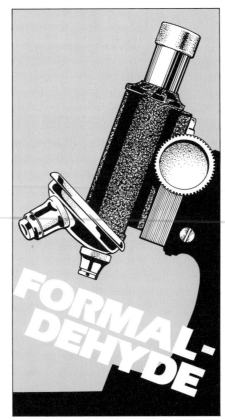

Formaldehyde is a resin used in home products that range from furniture to carpet adhesives. All told, they represent about 8 percent of the United States GNP.

0.1 parts per million of formaldehyde in the air as a safe level.

A level of 0.1 parts per million is a little lower than the voluntary standards in effect right now. "But we think it is well within reach of site-built homes, although it is harder to achieve in mobile homes," says Medford.

Maintaining home filtration systems

Besides these more insidious pollutants in the home, other more mundane air-

borne contaminants, such as dust, are caught by the filter of an air distribution system, serving to heat and cool—and sometimes even humidify or dehumidify—a home. Because of the tremendous volume of air that passes through the filter in your home's climate-control system, it's important to make sure that any filters in the system are cleaned and replaced regularly. A filter is most often located between the duct and the blower in a forced-air system. Check the condition of a filter by first turning off the power to the furnace, central air conditioner unit or heat pump. Then, access the unit and remove the filter from the unit. Hold the filter up against the beam of a strong light. If light shines through the filter, assume it is still good and put it back in place. If you detect only a little light, or no light, install a new filter at once; a dirty filter can be a health hazard. Some forced-air systems have sophisticated electronic filters. These can often be washed in a dishwasher; consult the owner's manual that comes with the forced-air system.

Also check the condition of the humidifier drum which is often attached to the supply duct on a forced-air system. If mildew has started to grow on the drum, in the drain pan under the drum or on any other parts, wash them in a solution of soap and water. Anti-mildew solutions are also available for humidifiers.

Window air conditioners also have filters that need to be cleaned periodically. When the air conditioner runs for a long period of time—such as during the summer months—make sure to wash the filter every week. The filter is usually found behind the air conditioner's front panel; both the filter and the panel are easily removed for cleaning.

Filtering indoor air with plants

Although the merits of indoor plants and their effects on the quality of indoor air are still being debated among experts, there are some who champion the use of plants as natural air filters.

As a first-line of defense against the pollution emitted by common household products like cleaners, insecticides, glues, air fresheners, hair sprays and shoe polish, plants have been shown to be remarkable natural filters of volatile organic compounds—particularly the formaldehyde in some pressed wood products. They are also effective filters of benzene and trichloroethylene, volatile organic compounds found indoors. Of particular note are philodendrons and spider plants, which have been shown to be excellent air purifiers. Other good natural filters include golden pathos, English ivy, pot mum and aloe vera.

ELECTRICITY 2

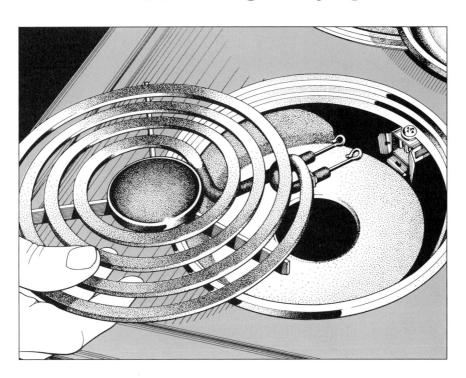

How to use
AN OHMMETER

Ohmmeters and VOMs are multipurpose tools that measure resistance and continuity.

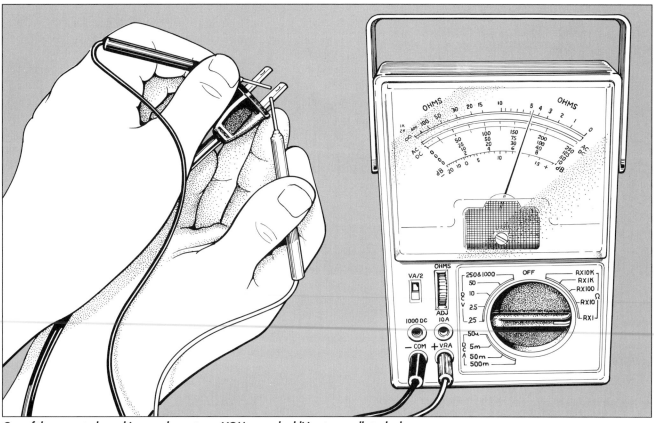

One of the many tasks making an ohmmeter or VOM a good addition to a well-stocked home electrician's toolbox is testing if a lamp cord or plug is conducting electricity. Always turn off electricity or unplug appliance from wall socket before testing.

Here's how you can test and troubleshoot electrical appliances like a pro—safely and easily—using an ohmmeter. An ohmmeter can test virtually every single electrical component in any appliance—small and major. This includes all power cords, switches, solenoids, relays, timers, thermostats and heating elements to name just a few. By simply placing the meter's probes on the component's wires or terminals, you can determine quickly and safely if the part is defective.

Some of the typical tests that you can perform include checking the water-level switch on a clothes washer, testing a thermostat of a refrigerator or freezer, and checking the heating element of a clothes dryer, electric range or oven. The owner's manual, which comes with each meter, provides more specific examples

and instructions. And, if you're concerned about receiving an electrical shock, don't be. When using an ohmmeter, double check to make sure the appliance is unplugged from the electrical outlet.

An ohmmeter can perform three vital electrical tests. One is to determine if a continuous, unbroken circuit exists. Another test measures the resistance to the flow of current. Every electrical component has a specified amount of resistance that is measured in ohms. Testing tells you if the component meets the original requirements set for it. Ohmmeters also can test for short circuits that make components inoperable.

The instrument shown in the drawings is a multitester known as a voltohm-milliammeter (VOM). Most people prefer a VOM over a straight ohmmeter because it expands their testing capabilities. A

VOM can test for continuity and measure resistance (ohms), voltage and current (milliamps). You can buy an adequate VOM for about $40. Regardless of whether you use a straight ohmmeter or a VOM, the continuity and resistance tests shown on these pages are performed the same way. Note, however, that the ohm scale on a VOM reads from right to left. At the highest end of the scale is the symbol for infinity (∞).

When the needle points to infinity, the meter isn't capable of measuring the resistance of the tested part (Fig. 1). Therefore, an open circuit (lack of continuity) exists and you need a new part. When testing for continuity, you aren't seeking an exact numerical value. A circuit is either open or it isn't. If it's open, the needle will point to infinity. If the circuit isn't open, the needle will point to a number.

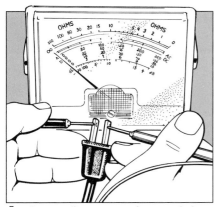

1 *When needle points to infinity symbol, there may be a lack of continuity. Note that the ohm scale reads from right to left.*

2 *With the leads removed from the jacks, use a small-blade screwdriver or knife to set needle exactly on the infinity symbol.*

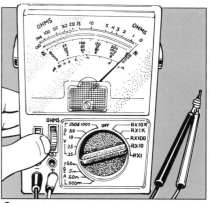

3 *Insert leads and tie together the probes with a rubber band. Adjust the needle exactly to zero with OHMS ADJ knob.*

A VOM is powered by one or more batteries. Keep the batteries fresh to ensure accurate readings.

Meter adjustments

The two holes, or jacks, in the face of the meter accept the test leads. Be sure to insert the red lead in the positive (+) jack and the black lead in the negative (-) jack. The ends of the leads have either metal probes, as shown, or alligator clips.

Before using a VOM or ohmmeter, you must adjust it to ensure accurate readings. First, *remove* the leads from the jacks and stand the meter upright on a flat, level surface. Insert a small-blade screwdriver or knife into the pivot point of the needle and turn it slowly until the needle rests exactly on the infinity mark (Fig. 2).

Next, use the ohms adjustment control knob to set the needle to zero; this will allow you to take accurate readings. Insert the leads into the jacks and tie together the probes using a rubber band. Rotate the knob until the needle rests on zero (Fig. 3). If you can't get on zero exactly, the batteries may be weak—replace them with new ones.

Most meters have a range-selector switch with three RX positions—RX1, RX10 and RX100. Some other meters have RX1000 (often designated RX1K) and RX10,000 (RX10K) settings for reading greater ohm values. To determine the resistance of a circuit or component, simply multiply the RX value by the number that the needle points to. For example, if the range-selector is set on RX1 and the needle points to 50, then the circuit has a resistance of 50 ohms. If the range-selector was set at X10, the circuit would have a resistance of 500 ohms.

When testing for continuity, start with the range-selector set at RX1. If the needle points to infinity, switch the selector to RX10 and then RX100. If the needle doesn't move off of the infinity mark, an open circuit exists.

Often when checking the resistance value (ohms) with the meter set at RX1, you'll get a reading on the high end of the scale. Since the high end isn't calibrated very precisely (see illustration on Page 66), switch the selector to RX10 and bring the needle into the lower, more precisely calibrated end of the scale.

Exact resistance

The exact resistance values of the parts of an appliance are printed on a wiring diagram glued to the appliance. Appliance manufacturers can also provide resistance values for specific parts. Another alternative is to check the resistance values listed in repair books. The reading that you get doesn't have to equal exactly what's listed in the book. For example, a repair book lists the resistance value of an electric range cooking element at 50 ohms. If you get a reading of 45 ohms (Fig. 4), that's close enough. A much lower reading of 10 ohms would indicate that a short exists in the element. When a short exists, the meter will display a low value—it won't point to infinity.

Also, when testing for continuity or resistance, it's important that the appliance's switch be turned on (even though the appliance is not plugged in). If the switch is left off, it will cause the needle to point to infinity indicating that there's an open circuit (Fig. 5), which may not be the case. If the appliance has two switches, such as a toaster-oven, be sure both switches are switched on (Fig. 6).

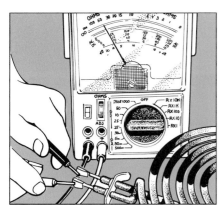

4 *To test the resistance value (ohms) of an electric range cooking element, place one probe on each prong of plug-in element.*

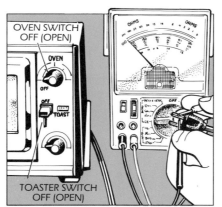

5 *Here, with both switches off, the meter points to infinity, indicating that there's an open circuit: an erroneous reading.*

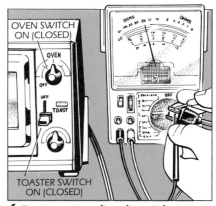

6 *For a correct reading, the switches must be on. If an open circuit still exists, then test the internal components of the appliance.*

How to repair
AN INCANDESCENT LAMP

Degree of difficulty: Easy   Estimated time: 1 hour   Average cost of materials: $10

Incandescent lamps are basically all alike. Aside from stylistic differences, every lamp includes the same electrical components—a plug, cord, socket and switch. If you have a lamp that has kept you in the dark too long, take heart, these are the only components that can wear out and each one is a quick fix.

Troubleshooting a lamp

When trying to locate a defective component, don't overlook the obvious. Always check the light bulb first. If you are satisfied that the bulb is not the problem, then go on to the plug. Look for any char marks that might suggest a faulty or loose connection.

If the plug is a screw-terminal type with a cardboard faceplate, pry the face off and look for loose wires. Also check for frayed insulation or any apparent break or split in the cord.

If the plug and cord seem undamaged, look to the socket and switch. Sockets and switches either work or don't work. If your lamp has a line switch attached to the cord, you can replace it without touching the socket. Most lamp switches, however, are contained in sockets. Short of investigating further, you should probably just replace the socket and switch and be done with it.

Dismantling a lamp for repair

Taking a lamp apart is not difficult. It's a simple progression from shade to plug. Start by undoing the lamp shade. Simply

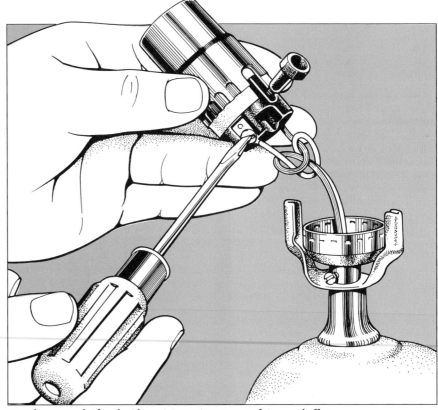

Most lamps can be fixed with a minimum investment of time and effort. Always disconnect the lamp from its socket before attempting repairs.

loosen the threaded cap, called a finial, and lift the shade up and off. Next, remove the bridged wire support, called a harp, by sliding upward the two metal ferrules on the harp bracket. Squeeze and

lift the two halves of the harp until they come free. You will then be able to remove the socket.

Each socket has four elements—an outer shell, insulating sleeve, socket and socket

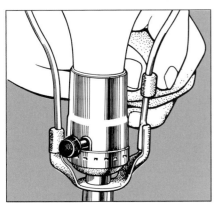

1 The harp supports the lamp shade and is joined to socket cap with two small ferrules. To free the harp, lift up the ferrules.

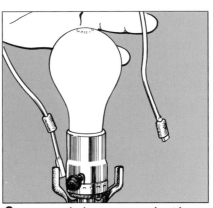

2 To remove the harp, squeeze the sides together and lift off the base. If harp is stuck, pliers may be required to free it.

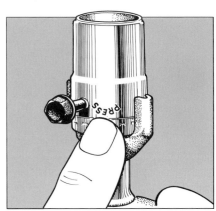

3 To remove socket, press and pull up where you see word PRESS on socket shell. If stuck, pry up with small screwdriver.

cap. To separate the outer shell from the cap, press in and pry up where you see PRESS stamped into the metal shell. If you can't free the shell with your fingers, use a small screwdriver. By removing the outer shell, you expose the insulating sleeve, socket and electrical terminals.

With the shell and sleeve removed, pull an inch or two of cable through the socket cap. Loosen the terminal screws on the socket and pull off the wires. Then use a small screwdriver to loosen the setscrew on the socket cap. Undo the Underwriter's knot in the cord and slide the cap off the wire. You are now ready to rebuild your lamp.

Replacing plugs and cords

Older cords with fabric covers should be replaced as a matter of course. Their rubber insulation and silk inner sleeves become hazardous with age. Zip cord is now the only cord approved for lamps by the NEC (National Electrical Code). Zip cord is stranded copper wire molded into flexible plastic insulation that offers long-term protection. The plastic insulation may be colored or clear and is ribbed on one wire and smooth on the other. The ribbed wire is the neutral wire—the smooth is the hot wire.

To avoid having to negotiate your new cord through the base and the threaded tube, tape your new cord to the old cord at the top of the lamp and pull them both through the lamp base. Once through, tie an Underwriter's knot (Fig. 7) in the socket end of the cord and install a plug on the other end.

The self-piercing plugs made for zip cord are literally a snap to use. They come in two pieces: a plastic body and a pronged insert. All you do is slide one end of the zip cord through the body and insert the unstripped cord into the prong slot. Make sure the smooth (hot) wire goes to the smaller prong, and squeeze the prongs together. Then push the prongs into the plug body until they snap into place. A small spike on each prong pierces the insulation and makes contact with the stranded wire.

Installing an in-line switch

When you open an in-line switch, you will immediately see how it works. One wire in the cord passes through uncut and the other is interrupted by the switch. Start by cutting the positive (smooth) side of the zip cord and peeling back about ¾ in. of this cut wire.

Lay the cord in the switch slot as shown in Fig. 8. Then press the separated wire into its slot and tighten the two halves of the body together. The switch prongs will automatically pierce the cord and make contact.

Replacing a lamp socket

To replace a lamp socket, start by pulling apart the two wires in the cord. You will need about 2 in. of separated wire. Strip ⅝ in. of insulation from each wire. Slide the old harp bracket and new socket cap over the cord and tie the wires in an Underwriter's knot. Then fasten the socket cap to the threaded tube with the setscrew provided. Next, tighten the hot wire around the brass screw and the neutral around the silver screw. Slide the insulating sleeve and outer shell over the socket and snap the outer shell in place. Then, replace the harp, shade and finial.

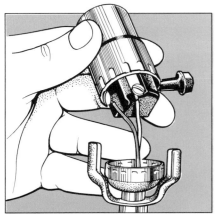

4 To expose the terminal screws, slide up the socket shell and insulating sleeve. Loosen terminal screws and pull off wires.

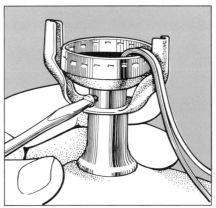

5 To remove socket cap, loosen setscrew and turn cap off threaded tube. Harp bracket and spacer will come off, too.

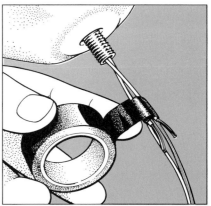

6 To replace the cord, tape end of new cord to socket end of old cord and pull both through threaded tube at base of lamp.

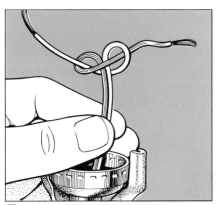

7 To prevent wire from coming off screws if cord is pulled, tie Underwriter's knot in end before attaching to terminal screws.

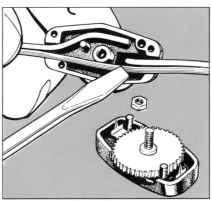

8 To install in-line switch, cut the smooth, positive wire and press it into place. Then screw switch sides together.

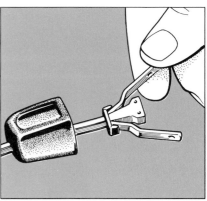

9 To install new plug, feed wire into plug body and slide end into pronged section. Squeeze prongs and snap into body.

How to fix
FLUORESCENT FIXTURES

Degree of difficulty: Medium   **Estimated time:** 1 to 1½ hours   **Average cost of materials:** $2 to $15

Fluorescent lighting is efficient and tubes have a long life. Most problems, however, arise when fluorescent tubes burn out. Replacement is easy, but sometimes either a starter or ballast will be the source of trouble. Before dismantling fixtures, be sure to shut off power.

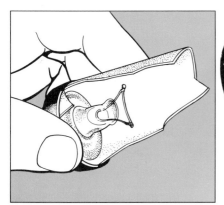

1 *The cathode filament charges the mercury gas. Fluorescent coating inside the tube changes the radiation to useful light.*

2 *Blackened ends indicate the tube should be replaced. Be sure the new tube matches the specs printed on the old tube.*

Dismantling a fluorescent light fixture can be a bit intimidating because, once you get past the tube, repair progresses from the mechanical to the electrical in a hurry.

Instead of the simple ON/OFF switch and familiar wire terminals characteristic of incandescent fixtures, what you'll find is an almost empty channel, a few meandering wires and the quintessential little black box. Somehow you expect more. If there were more, you reason, you might be able to figure the thing out.

The fact is, fluorescent lamps are not much like incandescent lamps. To achieve the high efficiency and long life they've become noted for, they're more complex.

Even so, completely diagnosing and repairing a troublesome fluorescent fixture is well within the reach of the average home owner.

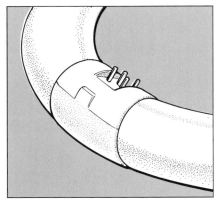

3 *Round fluorescent tubes are only different in shape. The four pins correspond to the two found at ends of a straight tube.*

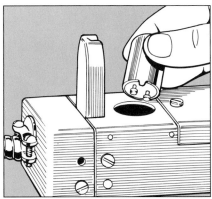

4 *Some units use starter switches. These have two contact pegs which lock into place when you press in and turn right.*

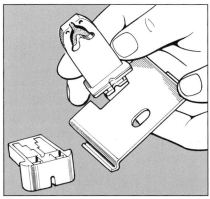

5 *Sockets mount to the channel with screws or by snapping into place. This design slides into a slot in channel cover.*

How fluorescent lamps work

Most of us have a fairly good idea of how an ordinary incandescent light bulb works. Turning on the lamp closes an electrical circuit which sends current through a metal filament contained inside a glass bulb. The filament burns white-hot and becomes luminescent much in the same way that an electric range burner glows red when it's on. In short, the filament is the source of light. When something goes wrong, it's usually a break in the circuit—a burned out filament or faulty switch. Fluorescent fixtures, on the other hand, rarely just quit working completely, but show their ill health by flickering, producing less than normal light, or having difficulty starting.

A fluorescent tube glows because a mixture of mercury and argon gas, sealed inside, is charged with electricity. The charge is generated by a cathode filament at each end of the tube. When enough electrons are generated, the gas conducts an electrical arc through the tube. The charged mercury vapors radiate invisible ultraviolet light and a narrow band of the spectrum that is visible as a blue-green glow. This radiation falls on a fluorescent chemical coating on the inside surface of the glass tube which absorbs it and radiates light at a useful level and color.

The amount of electricity needed to keep the gas glowing is a lot less than to get it started. When you turn on a fluorescent fixture, an initial voltage surge which charges the gas is sent across the filaments. Once current is established through the gas, the power is reduced to a normal operating level. Because the cathode filaments glow at full force only at start-up, repeated switching on and off can actually be less efficient and cause the tubes to fail sooner than simply leaving the light on. In general, fluorescent lamps last years and burn 5 to 6 times more efficiently than incandescent bulbs.

Starters

Some fluorescent fixtures require a separate component to control the initial voltage surge to the filaments that begins current flow through the gas. This switch is called a starter. If your fixture uses starters, you'll find one of these small cylindrical objects protruding from the lamp housing near each tube. When the filaments are hot enough to charge the gas, the starter switches off the high-voltage current. The charged gas then maintains the current flow at a reduced level. This 2-step ignition explains the familiar hesitation of older lamps when they're first turned on.

Ballasts

The heart of every fluorescent fixture, old or new, is its ballast (that black box you were wondering about). A ballast is a kind of current-limiting transformer that serves two essential functions. When a fixture is turned on, its ballast provides a high flow of current to preheat the cathodes. Once gas conduction has taken place, the ballast reduces the current to a stable operating level.

Modern fixtures have ballasts designed to charge the tubes instantly without the need for starters. These are called rapid-start fixtures. While there are many different fluorescent fixture types in commercial use, virtually all fixtures used in residential lighting are of the preheat type with starters or rapid-start design. Both have tubes with 2-pin ends.

Where to begin

If your fluorescent fixture is acting up, start by checking the tube. Most problems begin and end there. A tube will seldom go out abruptly, but will flutter and hesitate long before it fails completely. First, check the tube ends. A little gray discoloration is normal, but if the ends are black, the tube needs to be replaced.

To remove a defective tube, rotate it one-quarter turn and gently pull it down out of its holders. In the unlikely event your tubes have a single-pin configuration, push the tube in one direction against its spring-loaded holder and drop down the other end.

If the tube ends are not black, it may simply need to be reseated in its sockets or

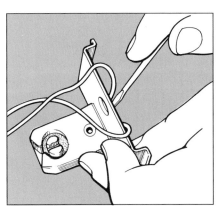

6 *Many sockets have push-in terminals. To release a wire, push a small screwdriver into the release slot next to the wire.*

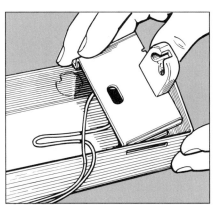

7 *When installing a socket mounted to a snap-in plate, slip one tab into its slot and spread the channel to accept the other tab.*

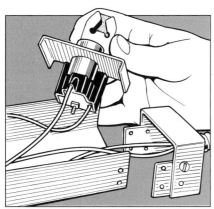

8 *The socket shown here contains the seat for starter. When replacing this type, make sure you get an exact matching part.*

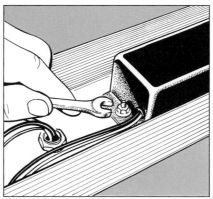

9 *Ballast is held in place by two mounting screws and nuts. It's a good idea to make a wiring diagram before removing it.*

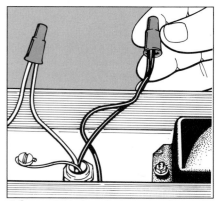

10 *Attach black and white wires from ballast to the corresponding house circuit wires. Ground wire is screwed to channel.*

the pins may need to be cleaned. The constant vibration a house endures can cause a tube to slip, thereby interrupting its contact with the socket. With the lamp switched on and the tube in place, try turning the tube slightly. If this doesn't work, remove the tube and inspect the ends. If you find dirt or corrosion on the pins, clean them and reinstall the tube. With fluorescent tubes you should look for little things. They can be temperamental. In some cases, you can get extra life out of a tube by simply removing it, turning it end for end and reinstalling. If nothing works, buy new tubes. As some fixtures are wired in sequence, you may have to replace both tubes, or two of four tubes within a fixture to correct the problem. If you'd like to ensure yourself several years of trouble-free operation, replace them all.

Starter problems
Because starters fail about as often as tubes, many electricians replace them each time they replace a tube. Problems that signify starter trouble are continuous flickering and tubes that only glow at their ends. If you have a tube that's flickering all the time, try reseating the starter. Remove the tube, press in on the starter and turn it to the right to seat it properly in place.

If only the ends of a fluorescent tube light up, don't bother reseating the starter. Simply replace it. To remove a defective starter, press in and then turn to the left.

Defective sockets and ballasts
There is a limit to the amount of money you should invest in a fluorescent fixture. This limit becomes a factor when the lamp sockets and ballast appear defective. If you shop around, you'll find that a new fixture can cost less than replacing the parts of an older fixture. However, older

fixtures can be completely rebuilt. A classic old desk lamp, for example, can continue to offer years of service with an electrical overhaul.

If you find that a lamp socket is broken or will no longer hold a tube against its contact, go ahead and replace it. When doing so, make sure the components you buy match the design and voltage rating of the originals. When in doubt, take the part with you for comparison.

To remove a defective socket, shut off the power and look for two mounting screws at the base of the socket. These screws are visible on some models but are concealed by a cover plate on others. Remove these screws to reveal the wire terminals on the socket. Disconnect the wires, fasten them to the replacement socket, and reinstall.

Some models have push-in wire connections and the wires will likely enter the front or back of the socket. To release each wire, slide a small screwdriver into the release slot next to the wire. Then, just slide the stripped ends of the loose wires into the new socket connectors.

Replacing a ballast
A defective ballast is signaled by a buzzing

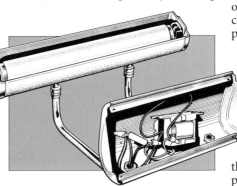

11 *This desk lamp is a preheat model, but it has no starter. It's turned on by holding the switch down until the light pops on.*

sound, sharp asphalt odor, tubes that glow only at their ends, or a black oily substance dripping from the fixture. When shopping for a new ballast, make sure you buy one with the same voltage rating and design characteristics as the original. Each fixture brand will have its own specific wiring diagram and installation procedures. Follow them carefully.

In general, the ballast is fastened to the channel by two or more sheet metal screws. You'll find up to eight color-coded wires disappearing under the ballast cover. Two of these, the black and white wires, should be attached to the corresponding black and white wires of the house circuit with wire nuts. The ground wire from the house circuit is generally screwed directly to the metal channel with a sheet metal screw. The remaining wires attach to the lamp sockets.

Start by undoing these wires from their sockets, taking care to note the position of each wire. It's a good idea to make a color-coded map of the wire connections so you have a reference when you're reassembling the unit. Then, undo the mounting screws and remove the ballast. Screw the new ballast in place and connect the new wires, keeping in mind the original wire connections and paying close attention to the wiring diagram supplied with the replacement ballast.

Other considerations
Before investing time and money in dismantling a fluorescent fixture and buying expensive parts, look for possible trouble spots outside the unit. A defective wall switch or a loose wire-nut connection are possibilities. These alternatives should be investigated if the fixture fails to come on at all. If some part of the fluorescent fixture works, you can usually assume that the external wires and switches are in good shape and the problem is within the unit itself.

How to install
TRACK LIGHTING

Degree of difficulty: Medium   **Estimated time:** 2 hours   **Average cost of materials:** $45 to $100

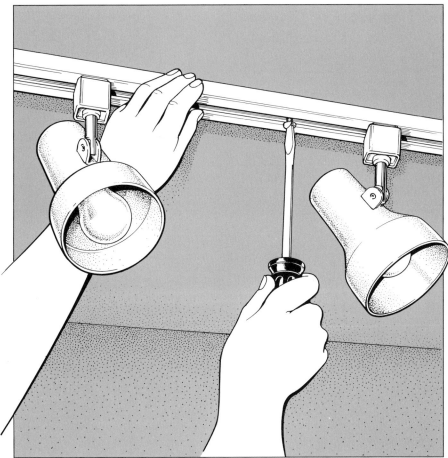

*Track lighting can add drama and style to a room or hallway.
For safe installation consult the instructions accompanying your model.*

When it comes to creating dramatic indoor lighting with a modest investment, track lighting excels. It can be used to highlight a wall hanging, spotlight a piece of sculpture, or simply brighten a darkened hallway. The effects are as varied as equipment options.

You'll find track lighting comes in many different styles and, because most units are modular, you'll be able to mix and match components to suit specific needs and the particular decor of the setting in which the track lighting is installed. While good lighting design does require some skill and imagination, installation is pretty basic, especially if you are simply replacing an existing switched light fixture, as described here. All you need are some common household tools, electrical tape and wire nuts.

Layout

Because you'll be dealing with an existing light fixture, your options will be limited to the location of those fixtures. For the best appearance, keep the track parallel to the house wall closest to the fixture. Do keep in mind, however, that you can install track lighting wherever you think it will work well. But if no wiring is in place for easy installation, you will have to fish new wiring through your walls and ceiling, which is a fairly complicated task suited for either an experienced home handyman with electrical know-how or a licensed electrician.

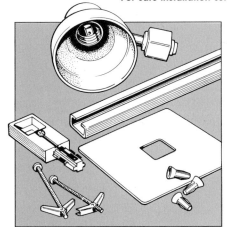

1 *Lighting kit includes lamps, track, hot cap, covering plate and usually some toggle bolts. You supply the wire nuts.*

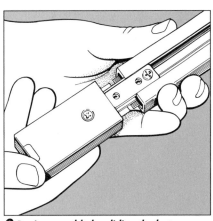

2 *Begin assembly by sliding the hot cap into one end of the track. Then tighten the fastening screw securely against the track.*

3 *Remove the back panel from the hot cap and install the kit's covering plate. This plate will conceal any standard ceiling box.*

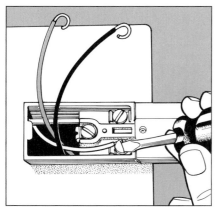

4 Attach pigtails to the hot cap as follows: white wire to silver screw, black to gold, and green to center grounding screw.

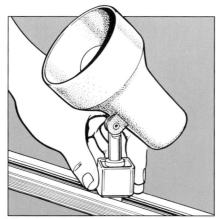

5 Slide the lamps into the track, then twist in place. Manufacturer's instructions will explain how to maintain proper polarity.

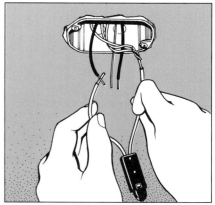

6 Turn off power and remove existing fixture. Using tester, check for current from each black wire to the white wires.

Assembly

Begin by sliding the hot cap that comes with your kit into one end of the track (Fig. 2). Attach it by tightening the fastener screw. Then screw the oversized covering plate onto the back side of the hot cap (Fig. 3). This plate is designed to cover the entire perimeter of a standard ceiling box.

Once the covering plate is in place, remove the top panel of the hot cap. This will reveal the binding screws that secure your electrical connections. Either cut 8-in. long insulated pigtails from scrap wire or buy already made pigtails from a hardware store. You'll need one white, one black and one green wire. Make sure the gauge of the wire you use matches the wire in your ceiling box and fulfills the manufacturer's requirements stipulated in the product literature.

Attach the white pigtail to the silver-colored screw, the black to the gold-colored screw, and the green to the center grounding screw (Fig. 4). Each end should wrap around the screw in a clockwise fashion. Make sure that the other ends of the pigtails run through the hole in the back side of the hot cap.

Finish the assembly by sliding the lamps into the track and twisting them in place (Fig. 5). The manufacturer's directions will explain the proper way to do this so you maintain electrical polarity. At this point you should also install the toggle bolts—used for attaching the track to the ceiling—in the track.

Electrical connections

Before you remove your existing light fixture, be sure to turn off the power to the circuit. Either switch off the breaker or unscrew the proper fuse. Make sure to test the circuit by turning the wall switch ON *and* OFF. When satisfied that the power has been cut, remove the light fixture and once again test for power, this time using a current tester (Fig. 6).

Depending on your home's wiring scheme, you will be confronted with two different situations: Either two black wires and a ground wire will be sticking down from the box—which indicates that the power supply is coming into the ceiling box—or a white, black and a ground wire will be there—which indicates that your switch box is receiving the power and your ceiling box is getting one 2-wire with ground cable from the switch. In the latter case, the white wire should be coded with black tape or a black ink mark. This designates that the white wire has been changed to function as a black (hot) wire. Be sure to check for current between the black (hot) wires and the white (neutral) wires with your tester. When you are satisfied that no current exists, you are ready to attach the track.

To do so, use an electric drill to bore a couple of holes in the ceiling for the toggle bolts, then push the bolt ears into the holes. Let the track dangle until you've made the connections as shown in Figs. 8 and 9. Be sure to use proper sized wire nuts. For added safety wrap the wire nuts with electrical tape after tightening them. Then stuff the wire connections into the ceiling box and tighten the toggle bolts to secure the track lighting in place. Turn on the power and flip on the light switch to test your work.

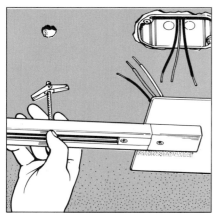

7 Lay out and bore ceiling holes for the toggle bolts. Install the bolts, push the ears through the holes, and let track dangle.

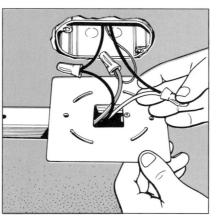

8 Using the proper-sized wire nuts, join black and white pigtails to the black wires in box, and green pigtail to ground wire.

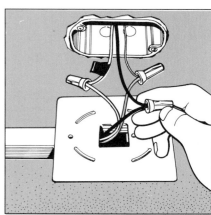

9 Sometimes a box will have a black wire and a white wire, coded with black tape or ink. Just treat the white wire as black.

How to hang
A CEILING FAN

Degree of difficulty: Hard   Estimated time: 3 to 6 hours   Average cost of materials: $75 to $200

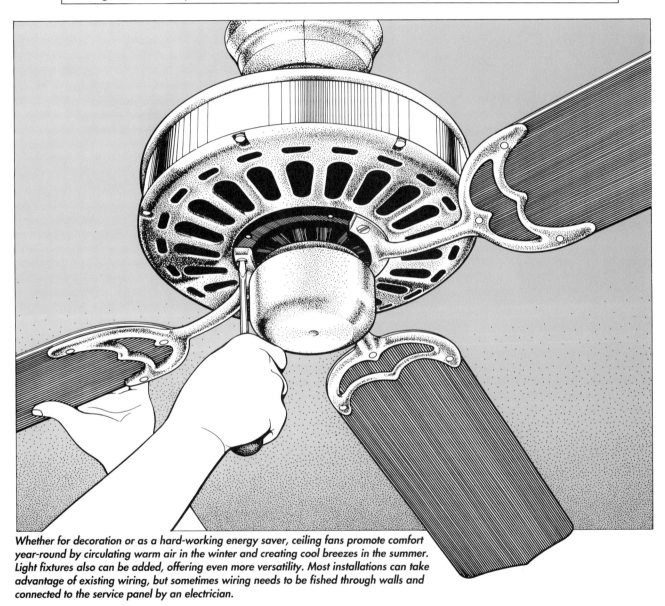

Whether for decoration or as a hard-working energy saver, ceiling fans promote comfort year-round by circulating warm air in the winter and creating cool breezes in the summer. Light fixtures also can be added, offering even more versatility. Most installations can take advantage of existing wiring, but sometimes wiring needs to be fished through walls and connected to the service panel by an electrician.

With such dramatic increases in energy costs over the years, people have been forced continually to look for new energy-saving devices. These may be high-tech problem-solvers like some solar components or low-tech solutions like adding more insulation to your home. But in between exists one of the oldest and most dependable ways to stretch your energy dollar: the ceiling fan.

These units have come a long way since the movie *Casablanca* when they were seen spinning over Ingrid Bergman's head in Rick's Cafe. They are available in many different sizes and styles and they're more efficient and affordable than in days gone by. Despite these improvements, the mechanism still works in the same basic way. It simply circulates the air already inside a room: It brings down the warmer ceiling-level air during the winter and brings up the cooler floor-level air in the summer. Without some means of mechanically moving this air you end up paying to heat or cool air that you never really feel.

To this end, all of the fans described here have reversing switches with at least three different speeds. Depending on the model, fans can be controlled by means of unit-mounted pull-chains; rheostat switches that control fan speed; remote control switches that turn the fan on and off *and* select speeds from anywhere in the room; and electronic wall switches that control fan speed and direction as

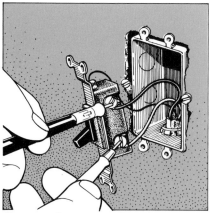

1 *Remove fuse or turn off breaker to proper circuit. Remove switch plate, pull out switch, check for current with tester.*

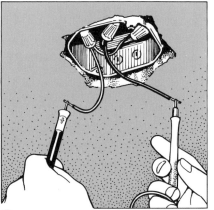

2 *Remove existing light fixture and then check white and black pigtails for current. If tester lights, current is present.*

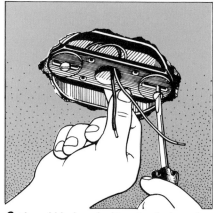

3 *Thread black and white pigtails through hole in fan's mounting bracket. Then attach bracket to outlet box.*

well as the light intensity on optional light fixtures attached to the fan.

Ceiling fans can be installed in nearly every area of the home. With the variety of mounting systems available, you can hang a fan from a flat 8-ft. ceiling or a 20-ft. cathedral ceiling. The minimum clearance height, however, is 7 ft. from the floor to the blades. And the tip of the blades should be at least 18 in. from the nearest wall. Never hang a fan where high humidity could damage the electrical functions or warp wooden blades, such as in a bathroom. And, of course, don't position the fan above the swing of a hinged door.

Installation is a reasonably straightforward job, particularly if the fan replaces an existing light fixture. Here we did just that, choosing a fan with a light so nothing was lost by the conversion.

Choosing a fan

It's important to choose the unit that's most appropriate for your situation. As mentioned before, there are many sizes and styles from which to choose. Get a feeling for what is available locally. Compare warranties and service as well as design and operating features. Ask yourself if a modern-looking fan will fit into more traditional surroundings, or if a western-style model accents a living room furnished in black leather and leopard skin throw rugs. Ceiling fans are also available with varying blade sizes, so choose one that complements rather than overpowers the dimensions of the room.

All of the residential fans we examined were fitted with light kits for a modest additional cost. But the method of control is a more complicated decision. It will determine how you operate your fan and, to some extent, the ease of installation.

If you are replacing a light fixture with a fan or fan/light combination, you can

switch the fan on and off using an ordinary light switch. Then, the fan speed and light fixture are regulated with pull chains hanging from the fan. The fan direction can be changed by means of a slide switch located on the fan housing.

If you would like to control the fan speed also from a wall switch, you can install a rheostat switch. Then, only the light fixture requires a pull chain. Of course, this arrangement can be reversed to control the light fixture with a rheostat and the fan with a chain.

All of these options are available without changing your fixture wiring.

However, if you want to control the fan speed and the light from a wall switch, then you can install a double rheostat. But you will have to run an additional electric cable between the ceiling and switch boxes for this function. Before deciding on your operating system, consult your owner's manual for specific instructions for the fan you have.

One very attractive alternative—and the one we chose—is to purchase a "com-

puterized" wall control. Sold with some models of the Casablanca Fan line, this unit offers the greatest control over the fan and light. Included are automatic light shutoff, random light patterns for home security and full control of speed and direction, all without changing existing fixture wiring.

Where to begin

Begin work by switching off power at the breaker panel, or unscrewing the appropriate fuse for the proper circuit. As an extra safety precaution, flip the light switch controlling the light fixture you'll be replacing the ceiling fan with on and off a few times to make sure the power has indeed been turned off. Next, remove the switch plate cover and the screws that hold the switch to the box. Carefully grasp the switch by the metal ears at the top and bottom, taking care not to touch any electrical connections in case the power was not shut off, and pull it out of the box. Then test for power before proceeding. Place one probe of a circuit tester on one

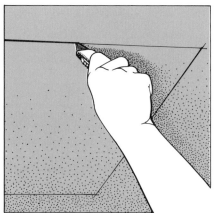

7 *Determine location of fan and position of joists on either side. Cut hole in ceiling from center to center of joist edges.*

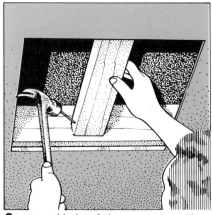

8 *Cut 2x4 block to fit between joists and position it so bottom of outlet box will be flush with ceiling. Toenail in place.*

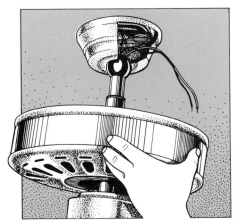

4 *Attach canopy to mounting bracket, then hang fan from canopy. Using wire nuts, join black wires then white wires.*

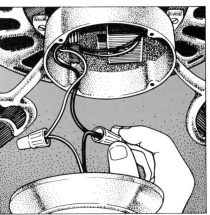

5 *To attach optional light fixture, remove covering plate on fan, and join pigtails with wire nuts. Screw fixture in place.*

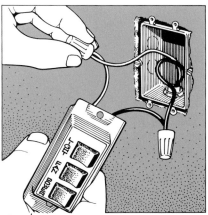

6 *To attach fan control unit to switch box, join pigtails with wire nuts, and screw unit to box. Attach face plate to unit.*

of the switch terminals, and the other probe to the second terminal. If the light on the tester does not light, the power is truly off, and the switch is safe to handle. Loosen the screws holding the wires and remove the switch. Separate the wires one by one to ensure that their bare ends can't contact each other.

Stand on a sturdy ladder and loosen the center post nut or screw that holds the light fixture and lower the fixture to expose the wiring. Carefully remove the wire nuts and test the wires as before to be certain the line is not "hot." Completely remove the fixture by undoing splices.

Weight considerations

Determine how firmly the electrical box is anchored to the ceiling framework. Though the fan we installed weighed 24 pounds, the owner's manual recommended a 50-pound test weight on the junction box. To see if our box could take this, we wired together several old window weights until they totaled about 50 pounds. We then attached the mounting

bracket that came with the fan to the electrical box. When we hung the weights from the bracket, we detected no movement in the box. It was solid. Of course, you can substitute any heavy object for the window weights. (If your box also withstands this test, then you can proceed as shown in Figs. 1 through 6. But if the box starts to pull away from the framework, you will have to reinforce it. To do so, follow the directions shown in Figs. 7, 8 and 9.)

Replacement installations

Temporarily remove the mounting bracket so you can feed the power wires through its center hole, then reattach it. Next, attach the escutcheon canopy to the mounting bracket. Keep in mind that some manufacturers may require preliminary assembly of certain fan parts. Consult your owner's manual for specific installation instructions.

Install the fan hanger system first. Run the fan wires through each piece, taking care not to damage the insulation on the

wires. Hang the fan from the escutcheon canopy, then connect the ground wire from the fan motor to the ground wire— or wires—from the power cables in the box. Make the connection with a proper size wire nut.

Connect remaining wires together; black to black, white to white, using proper wire nuts to hold them securely. You may want to wrap electrical tape around the connections for added safety. There may be an extra wire in the fan to provide a separate circuit for light control. We had no need for this because the control unit we used separated the functions internally. If you have no need for this wire, cap it with a wire nut and tuck it away. If you do need the wire, follow the manufacturer's wiring diagram supplied with the fan.

Next, attach the fan blades to the blade holders, then the blade holders to the fan. The blades are actually quite delicate in some respects and you should avoid handling them roughly or dropping them accidentally, since any warpage could cause the fan to wobble when it works. Spin the fan gently to make sure the blade path is unobstructed and all the mechanical connections are secure. Keep in mind that fan blades are matched and balanced at the factory, but you may have to switch the position of the blades to fine-tune the fan if it spins unevenly.

To add an optional light fixture, simply remove the cover plate on the bottom of the fan and install the fixture according to the manufacturer's instructions. Complete the job by wiring the control unit into the switch box.

New installation

If you don't have an overhead light fixture, you can still install your ceiling fan. It just takes a little more work. First, determine the location. Then trace the junc-

9 *Attach outlet box to bottom of support block using two 1½ in. No. 10 rh screws. Box comes with pre-bored mounting holes.*

10 *To gain access to wall cavity for running power cable, carefully pry baseboard from wall under new switch location.*

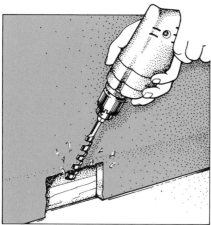

11 *Cut out small section of drywall behind baseboard. Then bore hole through bottom wall plate and floor for new cable.*

12 *Trace outline of new switch box, then cut hole. Feed cable through wall cavity from below, then through hole.*

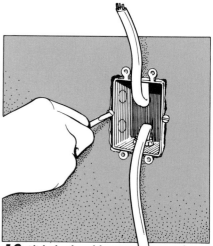

13 *Slide both cables into special cut-in box. Then push box into wall hole. Drive both side screws to tighten clamping ears.*

tion box on the ceiling and cut a hole in the ceiling at this point.

This hole provides a way to measure the distance to the adjacent ceiling joists and to determine in which direction they run. With this information established, draw a rectangle on the ceiling that spans the distance between the center lines of the adjacent joists. Joists most commonly fall on 16- or 24-in. centers. But in older homes, they can vary. Make the rectangle about 20 in. long in the other direction for working ease. Then cut out the opening with a utility knife or compass saw. Cut a 2x4 block to fit snugly between joists, approximately 1½ in. above ceiling height. This will allow for the depth of the outlet box, which should hang flush with the finished ceiling. Toenail the 2x4 to both of the joists using 8d common nails. Then attach a 4x4 octagonal box using two 1½ in. No. 10 rh screws.

Next, determine the position of the wall switch on the partition—not outside wall—nearest the fan. At the appropriate height, trace the outline of a "cut-in" switch box on the wall. (These boxes are called by different names, and some work differently than the one shown here. All, however, are designed to be mounted inside a precut hole without requiring additional support framing between the studs.) Carefully cut along the outline and remove the waste.

Then, using a flat pry bar, carefully remove the baseboard from the wall directly under the switch location. You can avoid damaging the wall above the baseboard by shielding it with a thin piece of wood as you pry. In some cases, the baseboard will also consist of shoe molding; pry it off first. Next, cut away the wall material behind the baseboard as shown in Fig. 11. The bottom wall plate should now be accessible. At a point

directly beneath the wall switch, bore a ¾-in.-dia. hole through the plate and floorboards into the basement. This hole provides access for the power cable coming up to the switch from the service panel in the basement.

If you live in a 1-story house, running the cable to the fan outlet box is a simple matter. Just climb up to your attic, locate the position of the box and remove a section of flooring—if it's in place—and some insulation. Once a path is clear from the box to the switch wall, bore a hole down through the top plates on the wall. Now you should have a clear path from the electric panel box to the switch and onto the ceiling fan box.

If you live in a 2-story house, however, the process is a bit more complicated. First, remove the baseboard on the wall directly above the first floor switch wall. Again, remove the wall material behind the baseboard, this time in a strip that is at least 10 in. wide. Next, using a reciprocating saw or a compass saw, cut out a 4-in.-wide section of the bottom plate

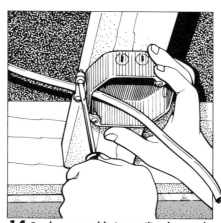

14 *Feed power cable into ceiling box and tighten connector. Patch ceiling around box by nailing new drywall in place.*

and subfloor. This should give you enough room to reach down into the cavity between the floor joists for the new wiring. It should also yield enough room to bore a hole through the top plates on the wall below.

With the wall plate and flooring cut out upstairs and the hole bored in the top plate, you should have clear access from your service panel to the switch and the ceiling box.

Once this is complete, simply string cable from the service panel to the switch, then another piece from the switch to the ceiling box. Be sure to leave about 5 ft. of cable at the service panel, and another foot at each end of the cable that enters the switch and ceiling box. Don't forget to check your local building codes for the wire gauge required for such installations.

Connecting wiring
It is strongly recommended to hire a licensed electrician to install the cable in the breaker or fuse box, and to make the individual connections inside the switch and ceiling box. But, if you've run the wires between the fixtures, the charge should be much less than if you had the electrician do the whole job.

In some cases, particularly in older houses, cutting holes in the ceiling and walls is a problem since walls are made of plaster. Plaster is harder to cut through because it is held in place by laths—usually wooden slats on which the plaster was originally applied. Since this poses more problems than for new houses where the walls are made of drywall panels (and where there are cavities to install new electrical wiring), it may be a better idea to have a professional do the work in such cases as well. Take note that ceiling boxes in older homes may not conform to the modern standards set for safe installation of a new ceiling fan.

How to troubleshoot
ELECTRIC RANGES

Degree of difficulty: Medium   Estimated time: 30 minutes to 1½ hours   Average cost of materials: $15 to $20

1 *A common problem with electric ranges is surface element failure. The first step in checking for the cause is to switch the element in question with its mate of the same size. Check other burners to see if a circuit breaker or blown fuse is the cause of the problem.*

When your electric range breaks down, don't complicate the problem by chasing down phantoms. The reason why an electric element doesn't work usually lies with a key part that can be easily tested.

Seldom will all elements (surface and oven) fail at once. But if they do, the problem is most likely a major electrical failure in the house or in the range.

Check the circuit breaker or fuse. Maybe an overload tripped the circuit breaker and resetting it or replacing a fuse will set things right. If not, you may need to seek help from a professional repairman to fix your range.

When there's surface element failure, usually only one element won't work. Under these circumstances, you know that you're getting current to the range and the problem is only confined to the element or to a component that controls the element.

Troubleshooting single-element failure is quite a simple procedure. Take the element from its original position on the stove top, remove another element of the corresponding size and put the non-working unit in its place. Then turn on the element to see if it works.

Turn the temperature control to high. If the problem element works, it's obviously okay. If it doesn't, purchase another from a hardware store.

Some ranges have only one element (and two or three hot plates). Since there is not another element to switch with the suspect element, you will have to test it with an ohmmeter (Page 66). The meter will either show resistance or it won't. If it doesn't (the needle stays on zero), replace the element with a new one.

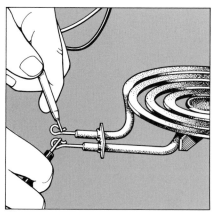

2 *To test an element with an ohmmeter, hold the probes to its terminals. You should get a zero resistance reading.*

Tracing element failure

If you have a bad element on your electric range, it's to your advantage to try and find out why it failed. About 85 percent of the electric ranges currently in use have surface elements that are pushed into and pulled out of the terminal blocks.

Elements of the remaining 15 percent have terminals that are screwed to power wires but work the same way.

If your range has push-on/pull-out elements, examine the terminals of the bad element to see if they're bent. Bent terminals indicate the element has not been reinserted properly—that it's been cocked when reconnected to the terminal block.

Bent terminals don't make good contact, causing arcing, and this could lead to element or terminal-block failure (as well as being potentially dangerous). Evidence of arcing shows up as a black coating on terminals.

Terminals might have a blue tinge to them. This is caused by grease—which has spattered on the terminal—being heated to high temperature. Eventually, this heated grease can cause the terminals to burn and lead to element and terminal block failure. This condition also can affect elements with screw-on terminals.

If terminals of push-on/pull-out elements are coated, shine a light inside the terminal block. If you see contacts that are burned or eaten away, replace the block and use fine sandpaper or steel wool to clean the ends of element terminals.

Electric range elements use Nichrome resistance wires, made of a nickel and chromium alloy. The wire is held inside an insulator and covered by a metal sheathing with a black oxide coating.

In time, the insulator can break down. This allows the Nichrome wire to touch the sheathing. The result is that the wire burns out, but before it does it may burn a hole through the surface of the element, causing it to fail.

"Bad" turns out good

Suppose that after swapping elements you find that the new element now glows brightly. The reason for your problem is either an element control switch that's worn out or defective, or a damaged control-to-element wire.

A damaged control-to-element wire is more likely if your range has a lift-up rather than a stationary top. As the top of the range is lifted and closed, the wires that carry current to the elements can be pulled apart or caught under the lift-up top and crimped.

If you spot a broken or crimped wire, turn off power to the range, strip insulation from the ends of the broken wire and twist loose ends together. Then, solder the wire and cover the splice with a ceramic wire nut. Caution: Don't use a plastic nut, which will melt when subjected to high temperatures caused by the range.

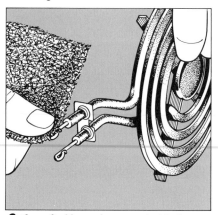

3 *If you find burned contacts inside the terminal block, replace it. Next, clean the element's terminals with steel wool.*

If you don't see a broken or crimped wire, it doesn't mean that one doesn't exist—only that you haven't found it. At this point, troubleshooting the element control switch will determine if the control is bad or if you have to look much harder for a damaged or severed wire.

Before starting, be sure that the power is turned off.

The first step in testing an element control switch is to get behind the control panel. With most ranges, this is done by removing screws holding the panel (console) in position and leaning the panel forward. With other ranges you have to remove screws from a cover at the rear of the console.

Examine the control switch that operates the element which isn't working and the one controlling the corresponding size element. Transfer "power" wires between the two elements. These power wires are normally colored red, black

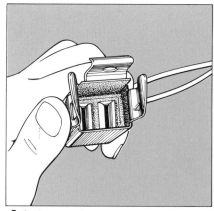

4 *If a heating element's terminals have a black or blue coating, check if the terminal block contacts have been burned.*

and/or white. They are the ones that don't bridge the oven controls, but originate from inside the oven's console.

To be on the safe side, use adhesive-backed labels or masking tape that you can write on to mark which wires connect to which terminals before disconnecting them.

Now, turn on power and turn both control switches to HIGH. If the element that did not work now glows, and the element that had been working doesn't, the control switch is bad. Again, turn off the power, replace the switch and reconnect the wires to their original positions.

Caution: When the power is turned on, be certain that you do not touch any wire or terminal connection.

If things are the same—that is, the bad element still isn't glowing, and the good element is still glowing and you've inspected the terminal block—a broken wire exists. Look for the cause of trouble once more.

Oven problems

When either the bake or broil element won't work, the cause is much the same

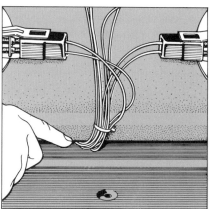

5 *The lift-up top on some ranges can easily pinch and damage wires. Check for this and replace any damaged wires.*

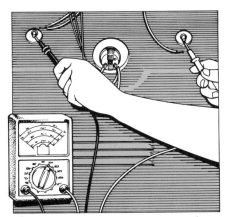

6 *Oven elements that can't be removed from the inside can be tested with an ohmmeter from behind the range.*

as when a surface element won't work—either the element is bad, a control switch is shot, or there's a bad wire.

Testing oven elements is a little more difficult than testing a surface element. You have to use an ohmmeter. Turn off power. From the inside of the oven, remove screws holding the nonworking element in place.

Then, carefully pull the element toward you, detach the terminals—they'll be held to power wires by spade connectors or screws—and remove the element. Place the ohmmeter leads on the element terminals. The ohmmeter should show resistance. If it shows zero, replace the defective element.

If the element cannot be removed from inside the oven, take off the rear panel. Test the element by holding ohmmeter probes against the element terminals.

Suppose the ohmmeter shows the element is okay.

So why doesn't it glow?

The cause probably is a defective oven selector control switch, which is used to select the BAKE and BROIL functions on your range.

Testing the selector control

As part of the wiring diagram for the range, which is probably pasted to the outer or inner side of the back panel, you will see an oven selector chart, similar to the one illustrated in Fig. 7. Using this oven selector chart and an ohmmeter, you can test the oven selector control switch to see if it works.

To demonstrate this, let's use the chart to test the bake and broil sides of a control. The chart points out that in the BAKE setting there should be continuity between contacts Ll and BK, PL and N, and PL and BR. You can use an ohmmeter to test between each of these contact positions.

Turn off the power and open the con-

trol panel to reach the contacts of the oven selector control switch. Disconnect the wires from the contacts. Make sure that you note which wire goes where.

Turn the oven selector control switch to BAKE. Then, hold ohmmeter leads first to Ll and BK contacts; then, to PL and N contacts; and finally, to PL and BR contacts. If you fail to get zero resistance in any of the three positions, replace the switch. The broil side of the control is tested the same way.

Turn the switch to BROIL and hold the ohmmeter leads first across contacts Ll and BR, and then contacts Ll and PL.

If the ohmmeter shows other than zero resistance in either position, replace the switch selector control with a new one.

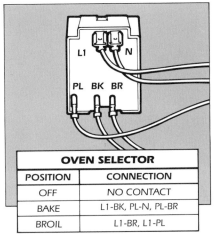

OVEN SELECTOR	
POSITION	CONNECTION
OFF	NO CONTACT
BAKE	L1-BK, PL-N, PL-BR
BROIL	L1-BR, L1-PL

7 *The oven selector switch chart tells which terminals control bake and broil functions. Check them for continuity.*

Testing the oven control

Another likely trouble area is the oven temperature control switch. When the control switch goes bad, one or both elements won't work.

In the event that both the broil and bake elements aren't working, however, there's one thing to do before testing the oven temperature control—check the clock-timer. It should be in the MANUAL position. If someone accidentally moved the clock-timer to the AUTOMATIC position, the element won't glow until the clock reaches the time set on the

timer. Move the clock switch to MANUAL. Now, check to see if broil and bake elements work.

If you have to test the oven temperature control switch, check the wiring diagram to determine which contacts are involved (Fig. 8). It points out that the oven temperature in bake mode is controlled by contacts 1 and 3, and the oven temperature in broil mode is controlled by contacts 1 and 2.

Using this information, here's how to check the switch: Turn off power and open the control panel. Disconnect wires from the oven temperature control switch. Turn the control to at least 300° F. Place ohmmeter leads across contacts 1 and 2 and turn the oven selector switch to BROIL. Then, turn the oven selector switch to BAKE and hold ohmmeter leads across contacts 1 and 3. If you don't get zero resistance in either or both positions, replace the switch.

An oven thermostat also can act up. Suspect a thermostat problem if the oven cooks food too quickly or not fast enough.

Test the temperature by placing an oven thermometer inside a heated oven and compare the reading with the setting on the oven knob. Both should be within 25° F of each other. If they aren't, try recalibrating the thermostat. Most thermostats can be recalibrated by making adjustments on the oven control knob itself or by inserting a screwdriver into the knob's hollow shaft. Most owner's manuals come with instructions on how to make adjustments for your particular model. Also check inside the oven to see if the thermostat sensing bulb—usually located near the back of the oven on the side—needs to be cleaned or replaced.

8 *If an oven's bake and broil elements aren't working, the cause may be the oven temperature control switch; its wiring diagram is at right. Note contacts 1 and 3 control bake; contacts 1 and 2 control broil.*

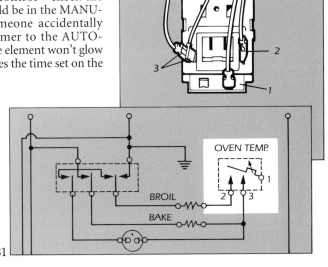

How to defuse the hazards of
ALUMINUM HOUSE WIRING

Degree of difficulty: Medium **Estimated time:** 3 to 6 hours **Average cost of materials:** $30

If your home is between 15 and 40 years old, you may be living with a potential fire hazard buried in your walls, namely aluminum wiring. It was used widely after World War II because it was inexpensive and copper supplies were inadequate. The shortcomings of aluminum weren't fully realized until the mid-1970s, after hundreds of thousands of homes were already wired improperly.

The trouble with aluminum is that it's not as good a conductor as copper. As a result, it expands more than copper when carrying a charge and contracts more than copper when not carrying a charge. This doesn't harm the wire itself, but eventually it can loosen terminal screws on receptacles, switches and some light fixtures. These loose connections cause increased resistance which in turn creates heat and sometimes sparks which can start fires.

Another problem with aluminum wire is oxidation. When dissimilar metals are joined—for instance when aluminum touches brass screws or copper wires—electrolysis results which corrodes the connections, further increasing resistance. To correct the oxidation problem, electrical component manufacturers started making copper-clad aluminum wire. This improvement, however, did little for the expansion-contraction problem. So finally, the industry responded by making switches and receptacles rated to accept aluminium and copper-clad wire as well as the traditional copper wire.

Because these newer devices are readily available, you can upgrade your aluminum wiring by simply replacing your old ones with new ones. Unfortunately, this is a relatively expensive undertaking. Your better choice is to splice new insulated copper pigtails between your aluminum or copper-clad aluminum wiring and the switch, receptacle or light fixture terminal screws. To avoid corrosion where the copper and aluminum meet, just pack each wire nut with a special anti-oxidation paste.

Identifying dangerous connections
The first thing to do is investigate your present situation. Shut off the power to a specific circuit at your fuse box or breaker panel. Then remove the cover plate

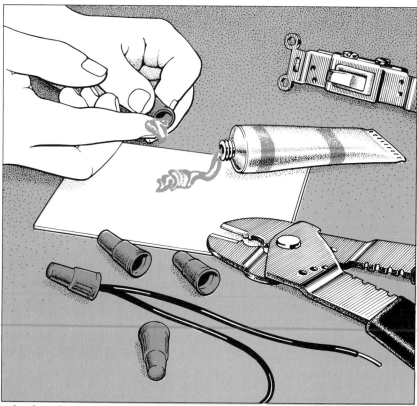

A few feet of insulated electrical cable, good wire strippers, a variety of wire nuts and some anti-oxidation paste are all that's required to upgrade your aluminum wiring.

from a receptacle and inspect the metal yoke that is screwed to the wall box. This yoke (Fig. 1) should have a wire rating stamped into its surface. If you see the letters CU-AL (copper-aluminum) this means the receptacle was designed for both copper and aluminum wire so it doesn't really make any difference what type of wire was used in your home. If you see CU and CU-CLAD this means the unit is rated only for copper or copper-clad wire.

If, however, no designation appears, then the receptacle is appropriate only for solid copper wire. To find out what wire you have, pull out the receptacle and inspect the wire ends. If you see aluminum colored wire or aluminum colored wire encased in a copper jacket, the receptacle must be upgraded with copper pigtails.

The way you install the pigtails depends on what type of electrical cable is com-

ing into the metal fixture boxes inside your walls. The drawings on the following page show the two different cables you are likely to encounter. The first is 2-wire cable without ground, which means just a black (hot) wire and a white (neutral) wire. The second type is 2-wire with ground which has the same black and white wires but also has a bare ground wire along for the ride.

Making conversions
To make the conversion, begin by shutting off the power to one circuit at the main service panel. For safety, post a note on the panel advising others not to switch on the power. Remove the cover plate and receptacle from the outlet box and disconnect the wires. Then cut 6-in. lengths of insulated cable that are the same gauge as the wiring used in your house. Usually this will be 12 gauge, though some circuits are still wired with 14-gauge cable.

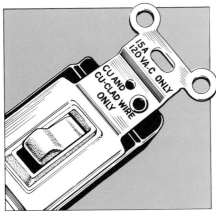

1 Newer switches and receptacles bear rating stamps indicating types of wire they accept. Switch above is rated for copper and copper-clad aluminum, not solid aluminum.

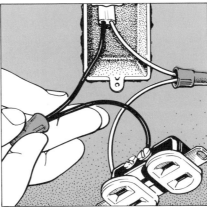

2 To adapt an ungrounded, end-of-circuit receptacle, splice new copper pigtails between terminal screws and aluminum wires. Use paste-filled wire nuts on wire ends.

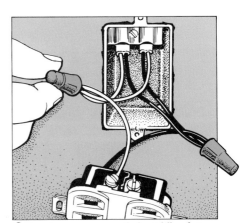

3 To adapt an ungrounded, middle-of-circuit receptacle, splice the new copper pigtails between each pair of like-colored wires and their proper terminal screws.

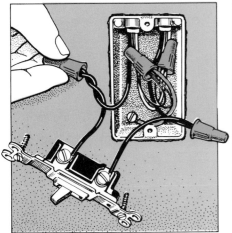

4 Because only the black (hot) wires are attached to a normal switch, add the pigtails only to the black wires. The other connections in the box remain the same.

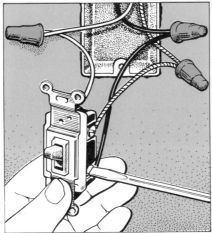

5 Three-way switches have three different colored wires. To avoid error, adapt only one wire at a time, making sure in each case that the pigtail goes to the original screw.

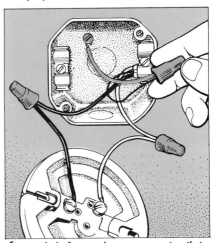

6 Most light fixtures have copper pigtails in place. But simple porcelain ones don't. Add pigtails to the terminal screws and between the bare ground wire and metal box.

Next, strip about ⅝ in. of insulation off both ends of the black and white pigtails. Then join these pigtails to the terminal screws on the receptacle. Be sure to note which side of the receptacle was attached to the black wire and which was attached to the white wire. When in doubt, remember that the black (hot) wires should always go to the brass-colored terminal screws.

With the receptacle ends attached, pack appropriately sized wire nuts with anti-oxidation paste and join the new copper pigtails to the ends of the existing aluminum wires, keeping the colors consistent: black-to-black and white-to-white. Make sure the wire nuts are turned down firmly on both wires. If a bare aluminum ground wire is present inside the box, just join a copper pigtail to this wire and then attach the other end of the pigtail to the back of the box using a grounding screw driven into the hole provided for it.

If there are two cables coming into the box, two white and two black wires, the retrofit is the same idea, except you'll have to use larger wire nuts that can accommodate two aluminum wires and the pigtail at the same time.

When upgrading switches, remember that the switch unit is wired only between the black (hot) wires. The white wires should already be joined together in the box. Leave the white wires undisturbed and simply add the pigtails between the ends of the black wires and the terminal screws on the switch.

If you are adapting 3- or 4-way switches you may find a red wire, or a white wire with black tape on it, inside the box. This coding is a matter of expedience to electricians, but it looks like a can of worms to just about everyone else. To keep from making a mistake, adapt only one wire at a time. If you're really worried about errors, use adhesive labels or pieces of masking tape to identify the wires you're working on. That way there's never any doubt about whether you'll connect everything up the right way.

All but the simplest light fixtures—the inexpensive porcelain utility lights—come with copper-stranded leads that are attached to the circuit wire with wire nuts. All that's required to adapt these fixtures is to simply remove the existing wire nuts, fill the nuts with anti-oxidation paste and reinstall them.

Remember, there is no need to panic if your house is wired with aluminum wiring. Discourage potential problems by following the steps outlined here.

One last note: Not all circuit breaker or fuse connections are a problem with aluminum wire. It depends on how the individual service panel was designed and outfitted. Inspecting and retrofitting these panels are jobs better left to a licensed electrician.

How to repair
A DOORBELL

Degree of difficulty: Easy   **Estimated time:** 2 hours   **Average cost of materials:** $10

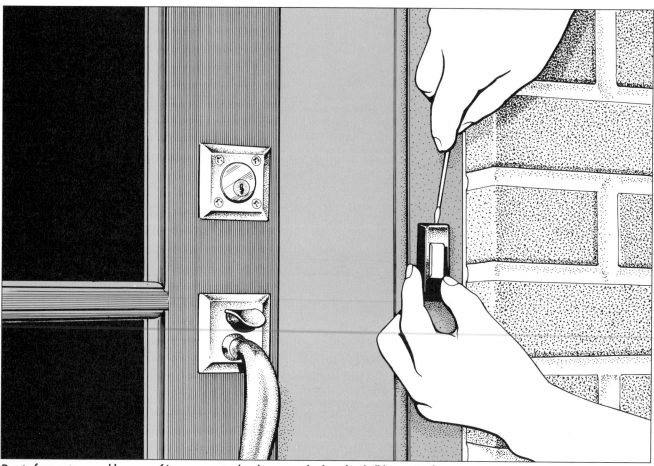

Due to frequent use and because of its exposure to the elements, a broken doorbell button is often the reason why a bell, chime or buzzer won't work. Fortunately, buttons also are easy to fix and replace. Gain access to connections and contacts by prying off the cover with a small screwdriver. If cleaning and testing the button don't solve the problem, then suspect the other components.

If your doorbell has had the life rung out of it, don't despair. Defective doorbells are easy and inexpensive to fix. And since a doorbell system uses low-voltage current to operate, there's little of the danger associated with regular work on other household electrical systems.

Doorbells also have few components, which makes problem diagnosis quick and easy. Every doorbell system is composed of a button, transformer and bell, buzzer or chime mechanism. Aside from a possible break in the wiring, a problem with your doorbell eventually will be traced to the faulty operation of one of these components. A little investigation will likely yield quick results.

Start with the button

Because the button gets the most physical abuse and is located on the exterior of the house where it's subjected to the elements, it's often the component that is most likely to fail first. If you press the button and hear no sound at all, it makes sense to start your investigation here.

Start by removing the button from the exterior trim. Buttons are either screwed directly to the trim (you'll see the screws right away) or snap-mounted to a base that's screwed to the trim. If you can't find the screws, you have the snap-on variety. Remove this type by gently prying under the button housing edge with a small screwdriver to pop it free.

The button is simply a spring-loaded switch that completes the low-voltage bell circuit allowing current to flow through the other components. You can determine whether the transformer and sound-generating unit are in working order and the wires are intact by bypassing, or jumping, the button. On the back of the button housing you'll see two wires connected to screw terminals. Remove one wire and briefly hold it against the other wire to jump the switch. If the bell rings, you know the rest of the system is fine and the button is at fault. Although you can attempt to clean the screw terminals and contacts, simply replacing the button is often the most practical solution. Install

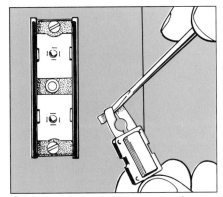

1 *Buttons with lights often have two brass spring tabs. Be sure they're clean and make contact with mounting plate terminals.*

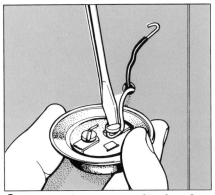

2 *Older-style buttons mount directly to the trim. Each of two low-voltage wires is connected to a brass screw terminal.*

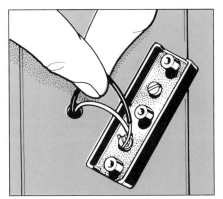

3 *To test the button, remove one wire and touch it to the other terminal. If the bell rings, you've got a defective button.*

the new button by fastening the two wires to it and reattaching it to the trim. If bypassing the button didn't cause the bell to ring, assume for the meantime that the button is in good operating condition and the problem is located in the transformer, the sound-generating unit or is caused by a broken wire.

Bells and buzzers

These mechanisms both employ a similar arrangement of coils and contact points to generate sound. Bells ring when current passes through electromagnetic coils which become energized and attract the clapper. As the clapper is pulled toward the coils, it strikes the bell. At the very instant the clapper strikes the bell, contact points on the clapper arm open, the circuit is broken and the coils lose their magnetism. Then, spring tension on the clapper arm returns it to its original position, the contacts close and the process is repeated for as long as the doorbell button is held down. Buzzers differ only in that they lack a clapper and bell. The sound they produce is simply a result of the electrical contacts vibrating as they open and close when activated.

If your bell or buzzer makes any sound at all—even a muffled, raspy hum, it's fairly safe to assume that both the transformer and button are in working order and the wires are not broken. In this case, your job is to check out the sound-generating unit.

Begin by using a thin-blade screwdriver to pry the cover from the bell or buzzer and inspect the wiring and contact points. Some units have covers that can be popped off by simply pressing at the top or bottom. If the sound was muffled, check for grease and dust clinging to the moving parts. Use an old toothbrush and a drop of rubbing alcohol to clean the components. After cleaning, resist any temptation to lubricate the moving parts. Dust has a greater tendency to cling to surfaces that are oiled than to dry surfaces and you'll only be shortening the time until the next overhaul.

Next, check the wire connections. If a wire is loosely connected to its terminal, tighten the screw. If the insulation on either wire is frayed or appears to be in bad shape, cut off the bad section, re-strip the wire end and connect it to the terminal. Clean the coils with the toothbrush

and rubbing alcohol. The contact points can be checked by pulling the clapper away from its seat.

If you see a buildup of dirt and tarnish, clean the contact points with fine sandpaper or emery paper. The striking surface of a matchbook or a nail file is a good substitute if you don't have any fine sandpaper on hand.

After you've checked the wires and connections, cleaned the entire mechanism, and dressed the points, reassemble the unit and try the doorbell. If it rings, the problem was simply a case of long overdue maintenance.

Cleaning and repairing chimes

Many modern homes feature doorbells that strike a series of chimes rather than ring a bell or buzzer. After years of reliable service, chimes will often sound in muted tones. In other cases, you'll hear only one note of the chime's 2- or 3-note sequence when the doorbell button is depressed. The rest may sound more like dull thumps than clear tones. This too can be caused by dust accumulation, but more often is the result of worn pads on the tone bar mounts.

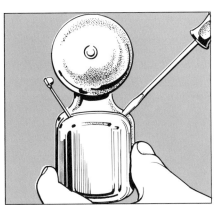

4 *Use a screwdriver to gently pry off the cover of a bell or buzzer. Some covers pop off when you press the top or bottom.*

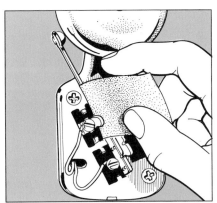

5 *Pull back the clapper to check the condition of the bell contact points. If necessary, clean them with a piece of fine sandpaper.*

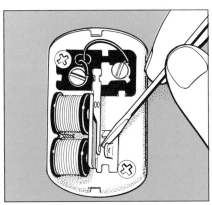

6 *Buzzer contact points also should be cleaned. Spread them apart with a screwdriver to check their condition.*

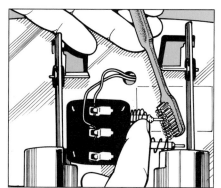

7 Use a toothbrush and rubbing alcohol to clean the parts of a bell, buzzer or chime. Don't lubricate to avoid collecting dust.

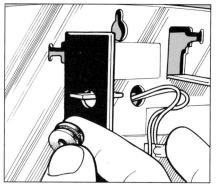

8 Rubber grommets in a chime unit isolate tone bar from its mounting. Get replacements if they're worn, hard or missing.

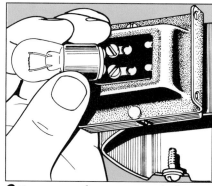

9 To test a transformer, remove the low-voltage wires and hold a 12-volt bulb to the terminals. If bulb lights up, all is well.

To clean a set of chimes, pop off the cover and look for dust around the plunger springs and tarnish buildup on the tips of the plungers. Again, use a toothbrush and rubbing alcohol to clean the plungers and return springs.

Next, check the rubber pads, or grommets, on the mounts of each tone bar. These pads insulate the tone bars from the mounts so that the tone bars can vibrate freely. If you find worn, hard or missing pads, you'll need to buy replacements. Check with a local hardware store or electrical supply outlet for the pads.

If you have trouble finding new pads, you may have to replace the entire chime. Remove the old chime by disconnecting the wires and loosening the screws in the mounting plate. Simply reverse the procedure when installing the new chime.

Checking the transformer
Every low-voltage doorbell system has a transformer that reduces the 110-volt household current to between 8 and 16 volts depending on the specifications of the bell, buzzer or chime unit. You'll find the transformer connected to a junction box, usually in the basement and often

near the electrical entrance panel, where it's wired to a 110-volt house circuit. The low-voltage wires are connected to the transformer by screw-type terminals and are safe to handle. The connections inside the junction box carry the full 110-volt house current.

To check if your transformer is doing its job, undo the low-voltage wires and hold the terminals of a 12-volt automotive bulb to the low-voltage terminals on the transformer. Don't test the unit by jumping the terminals with a screwdriver. Some models have built-in fuses that will blow with this procedure. If the bulb lights, the transformer is working. If not, you'll have to install a replacement.

Before attempting to remove the old transformer, shut off the house circuit that supplies current to the transformer. Find the appropriate circuit breaker at the main panel and switch it off. If your panel has fuses, simply unscrew the fuse. Then, remove the junction-box cover plate and disconnect the transformer wires that connect the unit to the house current. Undo the box connector that holds the transformer to the box and pull the unit out. Reverse this procedure to

mount the new transformer and, finally, reconnect to the 110-volt circuit and turn it back on.

Typical doorbell systems require either an 8-,10-,12-,14- or 16-volt transformer. While any brand will do, make sure the new transformer has the same voltage rating as the original when you go to purchase a replacement.

Checking the wires
If the three main electrical components of your doorbell system check out, and your doorbell still doesn't work, you probably have a broken wire. You can check this by disconnecting the two low-voltage wires at the transformer and holding the probes of an automotive continuity tester to each wire while a helper holds the doorbell button down. If the tester light comes on, the wires are intact. If not, you'll need to string a new set of matched low-voltage wires through the basement and attic, and behind walls. You can often attach the new wires to the old by taping them together with strong masking tape and then using the old wires to pull the new ones through walls and other blind spots.

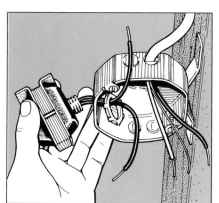

10 Transformer is connected to house circuit at a junction box. After shutting off circuit, disconnect wires and remove.

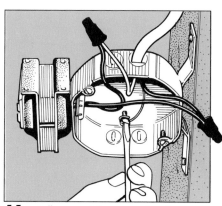

11 Install new unit by connecting the transformer wires to the incoming black and white wires. Ground is screwed to box.

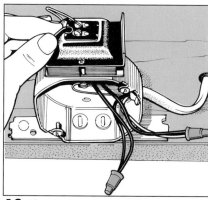

12 After you've connected the transformer to the house current, fasten each low-voltage wire to a transformer terminal.

How to install
LOW-VOLTAGE LIGHTING

Degree of difficulty: Easy   **Estimated time:** 4 hours   **Average cost of materials:** $65

When it comes to electrical projects, low-voltage landscape lighting is about as easy as it gets. Low-voltage outdoor kits have several real advantages over their 120-volt counterparts, at least from the home owner's perspective.

First, low-voltage outdoor kits are far less expensive to operate. A 6-head kit uses roughly the same energy as a single, 100-watt bulb.

Secondly, the complicated weather-and-hazard-protection measures required for 120-volt outdoor wiring can be dispensed with almost entirely. For example, low-voltage wiring need only be buried several inches deep, versus the 24-in. to 30-in. direct-bury requirements of 120-volt systems.

And finally, low-voltage outdoor kits are safe and easy to install, so much so that only a little or no knowledge of electricity is really required.

When shopping for a low-voltage landscape lighting kit, you'll quickly find that there are two distinct price categories. Retail outlets catering to the do-it-yourselfer offer inexpensive kits ($50 to $80), featuring a limited variety of lamp heads, usually six to eight in number.

Specialty lighting outlets, by contrast, are likely to offer a better quality system that may or may not come in kit form. These systems offer greater creative flexibility when it comes to mixing and matching heads for specific effect, but are substantially more expensive. A single head might cost as much as an entire kit at your local hardware store.

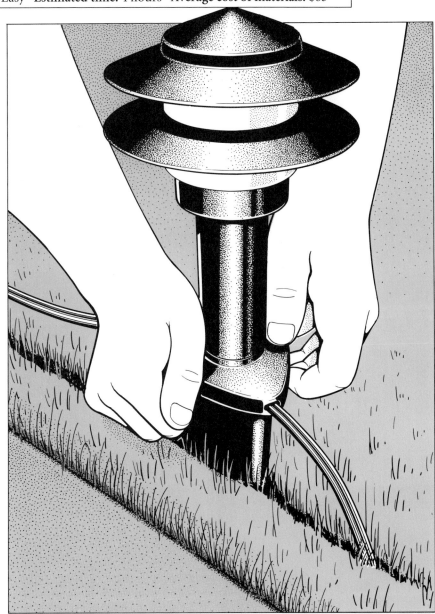

Low-voltage lighting kits make installation safe and easy. Installation requires little or no knowledge of electricity to brighten up gardens, patios and decks. Also, low-voltage lighting does not have to meet the stringent requirements set for burying cable in 120-volt systems.

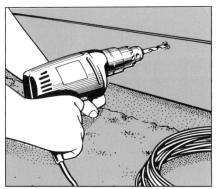

1 To bring cable from an indoor control box, bore a hole through rim joist or wall and feed the cable through the hole.

If you're planning a more elaborate landscape lighting design, the high-end systems are clearly worth considering. If you're not planning such an elaborate design, and you are a little timid around electricity anyway, the more modest kits are simpler and easier to install. And, as each landscape lighting kit is self-con-

tained, there is no chance that you'll install more lights on a system than it was designed to support.

The components
The model we've chosen is an 8-lamp kit. It has four floodlights and four 2-tier walk lamps. The kit also includes 100 ft. of

buriable cable, a control box that houses a transformer (voltage reducer) and a built-in timer. The timer automatically turns the lights on and off according to the times you set. The system's control box accesses house current via a standard 3-prong plug, so that no 120-volt wiring is required.

While the control box is weather-tight and can be installed outdoors, indoor installations are also worth considering. As most kits come with convenient 120-volt plugs, you'll be able to plug them directly into an outdoor receptacle. The problem, of course, is that an outdoor receptacle, having flip-up weather caps, is only water resistant when the caps are closed and sealed.

With a transformer plugged into the receptacle full-time, one cap will remain up, exposing the receptacle to driving rains. While most kits are installed in this manner, and are generally acceptable to local codes, an indoor receptacle would avoid the problem entirely. From a basement utility room or garage, it's easy enough to bring the low-voltage end of the system outdoors, leaving the higher-voltage end sheltered indoors. We've included both methods here. As with any outdoor installation, the receptacle you tap should be ground-fault circuit interrupter (GFCI) protected.

Planning and layout

Before purchasing a lighting kit, you'll want to consider factors of layout and design. Lamps to be positioned along a walk or drive are standard with each kit, as are floodlights. If you have a deck, you might also consider a kit that offers deck lights. Cable for the deck lights can be fed up through the deck and stapled along the underside, out of harm's way.

Also, some manufacturers offer a range of different heads that can be adjusted or focused in a number of different ways to yield more dramatic results. Plan your layout several ways, with these options in mind, before making your final selection.

Start your layout with a determination as to the best control box location. If sidewalks and other landscape obstructions will be a factor, position the box on the favorable side of the obstruction.

Measure from your control box location to each lamp location to determine how much cable and how many lamps and lamp styles you'll need. These factors will influence the type of kit you choose. Also, be sure to check your local codes to see if they have any specific requirements for low-voltage installations.

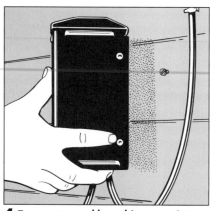

2 *Protect the cable drop by running it through conduit. Be sure to secure conduit to building with conduit strap.*

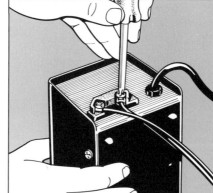

3 *To fasten low-voltage cable to control box, turn box upside down and bind each cable wire under a screw terminal.*

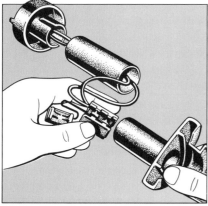

4 *To mount control box, drive screw into wall (and stud behind) leaving ⅛ in. of shank exposed. Hang box on screw head.*

5 *To set timer, adjust dial to current hour. Then lift pegs from timer and reset them in desired ON/OFF indicator slots.*

6 *Begin lamp assembly by sliding connector leads (attached to clip) through riser tube and into platform of stake.*

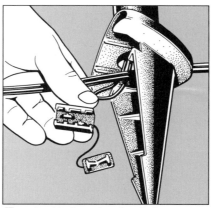

7 *Feed cable through stake platform to the desired location. Then remove cover from cable clip to expose contact points.*

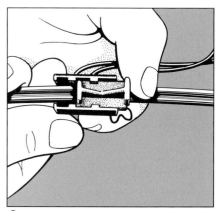

8 *Lay cable into channel on cable clip and slide the plastic cover into place so cable is pierced by contact points.*

Installing your kit

Begin the project by mounting the control box on a wall within a foot or so of the chosen receptacle. If mounting the box outdoors, position it at least a foot above ground. Then, to protect the cable from damage, encase it in conduit from the box to just below ground level.

The same is true if you're going for an indoor box installation. Bore through the rim joist or wall of your home and bring cable through the hole. Then, encase the exposed outdoor cable from the rim joist opening to below ground. You'll also want to caulk the cable opening.

With low-voltage wiring, the conduit need not be joined to a line box, or be weather-tight. The object here is to protect the cable from assault by sharp garden tools or pets.

Assembling lamp heads

All kits will require some lamp assembly, but don't be intimidated. It'll be a simple step-by-step procedure. In the case of the kit shown here, the walk lamps come in several pieces: a ground stake, extension riser, bulb socket and electrical leads (with self-piercing cable clip), and the globe. In this case, start the job by feeding the electrical leads through the riser tube and into the stake.

It's generally easier to make the cable connection before attaching the bulb and globe. Therefore, feed the cable through the opening in the stake platform and slide it through until it reaches the planned tap location on the cable.

The cable connections on most kits are incredibly easy. Each set of lamp leads contains a channel with self-piercing cable taps built-in. Just lay the cable into the channel and slide a small plastic shunt over it. As the shunt forces the cable down into the channel, the taps pierce a wire in each side of the cable and make contact. That's really all there is to it.

You'll then press the channel clip into a slot in the stake and tuck the cable neatly under the platform. With the electrical connection made, fold any excess lead wire into the riser and press the lamp socket onto the riser.

Follow this by inserting the bulb and twisting the globe onto the socket base.

When assembling a spotlight, you'll need to feed two leads through a bridge that spans the head and holds the bulb.

With the leads in place, press a bulb into the bridge and snap the bridge onto the head, with the bulb facing the back of the reflector. Then, snap the lens in place and fasten the head to its stake.

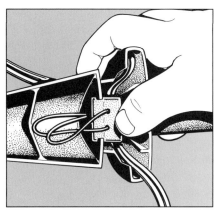

9 *Press the cable clip into its slot under the stake platform. Then, tuck the excess cable neatly into the platform recess.*

10 *Once the cable is secured, insert the bulb into the socket until you feel it seat against its contacts.*

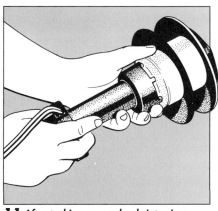

11 *After tucking excess leads into riser tube, slide the globe over the lamp socket tabs and twist until globe seats properly.*

12 *To install floodlights, feed wires through bridge and fasten bulb to center leg of bridge. Snap bridge onto lamp head.*

13 *Then, slide the lens into proper position over the floodlight's lamp head and snap in place. You should hear a click.*

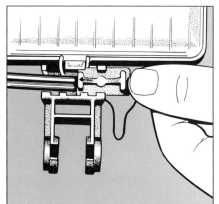

14 *Once again, lay the cable in the cable clip on the base of the floodlight and slide cover in place to make electrical contact.*

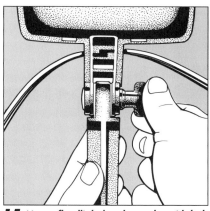

15 *Mount floodlight head to stake with bolt and wing nut. Bolt and nut allow for on-site adjustment of light.*

The electrical connection will resemble that of the walk lamps, but the cable will eventually be draped up one side of the stake and down the other when installed. If these cable loops are in a heavy traffic area, it's a good idea to tape them against each stake so they won't move over time.

Burying cable and setting heads
When it comes to burying the cable and setting the lamp stakes in place, you'll have several choices, and may wish to combine methods.

You might choose to slice through the sod and lay the cable into the trench. In this case, you dig a small hole for each

lamp stake. Then set the stake and replace the sod along the trench. In areas where frost heaving might push up the stake in winter, you can pack the stake hole with gravel, press the stake into the gravel and cover the gravel with sod.

If you use this method, keep in mind that newly laid sod requires a lot of special care. An easier and less destructive method is to slice into the sod with a flat-nose spade and pry the sod apart slightly. Then, use a paint stirring stick or dull putty knife to force the cable into the crevice so that it's well below sod level. To mount a stake in similar fashion, slice a cross in the sod with your spade, then press the stake into the intersection of the two lines of the cross. When the stakes and cable are installed, tamp shut the gap in the sod.

A deck lamp conversion
As mentioned before, special lamps are available to illuminate decks. These lamps are especially useful for illuminating stairs or in defining different deck levels with light. The kit installed here comes with instructions for a do-it-yourself conversion of a walk lamp into a deck-mounted lamp. The procedure is quite simple and is a reasonable alternative to buying a special deck kit.

To make this conversion, simply cut off a stake flush with its upper platform. Then, drill three small holes in the platform, attach the cable and screw the platform to the deck.

The cable can be brought up through a space between deck planks, or you can drill a hole through the deck and feed the cable up through it. The cable should be buried until it passes under the perimeter of the deck. Once under the deck, use a staple gun to staple it to the inner side of a support post and then to the underside of the deck timbers until you reach the lamp location.

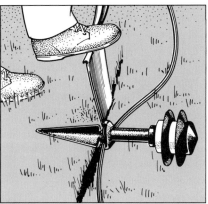
16 Lay cable, with lamps attached, along future path of lights. Slice through sod and pry seam open slightly.

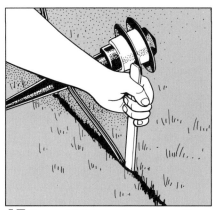
17 Force cable into spade opening with a paint stick or thin piece of scrap wood. Work gently to avoid damaging wire.

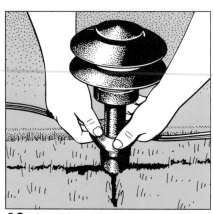
18 After making deep crosscut in sod, press stake into opening until its platform rests at ground level.

19 When laying cable along sidewalk or drive, pry the sod away from edge of asphalt or concrete.

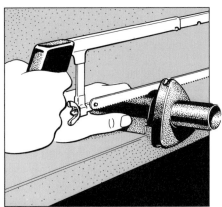
20 To convert a walk light into a deck light cut off stake flush with the bottom of the unit's platform.

21 Make the electrical connection and slide excess cable into fixture tube. Then screw platform to deck out of harm's way.

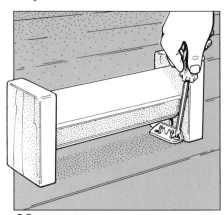
22 Dedicated deck lights also are available. To install, simply position where desired and attach brackets with screws.

How to repair
TELEPHONES

Degree of difficulty: Easy   Estimated time: 1½ hours   Average cost of materials: $8

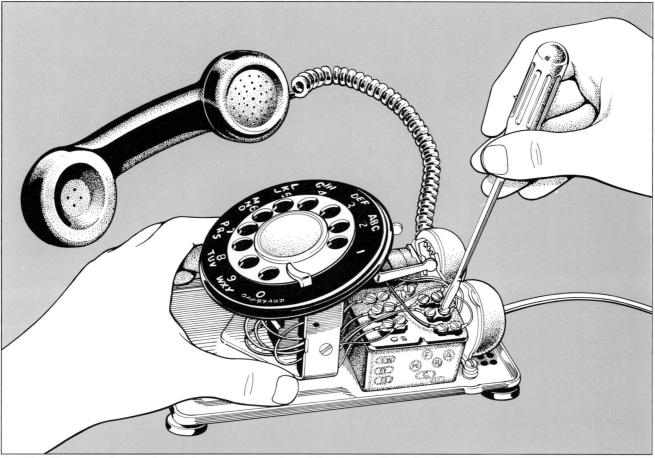

Considered by some to be more durable than newer electronic models, old rotary-dial and push-button telephones have stood the test of time—even in the face of planned obsolescence. And although their inside workings may look like a complicated tangle of wires and connections, malfunctions usually are easy to fix. Parts often can be transplanted from discarded phones.

In these days of planned obsolescence, it's nice to know that some things are built to last. Long before the introduction of the now-popular electronic telephone, the telephone company had installed millions of rotary-dial and push-button desktop phones. Both phones have an estimated life span of 25 years, but most have lasted years way beyond that and are still familiar fixtures in a lot of homes. However, the best thing about these old, reliable telephones is that you can often fix them yourself—something that's often more difficult to do with newer electronic phones.

The repairs for a rotary-dial or push-button phone are basically the same. Just don't be intimidated by the tangle of wires inside the phone. Besides, the wires are seldom the problem with a faulty phone.

Preliminary checks

Before you start to fix the phone, be sure that it's the phone that needs fixing. The problem could also be caused by the phone wiring inside the house walls, wiring outside of the house, or the equipment that's located at the telephone company's central office.

To check the problem phone, first unplug the phone from a modular jack or unscrew its wire connections from its connection box (phones are typically connected with four color-coded wires: red, green, black and yellow). Caution: Use an insulated screwdriver and take care not to touch any bare wire connections. The electrical voltage generated by a telephone when it rings is between 60 and 90 volts. Take the phone to a neighbor's house and plug it into or attach it to a wall jack. If the phone works properly, then the trouble is probably with the telephone wiring in your own house.

Next, borrow a phone that you know operates correctly and attach it to the wall jack at your house. Be sure that it's the same jack that the problem phone was connected to. Again, use an insulated screwdriver and take precautions against contacting any bare wire connections if

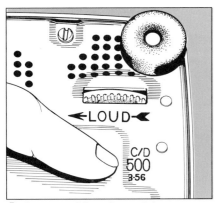

1 *Phone's model number and date it was manufactured are printed on its bottom plate. Note ringer's volume control knob.*

2 *The receiver is located behind the ear-piece cover. Be certain that the wires leading to receiver are fastened securely.*

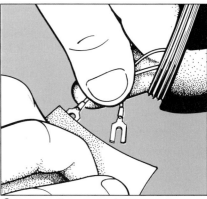

3 *Use very fine emery cloth or sandpaper to clean Y-shaped terminals of receiver. Clean back surface of the receiver, too.*

the phone does not have a modular jack. If the borrowed phone works okay, suspect a malfunction with your telephone. Also try connecting the phone to other jacks in the house to see if the fault is with the jack where the phone is installed.

Caution: Disconnect the phone's line cord from the wall jack before starting any repairs. If the cord is plugged in and the phone rings as you're working on it, you can receive a severe electric shock.

How's that?

One of the most common problems with older phones is reception quality. Voices may sound muffled or distant. First, unscrew the earpiece cover from the handset and lift out the receiver. The receiver is attached to the handset with two wires. Tighten the screws that hold the wires to the receiver (Fig. 2), taking care not to tighten the screws too much—wiring and connectors in older phones are sometimes brittle. Loose wires will cause bad reception, especially if the phone is moved while you're talking. If that doesn't help, then loosen the screws to free the two wires from the receiver.

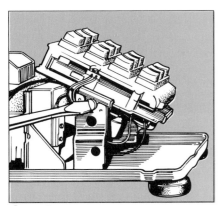

6 *In order to get contacts, you must remove the push-button panel, or rotary dial, by loosening the screws on each side.*

Use a piece of very fine emery cloth or sandpaper to clean the Y-shaped wire terminals (Fig. 3) and the contacts on the back of the receiver.

Reattach the wires to the receiver, place the receiver back in the handset and replace the earpiece cover. Now call someone and test the phone. If reception isn't improved, there are two more steps to take: servicing switch-hook contacts and replacing faulty parts.

Checking contacts

The switch-hook contact assembly consists of a series of make-and-break points. The contacts are located inside the phone and are protected by a removable transparent plastic dust-cover.

To expose the phone's guts, turn it upside down and loosen the two screws that hold the metal base to the plastic phone housing. The screws may be captive meaning that they can be loosened, but not removed and possibly lost. The switch-hook contacts are located behind the dial, in front of the switch-hook (Fig. 5). To work on the switch-hook contacts, remove the dial by loosening the screw on each side and pull it to one side (Fig. 6). Next, remove the clear plastic dust-cover that serves to

protect the inside switch-hook contacts.

Using a screwdriver, press the tab on top of the cover while squeezing its sides. Lift up to free the cover. Then, use an ear syringe or a can of compressed air to blow out dust and dirt from between the contacts (Fig. 7).

Press down on the switch-hook and release it slowly to open and close the contacts. If the contacts stick together, then further cleaning is necessary. Try using electrical contact cleaner that is available from an electronic parts supplier. Spray it onto the contacts as you did the compressed air. Then press down on the switch-hook and release it slowly to open and close the contacts a few times. Remember, though,

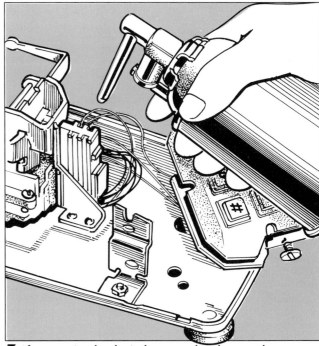

7 *After removing the plastic dustcover, clean between the contacts with a can of compressed air. Blow out all dirt and dust to prevent the contacts from sticking together.*

switch-hook contacts can be responsible for problems other than poor reception.

Replacement part remedies

Bad reception also can be caused by faulty cords. Modular cords—the kind you can unplug—are easy to test. Simply unplug the cords from the handset, phone and wall jack and connect them to another phone that is similarly equipped with modular connections. Also check for intermittent problems by wiggling the wires while you listen and talk.

If the phone's reception is clear, then the cords are okay. Buy a new receiver for the problem phone, reconnect the cords and test the phone.

Older phones have cords that are wired directly into the phone and handset. These cords are slightly more difficult to remove and you may want to install a new receiver right away. If this doesn't help, and you've already checked the switch-hook contacts, then the phone is probably beyond repair.

Telephone replacement parts are available at electronics parts suppliers and phone stores. You may also be able to transplant parts from other discarded phones. Look out for old phones that end up as inexpensive curiosities at garage and rummage sales—they're sometimes your best sources for parts.

When you go to a store, take the old part so that the salesperson can cross-check part numbers to ensure that you

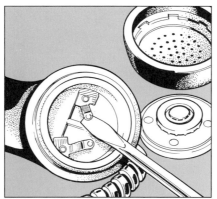

4 Unscrew mouthpiece and remove transmitter. Then, bend up the contacts slightly to ensure good contact with transmitter.

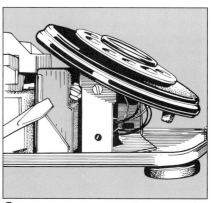

5 Here, we're pointing out the position of the switch-hook contacts. The contacts are protected under a plastic dustcover.

get the right match. In some larger outlets specializing in phone sales you may be able to run several tests using a phone diagnostics machine (you can attach your phone to the machine if your phone has modular connections).

Weak transmission

Do people have difficulty hearing you over the phone? Then the problem may be with the transmitting end of the handset. Unscrew the mouthpiece cover and remove the transmitter. Unlike the receiver, there are no wires attached to the handset transmitter.

Inside the handset are two metal contacts. Clean the contacts and the metal surface on the back of the transmitter with very fine emery cloth or some fine sandpaper. Then, bend up each contact slightly to ensure that they touch the transmitter (Fig. 4). Take care not to bend the contacts too much. Also check the contacts on the transmitter itself and clean them. Replace the transmitter and the mouthpiece and test the phone.

If the transmission quality isn't improved after taking these steps, then clean the switch-hook contacts, test the cords and, finally, replace the phone's transmitter.

More quick fix-its

In addition to transmission and reception problems, there are other troubles that can strike older telephones. The good news is that in most cases you can make the repairs yourself.

Here's a rundown of some of the most common problems with phones and some reliable remedies:

■ **Constant dial tone.** You pick up the handset, dial a number and get only a dial tone. Now what?

Disconnect the line cord from the wall jack and remove the phone's housing to expose its interior. Next, examine the network—the panel to which the tangle of interior wires are connected with either push-on/pull-off spade connectors or screw connections.

To test spade connectors, push down on each wire to make sure that they're attached securely to the network (Fig. 9). If the wires are fastened in place with screws, simply tighten each screw. Now test the phone.

If you still can't break the dial tone, switch the positions of the red and green

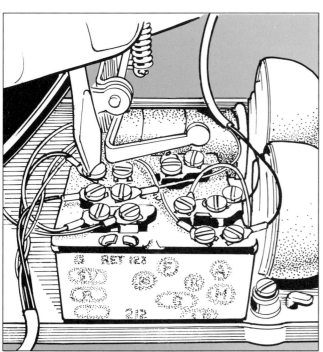

8 Rotary-dial phone uses screws to attach wires to the network. Tighten all screws to prevent trouble caused by loose wires. Also, clean away all dust and dirt that has accumulated.

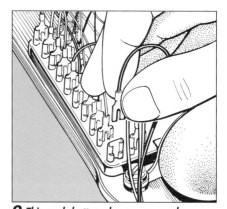

9 This push-button phone uses spade connectors to attach wires to the network. Push down on connectors to secure wires.

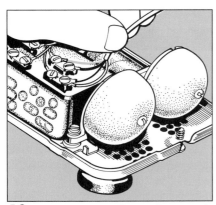

10 *Four wires connect line cord to network. Reverse positions of red and green wires to help break constant dial tone.*

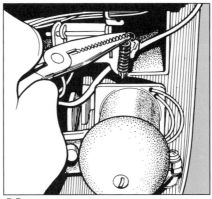

11 *Use needle-nose pliers to connect the switch-hook spring to the arms of the switch-hook. This will restore the dial tone.*

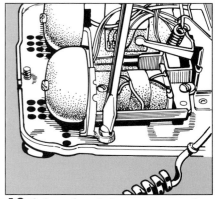

12 *If phone doesn't ring, you may need to replace the ringer assembly. Loosen screw on each side of ringer to remove assembly.*

wires on the network. This will reverse the polarity.

Be sure to switch the red and green wires of the line cord—the cord that connects to the wall jack. If this doesn't help, put the wires back in their original positions and clean the switch-hook contacts.

■ **Irregular dial tone.** This is another annoying problem that results in an on-again/off-again dial tone. Sometimes the phone works fine. Other times it's dead—no dial tone. This usually is caused by a defective line cord. Replace the line cord with a cord from a properly operating phone. If the substitute cord solves the problem, then buy a new line cord for your phone. Otherwise, service and clean the switch-hook contacts.

■ **No dial tone.** When the phone appears dead—no dial tone at all—check the line cord. Be sure that it's connected securely to the phone and wall jack. Then, substitute another cord.

If the line cord isn't at fault, then check the switch-hook spring. Be certain that the spring is connected to the upper and lower arms of the switch-hook (Fig. 11). Also, clean the switch-hook contacts.

If these repairs don't restore the dial tone, then the problem is probably a defective network. And, since a network can't be replaced, the telephone might have to be scrapped.

■ **No connection.** Let's say that you dial a number and the phone on the other end rings. But, when the party picks up, no connection is made and you hear a dial tone. As with so many other phone troubles, this one is caused by dirty switch-hook contacts.

However, if cleaning the contacts doesn't help, then check with the telephone company. A fouled circuit at their central office will prevent the connection from being completed.

■ **No incoming calls.** If your phone doesn't ring when someone calls, check the ringer.

First, make sure that the ringer isn't turned off. A ringer volume-control knob protrudes from the underside of the phone's base. Rotate the knob to full volume (counterclockwise) and have some-

one call you to see if it rings. If not, clean the switch-hook contacts. If the phone still doesn't ring, replace the whole ringer assembly with a new one.

The ringer assembly is fastened near the rear of the phone with two screws. Remove the screws and lift the ringer assembly from the phone (Figs. 12 and 13). The assembly consists of two bells, a coil, clapper and spring.

Note that the ringer has a part number stamped on it (Fig. 14). Use this number when buying a replacement ringer assembly from a store.

Install the new ringer, place the volume control on its loudest setting and have someone call you. Consider the phone beyond repair if a new ringer assembly doesn't help.

■ **Wrong numbers.** You should suspect a faulty rotary dial or push-button panel if you dial one number and are connected to another. First, loosen the screws on each side of the faulty dial or panel and lift it from the phone, but don't disconnect any wires yet. Lay the new, replacement dial or panel next to the faulty part.

Now disconnect one of the wires of the old dial or panel from the network and replace it with the same colored wire from the new part. Follow this procedure—disconnect an old wire, connect a new wire—until all the wires are attached. This is a foolproof way to avoid getting the wires mixed up.

If you come across two wires of the same color, you have a 50 percent chance of making the correct connection the first time. If the phone doesn't work, then reverse the positions of the same-colored wires or compare the destinations and origins of the wires when you begin.

After the wiring is completed, screw the dial or panel in place and test the phone. If it still doesn't work, it may be time for a new phone.

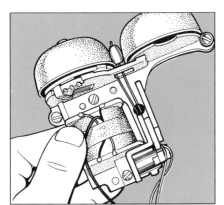

13 *Ringer assembly consists of two bells, a clapper, spring and coil. Mark wire positions before disconnecting the assembly.*

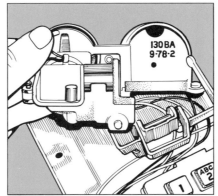

14 *Note that the model number is printed on the back of the ringer assembly. Use this number to buy the correct replacement.*

WALLS, FLOORS & STAIRS 3

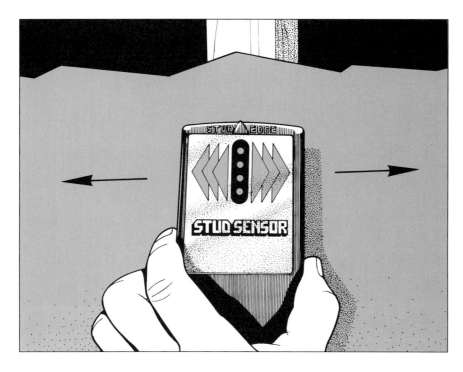

How to hang
WALLPAPER

Degree of difficulty: Medium **Estimated time:** 3 hours a room **Estimated cost of materials:** $100 a room

If you can survive scanning endless pages of wallpaper books and find a pattern that suits your decor, color scheme and budget, hanging the paper will come easy.

For your first job, choose a wallpaper that is easy to install, such as an inexpensive (less than $20 a roll) pretrimmed vinyl paper. Vinyl wallcoverings come paper-backed and fabric-backed, and both go up nicely. These papers don't stretch out of shape, even if you reposition them several times on the wall. Fabric-backed papers are more expensive and well-suited for bathrooms and kitchens, where humidity can be a problem. Fabric-backed vinyls can be scrubbed and easily stripped off the walls at a later date.

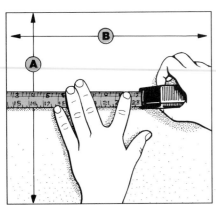

1 First, measure wall height, A. Now measure wall length, B. Multiply A x B and subtract door and window areas.

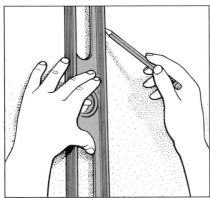

2 Use a level or chalk line to make a vertical layout line on the wall. Align the first strip of paper with this line.

With a little practice and some patience most people can become experts at wallpapering. Start off in a small room using inexpensive wallpaper before tackling bigger areas.

You can choose between prepasted wallpaper and those requiring adhesive. Prepasted paper only needs to be dunked or soaked in warm water to activate the paste impregnated in its back. Other wallcoverings are hung on the wall with an adhesive applied with a roller. If you use one of these papers, ask your wallpaper dealer for an appropriate adhesive.

Look for a paper with a pattern repeat or drop of 10 in. or less. Pattern drop or repeat refers to a pattern's length (a repeat or drop of 10 in. is a pattern that repeats itself every 10 in.). The larger the drop, the more paper is wasted getting the pattern to align between pieces.

You'll find the pattern repeat on the back of each pattern in your wallpaper sample books and on the roll's wrapping. By choosing a pattern with a small repeat for your first project, you can avoid excessive waste.

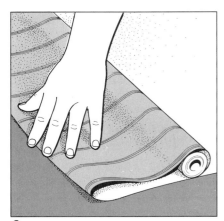

3 *Fold the roll back on the paper you just measured to the small scissor cut. Crease paper at cut and use as a cutting guide.*

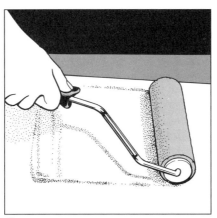

4 *Apply wallpaper paste using a paint roller or a wallpaper brush. Spread paste evenly over paper's back and edges.*

5 *To prevent paste from getting all over when you handle the strips, fold the paper back over itself (pasted sides together).*

Build success into your first attempt by choosing a simple bedroom. Don't try a bathroom, kitchen or two-story hallway the first time around.

Estimating paper

First, look in the back of the wallpaper book for a notice that tells you the area of each roll. Most rolls of American wallpaper contain about 36 sq. ft. of material. Allowing for waste due to the pattern drop and trimming, the roll covers about 30 sq. ft. A roll of European (metric) wallpaper contains about 28 sq. ft. and covers about 23 sq. ft. of wall (these are based on wallpaper with a drop under 18 in.).

To calculate how much paper you need, first find the wall area. Add the length of each wall, and multiply this total by the ceiling height (Fig. 1). Multiply the height of each door and window by its width. Add the door and window areas and subtract this from the wall area. This gives you the surface area to be papered. Add about 20 percent to the total papered area to allow for the few bad cuts and mistakes you'll most likely make (inevitable on your first job).

Divide this number by the area that your wallpaper roll covers, and that's the number of rolls you need.

Make sure the paper is from the same lot or batch. The batch number is stamped on each roll, and all the rolls should have the same number. If you have to order extra paper later, you might get a roll from a different batch run. The color or repeat pattern might not match exactly, even if you order the same pattern from the same store.

Clean the walls thoroughly and repair holes, cracks or dents. Wash or paint the room's woodwork and trim. Unless the woodwork is natural or its paint is in good shape, it may look dingy next to the new paper. It's easier to paint it now than after the paper is in place.

Turn off the electricity to the room, and remove the light switch and outlet covers. You could hit an outlet or switch wire with your razor knife while trimming the paper and get a shock, so leave the power off while papering. For added safety, post a note at the service panel advising others in the house that the circuit you turned off is meant to be that

way. Light the room with a lamp attached to an extension cord plugged into an outlet outside the room and work during the day to take advantage of natural light.

Next, size the walls. Sizing makes it easier to slide the paper around without tearing while you align the pattern. Because it seals the wall, sizing makes paper easier to remove at a later date.

Premixed sizing is easier to use, but more expensive than the type you mix. Either is simple to apply. Use a paint roller and pan to spread the somewhat watery solution. When it's dry, the wall is ready for papering.

When hanging a wallpaper with a light-colored background on a dark wall, you may be able to see the wall where there's minute misalignment between seams. Prime dark walls with a coat of inexpensive white latex primer or use a combination primer/sizing.

Layout: Getting started

Begin your paper layout by establishing vertical guidelines to help you position the paper. Even with guidelines there's sure to be some misalignment between

6 *Align first strip with vertical layout line. Smooth strip with wallpaper brush, working out from its center to the edges.*

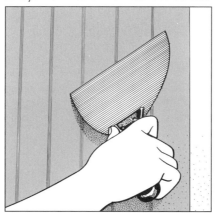

7 *If you work carefully, you can smooth paper with a broad knife. Pull knife gently across paper to avoid tearing it.*

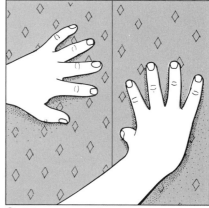

8 *Slide next piece of paper into position while adhesive is still moist. Smooth paper after pattern is aligned.*

9 *When working with small patterns, check alignment between strips using a level. This assures pattern stays even.*

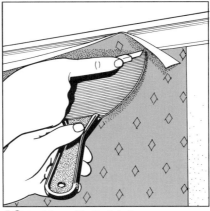

10 *Push broad knife tight into corner at ceiling (or molding). Run razor knife along broad knife to cleanly sever scrap.*

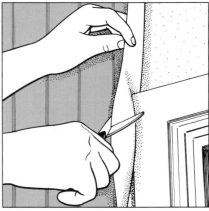

11 *Make diagonal relief cut from corner of window or door trim to paper's edge. This lets you work around projection.*

the first and last strip of paper you hang. To conceal this, lay out your job so you start and finish in an inconspicuous spot, such as over a door, a window or on the least conspicuous wall.

Hold up a roll of wallpaper where you want to begin the job. Make a pencil mark equal to the paper's width minus ½ in. Use a carpenter's level or a chalk line to make a vertical plumb line through this mark (Fig. 2).

Align the edge of your first strip to be parallel and about ½ in. inside this layout line. This prevents the line from showing through the seam, but ensures that the paper's edge is close enough for accurate alignment.

Don't cut the first strip by measuring it. Take the roll over to the wall and unroll enough paper to reach from the floor to the ceiling. Hold the paper in place at the ceiling and move it up or down so you have a complete pattern at the top (if your paper's pattern requires alignment).

Make a light pencil mark on the paper at the ceiling. Remove the paper, and place it on a flat surface. Trim the paper 2 in. above the mark you made at the ceil-

ing. Then, measure down from the ceiling and mark the height of the wall. Add 2 in. to this measurement for trim at the bottom. Make a small cut with a pair of scissors, fold across the paper at the cut, then use the fold as a guideline to cut the strip (Fig. 3). Test fit this strip.

To cut the second strip, unroll the paper and lay it next to the first strip. Move up the paper until the pattern matches (the wasted paper should always be located at the top of the roll). Cut the paper so it's 2 in. longer at the bottom, leaving some paper to trim at both ceiling and baseboard. Avoid cutting a large batch of strips until you've tested a few pieces of paper to see how the pattern is lining up.

Hanging paper

If you're using a prepasted wallcovering, use an inexpensive plastic container called a water box or trough. Fill this about half-full with warm water and place it on a plastic garbage bag covered by old towels to blot up spilled water. (A bathtub filled with water also works well for this job.) Let the strips of paper soak for the

amount of time specified by the manufacturer (usually less than a minute). Keep the paper rolled loosely from bottom to top and rotate.

Follow the manufacturer's advice for wallpaper that requires adhesive. A vinyl paste is usually a good choice because it resists mildew. If you have had a mildew problem in the room, buy a mildewcide additive and mix it in the paste.

Smooth the paste onto the paper's back with a paint roller or wallpaper brush (Fig. 4). Spread the paste evenly, including the edges. To keep the paste from getting over everything, fold the pasted side of the paper back on itself (Fig. 5). This also prevents the adhesive from drying out. Work ahead and paste up a couple of strips so one strip can soak while you work with the other.

Wait at least 5 minutes after brushing adhesive onto a strip of wallpaper for it to set, or "wet out" as it's called, before you hang it. Wallpaper expands when wet and contracts as it dries, so this wetting out lets it reach its maximum expansion and prevents bubbles from forming behind the paper once it's hung.

12 *Guide cut around window or door trim using broad knife. Trim away scrap before hanging next strip of paper.*

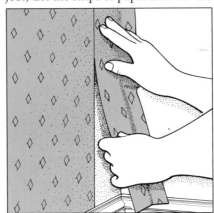

13 *Hang strip on an inside corner with about 2 in. of scrap on adjacent wall. Smooth paper toward corner and to seam.*

14 *Trim paper flush working with broad knife and razor. This leaves a small bit of paper overlapping in the corner.*

15 Start next paper strip with an overlap. Match the pattern and plumb the strip. Cut through top strip to remove overlap.

16 Overlap around outside corner should be under 1 in. Next strip should cover overlap. Then, trim strip flush to corner.

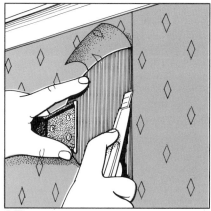

17 To make a double-cut joint, align the pattern with the strips overlapping. Press hard enough to cut both strips.

18 The overlap falls away, but you must peel back the top strip and remove the cut-off section. Then, roll the joint tight.

Have your ladder in place and your tools at hand before bringing the folded and pasted strip to your starting point. Unfold the top section and position the strip so it lines up with the plumb line. Don't forget that you allowed for an extra 2 in. at the top of the piece. Hold the top in place and unfold the pasted bottom section so it drops to the floor. Work your way down the strip checking alignment with the plumb line.

Press the strip firmly against the wall. Work out from the center of the strip using a brush or sponge to push air bubbles or wrinkles to the edges (Fig. 6). If you are very careful, you can use a broad knife (a 6-in.-wide scraper, also called a flat knife) to do this also (Fig. 7). Wipe off excess glue that oozes out of the edge of the strip. If you can't seem to push all the air bubbles out from behind the wallpaper don't worry, as the paper dries it will contract and the bubbles will often disappear by themselves. Hang the next strip and align the pattern by eye or with a level (Figs. 8 and 9). Use a seam roller to press the edge in place, and then again after each strip is hung to prevent the seams from opening.

Trim the paper at the top and bottom after you've hung several strips. This is best done using a broad knife and a razor knife. Press the knife into the corner where the wall meets the ceiling, and draw the razor along it (Fig. 10). Move the knife over as the razor reaches its end, then repeat the cut. Trim the paper at the floor the same way.

You have to negotiate around doors, windows, cabinets and other projections. To get the paper to lie flat next to these protrusions, use a pair of small, pointed scissors or a razor to make relief cuts. We'll use a window frame as an example. Carefully align the strip so it's plumb and its pattern matches the piece next to it. Smooth out the paper as much as pos-

sible. Make a 45° relief cut starting at the corner of the window trim, extending into the waste paper (Fig. 11). Then, finish smoothing the paper, and work out remaining wrinkles and air bubbles. Trim the paper flush against the edge of the opening the same way you trimmed up against the ceiling (Fig. 12).

Hanging outside/ inside corners
There's a great temptation to wrap a strip of wallcovering around an inside or outside corner, then continue on by butting the next piece of paper to it. This often results in a sloppy looking wallpaper job. Corners are very seldom square, and wrapping the paper around the corner will cause the pattern to run out of plumb. For best results, use a lap joint or double cut the seams.

To make a lap joint in an inside corner, trim the last strip so it's up to the corner and overlaps the adjoining wall by a couple of inches (Fig. 13). Push the broad knife into the corner and cut off the paper that overlaps onto the adjoining wall (Fig. 14). This leaves about ¼ in., or less, paper overlapping.

Make a plumb line on the new wall to align the first adjoining strip. This first strip on the new wall should wrap around the corner and overlap about an inch or so onto the wall that was just papered. Carefully match the patterns of the overlapping paper in the corner and double-check the new strip for plumb.

Trim the new strip flush in the corner. Use a light touch and a sharp blade in the razor knife to cut through the top strip only (Fig. 15). This overlaps about ¼ in., covering any gap between the new strip and the wall.

Next, add more adhesive to the joint by peeling the strip you just trimmed back and applying the adhesive with an artist's brush. Then smooth out the joint and sponge away excess adhesive.

Wrap the paper around an outside corner and trim it back so ½ in. of paper rounds the corner (Fig. 16). Mark a plumb layout line on the unpapered adjacent wall. Align the first strip with the layout line and trim it flush with the corner.

The inside and outside corner joints described here overlap. Some heavy papers will show a lump at the joint, and other vinyl papers do not stick well to one another. In these cases and anywhere you want a joint that butts perfectly, you can use the double-cut method.

Overlap the strips where you want the joint to be, then cut through both strips with a sharp razor guided by your broad knife. The trimmed piece will fall away from the top strip, but you have to peel back the top strip to remove the trimmed piece from under it (Figs. 17 and 18). Smooth the top strip back into place.

While the paste is still soft, sponge away excess paste from the wallpaper's face and woodwork. Go back several times with a clean sponge to be sure you get it all.

For an added touch, try border trim, applied using some of the same wallpapering techniques.

How to remove WALLPAPER

Degree of difficulty: Medium   **Estimated time:** 6 hours a room   **Average cost of materials:** $80 a room

Removing wallpaper is a messy job, but somebody's got to do it and that somebody will probably be you. Finding someone to do it is almost more difficult than doing it yourself. Professional paperhangers often don't want to have anything do with it. And when they do, they charge you a premium rate.

Fortunately, this job is more messy than it is difficult. It's a good example of the kind of grunt work home owners can do themselves. The job requires little skill and few tools, just scraping and patience. With the advent of improved wallpaper removing tools, teamed with time-proven methods, the job is easier than ever.

Different papers, different problems
Not all wallcoverings are created equal, meaning that some are more difficult to strip than others. The easiest to remove are the "strippable" wallpapers. They can be removed without tearing and without being loosened by water or steam.

Slightly more difficult to remove are old, untreated and uncoated wallpapers. They simply need to be wetted and scraped loose.

The most difficult to remove are the papers with vinyl coatings (washable wallpapers) or those with laminated surfaces of woven fabric or foils. Wallpaper that's been painted falls in this category. These papers are difficult to strip because water doesn't penetrate their surface as readily as with uncoated paper.

Stripping on drywall/plaster
Painted plaster is the easiest surface from which to strip wallpaper. Unpainted drywall is the most difficult.

Before you start, check to see what type of wall you have. Your stripping method depends on the type of paper and what's beneath it.

Most newer houses have drywall, and most houses over 50 years old have plaster. Plaster is rock-hard and appears smooth. Drywall is softer than plaster and is easily punctured. Its paper facing has a slight "tooth" that becomes more apparent after you've gained some experience distinguishing drywall from plaster.

You might see rows of small bumps or dents where wall compound covers the nails holding drywall to the framing.

The flip side of hanging wallpaper is removing it—a task that most professionals shy away from because it is messy and time-consuming. Fortunately, steamers can make the job easier.

Another telltale sign of drywall is a long but shallow lump where the compound covers the tape that hides the seam between sheets. But be careful here, because the tape may conceal a crack in a plastered surface, not a drywall seam.

If after looking for these signs you still can't tell which wall material you have, take a look at the material you find behind the faceplate for a light switch or outlet (you have to remove these faceplates to strip the wallpaper anyway).

Drywall is thin and a uniform thickness, usually ½ to ⅝ in., and is attached directly to the studs. Plaster varies in thickness and is applied over wood, gypsum or metal lath that's attached to the studs. The electrical box will fit through a hole cut into the drywall. Since plaster is applied to a wall and not installed as a

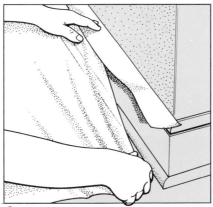

1 *Begin the job by turning off the electricity to the room and removing the telephone, electric outlet and switch plates.*

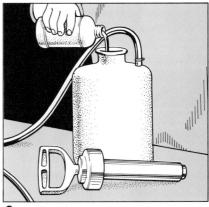

2 *Tape the drop cloth to the baseboard molding and unfold it into the room. Use masking tape at least 1½ in. wide.*

3 *Use a garden sprayer to soak uncoated wallpaper. Fill sprayer with a solution of wallpaper remover and warm water.*

sheet, you'll find it has been troweled right up to the box.

It's important to check what wall material you're working on in the part of the house where you'll be stripping. In an older house, the wall material may vary. If you're stripping wallpaper from a relatively recent addition to an older house, chances are the addition has drywall, while the rest of the house has plaster. Also, the plaster may have been entirely removed in rooms that have been extensively remodeled.

Paint seals plaster and drywall, and makes removing wallpaper easier. Removing wallpaper from unpainted or unsized (sizing is a solution applied before papering that further seals the wall surface) drywall is hard, because the glue used to attach the paper penetrates the drywall's face and forms a strong bond. You have to use water to soften the glue that holds the wallpaper, but this also softens the drywall paper facing. Be careful not to tear the paper face or taped joints of the drywall as you remove the wallcovering. If this happens, you'll have to

completely resurface the wall using spackling compound when you're through.

Preparing the area

First, prepare the room. Remove phones, pictures, lightweight furnishings, and move the heavier furniture and area rugs to the room's center. Cover remaining objects and the floor with drop cloths. Although old bed sheets will do in a pinch, wet globs of wallpaper could soak right through them and damage the floor or furnishing beneath. Water-resistant plastic or canvas drop cloths are better and prove to be a good investment for future projects. Plastic sheeting and combination paper/plastic drop cloths are another alternative. Although somewhat slippery to work on, these coverings can be disposed of at the end of the project. Next, turn off the electricity and then remove any remaining faceplates (Fig. 1).

To stop soggy wallpaper from hitting the floor, tape the drop cloth to the baseboard with heavy-duty masking tape at least 1½ in. wide (Fig. 2). Tape the drop cloth's edge to the baseboard and unfold

it into the room to cover exposed surfaces that might be damaged.

Stripping without steam

Old-fashioned wallpaper comes off easily if you get enough moisture behind it. It's held up with wheat paste adhesive, a substance easily softened by water. These porous papers absorb water, hastening the decomposition of the paste.

Stripping the paper is even easier if you mix some wallpaper remover in the water. The remover, sold at paint and hardware stores, has wetting agents that penetrate the paper and soften the paste. Some strippers also have enzymes that attack the wheat paste and dissolve it. Mix the remover in a pail or directly in a garden sprayer (Fig. 3). The sprayer should be clean and free of pesticide residue. Start applying the remover at the wall's top and work down. Work on 6-ft.-wide areas, soaking the area with the wallpaper remover solution (Fig. 4).

Another effective way of applying the remover is with a sponge mop or a paint roller (Fig. 5). A hand sprayer is effective

4 *Spray remover from the top of the wall down. Soak the paper during a 15- to 20-minute period, then soak a second area.*

5 *A floor mop can spread wallpaper remover. Soak the paper, but avoid letting the solution run onto the floor.*

6 *Apply the remover with a hand sprayer on hard-to-reach areas, such as a strip of paper between cabinet and window trim.*

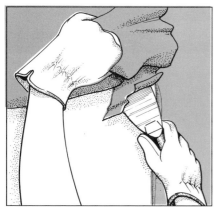

7 *The soaked paper should strip off the wall easily. If it doesn't, resoak. Use a wide, dull scraper to remove large pieces.*

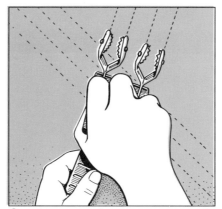

8 *Perforate painted or water-resistant wallpaper to prepare it for steaming. Holes allow the steam to penetrate the paper.*

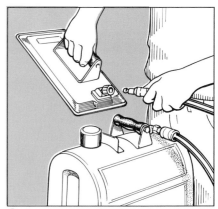

9 *Plug a steamer's hose into the tank and into the steam plate before letting it heat up. Parts are too hot to do this afterward.*

for spraying hard-to-reach areas (Fig. 6), such as the thin strip of wallpaper between a window casing and a kitchen cabinet.

The paper will darken as it absorbs water. Apply only as much solution as the paper can absorb. Excess solution just runs down the wall and onto the floor. Let the solution soak in, then resoak it.

Let the solution do the work. You'll have to rewet the paper several times during an hour period. A lot of water is needed to saturate it and adequately soften the glue. Prepare another section while the first is soaking.

Test that the wall is ready to strip. If you can easily run a scraper from the baseboard molding to the ceiling, the wall is ready (Fig. 7). Let the paper fall on the drop cloth. For plaster walls, use a broad knife scraper or wallpaper razor scraper. On drywall, use a putty knife with a dull edge to avoid gouging its paper face.

Preparing for steam stripping
Vinyl, foil-faced and other moisture-resistant wallpapers are designed to be cleaned. The challenge, then, is to get moisture behind their water-resistant face to soften the glue. Wallpaper remover is not as effective on coated papers as uncoated. The solution is to steam the paper loose, then scrape it off the wall.

You have to prepare these papers before steaming. The easiest way to get steam or water behind a coated wallcovering is to score the surface to allow moisture to penetrate. A good tool for this is a wheeled wallpaper scoring tool. This gadget (about $10 at paint stores) has small wheels with sharp spurs on them that make holes in the wallcovering ●Fig. 8). Its cutting depth is adjustable, so, with care, you can use it on drywall.

Painted wallpaper may be difficult to score. With several coats of paint, it can take on an almost canvaslike quality. Begin at the top of the wall, concentrating

on an area that you can reach comfortably, and work down. Score the paper thoroughly, crisscrossing the surface. Time and effort invested at this stage results in a cleaner strip because the steam better penetrates the paper. If the paper is old and there are several painted layers, most of the layers can be scraped off with a razor scraper. This is harder work than steaming off the individual layers, but it's much faster than trying to steam down through the individual layers.

Steam stripping
For about $20 a day, you can rent a wallpaper steamer. This tool has a small electric boiler tank that holds about 1½ gallons of water. It plugs into a standard 15-amp household outlet, but draws a lot of current, so use a heavy-duty extension cord rated to carry that amperage. The boiler connects to a perforated steam plate with a hose. When the tool starts producing steam, press its plate against the wall to loosen the paper.

First, snap the steamer's hose onto the tank and to the steam plate while the parts

are cool and easy to handle (Fig. 9). Remove the heavy steel stopper covering the tank's fill hole and insert a funnel. These tanks are hard to fill without a funnel because the fill hole isn't very large. Fill the tank with tap water (don't use wallpaper remover). Let the steamer heat up for about 10 minutes. Fill the tank again when it's half empty, so you won't have a long wait for the water to boil.

Wear heavy work gloves, old clothing and especially an old pair of shoes or work boots. Stepping around all day in piles of soggy wallpaper will quickly ruin a pair of sneakers. Most importantly, avoid touching the hot hose or steam plate. You can't turn off the steam without shutting down the boiler, so rest the steam plate on a heavy towel when changing areas or taking a break.

Hold the steam plate at the top of a wall and follow a wallpaper seam (Fig. 10). When the seam is loose, work onto the perforated area. Gently pull a corner of paper toward you when it starts to come loose. Move the steamer ahead as you pull the paper off the wall. If the paper does

13 *Let a portable steamer heat up, and use it as you would a rented steamer. It weighs about the same as steam plate and hose.*

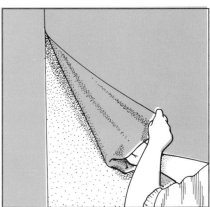

14 *Pry up one corner of the strippable wallpaper using a putty knife or scraper. Slowly peel the paper off the wall.*

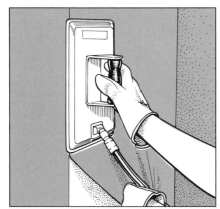

10 *Start steaming the wallpaper along a seam. Hold the steam plate on the wall for 10 to 20 seconds or until the glue softens.*

11 *Hold steam plate over perforated areas. Use a razor scraper or flat knife to scrape softened paper off the wall.*

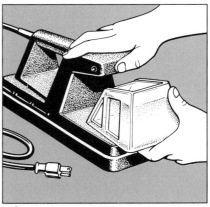

12 *You may consider buying a portable steamer instead of renting. Tool combines water tank and steam plate.*

not readily come off, steam the area more thoroughly. Allow the steam time to penetrate. If you rush the process, you'll have to scrape off a lot of small pieces.

Even when you are patient, however, the wallcovering may separate from its backing. Give the remaining paper a second shot of steam and pull it or scrape it off with the razor scraper or knife (Fig. 11).

The procedure is basically the same for painted wallpaper. Work a small area to allow the steam longer to penetrate. If you uncover another wallpaper layer, just attack it the same way as you did the previous one.

If, as you progress, the steamer seems to be working less efficiently than it should, check that the tank isn't low on water or that the steam plate hasn't been clogged with bits of paper. Then lightly scrape off any paper stuck to the steam plate using a broad knife.

If you are removing the paper from several rooms or you need the steamer for a couple of days, consider buying a portable, hand-held model (Fig. 12). It costs about $50 at hardware stores and home centers.

It's used the same as the rented steamer, but it is less cumbersome, even though it weighs about the same.

Plug it into a 3-prong outlet or extension cord, fill its tank with water, and a minute later, it's ready to use. Its steam plate area is smaller than the rented steamer, but there's no hot hose to worry about (Fig. 13). For added safety against electric shock, make sure the circuit is protected by a ground-fault circuit interrupter and attach the steamer to a heavy-duty extension cord.

Removing wallpaper from a ceiling
This is the worst stripping task because of the additional challenge of working overhead. Set up a pair of stepladders, spanned by a short section of scaffold or painter's adjustable plank (either may be available at your tool rental center). Working on the planking or scaffolding will save you countless trips up and down a ladder.

Observe several precautions when stripping the ceiling. First, wear goggles to keep pieces of wet paper, condensing

steam and drops of wallpaper remover out of your eyes. Also, watch your step—it's easy to step off your scaffold when looking overhead. Keep the scaffolding clear of slippery bits of paper and work with it aligned in the direction you are stripping. You can insert a pole into the wallpaper scoring tool so you can puncture the paper from floor level or the scaffold.

Strippable wallcoverings
Strippable wallpapers simply peel off the wall when gently pulled from a corner (Fig. 14). At a seam, lift the corner of the wallpaper with a putty knife or scraper and pull toward you. Carefully remove the adhesive left on the wall with a fresh blade in a razor scraper. Since the paste is dry and hard, most of the heavy residue can be scraped off. Then wash the walls with warm water and detergent.

Cleanup
Once the paper is off the walls, most of your work is done. After each wall is stripped but is still moist, wash off remaining paste and paper bits. Use a large sponge soaked in a warm solution of TSP (trisodium phosphate) and water (Fig. 15). If phosphate-based detergents are banned in your area, use a powerful household cleaner instead.

Remove the masking tape and drop cloth from the baseboard, and then pick up the four corners of the drop cloth to keep the water from running out (Fig. 16). If the drop cloth is disposable, simply tie or tape the cloth around the debris as if it were a giant garbage bag and throw it out. Otherwise, scrape the debris into a trash bag and rinse off the drop cloth.

The walls are now ready to be painted or covered with wallpaper again. Patch any defects with spackling compound, sand repairs smooth and coat the walls with primer—or sizing, if you are going to hang wallpaper.

15 *Wash glue residue and bits of paper off the wall using a solution of TSP and warm water, or use a household detergent.*

16 *To complete the job, fold up debris in disposable drop cloth and throw it out. Let the walls dry before painting them.*

How to paint
WOODWORK AND WALLS

Degree of difficulty: Medium   **Estimated time:** 6 hours a room   **Average cost of materials:** $50 a room

Window sills, door trim, crown moldings and baseboards require a durable, protective finish. A good, long-lasting paint job on woodwork and trim involves careful brush work and that takes a little practice. It's worth the effort, though, to learn how to prepare and paint woodwork correctly because it really brightens a room. Done properly, a good paint job lasts for many years and withstands repeated cleanings.

In any painting project, first prepare the surface by cleaning and patching it, then paint it. If you're painting the walls and woodwork, begin by patching the walls and the trim so all surfaces are smooth. Paint the trim first, then paint the walls. It's easier to wipe a little wall paint off woodwork than to get trim paint off a wall.

Wash the woodwork with a solution of water and a scouring detergent or trisodium phosphate (TSP). If phosphate cleaners are banned in your area, use a good household cleaner. Rinse the woodwork and let it dry.

Choosing paint

Latex or vinyl (water-based) paints are the predominant choice for the home painter and are best for walls. However, latex semigloss and enamel (glossy) are not as abrasion resistant as oil-based paints (especially important on window sashes, handrails and sills) and can't be cleaned as many times as oil-based paints. Latex trim paints dry quickly, and this makes it difficult to avoid lap marks— even for experienced painters. These paints dry to a softer and more flexible film than oil-based paints. Objects placed on latex paint can stick in place if left for a long time, even after drying.

On the plus side, latex paint is easy to clean up. Spills wipe up with water, and brushes can be quickly washed in the sink. And because it doesn't contain petroleum-distilled solvents, latex paint is often considered less of a threat to the environment.

Oil-based paint provides a tough, durable finish that's ideal for woodwork. It dries slowly to a hard surface. This paint comes in four levels of gloss: flat, eggshell, semigloss and gloss. You clean up oil-based paint with paint thinner (also

Painting is among the most popular do-it-yourself projects. The investment in time and equipment is minimal compared to the dramatic change created by a fresh coat of paint. Adequate preparation and the right tools are important for achieving professional-looking results.

known as mineral spirits) which is available in different quantities.

How much paint for trim?

Most trim paints cover between 350 and 400 sq. ft. of surface per gallon. Painters allow about 8 sq. ft. of paintable area for each window and about 25 sq. ft. of area for each door. Extra paint will be need-

ed for the window's trim or casing, as well as its jamb.

To determine the surface area of base and ceiling molding, estimate it at 6 in. wide (regardless of actual width) and multiply this times its length in inches. Divide this number by 144 to arrive at the square-foot surface area. The average room does not typically require a lot of

1 *To allow paint to drain back into the can, punch a few holes in the lid groove with a 4d finishing nail. Keep groove clean.*

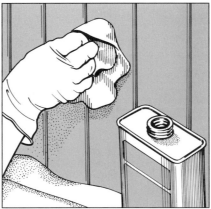

2 *Degloss shiny surfaces with chemical deglosser (paint adheres best to a dull surface). Solvent also degreases and cleans.*

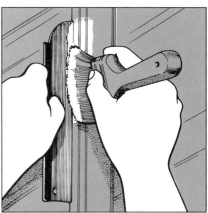

3 *Fill any cracks or screw holes in the woodwork with spackling compound. Use wood filler for deep holes and cracks.*

trim paint. A quart will usually do it. If you need 3 quarts, buy a gallon.

Brushes, buckets, rollers and trays
The material your brush is made from should be determined by your choice of paint. A brush with polyester or nylon bristles is suitable for latex or oil paint. If you're going to buy only one brush, make it polyester.

Brushes made from hog bristle (sometimes called China bristle) are best with oil paints and get limp when used with latex paint. Good quality bristle brushes are expensive. Don't buy inexpensive bristle brushes, though. They lose their bristles.

For a quick touch-up, use a small, inexpensive foam brush. Avoid the wide foam brushes because they tend to drip when loaded with paint.

Consider brush shape when you're buying your supplies. A sash brush with its bristles cut at an angle is designed for painting thin areas and getting into hard-to-reach corners. It's your best choice for cutting in (painting up to a line) and

painting windows. A square-cut brush is best for painting door panels or wide trim. Brushes with a long, pencil-style handle give you a good grip and provide balance.

You should own at least three brushes: a 1-in. and 2½-in. sash brush and a 2½-in. straight brush. Buy the best brushes you can afford. Properly cared for, they will last indefinitely.

You can use a paint roller to work wide sections, such as flat doors. Use a roller with a nap length recommended on the paint can.

Open paint cans by prying around the lid with a wide-tip screwdriver. Pour the paint into a paint pail or a clean paint can and stir it to make sure it's evenly mixed. You can pour some of the paint back into the paint can and work out of that, or work out of the pail. If you use the can, don't fill it back up right to the rim. It's a messy and inefficient way to work with paint. Also, puncture the lid of the can in several places using a 4d finishing nail to help drain paint back into the can after it drips from the brush (Fig. 1).

Prepare the woodwork
Paint sticks better to a dull surface. One way to remove its gloss is with a chemical solvent deglosser (Fig. 2). Rub on the deglosser with a clean rag. This is strong stuff, so allow plenty of ventilation.

You can also use 120-grit sandpaper with a sanding block or an electric palm sander to dull a surface or smooth out chipped areas. Feather any rough areas until smooth.

Remove several layers of deteriorating paint with a heat gun or chemical stripper. Your paint store should have a variety of chemical strippers on stock, among them low-odor and water-soluble types. Stripping is a messy job, so protect the floor and surroundings by putting down a drop cloth. Wear old clothes and protective glasses.

Let the gun heat up and hold it about a foot from the paint. When the finish bubbles up, scrape it away using a paint scraper. Move the gun slowly forward, and you can keep the paint hot without burning it. Keep a fire extinguisher handy

4 *Wrap sandpaper around a sponge to sand a curved area, like window or door trim. Sponge takes on molding profile.*

5 *Rub sealant on glass before painting. Afterward, scrape the window clean with a retractable razor scraper.*

6 *You can also keep glass free of paint with a trim guard. On bare wood windows allow some paint to seal against glass.*

7 *Begin painting a window from the inside out. Paint the sides of the muntins, then paint the front surfaces.*

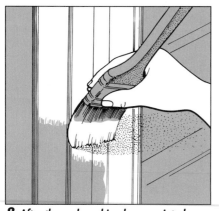

8 *After the sash and jamb are painted, paint over the window trim. Begin next to the jamb, then do the outside edge.*

when using a heat gun, and don't set the gun down on a flammable surface.

Apply chemical strippers with an old paintbrush. When bubbles appear, use a scraper and steel wool to remove it. Clean off the residue on the scraper using the sides of a sturdy cardboard box. A second application is often required. Let the surface dry, then sand it lightly.

Fill holes and cracks

Most trim has some cracks and holes in it that should be filled with spackle or wood filler before applying paint. Spackle and premixed or 2-part fillers are applied with a small putty knife (Fig. 3). Just overfill the hole or crack, smooth the filler and let it dry. Sand the filler flush, and it's ready for paint (Fig. 4). You might have to use two coats on large repairs since some fillers shrink.

Protecting window glass

When you're painting windows you can use masking tape or a wipe-on protective film that's dispensed much like deodorant (Fig. 5). Another option is to skip this step and scrape off any paint from the glass with a razor. It's a case of spending your time masking or scraping, but if you paint carefully, you will spend less time with the laborious task of scraping.

Apply the tape or film only after thoroughly dusting the corners of each window pane. The crevice tool of a vacuum cleaner works well.

If you paint the windows without tape or film, you can use a trim guard to protect the glass area. These come either as a small, triangular-shaped piece of metal or a metal strip with a plastic handle. Tightly hold the guard against the muntins while you paint them (Fig. 6). After each use, check for paint on the back side of the guard and wipe it away.

Hardware and what to do about it

Should you remove hardware or should you paint over it? A purist will remove hardware. And of course, that's the right answer. But for practical purposes, it's not always the most realistic one.

If a window lock is covered by several layers of paint but works properly, decide how much time you want to spend on the window. You will crack the existing paint if you remove the lock, and this also leaves

a dent in the paint the shape of the lock. Unless you replace it with the same type, you will have to sand away the paint buildup in this area. If the hardware is not painted, it may be easier to remove it rather than paint around it.

Painting windows

Paint windows from the inside out. Begin painting the thin vertical and horizontal dividers between the panes in double-hung windows (Fig. 7). The same holds for painting casement windows.

If your window has a removable window grille, take it out for a much easier job. Use a 1½-in.-wide sash paintbrush, and don't drag your brush back across the edge because this will cause a run in the paint.

If you are painting a double-hung window and the upper sash is movable, reverse the position of the inner or lower sash and the outer or upper sash. Paint the lower half of the outer sash first, then paint the inside sash, but don't do the top edge where the lock is. Save that until last.

Return the sashes to their normal positions, but don't close the window completely. Then paint the top of the outer sash and the top edge of the inner sash.

Switch to a 2½-in.-wide brush and paint the window frame from the inside out, moving the sash cord, if there is one, out of the way. Next, paint the window casing (Figs. 8 and 9). Cut in a nice, clean line where the casing meets the wall. Then paint the sill and the apron, which is the trim beneath the sill. When the paint is dry, scrape it off the glass with a razor scraper (Fig. 10).

Of course, if the upper sash is painted shut, you won't be able to move it. In this case, paint the upper sash from the inside out and then open the lower sash and paint it. Leave it slightly open to ensure the paint will not get dirty at the bottom of the sash.

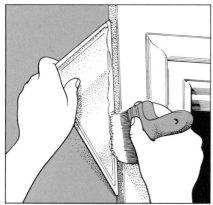

9 *Use a trim guard to protect the walls when painting woodwork. Hold the guard tight in the corner between trim and wall.*

10 *Run a razor scraper down the joint between the glass and frame, then scrape away the paint working toward the sash.*

11 *Start painting a paneled door by outlining the molding around each panel. Use a 2½-in.-wide square-tip brush.*

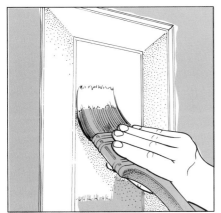

12 *Next, work from the top down and paint the panel's face. Work the paint into outlined area to prevent lap marks.*

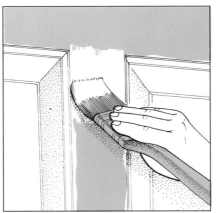

13 *Paint the stiles between the panels. For a smooth finish, feather out the paint at the intersection of stiles and rails.*

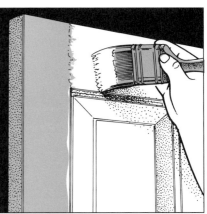

14 *Paint the top and bottom rails and then the outside stiles. Paint the long surfaces with a continuous stroke.*

Painting a panel door

Like a window, paint a panel door from the inside out. Paint one small section at a time to avoid creating lap marks. A 2½-in.-wide brush should be used for the best painting results.

Start with the decorative edge molding surrounding the door panel followed by the panel itself (Figs. 11 and 12). Then paint the stiles between the panels (Fig. 13). Next, paint the top and bottom rails (Fig. 14) and work down the remaining stiles. Finish by painting the edges, cutting in cleanly around the hinges and avoiding drips (Fig. 15).

After the door is painted, do the doorjamb. Start on the inside (doorstop) and work out. Finish by making the cut along the outside edge and the wall.

When painting moldings, don't get too far ahead on one part of the molding. You don't want the paint to begin to dry or set up before you can finish. If you find your brush drags or sticks to an area where you have painted, don't try to smooth over it by brushing into the area. You'll just make it worse. In this case, let the lap mark dry, then sand it and repaint.

Ceiling molding and baseboard trim

To make a clean cut along a ceiling molding and the wall, hold your brush at an angle to the work surface and work away from the area you're painting. Don't set the ladder too close to the work. Move it often so you can easily reach the area you're painting. You can't paint a straight line if you have to stretch.

Painting walls and ceilings

Painting walls and ceilings alone is the most popular do-it-yourself project for two very good reasons: Learning to paint large areas is relatively easy, and your investment in paint and equipment is minimal compared to the dramatic change created by a fresh coat of paint. The secret to a professional-looking, long-lasting paint job is preparation. Unless your walls and ceilings are in unusually good condition, you will probably spend more time preparing to paint than actually painting.

Painting equipment

Many time-saving painting gadgets are now on the market. Some are designed for professional use, but many can be economically used by the weekend painter. You'll find the best selection of paint equipment in a store that sells to painting contractors and also to consumers. A word of advice: Buy good quality equipment and paint.

Invest in a couple of canvas drop cloths. These are heavy enough to withstand rugged foot traffic and will save your carpeting or hardwood floors from wear and tear. Paint spatters are absorbed in a canvas drop cloth, unlike plastic, on which they dry, then flake off in a snowlike flurry. An 8x10-ft. canvas is convenient to move around and costs about $30. Buy more than one drop cloth if you're painting a large area at one time, such as the entire top floor of a house. It's inefficient and messy to constantly have to move one drop cloth as you paint.

Plastic drop cloths cost from $3 to $5. If there's a choice, go for the heaviest (highest mil number) plastic drop cloth. You can use these alone or under old sheets, blankets or draperies. Check that you do not have a slippery combination because some fabrics will slide on plastic, making a nice scene for a disaster.

Even though most of your painting will be done with a roller, you still need a brush to cut in or apply paint in the corners. A 2½ -in.-wide brush is the best tool for cutting in. It carries enough paint for easy coverage but is lightweight and easy to handle. Nylon or polyester bristle brushes can be used with latex or oil (alkyd-based) paints. Remember that bristle brushes go limp from the water contained in latex paints.

A 9-in.-wide paint roller is a good choice for the do-it-yourselfer intent on

15 *Paint door's side, top and bottom edges. Cut in cleanly around hinges, avoiding drips. Next, paint the doorjamb.*

16 *Turn off the electricity and remove switch plates and outlet covers. Store them and their mounting screws in a plastic bag.*

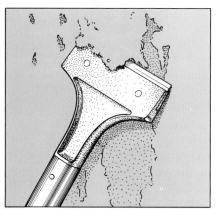

17 *Scrape off loose paint, dirt, old wallpaper glue and high spots with a razor scraper. Change the scraper blades frequently.*

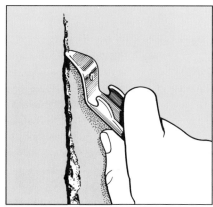

18 *Widen small cracks in plaster walls into a wedge shape with a bottle opener. An old screwdriver blade also works well.*

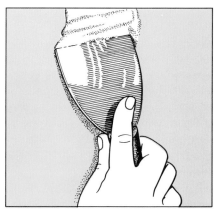

19 *Apply spackle to the crack with a putty knife. Press in spackle with blade at 30°. Scrape off excess with the blade at 45°.*

painting large areas. Buy a roller handle that accepts a screw-in extension pole. The roller handle's frame should be stiff enough to resist flexing. A cheap handle will flex, leaving an uneven coat of paint, and the roller will keep running off the handle. A stiff handle frame allows the roller to be worked easily into the corners of walls and ceilings.

Most good quality roller handles are sold without rollers (sometimes called covers or sleeves). Buy a roller labeled for walls and ceilings or one with a nap between ⅜ and ½ in. long. If you're painting a heavily textured surface, such as walls and ceilings that have received a stucco treatment, get a roller with a longer nap (more than ½ in. long).

The roller should fit snugly on the handle. The better quality rollers have a plastic core and will provide years of service if you clean them properly. You'll also find a cheaper line of disposable rollers with cardboard cores. Some are made of a spongelike material.

Purchase a sturdy metal roller pan. Inexpensive plastic pans are flimsy and flex when you pick them up, spilling the

paint. A metal pan is sturdy and has legs or corner brackets so you can hook it over the top of a ladder.

If you're painting several rooms the same color, use a 5-gallon paint bucket with a lid and a roller screen that hangs in the bucket. You can buy a roller screen at paint stores that sell to professionals. The screen hooks over the bucket's edge and hangs in the container.

Fill the bucket with a couple gallons of paint, dip the roller into it, and work the roller up and down the screen to push out excess paint.

Screw an extension handle into the roller handle, and you can paint the walls and ceilings without using a stepladder. The extension handle also allows you to spread paint on the roller without bending over. When it's time to take a break, just drop the screen into the bucket, snap on the lid, and then wrap the paint roller in aluminum foil.

How much paint for walls and ceilings?
Figure 1 gallon of paint to cover about 350 sq. ft., slightly less if the walls are unpainted drywall. To estimate the

amount of paint you need, determine the paintable wall and ceiling area. Add the length of all the walls and multiply this by the ceiling height. From this figure, subtract 20 sq. ft. for each door and 15 sq. ft. for each window. Divide this figure by 350 to find how many gallons of paint you need for the walls. Multiply the ceiling's length times its width to determine its area and divide it by 350 to arrive at the required number of gallons.

Wall and ceiling paint is sold in gallons and quarts, so round your paint estimate to the nearest quart. For example, if you need 1.33 gallons, purchase 1 gallon and 2 quarts. If you need more than 2 quarts, buy a gallon. You can use the extra paint for touching up later on.

You will need two coats of paint to cover dark colors or heavily patched walls. In this case, use a high-hiding (high solids content) wall primer, which is less expensive for the first coat. Ask your paint store for tinted primer—to bring the primer close to the final paint color so you avoid applying more coats than necessary.

Generally, flat latex paints are the best choice for the do-it-yourselfer to use on

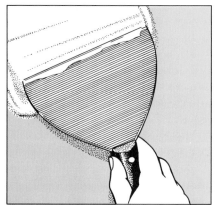

20 *Use drywall joint compound on small cracks and as a top coat for large cracks. It hardly shrinks and is easy to sand smooth.*

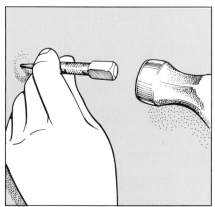

21 *Drive in protruding drywall nails with a nail set. Place a new nail above the popped nail, then fill the combined nail hole.*

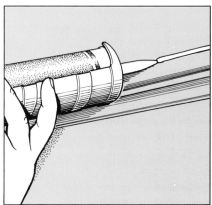

22 *Fill gaps between walls or ceiling and moldings with inexpensive latex caulk. The caulk should be a thin, even bead.*

most walls and ceilings. Flat paint is easy on the eyes since it reflects minimum light.

In heavy traffic areas, like the kitchen, bathroom, hallway or a small child's bedroom, consider using a semigloss paint that can withstand several washings. Alkyd-based paint (flat or semigloss) is a good choice in the bathroom, especially if you like to take long, steamy showers, because it has good resistance to mildew. If mildew appears, it's easily removed with bleach and soapy water. The tough surface of alkyd semigloss finish withstands this kind of washing and is generally a better choice in heavily used areas.

Quality paint gives better coverage and stands up better to washing than economy paints. Most good quality paints offer 1-coat coverage under normal conditions and are actually easier to spread and level than inexpensive paints. The cost of even the most expensive paint is modest compared to the value of the labor involved in preparing and painting the walls and ceiling. Given the extra durability and better finish offered by quality paint, it makes sense to spend the extra $15 to $20 per room to buy it.

Getting ready

For big paint jobs, move as much furniture as you can into other rooms. What can't be moved easily, place in the room's center at least 3 ft. from the walls. If it's a large room, stack furniture in two areas so there's ladder space in between.

Cover household furnishings and anything else left in the room with old bed sheets or plastic drop cloths taped closed. Completely cover wall-to-wall carpeting and hardwood floors with drop cloths, and remove area rugs. For optimum coverage, drop cloths should overlap each other by at least 1 ft., and they should reach well into corners and under radiators.

Paint sticks better to a clean surface, so thoroughly dust ceiling corners, baseboards and inside closets. Use a rag wrapped around a broom or a vacuum's crevice tool and duster nozzle to reach difficult areas. Wash dirty walls and ceilings, rinse them with water, and let dry.

Remove electrical switch plates and outlet covers. Store the plates, covers and mounting screws in a plastic sandwich bag (Fig. 16).

Before painting, make repairs to the drywall and plaster surfaces so they are completely smooth and free of cracks and holes. Caulk the gaps between the walls or ceiling and the baseboards (Figs. 17 through 22).

Protect exposed woodwork and such fixtures as thermostats from the fine splatter tossed by paint rollers by gently applying 1-in.-wide masking tape to them. For

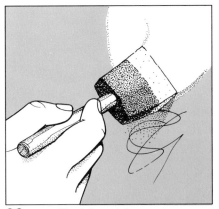

23 Stains bleed through latex paint, so hide them with shellac-based primer. Apply the primer with a foam brush.

maximum protection, use a flat knife to tuck masking tape into the corner where wall-to-wall carpeting meets the baseboard. The mastic used on masking tape will set if left in place too long, so remove all tape as soon as the paint has had a chance to dry.

If it's feasible, remove hanging chandeliers and wall fixtures. Otherwise, wrap them in plastic bags taped closed. Tape carefully, making sure that paintable surfaces are not covered with tape.

If there are any ink or marker pen stains, cover them with a stain killer such as BIN, a widely available pigmented shellac (Fig. 23). To save cleanup time, line the paint pans with aluminum foil. Dispose of or recycle the foil when you're finished with it.

Paint the ceiling first

Paint the ceiling before you paint the walls. Since the paint roller cannot reach into the corners or paint right up to the woodwork, the first step is to cut in the ceiling (apply about a 2½-in.-wide band of paint around the ceiling) using a 2½-in.-wide brush. You may want to use an

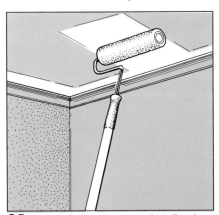

25 Use a 4-ft.-long extension handle when painting ceiling and walls. The extension screws into the roller handle.

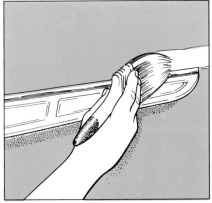

24 Hold an edge guard against the wall while you cut in the ceiling. Clean the guard occasionally by wiping it with a rag.

edge guard while cutting in the ceiling (Fig. 24). Wipe the guard frequently to avoid getting paint on the wall.

You don't have to complete the cutting in before you start rolling. One painter can cut in the ceiling, while another rolls on the paint. Allow the cut-in person to get a head start, then begin rolling. Don't let the painter cutting in get more than 20 minutes ahead of the painter using the roller. Should the painted band dry, the paint applied by the roller then acts as a second coat, and this 2-coat area becomes a lap mark.

If you use the same color on the walls and ceiling, it's not as difficult to make accurate cutlines where the ceiling meets the wall.

Regardless of whether the walls and ceiling are the same color, paint the cut-in line as heavily as you can without dripping. Spread the paint evenly, but don't brush it too much. Use a damp rag to wipe off the walls.

To paint the rest of the ceiling, use a 4-ft.-long extension handle screwed into the roller handle. Start rolling at one end of the room, and work the roller back and

26 To paint a large area, hang a roller screen in a 5-gallon paint pail filled with a couple of gallons of paint.

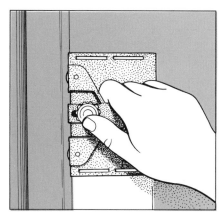

27 Cut in around door and window trim with a wheeled paint pad. If trim is wavy, however, pad leaves a wavy cutline.

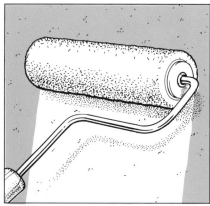

28 Use a roller with a nap length more than ½ in. to paint rough surfaces, like textured stucco walls or ceilings.

29 Spin dry a roller after you wash it. Hold it in a bucket and pump paint spinner handle. Spinner also works on brushes.

forth parallel to the longest wall (Fig. 25). Work your way across the ceiling in 3- or 4-ft.-sq. patches. When you reach the opposite wall, go back to the first wall. This technique lets you spread paint into new areas, but prevents lap marks.

Dip your roller in the paint, but don't submerge it, to avoid getting paint inside the roller (Fig. 26). This can cause runs and drips when the paint begins to leak out. Dip frequently, and don't be stingy. If you try to spread the paint too far, you will not get even coverage. Similarly, don't roll on paint too heavily. This can leave lap marks and runs.

When you are finished, move everything to the center of the room so you have free access to the walls.

Cut in and paint the walls

With the ceiling painted, start cutting in the corners of the room. Spread paint about 2 in. out from the wall-ceiling corner. Outline one wall at a time, working along the ceiling and into the corners. Then cut in around door and window trim and cabinets.

Instead of a paintbrush, a paint pad with wheels on one edge can roll along the side of the trim to help make a clean cut (Fig. 27).

The roller person can use the extension handle when painting the upper half of the wall, then remove the handle and finish the wall. Overlap your strokes in the wall's center since this area takes most of the abuse and it's the part that most people look at.

With a little practice, you can use the handle to paint the entire wall, which saves time and makes for an even paint job. Roll the upper third of the wall and work the roller down. Step back a bit to roll the center, then move closer to paint the lower section. Roll out small sections to avoid lap marks. Use a long nap roller for textured walls or ceilings (Fig. 28).

Take off your shoes if you have to walk off the drop cloth onto an area that is not protected. Otherwise, the paint on your shoe soles can easily be tracked onto clean floors. If you happen to track paint onto the floor, the sooner you clean it up the better. Depending on the paint, use a rag dampened with thinner or water.

Cleaning up latex paint

Latex paint is water soluble, so wash out the brushes under a steady flow of warm water until all the paint is removed. Then soak the brushes in warm water and mild liquid soap. Towel dry the brush, and use a spinner to remove excess water. This device grips the paintbrush or roller and spins it as you pump the spinner's handle. Before you wash out the rollers under a stream of warm water, slice the paint out of them with a paint stirring stick. Then spin the roller while holding it in a paint can or in a bucket (Fig. 29).

Cleaning up oil-based paint

Oil-based paints require paint thinner for cleanup. Hang brushes in thinner using brush hooks or bent wire coat hangers. You can use handle clips for long-handled brushes (Fig. 30).

Fill the container with paint thinner to where the brush bristles can hang about halfway into the solution. It's important to keep the tip of the bristles off the bottom of the container, where pigment residue settles. To store the brush for a couple of days, dip it in the spirits and work out most of the paint by spreading the bristles with your fingers. If you're concerned about getting the mineral spirits on your hands, wear a pair of rubber gloves. When you're ready to paint again, squeeze out the excess thinner from the brush. Then use a paint spinner to spin dry the brush.

Clean the brush completely at the end of the paint job. Use a brush comb to

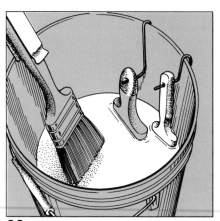

30 Suspend brushes in thinner at the end of the day. Keep the paintbrushes off the bottom by using brush hooks or clips.

work out any stubborn paint deposits in the bristles, especially those that accumulate near the ferrule (the metal band where the paintbrush handle and the bristles meet).

You can clean or discard a roller used with oil-based paint at the end of the job. To clean it (or store it overnight), force out excess paint from its nap using a stirring stick. To clean it, pour some paint thinner in the pan and work the roller around in it. Force out the remaining residue, then wash the roller in soap and water. Blot it dry, then let it air dry. Wrap a paint roller in plastic or aluminum foil overnight to keep it from hardening.

Equipment cleanup

Clean buckets and pans with thinner or water. Store painting tools in the wrappers they came in. Store drop cloths in a dry area—someplace where mildew is not likely to form on them. Finally, keep a brush and some paint handy even after you clean up. You can touch up any scuffs accidently made when moving the furniture back in place.

How to repair holes in DRYWALL

Degree of difficulty: Easy   Estimated time: 2 hours   Average cost of materials: $15

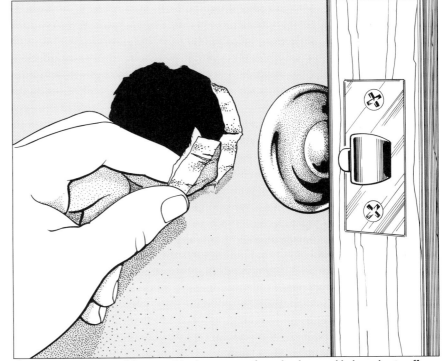

1 *Begin by removing all loose and broken gypsum from the damaged hole and strip off any torn or frayed paper. Also, vacuum away all dust, then dampen the edges.*

The material most widely used on interior house walls is gypsum wallboard, also known as plasterboard or drywall. This product consists of a core of gypsum faced on both sides with tough paper. Although it serves its purpose well, it is relatively brittle and can puncture when struck by a sharp blow. But patching a hole is not a difficult task and you'll obtain a neat, sound repair by using one of two basic methods. Both make use of ready-mixed joint compound which is available in different quantities at hardware stores and lumberyards.

Small holes

Holes up to about 4 in. in diameter are patched with the wire mesh backup procedure. Begin by cutting a piece of ordinary wire screening slightly larger than the hole to be repaired. Thread a length of string through the center of the screen.

Next, moisten the edge of the hole and the perimeter of the back side of the opening. Then, using a narrow putty knife, apply compound to the edge and around the back of the opening. While holding onto the string, curl the screen and fit it through the hole in the wall. Pull on the string to draw the screen up against the back of the wallboard. Tie the string around a pencil or a length of dowel that spans the opening.

Apply a layer of compound to the screen but not flush to the surface of the wall. When the screen has been coated overall, twist the pencil slightly to increase the tension on the screen. Allow this first layer to set, then cut the string to remove the pencil. Apply a second layer of compound so the patch will be flush to the surface of the wall. When this flush coat has set, apply a final thin coating of compound over the patch and slightly onto the surrounding wallboard. When the compound is dry, sand the patch with 220-grit abrasive paper.

Large holes

Holes larger than 4 or 5 in. are best repaired with a plug cut from a scrap of

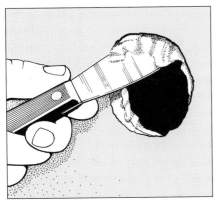

2 *Use a putty knife to apply joint compound to the edge of the hole and back surface of damaged panel.*

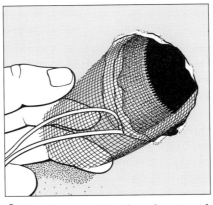

3 *Thread a strong string through a piece of wire mesh screening. Then curl the mesh and pass it through the opening.*

4 *Pull the mesh against the back of the wall, tie the string to a pencil, then apply a layer of compound over the mesh.*

wallboard. First, trim the hole square then cut a piece of board about 2 in. longer on each side than the hole size.

Mark off a centered area on the back of the patch ¼ in. smaller on each side than the hole in the wall. Cut through the paper surface and slightly into the core. Snap the board on each score line and carefully peel away the core material so

that only a paper flap remains. Use 120-grit paper to sand the outer edges of the flap until they taper to a point. Dampen all surfaces that will be bonded. Then, apply joint compound to the back of the patch flap and edges of the hole.

Press the patch into place and use a wide-blade knife to work the flap flush to the wall and to squeeze out excess com-

pound. Allow the compound to dry and then apply another thin coat of compound, extending about 1 or 2 in. beyond the patch area. When this is dry, sand smooth. Cracks in walls and ceilings can also be repaired before painting. Use a can opener or a putty knife blade to widen the crack. Then fill it with compound and sand smooth.

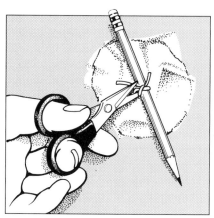

5 *When the first layer of joint compound has dried thoroughly, cut the string close to the mesh, and remove the pencil.*

6 *After the second layer of compound has set, apply a thin final layer, feathered to slightly overlap the surrounding surface.*

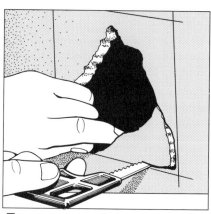

7 *To repair a larger hole, first square off the hole with a keyhole saw. Be sure to avoid wires or pipes with the saw.*

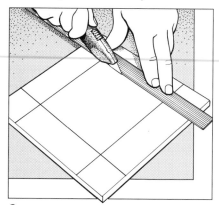

8 *Cut the wallboard plug to size and mark the back. Then cut through the paper facing and partly into the gypsum core.*

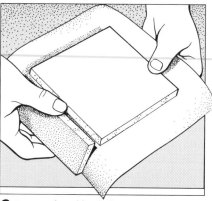

9 *Snap and peel back the waste segments, leaving the center and the overhanging front facing paper intact.*

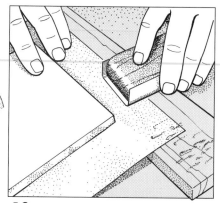

10 *Sand the edges of the flap to a taper at the outside edge. This feathering makes the patched surface less noticeable.*

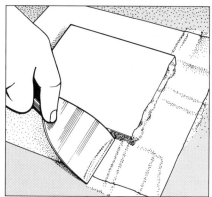

11 *Dampen the wall surfaces that will receive compound, then spread it on the flap. Apply extra compound in the corners.*

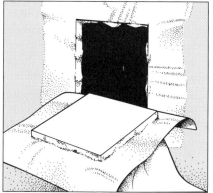

12 *Apply a thin layer of compound on the wall surface and hole edges, then slide the plug patch into the opening.*

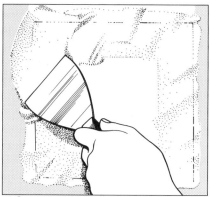

13 *Use a wide-blade knife to press flap against wall. Force out excess compound, then cover entire patch.*

How to locate
FRAMING STUDS

There are at least eight different ways to locate framing members behind walls and ceilings.

Most house walls are built using vertical 2x4 studs. And as long as they serve their primary purpose—namely, holding up the house—we rarely think about them. But when we do work on the walls, whether putting in a new window or simply hanging a heavy painting, we need to know the precise location of these framing members. And, we usually want to find them easily without tearing the wall apart.

Fortunately, every wall carries some telltale clues that make this job easier.

If you do a lot of remodeling and repair work, your best bet is to invest about $20 in an electronic stud finder. The one shown in Fig. 1 is available in hardware stores, home centers and through mail-order tool catalogs. All you do is move the sensor across the wall and when it passes over the stud, the lights on the unit come on. It operates on a simple 9-volt battery and will accurately establish both outside edges of the studs. This device was designed primarily for working on drywall or wood-paneled walls. But it also functions well on plaster walls as long as wood lath was used. Metal lath confuses the instrument.

If you'd rather take a lower-tech approach, Figs. 2 through 10 give you some sensible options.

The easiest of these is simply tapping your knuckles across the wall and listening for a change in sound. While this will generally yield the rough location of a

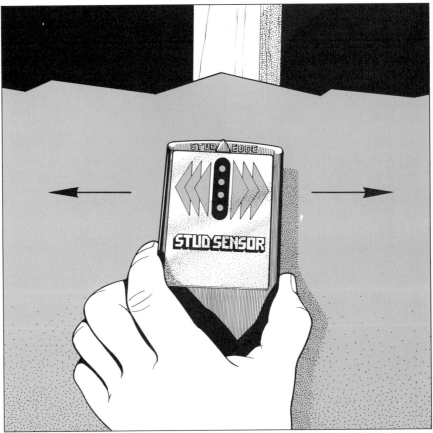

1 An electronic stud finder is a great tool for locating the exact position of wall studs. As you move the tool across the wall, the lights indicate the stud edges.

2 Using your knuckles, lightly tap along a wall and listen for a change in sound. A solid thud will be heard over a stud.

stud, it will not clearly define both edges. To find the center of the stud, you can probe the wall with a small nail. Usually, you can use a 4d finishing nail and repeatedly drive it into the wall until it hits the stud. Then measure over 1½ in. to find the other edge of the stud. (Studs are called 2x4s but their actual width is generally 1½ in.) Drive the nail again to ensure that you have found the other side of the stud and then mark the wall lightly. These small holes can be easily hidden with caulk and touch-up paint. If you're planning to repaint, use the patching instructions described on Page 111.

This method works on plaster walls too, but you do run the risk of cracking the brittle plaster. A better option is to drill repeated ⅟₁₆- to ⅛-in.-dia. holes across the wall's surface. When the bit meets resistance beyond the depth of about 1 in.,

you'll know you've found a stud. You should, however, remember two important cautions when drilling into any wall: Be sure to use a double-insulated drill connected to a circuit protected by a ground-fault circuit interrupter (GFCI), and avoid drilling in any areas where there may be concealed electrical wires or water or gas pipes. You should always check the other side of the wall you plan to work on for water and gas fixtures—an obvious but often overlooked precaution.

If you'd rather not put small holes in your walls, careful visual inspection may do the trick.

By shining a light at a low angle across drywall, you can often see bumps or depressions where nails are driven into the studs. Flaws not apparent during the day will sometimes appear at night when they aren't washed out by strong daylight.

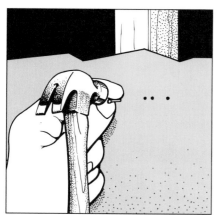

3 *After sounding out general stud location, find precise position by driving a small nail into wall until it meets resistance.*

You'll get the best results if you work in a darkened room or in the evening.

Visual inspection of the baseboard can also reveal depressions over finishing nail heads. Often the filler will shrink after it has dried and become noticeable if you

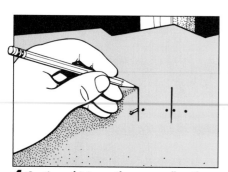

4 *Continue driving nail across wall until you pass over other edge of stud. Mark both edges on the surface with a pencil.*

specifically look for it. Of course, you can also carefully remove the baseboard and check for stud markings or nails underneath. In some cases the drywall will not abut the floorboards completely so you can see exactly where the studs are.

Another good option is to remove outlet cover plates. Generally, the boxes underneath are nailed to studs. Once the

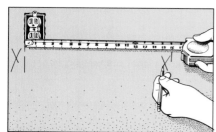

5 *Outlet boxes are usually nailed to studs. Remove cover plate to see where stud is, then measure and mark 16 in. to next stud.*

cover is off, you can see which side the stud falls on and then measure over in increments of 16 in. to find where other studs fall. Remember that these stud locations must be confirmed—by probing with a nail—because you cannot depend on all studs being located on the typical 16-in. centers.

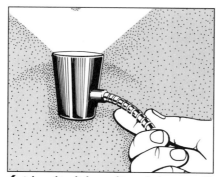

6 *A low skim light used in a dark room will often reveal depressions or bumps where wallboard nails are driven into studs.*

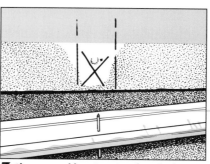

7 *Clues to stud locations are found when baseboard is removed. Wall may be marked or have exposed nails over studs.*

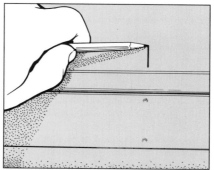

8 *Baseboard nails are usually driven into studs. Look for nail-head depressions. Confirm location by probing with small nail.*

Magnetic stud finders

One last device that is for locating hidden framing members is a simple magnetic stud finder. This simple, inexpensive device has a pointer that reacts when the tool passes over the nails or screws used to secure drywall panels in place. These

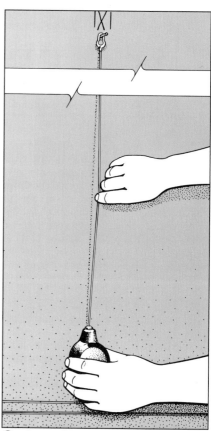

9 *When stud location is pinpointed at top and bottom of wall, snap a chalk line between the two to mark length of stud.*

finders will work well if the nails are close to the surface and if you have the patience to thoroughly scan the wall inch-by-inch. They will not, however, work on any paneling that is installed with adhesive or on plaster walls.

Using one of the methods described here should help you locate your wall studs. But keep in mind that many will also work well if you want to find ceiling joist locations. And remember, you can sometimes take a peek into attics and crawl spaces to find joist locations.

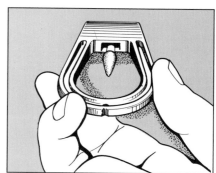

10 *A simple magnetic finder has a built-in pointer. This indicates the hidden location of nails used to attach wallboard.*

How to hang and finish
DRYWALL

Whether you're remodeling an old room or adding on a new one, being able to install and finish drywall properly can save you money. And the job is well within the abilities of most home owners. When hanging drywall ceiling boards, a 40-in.-long 2x4 tack-nailed to wall studs helps support the panels while you work. To reach the ceiling, stand on scaffolding made from planks supported between two sawhorses.

Drywall—also called wallboard, gypsum board or plasterboard—is probably the most versatile and forgiving wall surface available today. It's inexpensive, comes in a wide variety of sizes, and is much easier and less costly to apply than plaster. However, working with it can be extremely frustrating—especially in the finishing stages—because it does require real facility with at least three different compound knives. These and other basic tools are shown in Chapter 6. With a minor investment, these simple tools will provide excellent results at a fraction of what a professional would cost to do the work.

The individual drywall panels—or boards as professionals call them—come in a variety of sizes. The common width is 4 ft., but the length varies by 2-ft. increments from 8 ft. to 16 ft. The thickness of the boards also varies: beginning at ¼ in. and progressing in ⅛ in. increments to ¾ in. By far the most common size is ½ in. thick by 4 ft. wide by 8 ft. long.

Each board consists of a gypsum core covered with heavy-duty paper on both sides. The ends of the boards are cut off square with the gypsum core exposed.

The long edges, however, have a built-in tapered depression that's about 1½ in. wide. These depressions are designed to

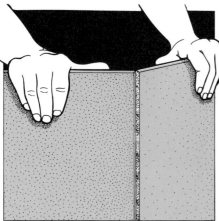

1 To cut the boards, score the paper surface with a utility knife, then snap from behind using your thumbs and one knee.

accommodate the paper tape and joint compound that seals the joint between boards and creates a seamless surface.

It's very important to keep these edge differences in mind. Because the butt ends have no depression, the tape and compound that cover them will sit exclusively on the surface, which creates a slight bulge. For this reason, you should plan your installation to minimize or eliminate the butt joints. You can do this by ordering various length boards to do specific areas of a room. If you are installing drywall in a bathroom or another area that is subjected to moisture, purchase special water-resistant drywall for the job. Of course, larger boards are heavier and more unwieldy, particularly when working on the ceiling.

Scaffolding

When working on ceilings you'll need to set up a system that supports you while you work. Professionals use a mechani-

2 Using a caulking gun, apply panel adhesive to the edges of underlying framing members before the board is installed.

cal drywall lift that supports the boards, but a do-it-yourselfer can take a more modest approach. And with a little help from a willing friend, you'll be more than able to handle the job.

For small jobs, a stepladder works well. But for larger areas it's better to use scaffolding. Lay planks between two sawhorses which can be rented, purchased or constructed from wood. You can also lay the planks between the steps of two stepladders and secure the planks in place with C-clamps. This allows the platform's

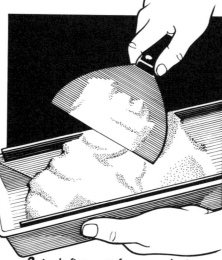

3 Apply first coat of compound using 6-in. knife. For better control, be sure to scrape compound off both corners of knife.

height to be adjustable. Whatever system is used, make sure to protect the floors from possible damage.

Cutting the boards

Starting with the ceiling, plan your boards so the length runs across the joists. If your ceiling joists are on 24-in. centers, it's best to use ⅝-in.-thick boards. But if the joists are on 16-in. centers—which is much more likely to be the case—½-in.-thick boards are the standard. The same is true for the walls. Make sure that you have nailing surfaces at the end (or ends) of the board where it intersects with the room walls.

Cut the board to length using a utility knife and metal straightedge. Once you've cut the surface paper, break the board from the back as shown in Fig. 1. If this edge is ragged, you can sand it flat using 60-grit sandpaper. It does not have to be perfectly smooth; your goal is simply to make the board fit. Also mark the location of any electrical light boxes in the ceiling and cut out a matching hole in the board using a compass saw.

Before raising the board, apply panel adhesive to the bottom edges of the joists

4 Press tape into first layer of compound using your fingertips. Then smooth tape across length of joint with a 3-in. knife.

using a caulking gun. The adhesive improves the bond and reduces the number of nails that are required.

Hanging the boards

To help hold the board in place, it's a good idea to tack-nail a 40-in.-long 2x4 to the wall as shown on Page 115. When positioned just 1 in. below the ceiling, it helps support one end of the board, which takes much of the strain out of the job. (Once the board is nailed, simply move the cleat to support the next board.) You can also set up a T-shore—a drywall panel support made from a 2x4 3in. longer than the distance between the ceiling and the floor. The 2x4 is fitted with two wooden blocks at each end. The end of the T-shore that abuts the ceiling should be padded with carpeting or cloth so the boards don't get damaged. Again, it's suggested that you have someone help out with this procedure since the boards are very awkward to handle.

Once you've decided what support method to use, attach the drywall board with 1⅝-in.-long drywall nails. Drive these nails 8 in. apart around the perimeter—and across the face of the board—into every joist that the board covers. Dimple—or slightly recess—the nail heads into the surface paper. This creates a depression that can be filled with joint compound later.

You can also use drywall screws in tandem with an electric drill fitted with a drywall-screw countersink. The countersink provides a fast and efficient way of attaching the drywall. When using a countersink, the drywall screw is drilled into the wall at a perfect depth. The countersink will contact the board and begin making a clattering noise once the screw is seated. With a little practice, this method works the best for jobs where you're installing a lot of drywall.

5 *After tape is smooth, apply another layer of compound using a 6-in. knife. Use just enough compound to cover tape.*

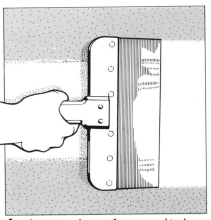

6 *When second coat of compound is dry and sanded smooth, apply final—very thin—skim coat using a 10-in. knife.*

Walls

Use the same technique to hang the wall boards, making sure to plan your material to minimize butt joints. Areas over a door or window are good places for such joints because they're less noticeable. One way to avoid butt joints completely is to install the boards vertically. Professionals, however, strongly recommend that you run your boards horizontally. It makes finishing easier because much of the tape and compound are applied horizontally, near the level of your waist. By doing the joints vertically, you have to move up and down a ladder continually, which makes the work harder and using the knives much more awkward and much less controllable.

Be sure to push the upper wall board tight against the underside of the ceiling boards. When the ceiling boards bear directly on the wall boards, the chance of cracks appearing later is drastically reduced. Complete the walls by installing the lower boards. If your ceiling height is 8 ft. or less, a second board around the perimeter of the room will do the job. But if your ceilings are higher, as is the case in many older homes, a third, partial board will be required. Install it the same way as the others.

Knives and compound

The finishing process is basically a 4-step endeavor. First, apply a layer of joint compound. Next, embed paper tape in the compound, directly over the joint line. Then the tape is covered with another coat of compound. And once this coat is dry, the joint is skimmed with a final—very thin—layer of compound. That said, you should know that there are as many ways to do this as there are professional drywall installers. But the 3-knife method—using 3-in.-, 6-in.- and 10-in.-wide blades—is a good one for beginners.

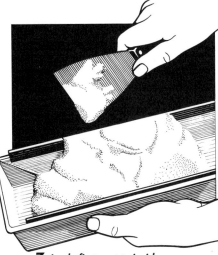

7 *Apply first coat to inside corners using 3-in. knife. For better control, scrape compound off outward corner of knife.*

When buying these knives, look for blades that are extremely flexible. Blades that are stiff may work well for scraping off old wallpaper but they are inappropriate for applying compound. You should be able to push the flat side of the blade against the palm of your hand and have the blade bend easily under pressure. When pressure is released, it should return to its former straight shape. If the knives are not flexible, you'll have quite a struggle on your hands.

The best joint compound is the premixed variety that comes in plastic pails—usually in 1-gal., 2½-gal. and 5-gal. sizes. Dry compound, that you mix with water, is also available and often less expensive than the premixed variety. But it is extremely difficult to mix to a smooth texture without the proper equipment. And, smooth joint compound is absolutely crucial to the properly performed finishing process. The best way to carry the compound from joint to joint is with

a plastic or metal pan like the one shown. Each time you load the pan with compound, be sure to mix the compound slightly with a knife.

These pans have a sharp blade on both sides for keeping the knives clean. Every time you remove your knife from the wall, whether to deposit excess compound in the pan or to get a new load, always scrape off both sides of the knife blade on the pan blades.

Joint sequence

Begin on the ceiling and do all of the tapered joints first. When you're finished, move to the tapered wall joints. Return to the ceiling and do any butt joints, followed by the butt joints on the walls. Then tape the corner joints between the walls and the ceiling followed by the corner joints between the walls. Finally, cover all the nail heads with compound only.

To begin a tapered joint, use a 6-in. knife and put a generous amount of joint compound on the blade. Then, clean off each corner of the knife slightly as shown in Fig. 3. This cleaning step is important—especially when working on the ceiling—because it allows some room for the compound to spread across the knife without falling off, which, when working on the ceiling, means falling on you. Hold the knife at a 30° to 45° angle to the surface and run it down the middle of the joint, pressing the compound into the depression. Work in smooth, steady strokes. Remember that your goal is to apply the compound as smoothly and evenly as possible.

Once the whole joint is covered, go back to the beginning and wipe off the excess using the same 6-in. knife. Do not press so hard that you scrape all the compound out of the depression.

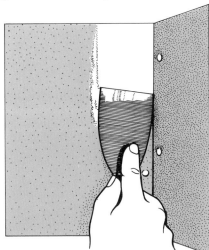

8 *Press knife loaded with compound into the corner and then pull down length of joint. Use surface of adjacent wall as guide.*

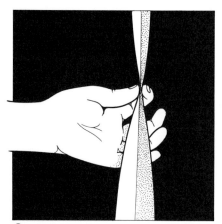

9 *Cut joint tape to match length of corner, then fold tape in half. Tape has depression in middle to make precise folding easy.*

Pull out a length of tape equal to the joint length and tear it off the roll. Then carefully press the tape into the compound with your fingertips. Once the entire joint is covered, return to the beginning of the joint and carefully smooth the tape into the compound using light pressure on the 3-in. knife. Once the paper is embedded, go back over the joint with the 6-in. knife to completely smooth the tape and remove the slight ridges that often result when the tape is embedded. Again, clean the knife every time before you put it back on the wall—this is crucial for a perfect job.

If, after the tape is smooth, you notice a bubble underneath the tape, stop, remove the tape from the whole joint and throw it away. Your problem is too little compound under the tape for the tape to stick properly. Do not try to lift the tape and put more compound underneath it; you'll spoil the whole joint and the job

will be botched. It's simply better to start the procedure over.

Once the tape is embedded smoothly, cover it with another layer of compound using the 6-in. knife. Then smooth the joint with the 10-in. knife. Leave just enough compound to completely cover the tape. Move onto the remaining tapered joints and when they're done, stop for the day. Let the joints dry overnight, then smooth them by sanding lightly with 120-grit sandpaper. If you've done a reasonably good job, the sanding will be minimal. Remember, your goal is to achieve the smoothest surface possible before adding more compound.

Professionals will often omit this sanding stage. But for the beginner, it's well worth the effort because each ensuing coat of compound will be easier to apply. Whenever sanding the compound, be sure to wear safety goggles and a respirator. Also provide adequate ventilation. The dust is very fine and very irritating.

Butt joints

The second day, finish all the butt joints. This takes considerably more finesse because the built-in taper is not available. Begin in the same way as before. Apply the underlaying compound using a 6-in. knife. Then smooth the compound with a 10-in. knife. Embed the tape as before, directly over the joint line. Smooth it in place with a 3-in. knife, followed by a 6-in. knife. Add a layer of compound and smooth it with the 10-in. knife. For this step, the wider knife is crucial because the compound must be feathered at least 5 in. away from the joint on both sides. As mentioned before, you are creating a surface bulge with a butt joint, so it should be as smooth and as gradual as possible.

Once all the butt joints are all taped, wait overnight until they have dried and then sand them to a smooth finish.

Corner joints

In many ways corner joints are the least crucial because they don't show as much irregularity as a flat surface. The biggest problem is that when working on one side of the joint, your knife will often foul the adjacent surface.

Begin by applying the compound to both sides of the joint with a 3-in. knife as shown in Fig. 8. Smooth it with a 6-in. knife. Then cut off a piece of tape the length of the joint and fold it as shown in Fig. 9. Press it into the corner with your fingertips. Then smooth each side with the 3-in. knife followed by a 6-in. knife. At this point, top coat only one side of the corner. Do the remaining corner joints in a similar fashion and let them dry overnight. The next day, top coat the other side of each joint and let these dry overnight. On outside corner joints, join two boards with corner bead—a metal, L-shaped channel that is covered by successive layers of joint compound.

Skim coat

Lightly sand the whole job. Now using the 10-in. knife, apply a very thin skim coat of compound to each joint. Clean the knife every time you return it to the pan. If you ever see the knife dragging anything in its wake, be sure to stop and remove the debris immediately. Once the entire surface is skimmed, wait a day for it to dry, then carefully sand the whole job with 180-grit paper and touch up any imperfections you find with fresh joint compound. Apply sealer to the drywall before painting.

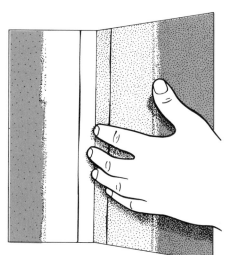

10 *Carefully embed folded tape into compound. Do not try to smooth with fingers, just make sure that tape will not fall.*

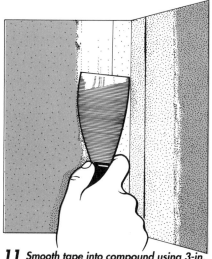

11 *Smooth tape into compound using 3-in. knife and adjacent wall surface as guide. Smooth one side and then the other.*

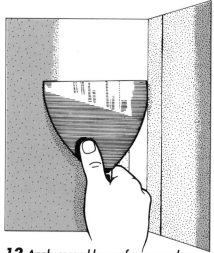

12 *Apply second layer of compound over tape using 6-in. knife. Let dry and sand first side before coating second side.*

How to install
SOLID WOOD PANELING

Degree of difficulty: Medium   **Estimated time:** 10 hours a room   **Average cost of materials:** $20 a panel

Solid wood paneling is available in many varieties, including pine, cedar and redwood.
Depending on your taste, it can be painted or coated with a natural or synthetic varnish.
Paneling can add a comfortable ambience to rooms throughout the house.

Home owners have long appreciated the warmth, versatility and value of solid wood paneling. Often reserved for family rooms and studies, wood paneling has long been the material of choice for comfortable, lived-in spaces. And today, it is moving more and more into living rooms and dining rooms.

Selecting paneling
Installing solid wood paneling is almost as easy as using veneered 4x8-ft. sheets. Though they make covering walls relatively easy, they are cumbersome and are limited to vertical application. Solid paneling is available in many milled styles, including square edged for board-on-board and board-and-batten applications, and tongue-and-groove with a V-milled edge or a beaded edge. It's also available in rustic patterns and more finely finished milled variations.

It can be had in many different wood species, including several varieties of pine, redwood, oak, ash, cherry and walnut. Ease of installation and availability depend on the type of wood and style of paneling. Most lumberyards stock pine, cedar and, sometimes, redwood. If they don't stock hardwoods, they often can order them for you. While hardwood paneling looks luxurious, it's much more difficult to install. Nail holes, for instance, have to be predrilled.

Some lumberyards will carry the material as open stock while others will sell it in packages of random lengths. Its thickness may vary from $\frac{5}{16}$ to $\frac{3}{4}$ in.

Since boards may be stored in outside warehouses, it's important to let them adjust to the humidity of the room in which they will be installed. This reduces

119

1 *To remove baseboard, gently drive a pry bar between the trim and wall. Then pry away board at all nail locations.*

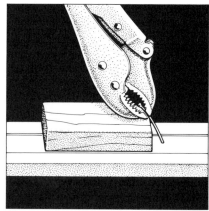

2 *Use a pair of locking pliers to pull nails out the back of trimwork. This way, it can be reused after paneling.*

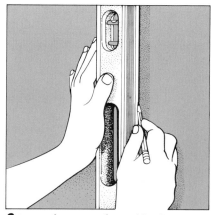

3 *Locate the center of a stud by driving a nail into the wall. Then mark a plumb line from the nail hole using a level.*

shrinkage and expansion after installation. Store boards in the room for a week to 10 days before you install them.

Separating stacked boards

Use 1-in.-thick stickers (wood slats) to separate the stacked boards to allow air to circulate between them. Tongue-and-groove boards should be pre-stained to avoid unstained tongues revealing themselves in the event of shrinkage. And in locations with high-heat and high-humidity conditions—such as bathrooms and kitchens—the backs of the boards should be sealed prior to installation.

For this example, we installed V-jointed tongue-and-groove boards vertically. The home owner chose knotty pine, which was sold as open stock at the local lumberyard. Though sold as No. 3 grade (the grade below A, B, C Select, No. 1 and No. 2 softwood boards), the material was clean and straight, yet relatively inexpensive for interior wall covering.

If you go this route, buy enough extra material so you can eliminate unusable sections of boards.

Removing trimwork

Begin by removing trimwork on the walls to be paneled. Using a flat pry bar, pull the baseboard away from the wall. Pull the nails out from the back with a pair of locking pliers. This saves the surface of the baseboard in case you want to reuse it.

Pull casings from doors and windows the same way. Remove light and outlet covers and edging from heat registers. If you have radiators or baseboard heaters, call a heating contractor to remove them temporarily.

Next, locate the studs by tapping across the wall with a hammer or by using one of the stud-finding methods described on Page 113. If you use a hammer to find

studs, you'll notice a solid "thunking" sound when you pass over each one. Using a 6d nail, drive test holes to find the center of each stud. Mark the nail hole and then draw a plumb line through it with a level, going from the floor to the ceiling (or however high you are installing paneling). Then, drive a nail into the studs at the top and bottom of the line to double-check stud location. Correct the lines as necessary to correspond to the center of the studs.

Providing a nailing surface

Next, you must provide a nailing surface for the paneling because the majority of the boards can't be nailed to studs. Also, a nailing surface must be provided for door, window and duct openings.

To provide a suitable nailing surface for the paneling and various openings, nail 1x3-in. furring strips to the studs horizontally with 8d common nails. Space the furring 2 to 3 ft. apart. Shim the strips where necessary to make up for the dips in the wall.

One drawback to this is that the floor space of the room will decrease by the thickness of the paneling and the furring strips (as much as 1½ in.). To avoid this problem, you can cut away wall material where the furring is nailed to the studs.

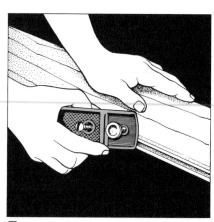

7 *Using a block plane, remove wood from the grooved edge of the board. Work down to the scribed line, then test fit.*

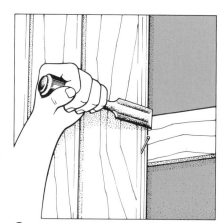

9 *To wedge over a board with a bad crook, drive a chisel into the furring strip next to it, lever into place, then nail.*

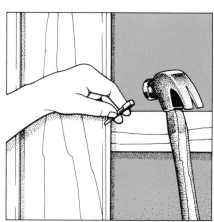

10 *Nail boards through the tongue with 8d finishing nails. Leave their heads above the surface and then bury them with a nail set.*

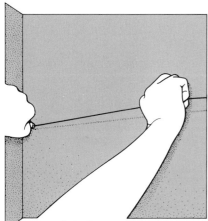

4 *To mark the location of the furring strip nailers, snap a horizontal chalk line at intervals of 2 to 3 ft.*

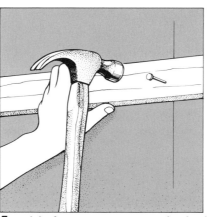

5 *Nail the furring strip to every stud with 8d common nails. To save space, cut away wall material behind the furring.*

6 *Hold the first piece of paneling plumb at the inside corner. Use a compass to scribe the board.*

Fastening to masonry

When working on masonry or concrete walls, the simplest alternative is to face-nail 2x4-in. furring for the paneling directly to the walls. Cut nails are the simplest type of masonry fastener for this

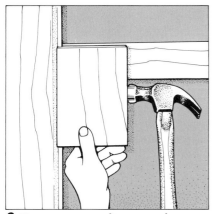

8 *Hammer on a paneling scrap when you tap a board into place. Put the scrap's grooved edge over the board's tongue.*

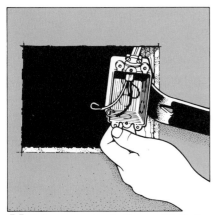

11 *Relocate an electrical box so it's flush with the paneling's surface. First, gently pry it loose from the wall.*

type of job. These wedge-type fasteners are driven like common nails, but with a heavier hammer (about 2 lb.). They are made of hardened steel and are therefore more brittle than regular nails: Wear safety glasses when driving them. If you have hollow concrete block walls, you can also use toggle bolts to fasten furring strips in place.

If you're paneling the ceiling, the boards can be attached directly to the ceiling joists through the drywall or plaster, providing they are running perpendicular to the floor joists. If parallel to the joists, you'll have to install furring strips over the ceiling.

Relocating electrical boxes

Should there be an electrical box in the ceiling, it will have to be lowered to accommodate the paneling.

Turn off power to the room at its source and cap all exposed wiring with wire nuts. Cut out a 16-in.-square section of the ceiling from around the electrical box. Remove the box and attach it

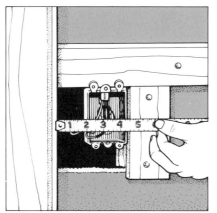

12 *To scribe for an electrical box, take measurements from the board's side to the box side and from the floor to the box top.*

to a 2x4-in. block that has been cut to fit between the ceiling joists. Hang the box so it will be flush with the paneling on the ceiling.

Relocating an electrical box on a wall is very similar. You can replace an existing box with a box that grips the paneling from behind or you can use a box with holes that allow you to screw it into the wood paneling.

In this case, we just removed the box and reattached it to furring material fastened to the stud by the box opening. If you are fastening the boards directly to the wall, you can buy extension collars for electrical outlets and switches that save the trouble of moving the box. If you have a forced-air heating or cooling system, you'll have to have a heating contractor fabricate the extension collars for the registers.

Beginning at an inside corner

Once the nailing surface has been prepared properly, begin by nailing a board at an inside wall corner.

Hold the grooved side to the corner, plumb the board with a 4-ft. level, and scribe the edge in the corner with a compass, using the wall as the guide. If necessary, rip off extra material. Then, use a block plane to work down to the scribed line. Fasten the board by nailing it through the tongue into the furring with 8d finishing nails.

Leave the nail heads above the surface and sink them with a nail set just below the surface.

Tap the next board in place; use a scrap block cut from the grooved edge of a piece of paneling to avoid crushing the tongue.

If a board has a crook, drive a chisel into the furring strip next to its tongue and pry it against the next board. Maintain pressure on it until you drive a nail near the pry point. If the crook is bad, start a face nail and a tongue nail before

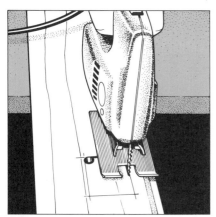

13 *Cut out a box or switch opening with a saber saw. First bore a starter hole at the corner of the opening.*

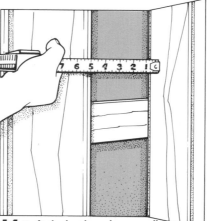

14 *To fit the last board on a wall, measure from board's edge to wall opposite at both its top and bottom.*

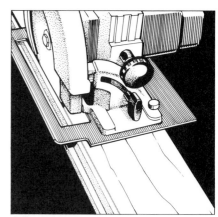

15 *Hold the last board in place, then scribe-fit it. Rip off the waste and then plane down to the scribed line.*

you begin to pry the board, then sink both nails before releasing pressure. After you've installed four boards, measure the distance from the tongue on the fourth board to the corner you're working toward, both at the ceiling and floor. If the measurements differ, adjust the spacing of the boards so the difference gradually disappears.

Scribing a window cutout

To scribe the cutout for a window, measure the distance between the edge of the face of the last board you installed to the outside of the nearest window jamb—measure at the top and bottom of the window. Then, measure from the floor to the bottom of the window stool and to the top of the window head jamb. Transfer your measurements to the board and cut the waste away with a saber saw.

After all the boards are in position on the wall, apply extension jambs to windows and doors. These wooden strips will bring the jamb flush to the face of the wood paneling.

Applying the last boards

To apply the last board at an inside corner, measure from the edge of the previous board to the corner at the ceiling and the floor. Transfer these measurement

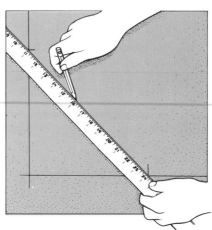

16 *For diagonal paneling, mark horizontal and plumb references. Measure each 12 in. in, connect marks.*

marks to the top and bottom of the board. Now, hold the board about 1 in. from the corner, parallel to the board next to it. Set your scribe to touch the wall and the top measurement mark, then run it down the length of the board.

Rip the board as necessary, then plane off the excess, leaving half the line for a tight fit. Remove the back side of the groove, press the board in place, and then face-nail.

Finish outside corners by cutting the last board flush with the adjoining wall. Sand the edge of the board smooth and flush with the adjoining wall.

For diagonal pattern paneling, begin by laying out a reference line. For a 45° angle, measure 6 in. from the corner and mark a 2-ft.-long plumb line. Next, measure 1 ft. up from the floor and mark an intersecting horizontal line. Measure and mark 1 ft. up on the horizontal line and 1 ft. along the plumb line. Connect your marks, extending the line from the corner to the floor. Cut a 45° angle on the end of a board, with the long point on the tongue side. Then, cut the piece to fit tight to the corner and floor while being parallel to the reference line. Blind-nail through the floor plate into the corner stud.

While diagonal paneling does not require furring—if it runs from floor to ceiling—it does require careful cutting and fitting. For those boards used on long diagonal runs, you should try to cut them so their ends fall on the center of a stud.

After paneling and extension jambs are in place, apply window and door casing, and then baseboard trim. Fill nail holes with wood filler, then lightly sand the walls with 220-grit sandpaper.

If you're planning on painting the paneling, you should prime it with an alkyd primer before applying subsequent coats of paint.

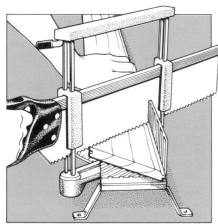

17 *Use a miter box to cut the diagonal on the end of a board. Note that the long point of the angle is on the tongue side.*

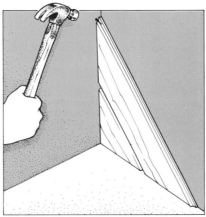

18 *Nail boards through the tongue into the corner stud and along the plate. Baseboard covers nails along the floor.*

How to install TRIMWORK

Degree of difficulty: Medium Estimated time: 5 hours Average cost of materials: $70

Trimming a window is more complicated than for a door, even though the two jobs share the same techniques. Successful trimwork can be accomplished with only a miter box, backsaw and marking tools.

Installing trimwork—which means installing casing, baseboard, shoe molding and ceiling molding—is not very difficult, though it can be time-consuming. In this respect, it's very much like taping drywall panels together.

The two jobs also share other similarities because, taken together, they represent the bulk of what is seen on the interior of a house. A poor job of either will never be out of view.

Of course, very little goes wrong with existing trim, especially if your house is new. But, if you plan to add on or convert a basement or attic to usable living space, knowing the ins and outs of this finish trade will be invaluable when you undertake to do so.

You can trim a room with a small selection of hand tools—basically a hammer, nail set, coping saw, block plane and a few sharp chisels. You also need a miter box. Both the old-style, hand-powered boxes and the new electric tools are generally available at tool rental shops.

Depending on your local supplier, baseboards, casing and ceiling or crown moldings come in different sizes and shapes. But the ranch (clamshell type) and the colonial style are by far the most common. We used the colonial variety on this job. Both types are available in clear stock, if you plan to stain or cover with a clear finish, and in finger-jointed sections, if you paint.

There are no hard-and-fast rules about the order in which you trim a room, except at the point where the baseboard abuts a door casing. Obviously, the casing must be nailed in place first. (*Note*: Because trimming a window is more involved than a door, we chose the window as the basis of our illustrations. But the techniques for casing a window are in every way identical to casing a door.)

Begin by checking the relationship between the outside edge of all window jambs and doorjambs with the wall sur-

1 *Using a square, check to see if the jambs are flush with the wall surface. If not, measure the difference with a ruler.*

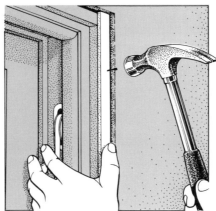

2 *If jambs are recessed from the wall surface, glue and nail extension jambs in place. If jambs project, plane them flush.*

3 *Cut stool to length and mark centerline. Then, mark center of window sill. Hold stool against sill and align marks.*

faces next to them. Use a square and ruler as shown in Fig. 1. If the jamb is within 1/16 in. in either direction, it's fine; the trim will be able to lay flat against both surfaces. If it projects more, plane the jamb flush. If the jamb is recessed, rip a thin wood shim. Then, glue and nail it onto the jamb so it's flush with the wall. These shims are called extension jambs.

Doors and windows

Once the jamb is flush with the wall around it, mark the reveal; that is, the part of the jamb that will remain uncovered by the casing. Measure from the inside face of each jamb across the edge and make a mark at the 3/16-in. point. Do this at the bottom and top of both side jambs, and at both ends of the top or headjamb. These marks define the position of the inside edges of all casing boards. The reveal is basically cosmetic. But it will allow you to adjust your casing boards slightly if you cut a miter a little too long or too short.

The next step is to measure for the window stool. The stool is the piece which fits over the window sill, extending beyond the casing on each side of the window. Window stool is available at lumberyards, pre-shaped to fit over the traditional downward-sloping sill. It must, however, be notched to fit between the jambs or it won't slide into place. To fit the stool, first measure the distance between the window jambs. Then, add twice the reveal, plus twice the casing width, plus 2½ in. Your goal is to have the stool extend 1¼ in. beyond each side casing. Cut the stool to this length. Next, mark the edge of the stool at the centerline of its length. Also, mark a centerline on the sill between the jambs. Hold the stool against the sill with these marks aligned and then mark the location of the inside edge of both jambs.

Make sure the lower sash of the window is closed, then measure the distance from the stool to the sash. This determines how deep the notch should be on both ends. Cut the notches by hand, keeping the saw blade to the waste side of the line. Next, trace the profile on the front edge of the stool to both ends. Cut the ends to this shape with a coping saw. Then, sand smooth and nail the stool into the sill and jambs.

Casing

Using a miter box set to 45°, cut one end of the head casing so that the long point of the angle is at the thickest part of the headjamb with the short point of the mitered cut on your reveal mark. Then, mark the other end of the head piece at its reveal mark. This establishes the short point of the second miter. Carefully make the cut, keeping the saw blade to the waste side. Align the head piece between the reveal marks, then nail it to the jamb using 4d finish nails. The short points of the miters should be 3/16-in. above the

inside edge of the headjamb, so that the reveal is uniform on the sides and top.

Next, measure from the stool to the top of the head casing at both ends. Cut and miter the respective side casings. Apply glue to both members of each miter joint,

7 *Using a miter box, cut a closed miter on both ends of the sill apron. Hold the board firmly while making the cut.*

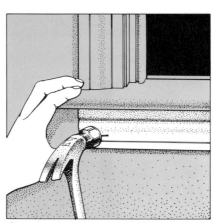

9 *Nail the finished apron under the sill. Note that ends of apron should align with outside edge of both side casing boards.*

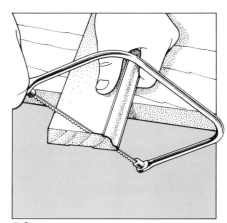

10 *Inside corners on baseboards must be coped. First, cut open miter on end, then back-cut profile slightly with coping saw.*

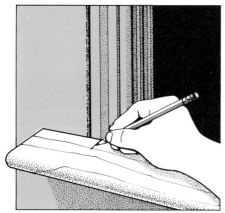

4 Mark stool—at both ends—where inside edge of jamb falls. Remove stool and cut the notches with a backsaw.

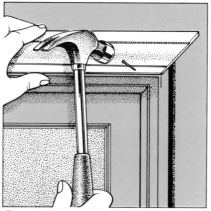

5 Carefully miter both ends of the head casing. Then, nail the lower edge to the headjamb using 4d finishing nails.

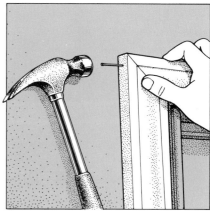

6 Cut side casing and apply glue to miter. First, nail casing to jamb, then nail miter together with a 4d finishing nail.

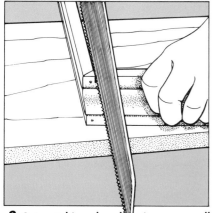

8 Cut matching closed miters on small sections of casing. Glue and nail to apron ends. Cut ends flush.

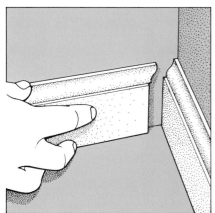

11 Nail square-cut baseboard in place first. Then, test-fit coped cut. If necessary, refine profile cut with sandpaper and rasp.

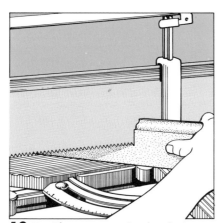

12 Outside corners require closed miter on both baseboards, if wall corner is square cut at 45°. If not, bisect angle.

then nail the sides to the jambs with 4d finishing nails. Also, drive a nail through each miter as shown in Fig. 6, then nail the casing boards to the wall surface with 6d finishing nails. These should be positioned about ½ in. in from the outside edge of the boards so you'll be sure to hit the jack studs within the wall.

Now measure for the apron, which is the trim piece that runs underneath the stool. Generally, its length matches the measurement between the outside edges of both side casings. Cut a piece of casing to this length with a closed miter on both ends. (A closed miter means that the angle is cut so the face is longer than the back. An open miter is cut so the back is longer than the face.) Next, cut a closed miter on two small scraps of casing. Glue and nail one on each end of the apron. When the glue is dry, carefully cut the ends flush with the back of the apron, as shown in Fig. 8. Nail the apron into wall studs using 6d finishing nails.

Baseboards

Once you've finished the windows and doors, turn your attention to the baseboard. Locate the wall studs and lightly marking their positions on the floor or wall. If the drywall is up off the floor more than an inch, fill in the gaps with strips nailed to the floor plate. (These don't have to fit perfectly; you just need some solid backing for the baseboard.) There are four basic cuts involved in applying baseboard. The first is a square cut. This is used on ends that abut a door casing or other trim board that extends to the floor. The second is a closed miter that is cut on ends of both boards that meet at an outside corner (Figs. 12 and 13).

The third is an open miter. It's used along with a closed miter when you need to splice together two boards in the middle of a wall. And the fourth is a coped open miter that fits over a mating baseboard on one side of an inside corner (Figs. 10 and 11).

The straight cuts should be made with your miter box set at 90°. Any board that has a straight cut on both ends can be nailed to the wall immediately. Use 6d finishing nails driven into the studs along the top of the baseboard and into the plate along the bottom.

The open and closed miter cuts that form a splice are cut with the miter box set at 45°. Always cut the open miter on the first board you nail to the wall.

Then, cut the closed miter, apply glue to the splice joint and nail the board onto the wall. When the glue dries, you can sand the joint smooth.

When making the matching closed miters for an outside corner, keep in mind that very few house walls meet at a precise 90° angle. For this reason, it's wise to check each corner with a sliding T-bevel square and protractor. Just place the square around the corner and lock it in place, then read the angle against a protractor. Bisect this angle, that is, divide it by two. The resulting number is the angle that should be cut on each of the boards. Nail the boards to the wall, being sure to glue the joint.

The coped miter is used on one board of an inside corner and requires two cuts.

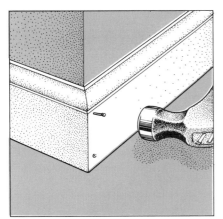

13 *Glue miters together and nail with 4d finishing nails. Blunt tips of nails before driving to prevent splitting wood.*

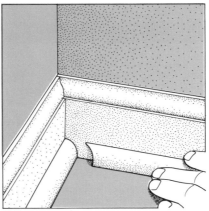

14 *Shoe molding is cut just like baseboards. However, it is usually nailed in place after the floor covering is installed.*

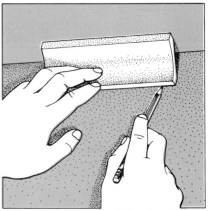

15 *To establish a straight line for ceiling molding, scribe bottom edge of scrap molding at wall ends. Snap chalk line.*

First, make a 45° open miter. Then, cope the end, following the mitered cut's profile where it meets the face of the board. You should under-cut, or back-cut, the cope slightly so the front edge of the board is longer than the back. This allows a small amount of stock that can be filed easily or sanded to make the joint fit tightly. Test your cut against the baseboard that is already in place, and then nail it to the wall.

If you plan to add a shoe molding over the baseboard, cut and fit it now, even though you may not install it yet. All the cuts and installation techniques for shoe molding are the same as for baseboards. Whenever possible, plan your installation sequence so you have only one mitered or coped cut on each board. By doing so, you can adjust the cut so that it fits perfectly before you actually cut the entire board to length.

Ceiling molding
Ceiling molding went out of fashion somewhat in the past 30 or 40 years. But

it's not much harder to install than a baseboard, and it can add something special to any room.

It does have one complication: Instead of laying flat against the wall surface, ceiling molding bridges the corner between the wall and ceiling at a 45° angle. Begin by cutting a scrap of ceiling molding approximately 5 in. in length. Hold the scrap against the ceiling in one corner of the room and lightly mark the wall below it. Do the same thing at the other end of the wall. Then, chalk a very light blue line between these points. Make sure the scrap block will fit between the line at every point on the wall. If it is too tight in some places, snap a new line lower than the first. The molding is difficult to nail in place without it moving up or down. The line provides accurate reference.

Keep the bottom edge of your molding on the line, then nail it into the studs. As with the baseboard and the shoe molding, miter the outside corners and cope the inside corners. But keep in mind when you cut the ceiling molding, you must

hold the lower edge firmly against the fence because the top edge does not bear on the fence. The installation techniques are the same as for the baseboard and shoe moldings. Prefabricated ceiling molding is another option. It comes in varying styles and lengths, and can look pretty convincing as a stand-in for the real thing.

Filling small holes and gaps
The material used to fill nail holes and small gaps in joints depends on the finish you use. For instance, work that is to be stained is much less forgiving than paint-grade work. Any glue on the surface will show up as light blotches after the wood is stained.

The same is true for many wood fillers, unless the filler comes colored to match various stains. Paint-grade work is much more forgiving, since any filler will be completely covered. Painting also allows you to caulk areas where the trim is not flush to the wall or ceiling. Remember that oil-based paints work best on woodwork. Latex semigloss and enamel (glossy) are not as abrasion resistant as oil-based paints. This is especially important on window surfaces that are frequently subjected to moisture from the outdoors. Oil-based paint provides a tough, durable surface that's ideal for woodwork, and is available in four varieties: flat, eggshell, semigloss and gloss. It dries slowly to a very tough surface.

No matter which way you finish the trim, set all nail heads, apply some kind of filler—either spackling compound or wood filler—and lightly sand any blemishes with 220-grit sandpaper.

One way to sand intricate woodwork is to wrap a piece of sandpaper around a sponge. Sand the woodwork as you would normally—the sponge will take on the profile of curved sections.

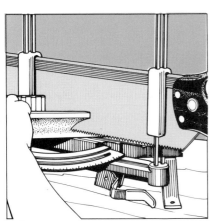

16 *Outside corner on ceiling molding requires closed miters. Keep in mind that top of molding is held away from saw fence.*

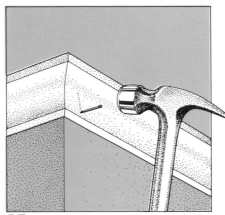

17 *Join outside corners with glue and 4d finishing nails. Nail as close to corner as possible but avoid nailing through miter.*

How to install
A TOWEL BAR

Degree of difficulty: Easy Estimated time: 1 hour Average cost of materials: $10

It often seems that where you want a towel bar is exactly where it's the most difficult to install. Rarely can you find wall studs—or other appropriate solid members—in the right position. And if you do attach it directly to your plaster or drywall, one quick tug can bring the whole thing crashing to the floor, leaving behind some unsightly holes that you'll have to repair.

Of course, this is a long-standing problem, one that various manufacturers have solved by creating quite an array of fasteners for handling the job. Three of the best are shown at the right: a clever plastic anchoring device called a toggler, a standard metal expansion bolt often referred to as a molly bolt, and the tried-and-true toggle bolt with its winged nut and standard machine screw.

Your choice of a fixture is usually determined by your taste. Any fixture can be installed anywhere. But common sense does dictate some preferences. For example, if you want a towel bar installed on ceramic tile, it's better to go with the adhesive-backed unit like the one shown in Figs. 1 through 4. Drilling through ceramic tile to install a dedicated fastener can be tricky—you risk breaking the wall tile. Another type of self-adhering towel bar fixture features peel-away tape that holds the unit to the wall. The one disadvantage of this variety is its inability to support heavy loads.

By far the more common problem is attaching towel bars to drywall or plaster

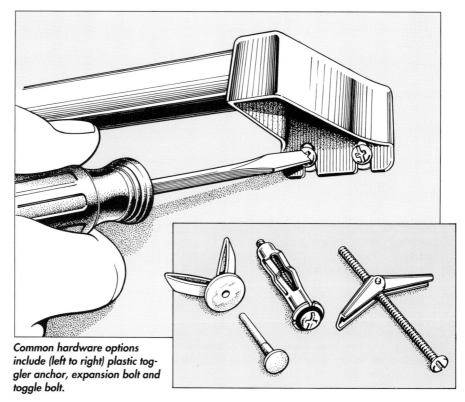

Common hardware options include (left to right) plastic toggler anchor, expansion bolt and toggle bolt.

walls. These hollow-wall applications, as they are called, require you to supply a piece of hardware that can be attached firmly to the wall. Then you simply hang your towel bar from this hardware. The principle employed by all such fasteners is basically the same: They are designed

to be inserted through the wall surface and then to expand on the other side for a strong grip that will withstand a reasonable amount of weight.

The metal expansion bolts shown in Figs. 7, 8 and 9 are sized according to the approximate thickness of your wallcov-

1 To install adhesive-backed holders on ceramic tile, first clean off all the residue from the surface using denatured alcohol.

2 Position the assembled towel bar on tile, level in place, then lightly mark an outline of the end brackets using a soft pencil.

3 Using your fingertip, apply water to the adhesive pads. Keep applying water and rubbing until the adhesive starts to thicken.

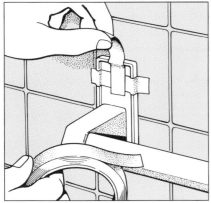

4 Press the end brackets inside the traced guidelines. Hold steady for 1 minute, then tape in place for 24 hours.

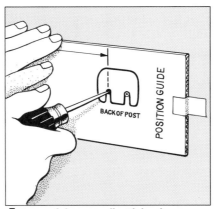

5 To attach bar to wall with hardware anchors, locate anchor holes using an awl and the template supplied with towel bar.

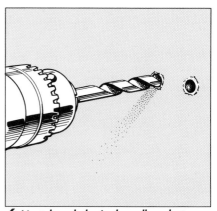

6 Next, bore holes in drywall or plaster using electric drill and drill bit sized to match the specific anchor you are using.

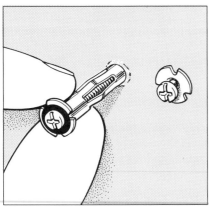

7 Slide expansion bolts into holes and press sharp ears on surface flange into drywall or plaster. Ears prevent screw from turning.

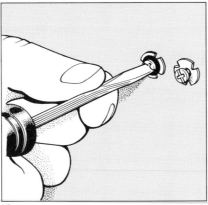

8 Turn screw heads clockwise until black indicator washer falls off. This signals that anchor is fully expanded and seated.

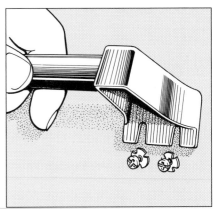

9 Once anchors are seated, turn out screws to accommodate bracket flange. Slide bracket over screws, then tighten screws securely.

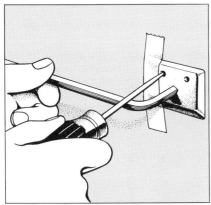

10 To hang bar on hollow-core door, as we did here, hold bar against door, level in place, then mark screw locations with awl.

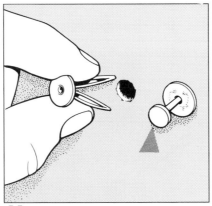

11 Bore proper-sized clearance holes in door and insert plastic anchor in holes. A separate push pin seats anchor.

12 Insert screws through holes In brackets, then thread screw tips into holes in anchors. Tighten screws until bracket is held securely.

ering and the amount of towel weight that needs to be support. Once the anchor is inserted into its hole, tightening the screw causes the side walls to expand outward and thus seat against the inside surface of the wallcovering. Once the anchor is seated in this way, the screw can then be removed.

The toggle bolt, on the other hand, is simply pushed into the wall, wings first. By tightening the screw, the wings are drawn against the inside surface of the wall. The one big drawback to this kind of anchor is that the screw cannot be removed once in place. If it is, the wings simply fall down behind the wall.

The toggler is also sized according to the thickness of the wall. To seat it, simply push it into a hole in the wall as shown in Fig. 11. Then push the set pin until the wings expand inside. Remove the pin and screw your towel bar into the plastic inserts, using self-tapping screws of the proper diameter and length.

How to regrout
CERAMIC TILE

Degree of difficulty: Easy **Estimated time:** 3 hours **Average cost of materials:** $25

Ceramic tile, whether on a bathroom wall or kitchen countertop, is a wonderful building material. It's durable, easy to wipe clean and comes in so many different styles and colors that it's a decorator's dream. It does, however, have one major drawback, namely the grout between the tiles.

Sooner or later these grout joints will deteriorate, becoming stained or cracked. This is particularly true on tub and shower walls, where the heavy exposure to water speeds the deterioration process.

Fortunately, replacing the grout is a pretty easy job and all the tools and materials required are available at most hardware stores and lumberyards. You'll need a bag of dry grout, a grout removal tool, and a rubber-faced trowel for applying the grout, plus a bucket for mixing the grout, a large sponge and a few clean burlap or terry cloth rags. In this job, we regrouted tub and shower walls, but the same basic techniques apply to regrouting any ceramic tile joints.

Where to begin

Start by turning off the shut-off valves below the floor that supply water to your tub or shower. Strictly speaking, you should be able to complete the job without shutting off these valves because there is no need to ever turn on the tub or shower faucet. But, if a faucet is turned on by accident when you are working, you could have quite a messy situation on your hands.

Next, remove the tub spout from the wall. Turn the spout counterclockwise using either slotted pliers or a pipe wrench (Fig. 1). Be sure to cover the jaws with masking tape to prevent damaging the chrome on the spout. Then remove the faucet handles, sleeves and escutcheons as shown in Figs. 2 and 3. Also remove the shower head and the escutcheon behind it that rests on the wall. By removing these fittings, you will have complete access to all the old grout.

Next, start scraping the old grout from the joints. The grout removal tool shown in Fig. 4 is a clever device. It fits comfortably in the hand and its blade is coated with carbide granules that do a great job of cleaning the joints. Remove the grout to a depth of at least ⅛ in. or until

Ceramic tile is durable, easy to clean and comes in a wide assortment of colors. Grout between tiles, however, gets old. Apply new grout with a rubber-faced trowel.

the old grout is no longer cracked or crumbling. This job will take some time—in this case several hours—but it is crucial for obtaining the best results.

Once you are done removing the grout, vacuum all the joints clean using a vacuum equipped with a crevice-cleaning tool and then wash the wall with a wet sponge. Dust and debris may cause new grout to bond poorly.

Now, mix your dry grout with water according to the directions on the bag. Apply the grout using a rubber-faced trowel as shown above. Spread the grout diagonally, across the surface of the tile, forcing it into the joints as you go. Work in sections no larger than 15 to 20 sq. ft. at a time. Otherwise, you run the risk of the grout hardening before you can remove the excess.

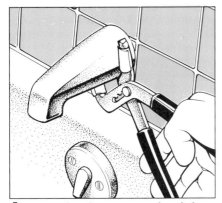

1 *Remove the tub spout using slotted pliers or a pipe wrench. Wrap masking tape around the jaws to protect the spout.*

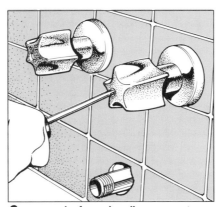

2 *Remove the faucet handle screws using a screwdriver. Some handles have a covering plate over a screw that must be pried off.*

3 *Remove the faucet escutcheon and sleeve by hand, turning counterclockwise. When stuck, use pliers or a pipe wrench.*

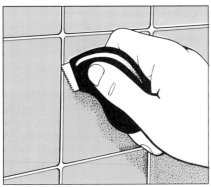

4 *Scrape the old grout from each joint using a grout removal tool. The tool has a blade that's coated with carbide granules.*

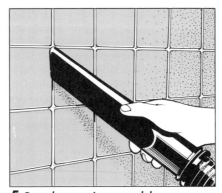

5 *Once the grout is removed, be sure to vacuum all dust from the joints. Dust and debris cause new grout to bond poorly.*

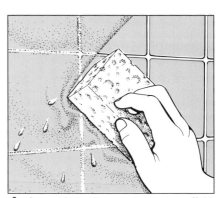

6 *After applying the new grout, wipe off the excess from the surface of the tiles using a wet sponge. Rinse the sponge often.*

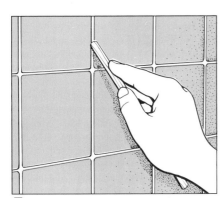

7 *Shape the fresh grout joints with a wet finger or a ¼ in.-dia. wood dowel. This will yield a uniform joint appearance.*

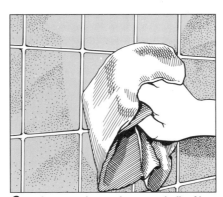

8 *As the grout dries, it leaves a chalky film on the tiles. Remove this film by rubbing the surface with burlap or terry cloth.*

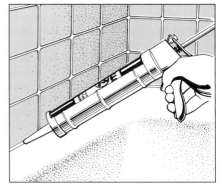

9 *After grout has cured overnight, apply silicone caulk where tiles abut the tub, and around spout, faucets and shower head.*

After you have applied the grout to the tiles, use the rubber trowel to remove excess grout. Then wash down the surface with a wet sponge. Do not rub so hard that you remove the grout from the joints, just clean the surface of the tile.

Next, smooth out all the grout joints using either your finger or a wood dowel as shown in Fig. 7. The finished grout joint should fall just below the surface of the tile, so it forms a very slight depres-

sion. After all the joints are shaped, let the grout dry for 15 to 20 minutes, or until a dry haze forms on the surface. Then buff the surface with burlap or terry cloth rags and you are done with the grouting. To finish up the job, just replace the fittings you removed earlier and apply a generous bead of caulk around the spout, faucets and the shower-head escutcheons. To ensure that the seam between the wall and the tub is watertight

and to allow for shrinkage, fill the tub with water and apply a generous bead of silicone caulk to the joint between the tiles and the tub. Allow the caulk to dry.

Finally, it's a good idea to damp-cure your new grout job. All this means is thoroughly wetting down the wall every 8 hours for two or three days. This step improves the bonding properties of your new grout and ensures that the repair will be long-lasting.

How to install
VINYL SHEET FLOORING

Degree of difficulty: Medium **Estimated time:** 6 hours **Average cost of materials:** $150

Vinyl sheet flooring is durable and able to stand up to a lot of wear and tear. It offers an easy-to-clean surface that is ideal for kitchens, bathrooms and playrooms. Often, the toughest part about installing vinyl flooring products is selecting a pattern and finish from the wide assortment available. Some manufacturers offer do-it-yourself kits which walk you through installation step-by-step.

They say that what goes up must come down. And, if it comes down inside your home, it comes down on the floor. This makes your floor one of the most abused components of the house. Not only is it expected to suffer dirty boots, high-heeled shoes and everyday spills and grime, it's expected to bounce back to its wonderful original appearance with a minimum of drudgery.

One answer to these demands is a vinyl floor covering. Vinyl flooring is durable, easy to maintain and comes in a wide variety of styles and colors. And, it's not that difficult to install. In fact, some manufacturers offer an installation kit that costs about $10 and is designed to take you through the process step-by-step. It includes paper for making full-size templates, markers and tape. If you buy the kit and flooring from the same manufacturer and you make a mistake, the manufacturer will replace the flooring and kit free of charge. There are some restrictions to this policy, however, so be sure to read the fine print.

About vinyl flooring

The decorative pattern on the flooring may be either printed on, or the result of colored pieces of vinyl inlaid in the backing layer. While both varieties have a durable wear layer on top (generally urethane), the inlaid variety is typically a better bet for use in halls and other high-traffic areas of the house.

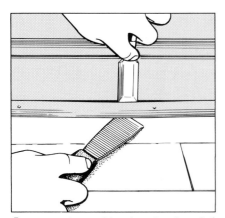

1 *Remove shoe molding from baseboard. If there isn't any, you can lay flooring to trim and conceal edge with new molding.*

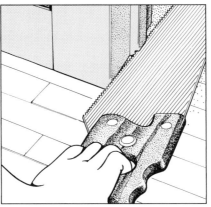

2 *Where required, trim casing and doorstop with a sharp handsaw so new underlayment and flooring can fit in neatly.*

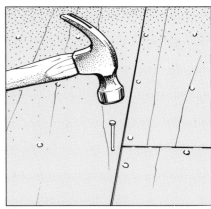

3 *Secure plywood underlayment with 4d ringed flooring nails. Space nails 3 in. apart at edges and 4 in. apart elsewhere.*

Today, most vinyl flooring products are called "no wax" floors. The tough top wear layers don't require the protection of wax to maintain their gloss. After a period of time, however, they may need an application of an acrylic floor dressing to restore their original appearance. There are exceptions. Some manufacturers claim that a power buffing is all that's necessary to revive a dull top layer in some of the coverings they make.

The floor-backing layer is a composite material that's made of mineral fibers and vinyl, and may vary from product to product. Most manufacturers offer a line of soft vinyl flooring that's appropriate for loose-lay installations. However, for heavy traffic, a permanent installation with a firm-back vinyl flooring is highly recommended.

Vinyl flooring is typically available in 6- and 12-ft. widths. The 6-ft. width is easier to handle but the 12-ft. width may enable you to cover your floor with few or no seams. It's always a good idea to discuss the plans for your project with your dealer to get the flooring product that best suits your installation requirements.

Surface preparation

Vinyl flooring can be installed over concrete, wood or an existing resilient floor. If your floor is concrete, first make sure it's clean and free of paint, oil and dust. Use a latex patching compound available at your flooring dealer to level any uneven spots before beginning the job.

To install vinyl flooring over a wooden subfloor, first make sure that the floor is firmly fastened to the joists. Rock back and forth over questionable areas to locate trouble spots and renail with 8d ringed flooring nails where necessary. Then, cover the floor with ¼-in. exterior-grade underlayment plywood, staggering the joints at the panel ends. Fasten the plywood with 4d ringed flooring nails. Space the nails 3 in. apart at the panel edges and 4 in. apart elsewhere.

Fill the joints with latex patching compound; sand when dry with 120-grit sandpaper and thoroughly vacuum up all dust.

If you intend to install new flooring over old, first check with your dealer to find the types suitable for this purpose. Use flooring nails to secure any loose areas and thoroughly remove all wax and

dirt with steel wool and an appropriate cleaning agent available from your dealer. Never sand a resilient floor as it may contain asbestos fibers that can be released into the air.

Finally, the flooring material and the room should be kept at 65° F. to 70° F. for two days prior to the installation.

Getting started

For our project, we installed a vinyl floor in a kitchen with a wood subfloor. To begin, remove all free-standing appliances from the room. If you have a gas range, call the gas company to have them disconnect it. If the gas range is built in, then have the gas company shut off the gas to avoid the danger of a pilot light igniting the fumes from the adhesive.

Next, remove any shoe molding from the baseboard with a flat pry bar or chisel (Fig. 1). Pull the nails through from the back side of the molding with locking pliers. This protects the exposed surface of the molding from damage so it can be reused later. If you don't have a shoe molding, then plan to lay the new floor to the edge of the baseboard. After it is in

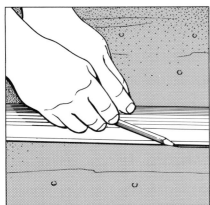

7 *Draw a line on the floor to indicate seam position. Measure from seam line to walls to double-check dimensions on drawing.*

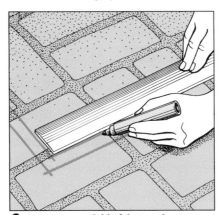

8 *Use a water-soluble felt-tipped pen to mark cutting lines on flooring. Mark rough cutlines 1½ in. outside finish cutlines.*

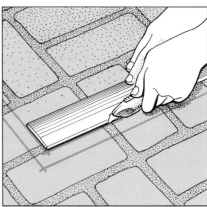

9 *Carefully cut flooring on rough cutlines with a linoleum knife or utility knife fitted with a sharp, linoleum-cutting blade.*

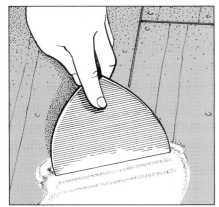

4 *Use a wide putty knife when applying latex patching compound to the seams in the plywood underlayment.*

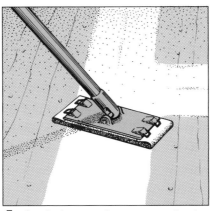

5 *After the latex patching compound is dry, sand with 120-grit sandpaper. Using a pole sander makes it quick and easy.*

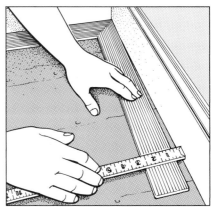

6 *Use a framing square and ruler to determine how far out of square the corners are. Record the information on your drawing.*

place, you can add the shoe molding to cover the edge of the vinyl. For floors with vinyl base trim, pry away the trim with a putty knife.

Making a scaled drawing

Use graph paper to make a scaled drawing of the floor showing doorways, closets, cabinets and walls. Make sure to double-check all measurements and note them on the drawing.

Because we used 6-ft.-wide flooring, our floor required one seam. If you must have a seam, plan to locate it in a place that minimizes waste.

Mark the finished height of the new floor on the casings and doorstops. This should include the thickness of the underlayment plywood plus the thickness of the vinyl flooring. Then, saw to the waste side of these lines with a handsaw to make room for the new floor (Fig. 2).

Install the plywood underlayment with 4d ringed flooring nails as described here (Fig. 3). Be sure to use exterior grade plywood to resist damage from water that may seep through the flooring. Then, fill the seams with latex patching compound,

sand with 120-grit sandpaper and vacuum the area (Figs. 4 and 5).

As you install the plywood, you'll find out just how square the walls are. Make note of these variances on your drawing so the vinyl will be cut accurately. You can measure the deviation from 90° by placing the short leg of a large steel square against one wall and in a corner.

Then, depending on whether the angle is lesser or greater than 90°, measure the width of the gap at one end of the long, 24 -in. leg of the square (Fig. 6). This represents the deviation from 90° over 24 in. Make a note of the deviation and transfer this information to your drawing.

If you're planning a seam, mark the floor to indicate the end of the first sheet (Fig. 7). Measure from the seam to the wall at several points and compare with your drawing to check the placement of the cutting lines.

Next, transfer the measurements from your drawing to the flooring material. Use a water-soluble felt-tipped pen and a straightedge ruler to accurately mark the exact cutting lines (Fig. 8). Plan for the finished seam to occur on a straight,

continuous line in the pattern but allow for a little excess on the waste side of the seam for trimming.

When marking the lines on the second piece, make sure that the pattern will line up along the seam. Allow for about 2 in. of overlap so the pattern can be aligned across the seam. Then, draw additional lines 1½ in. outside your finish cutlines. These are rough cutlines—the final trimming takes place with the material in position. Cut to the rough cutline with a linoleum knife or a utility knife fitted with a linoleum-cutting blade (Fig. 9).

Roll out the flooring and position the seam edge on the seam line. Let the excess flooring run up the walls. At any of the corners, make a diagonal cut from the exact cutline to the corner of the flooring so the material can relax against the wall (Fig. 10).

Double-check that the seam is properly positioned and have a helper stand on the flooring to make sure it doesn't shift by accident.

Then, press the flooring in place around the perimeter and trim to the finished cutline (Figs. 11 and 12). Leave a

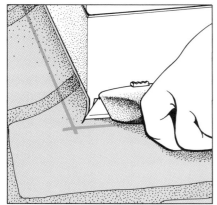

10 *After rolling out flooring and positioning correctly in relation to seam line, make diagonal relief cuts at all corners.*

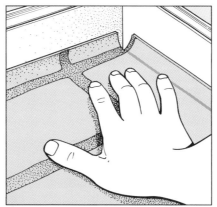

11 *Press vinyl flooring down into corners. Have a helper stand on the flooring to make sure that it doesn't shift.*

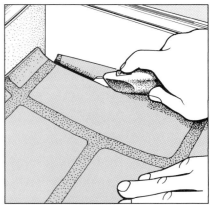

12 *Cut the flooring to the finish cutlines. Where it will be covered with shoe molding, leave a ⅛-in. space for expansion.*

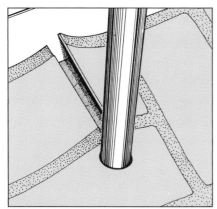

13 To fit around a pipe, cut an appropriate-size hole at the correct position. Then cut a straight line from edge to hole.

14 Spread adhesive with a finely notched trowel and stop 12 in. from seam. Avoid lumps which will show through flooring.

15 After installing both pieces with overlapping seam, use straightedge to cut seam along line in flooring pattern.

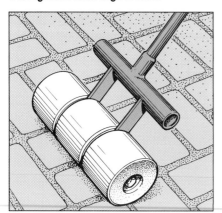

16 To firmly bed the flooring in the adhesive, use a 100-lb. roller that can be rented. Roll across floor in both directions.

Gluing it down

Your dealer will be able to tell you which adhesive is best suited for your particular floor. Some flooring can be stapled around the perimeter with ½-in. staples which will be concealed by the baseboard molding. Other types require a band of adhesive around the perimeter. Our flooring was set in adhesive over the entire floor surface.

To begin, reroll the flooring, pattern side in and set it aside. Then, apply the adhesive to the underlayment with a finely notched trowel as per manufacturer's instructions. Spread the adhesive as evenly as possible to avoid bumps that will show through. Stop the application about 12 in. away from the seam line (Fig. 14).

Carefully unroll the first piece of flooring onto the adhesive. Avoid sliding the material as this can cause lumps. Press down on the flooring as you go. Then, unroll the second piece, position the seam exactly, and press the flooring in place.

To cut the seam, place a straightedge along a continuous line in the pattern that's in the overlapped area of flooring. Cut through the two layers at once with

a utility knife. Avoid leaning the knife to one side or the other when making the seam cut (Fig. 15). Then, remove any waste and peel back the seam edges of the flooring.

Some manufacturers require a special seam adhesive. Apply the adhesive as evenly as possible with the notched trowel. Press both pieces into place and wipe away excess adhesive with a damp rag.

Next, roll the floor in two directions with a floor roller (Fig. 16). A 100-lb. roller can often be rented from the flooring dealer. Apply seam sealer to the seam, leaving a ⅛- to ¼-in.-wide bead on the surface (Fig. 17).

Finally, reinstall the shoe molding or baseboard and set the nails (Fig. 18). Where the new floor adjoins another floor, screw in metal trim strips to finish the seam (Fig. 19). Allow the adhesive to set for at least 24 hours before walking on the floor. Use pieces of plywood to protect the floor when you move heavy appliances back into place so you avoid putting any holes in the new flooring. Have the stove reconnected by your gas company, if necessary.

⅛-in. gap between the flooring and the baseboard or wall to allow for expansion. Then carefully fit the flooring material under the door moldings.

Unroll the second sheet of flooring, allowing it to overlap at the seam and position it for an exact pattern match. Trim to the finish cutlines in the same way as with the first sheet of flooring.

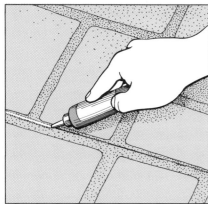

17 Apply seam sealer to seam. Use applicator provided and leave a ⅛- to ¼-in.-wide bead on the flooring surface.

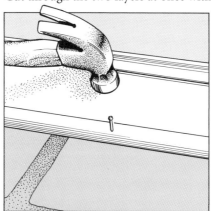

18 Replace the shoe molding by securing with 4d finishing nails. Then, set all nails below the surface with a nail set.

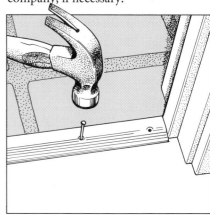

19 Where the new flooring joins another floor at doorways, nail a metal finish strip in place over the flooring edge.

How to install
SLATE FLOORING

| Degree of difficulty: Medium **Estimated time:** 10 hours **Average cost of materials:** $100 |

Slate flooring is an ideal choice for foyers and other areas subjected to frequent exposure to moisture. Once requiring special framing for installation, modern developments have made slate relatively easy and inexpensive for home remodelers intent on enhancing the style and function of flooring. Tile is spaced with small spacer blocks which match grout thickness.

In many ways, slate is the perfect material for a foyer floor. It's durable, easy to maintain and has an elegance that tastefully accents just about any adjacent floor material. While slate may not be suitable for some rooms in your house, because of its cold feel and unyielding surface, it is entirely appropriate for a foyer which is used primarily for entering and leaving the house and is often exposed to a great deal of moisture.

Traditional slate floors are set in concrete and the subfloors that support them must be lower than the surrounding floors to accommodate this extra thickness. The floor framing must also be

strong enough to carry the extra weight. Because of this, a traditional installation is a difficult and expensive remodeling proposition. Fortunately, today's slate floor tiles are available in a fairly uniform ¼-in. thickness and can be successfully installed over a standard wood or plywood floor using mastic instead of concrete. As such, slate becomes a relatively low-cost, high-quality floor option for home remodelers.

For this example, we installed slate in a foyer that was formerly covered with carpeting. We purchased the slate from a local stone and masonry dealer and it came in boxes which contained 10 sq. ft.

each. In addition to the slate, you'll also need the following to undertake this job: proper mastic, some latex grout, a ¼-in. notched trowel—to spread the mastic—and a flat-bottomed pointing trowel, called a Dresden trowel, to apply the grout. For a small area, like our 25-sq.-ft. foyer, these tools and materials cost less than $100.

Preparation
Proper floor preparation is the key to a successful slate installation. What's required depends on the type and condition of the flooring surface. In our case, we had to remove the shoe molding and

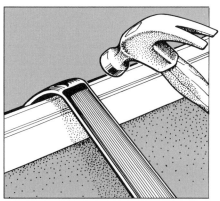

1 *Remove shoe molding and baseboard by driving pry bar behind one end of board, then moving along length of wall.*

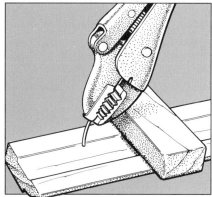

2 *To avoid damaging trim boards, pull out nails from back side using locking pliers and small wood block for leverage.*

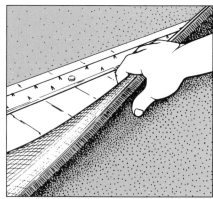

3 *To remove carpeting, cut it to line where slate will end using a sharp utility knife. Then pull it away from tack strip border.*

baseboard first, then cut the carpeting and pull it away from the tack strip as shown in Fig. 3.

To remove the shoe molding, insert a flat pry bar behind the piece at one end and carefully pry it away from the wall. Continue moving along the wall with the bar until the whole piece is free. Then pull out the finishing nails from the back side of the board using locking pliers and a small support block.

Once the shoe molding is removed, do the same for the baseboard. If you proceed carefully, you should be able to use the same trim after the slate is installed. Next, cut the carpet where you want the slate to begin with a sharp utility knife and straightedge guide. Then, pull the carpet off the tack strips and pry the tack strips off the floor.

At this point, inspect your existing subflooring for any potential problems. Keep in mind that the tiles are rigid and, therefore, any resilience in the floor below can cause trouble later on. The slate may crack if the floor gives a great deal, and if the floor moves just a little, the grout can fracture and break.

Problem solving

Your most common problem will be loose plywood or floorboards. These must be renailed with 8d common or box nails driven into the floor joists underneath. Another potential problem is material on the surface of the subfloor. For instance, if you don't have carpet but do have resilient floor tiles or linoleum, these will have to be removed and the adhesive underneath scraped away. This is a very time-consuming and annoying job. Also, if you have floorboards covered with paint or varnish, the finish must be removed by sanding with coarse-grit paper or scraping with a hand scraper.

For these reasons we recommend covering the existing floor with ¼-in.-thick underlayment plywood. The cost is minimal considering the square footage that's usually involved, and it's the best way to achieve a sound surface.

To install the underlayment, cut the plywood panel to size and then attach it with flooring nails driven in a 4- to 6-in.-sq. nailing pattern.

Sink the nail heads slightly below the surface of the plywood and then fill these

depressions with floor patching material. When the patching material is dry, sand it smooth using 100-grit paper, then vacuum all the dust from the floor. Wear a dust mask or respirator when sanding the patching material.

Keep in mind that most foyers are small and, therefore, a single sheet of plywood would cover the area without a seam. But if your area is larger, simply butt the adjoining panels together and nail along the seam in a slightly tighter pattern. Fill with patching material and sand smooth. Make sure that you stagger the seam so it doesn't fall directly over any seam in the subflooring material underneath.

In addition to a firm surface, you'll need to make sure that the structure of the floor will not flex. If it does after installing the slate, the grout between tiles will crack—allowing moisture to penetrate the plywood underlayment and the tiles to loosen.

Watch as a friend walks across the underlayment. Check to see if the floor gives under the weight. If the floor is rigid, you can proceed to the next step. But if it's bouncy, you'll have to strengthen the

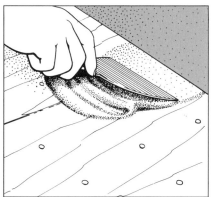

7 *Set nail heads below surface. Fill holes and seams with patching compound. Let dry and sand smooth with 100-grit paper.*

8 *Bottom edge of casing must be cut off to accommodate slate. Place tile against casing and scribe proper cutline on surface.*

9 *Cut casing board using a sharp handsaw. Make sure to keep blade parallel to floor and cut on waste side of scribed line.*

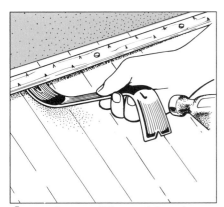

4 Pry tack strips off floor and discard. Resilient floor tiles and linoleum must also be removed to provide stable surface.

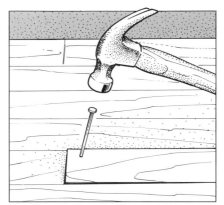

5 Be sure to renail any loose subfloor boards or sections of plywood subfloor panels. Use 8d common or box nails.

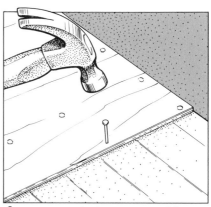

6 In most cases it's best to cover subfloor with underlayment plywood. Install with flooring nails driven in 4-in.-sq. pattern.

structure below. To do this, go into your basement and locate the floor framing under the foyer. In this case, plan to increase the strength of the floor by running blocking between the joists on 24-in. centers.

First, cut a block from the same size floor joist material to length, so that it fits snugly between two joists. Mark square lines on the side of the joists at the desired locations. Then nail through the joist into the blocks with 12d common nails. If it is impossible to nail through the joists, toenail the blocks in place with 10d common nails. Make sure to hold the blocks to the square lines and tight against the underside of the floor above.

Install blocks on 24-in. centers between all of the joists in the foyer. Secure the blocks with joist hangers. Then, nail down through the floor into the blocks with 8d common or box nails.

Your last preparation task is to cut off the bottoms of any door casings so the tile will fit underneath. First, place a piece of flooring next to the casing and scribe a line on the casing. At a doorway to an adjacent room, continue the line onto the

jamb, stopping at the doorstop. Cut the casing with a handsaw, making sure to keep the blade on the line's waste side.

Test to be sure the flooring will fit below the casing with 1/16 in. to spare—for the thickness of the mastic. Some fine cutting may later be involved but it's the best way to achieve a sound surface.

Layout

Begin by establishing the center point of the room. Measure the distance from one wall to the opposite wall at both ends of the room. Place a mark on the floor at the halfway point between the walls and make a similar mark on the floor at the other end of the room. Then strike a chalk line between your two marks and find the center of your line. Place one edge of a framing square on the chalk line at the center and mark a pencil line along the blade. Lengthen this line—from wall to wall—by snapping another chalk line perpendicular to the first one. Use your pencil mark as a guide.

With these reference lines in place, open a package of tile. Usually the manufacturer will supply a drawing of a ran-

dom pattern. We followed their suggestions, but feel free to create a pattern of your own. Keep in mind that traditional methods call for grout lines that are 3/8 to 1/2 in. wide, though you can reduce or enlarge this spacing for special effects. Scatter tiles of a different color to maintain a random appearance.

To achieve your final layout, cut small wood spacer blocks that match the thickness of the grout joint you prefer. We used 3/8-in.-wide joints.

Beginning at the reference lines, lay the tiles across the floor in both directions. Slide the wood spacers between the tiles to maintain straight, even grout lines. Adjust the tiles as necessary to make the borders as uniform as possible. Once all the full tiles are in place and you like the pattern, measure the pieces that are required to fill in the floor. Cut the tiles with a circular saw and masonry cutting blade, being sure to wear goggles and a respirator, as the dust from the slate is noxious. If you can, do all of your cutting outdoors. Otherwise, open windows and doors adjacent to the area where you are working.

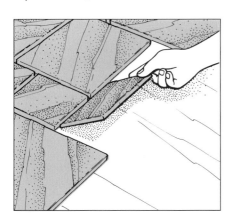

10 Lay out tiles on dry floor to match manufacturer's pattern or one of your choice. Be sure to balance perimeter tiles.

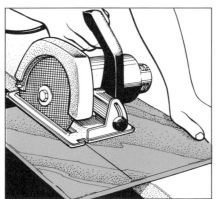

11 Use a circular saw and masonry blade to cut perimeter tiles. Be sure to wear eye protection and respirator while cutting.

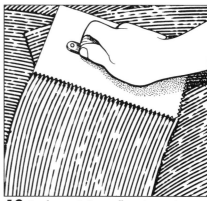

12 Apply mastic in small sections using notched trowel held at 45° angle. Use a sweeping motion to get best coverage.

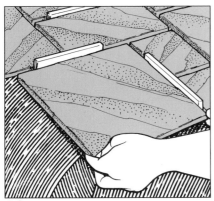

13 Set tile into mastic and press into place with slight twist. Use wood spacer blocks to maintain uniform grout spacing.

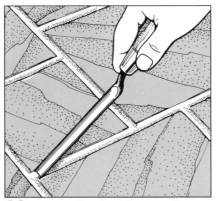

14 Let mastic dry, then fill joints with grout using pointing trowel. When voids are filled, smooth surface with trowel.

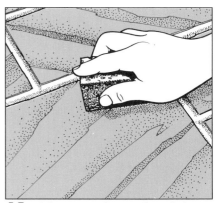

15 While grouting, keep surface of tiles clean. Wipe with damp sponge to prevent grout from hardening on surface.

When satisfied with the fit of all tiles, pick them up and lay them out in the same pattern in an adjacent room. By doing this, you can avoid searching for the tile you want after you've applied the mastic to the floor.

Mastic

Begin in one corner, spreading the mastic in a 2- to 3-ft.-sq. section. Hold a ¼-in. notched trowel at a 45° angle to the floor, and work the mastic onto the floor with a sweeping motion. Press the appropriate tiles firmly into the mastic with a slight twisting motion. Place your spacer blocks between the tiles to maintain straight and even grout lines, and remove them once the tiles are down. Work backward toward an open room or doorway to avoid kneeling on the tiles. Continue spreading the mastic and installing tile until everything is properly in place. Allow the tiles to set for 24 hours before continuing the job.

Grout

Begin by cleaning all joints and the surface of the slate with a damp cloth. Then, read the mixing directions on the grout container. Keep in mind that the Building Stone Institute recommends the use of a latex grout for slate floors. Slowly add water to the grout while mixing until it obtains the texture of damp sand. Then carefully begin working the grout into the spaces between the tiles with your flat pointing trowel. Be sure to fill all of the spaces completely, then smooth the surface of the grout with the trowel. As you work, clean the grout from the adjacent slate surfaces with a sponge and clean water. Change the water often and rinse the sponge frequently.

Be sure to clean the tile as you go, before the grout has a chance to dry. If the grout dries on the slate you can only remove it by washing the surface with an acid bath, so try and avoid this step if you can. Be familiar with the open time of the grout and mix only a usable amount.

After the grout is dry to the touch, sprinkle sawdust over the tile. Then rub the surface briskly—in a circular motion—with a clean burlap cloth. Let the joints harden for at least three days before you attempt to walk on the floor.

At this point, wash the floor again with clean water and wipe it dry with an absorbent cloth. If you still have grout stains on the floor, you will probably have to resort to the acid bath.

Acid bath

Begin by saturating the joints with water to prevent the acid from penetrating the grout. Then, mix one part muriatic acid to nine parts water. Be sure to wear rubber gloves, goggles and a long-sleeved shirt for this whole operation so you don't get burned. If acid should accidently splash on exposed skin, rinse the affected area immediately under a stream of water from a tap or garden hose.

Wash the surface of the slate thoroughly, but don't work the solution into the grout. After the floor is clean, wash the floor several times with clean water to neutralize the acid.

It is not necessary to seal the slate, but many people choose to apply a chemical sealer at this point to help protect the grout from stains. Chemical sealers are available in matte or gloss finish and are easy to apply. Follow label instructions for the brand you buy.

Simply allow the floor to cure for 30 days, then apply the sealer to a clean floor with a large cloth or paintbrush. First, apply a thin, uniform coat and let the floor dry for 2 hours before adding a second coat. To avoid leaving marks, be sure to stay off the floor for a full 24 hours after applying the second coat.

When everything is dry, reinstall the baseboard and shoe molding. Set the nail heads, fill the holes and touch up all marked surfaces with paint. Because we were replacing carpet, we had to add a metal trim strip between the remaining carpet and the new slate floor. These inexpensive trim strips are available in a variety of colors and styles at stores that sell carpets and floor coverings.

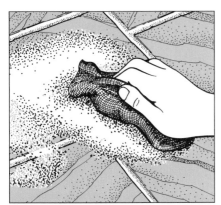

16 When grout is dry to touch, sprinkle sawdust on tile and rub with burlap cloth. This removes residue from grouting job.

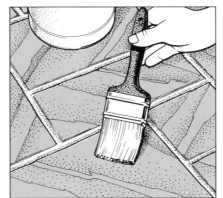

17 If you want to seal the floor, wait 30 days, then brush on a thin coat of commercial sealer. Let dry and apply second coat.

How to carpet
A STAIRWAY

Degree of difficulty: Medium   Estimated time: 5 hours   Average cost of materials: $80

Applying new carpeting to a stairway is a simple way to freshen up your home's interior appearance. First remove any old nails or tacks that may remain after pulling off the old carpeting. You can use a continuous runner or several pieces of new carpeting, but keep in mind that the pile on each piece should always lay facing toward the bottom of the stairs so that the carpeting doesn't suffer from excessive wear.

There are lots of good reasons for carpeting a stairway. Stairs leading directly from a living room or central hallway can look more attractive and inviting when carpeted. And a carpeted stairway will also quiet your home, not only by softening footsteps, but by partially absorbing sound waves passing from one floor to the other. Carpeted stairs are safer, too, lessening your chances of slipping and falling.

It's easier to carpet a stairway than a large room. There's no need to stretch a cumbersome expanse of carpeting into place, and it's easier to measure and make adjustments in position. Also, there are no tricky seams to join.

Avoid using utility-grade carpeting. Stairways get heavy wear, especially along the tread nosing. Choose an easy-to-clean variety with a dense pile. Carpet with attached cushion backing is cheaper and easier to put down, but isn't recom-

mended for stairways. For this reason, we are describing the installation of a conventional carpeting—with a jute backing—placed over separate sponge or felt padding.

Since you'll require a long, narrow runner, you may be able to buy remnants of high-quality carpeting for considerably less than the going rate for a room-size piece. It isn't necessary for the runner to be in one, continuous length. Two or more sections can be used, placing the seam under the tread nosing where it will be unnoticeable.

Whether you use a continuous runner or several pieces, keep in mind when purchasing the carpet that the pile on each piece should always lay facing toward the bottom of the stairs. Both ascending and descending, the pressure of your foot is mostly toward the tread nosing, so unless the pile faces the same way, wear will be excessive—perhaps as much as doubled.

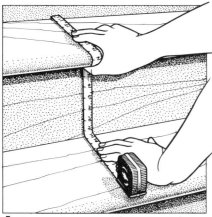

1 *Measure step around the nosing to bottom of riser. Multiply by number of steps to find runner length. Allow extra if runner pieces will be joined under nosing.*

You can determine the direction of the pile simply by running the palm of your hand lightly across the carpet surface.

Which installation method?

The most common method for carpeting stairs—and the one we describe in this example—applies to a stairway that has one closed side wall and open balusters at the other side. Both edges of the carpeting are rolled under and tacked in place, with the rolled edges either set back 1 to 3 in. from the wall and balusters, or butted directly against them. The illustrations in this example show the carpeting set 1 in. from the wall and balusters, with a 1¼-in. roll-under at the edges.

However, if your carpeting is a type that will not unravel, you can butt the uncut edge directly against the side wall without roll-under. In fact, with this type of carpeting, you are able to butt both cut edges in a stairway that's enclosed within two walls.

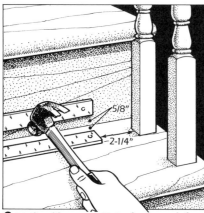

2 *Nail tackless strips ⅝ in. from crotch for carpet of average thickness. Setback of 2 ¼ in. allows 1 ¼-in. roll-under and 1-in. space between carpet and baluster.*

5/8"

2-1/4"

3 *Cut padding the same width as tackless strip. Staple first to back of tread against strip; pull padding tight and staple under nosing, then at bottom of riser.*

Our method calls for wrapping the carpeting tightly around the tread nosing. Another method—called a waterfall

4 *Cut carpet 2½ in. wider than finished width. Score the length of the runner 1¼ in. from each edge using a straightedge and awl. Fold carpet over and press flat.*

installation—allows the carpet to fall directly from the leading edge of the nosing to the crotch below where the tread and riser join. While this method is simpler, we consider it less desirable from a safety standpoint and less attractive, especially if one side of the stairway is open to view. Still another method, known as cap and band installation, is illustrated on Page 142.

Measuring the stairway

Determine the total length of the runner by measuring one tread and one riser, wrapping the tape measure around the nosing as shown in Fig. 1. Add 1 in. to allow for the thickness of the padding that will wrap around the nosing. Then multiply this amount by the number of steps making up the stairway. Remember that you will have to allow for additional carpeting if your runner will consist of two or more sections, since each section must adjoin under a tread nosing.

To calculate the required carpet width, measure the distance from the wall to the base of the balusters, or whatever portion of the step you will be covering. Add 2½ in. for rolling the edges under—1¼ in. for each side. Since you will probably need to trim at least one edge along the runner's length, allow an additional inch for this. If the carpeting you purchase has irregularly cut edges, make sure you will have enough carpeting to trim a straight line for the entire length of the piece.

A stairway that includes a landing is measured as though the landing were a deep step. Ideally, you will want to cover the landing and the first riser above it in one piece. However, if this won't work with the carpet dimensions, include this first riser in the runner with the steps above it.

Winder steps—wedge-shaped steps that turn a corner—will require carpeting approximately 50 percent wider than your runner and will produce considerable waste. This is because each step and the riser above it must be covered with a separate piece. For the sake of appearance, carpet life and safety under foot, the pile on each step should be at right angles to the nosing and facing downstairs.

Preparing the stairs

If your stairs have been previously carpeted, remove old nails or tacks that may

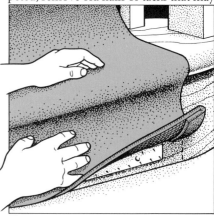

5 *Secure bottom edge of runner to tackless strip on first riser, butted flush against the floor. Place three carpet tacks through each doubled-over edge into riser.*

remain. Check treads and risers and secure any that are loose using 8d finishing nails and glue. If you don't plan to carpet the entire width of the stairway, you may want to refinish those portions of treads and risers that will be exposed, sanding and coating them with either a natural or hard-wearing finish coating. Remove any quarter-round or other molding nailed against the wall, in the crotch or under the nosing.

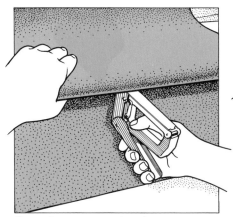

6 *Snugly press carpet into the corner against underside of the nosing and staple into bottom of the tread. Start from center of stair and work toward each side.*

Mounting tackless strip

Our installation shows the use of tackless strips to secure the carpeting in place. These are ¼-in.-thick by 1-in.-wide lengths of plywood with pins protruding from the face at a 60° angle. The strips are installed with the pins pointing against the pull of the taut carpeting.

If you plan to roll under both edges of the carpet 1¼ in., cut the tackless strip 2½ in. shorter than the finished width of the runner. Nail one strip to the riser, ⅝ in. above the tread with the pins pointing down. Nail another strip to the tread, ⅝ in. from the riser with the pins pointing back.

The ⅝-in. dimension will produce a tight, secure angle at the crotch with carpeting of average thickness. But before nailing all the strips in place, test-fit a piece of carpeting at the crotch as shown in Figs. 7 and 8. If your carpet is either thicker or thinner than average, you may have to increase or decrease the ⅝-in. dimension slightly. When you're satisfied with the crotch fit, nail all the strips in place, including one at the bottom of the first riser.

Installing padding

Cut the padding to the same width as the tackless strips. Then measure the distance from the strip on the tread, around the nosing, to the strip on the riser. Cut each piece of padding about ½ in. undersize, since it will stretch as you pull it tight.

If you are using felt padding, the waffled side should face outward. With sponge-rubber padding, the fabric webbing should face outward. Staple the padding to the tread, then under the nosing and then to the riser. A bit of space remaining between the bottom edge of the padding and the tackless strip on the riser is nothing to worry about.

7 *Work carpet tight around nosing, then into space between strips using a blunt cold chisel. Keep equal space between carpet edges and the wall and balusters.*

Cutting and rolling edges

Lay the runner out flat in order to cut it to width. Carpet with a looped pile, that is, with adjacent strands joined at the tops should be cut from the face side. Cut-pile carpeting, where all the strands are unjoined at the tops, is cut from the backing side. Make pencil marks or small cuts at the width required, allowing for roll-under. Then, place a straightedge—a long, straight board will do—on the marks and

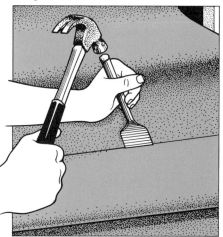

8 *Drive the carpet into the crotch with the cold chisel to tighten carpet and secure it to tackless strips. Start from the center of the crotch and work toward each side.*

cut the carpet with a sharp utility knife. If you are cutting from the face side, separate the pile and cut between the rows of loops.

With the carpet face down, pencil-mark 1¼ in. back from both edges for the roll-under. Place the straightedge on the marks and score the jute backing with a sharp awl. Your scored lines should form a substantial depression in the backing, but be careful not to cut all the way

through. Fold the edges back on the scored lines and walk them flat.

Installing the carpet

Spread the runner up the stairway, keeping the edges rolled under. Secure the bottom edge to the tackless strip on the first riser and pull it onto the pins. Press the carpeting against the riser and be sure to work it snugly into the joint under the nosing. Staple the carpet to the underside of the nosing, starting from the center of the runner and working outward.

To attach the carpeting securely through the padding and into the tread, which is probably hardwood, you'll need a heavy-duty stapler. Most electric staplers won't do the job. You can rent an industrial-grade stapler, electric or hand operated, either from your carpet supplier or a tool rental outlet for a reasonable price. Make sure the stapler is capable of driving a ⁹⁄₁₆-in. staple all the way home into hardwood.

Caution: Before using the stapler, read the instructions accompanying it for specific safety instructions and correct usage. Power staplers can be dangerous if used carelessly.

After the carpet has been stapled under the first tread, drive ½-in. carpet tacks at the lower left-hand and lower right-hand corners, through the roll-under, into the riser bottom, as shown in Fig. 9. Place two additional tacks into the riser along both of the rolled-under edges.

Work the carpeting tightly around the nosing and against the tread surface with your left hand. With your right hand, press the carpet into the crotch using a wide, blunt cold chisel. Work from the center of the crotch toward each side, making sure the rolled-under edge remains equidistant from the balusters and the wall. Then force the carpeting into the crotch with the chisel and a

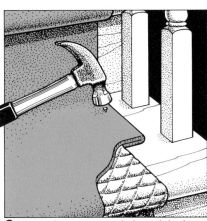

9 *Place a long carpet tack through both doubled-over edges into the crotch, and drive them home with a nail set. Drive two tacks into treads at each edge.*

141

hammer. This will pull the carpet tight across the tread and secure it to both tackless strips. Drive 1-in. carpet tacks into the crotch through the roll-under at each side and set these tacks with a nail set. Use a hammer to drive two ½-in. tacks through the rolled-under edges into the surface of the tread.

Continue up each stair following the same method. When you reach the top, extend the carpeting up the last riser and staple it at the top of this riser.

Cap and band stair carpeting

You may wish to wrap carpeting completely around your stair treads either for the full length of the stairway, or on just the first two or three steps that are exposed on an otherwise enclosed stairway. This method is called cap and band installation—the cap being the tread covering and the band a separate piece applied to the riser. You can, if you wish, cut the tread carpeting to fit around balusters. Start the installation procedure from the top riser. Use tackless strips on the treads, but not on the risers. Cut padding to the full height of the risers and staple it in place, 1¼ in. back from the risers' open sides. Cut carpeting to full riser height and 1¼ in. wider for roll-under at the open side. Score the carpeting with an awl and straightedge, 1¼ in. back from the edge, and fold flat. Staple the carpet to the riser along the top and bottom edges, and secure the rolled-under edge with three ½-in. carpet tacks. Secure tackless strip to the treads, ⅝ in. from the crotch. Measure and cut padding to fit against the tackless strip and around all the exposed nosing. Then use an industrial-grade stapler to staple the padding at the back and under the nosing,

cutting miters at the corners. Measure and cut the tread carpet pieces and secure them to the tackless strip. Miter the corners, then staple the carpeting under the nosing.

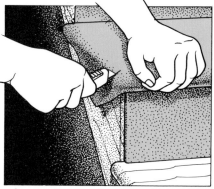

After riser is covered, secure tackless strip and padding to the tread below. Cut carpeting to size and attach it to the tackless strip. Make diagonal cuts at corners.

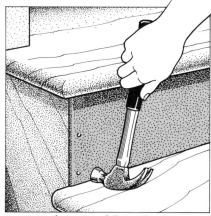

Cut carpet for riser to full riser height. Score carpet at end of riser, and fold against edge of padding. Staple at top and bottom of riser, and tack rolled-under edge.

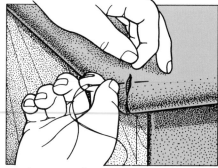

Staple carpet to bottom of tread under all exposed nosing. Sew miters at front and back corners with large needle and heavy thread that matches carpet color.

Reviving a worn runner

Stairway carpeting usually shows its first signs of wear along the leading edges of the treads. Carpet people call it "grinning." If your stairway is beginning to grin at you, and if the runner is of one piece, you may be able to revive it. Remove the runner, then shift it toward the bottom of the stairway approximately 2 in., enough to reposition the worn areas so they are out of sight under the nosing of the treads and at the top of the risers. Reinstall the carpeting as described on the previous pages. It will now be too short to reach the nosing of the floor above, so leave the top riser uncarpeted, or install a matching piece.

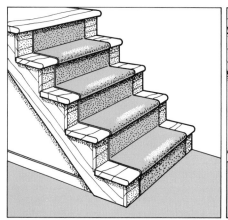
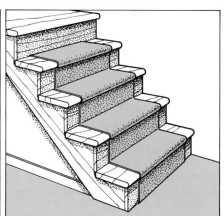

Make the wear disappear from tread edges of a one-piece stair runner. Shift the entire length of carpeting toward the bottom of the stairway so worn areas are under nosing.

How to install
A FOLDING STAIRWAY

Degree of difficulty: **Hard**   Estimated time: 8 to 12 hours   **Average cost of materials:** $250

A folding stairway can alleviate the problem of limited access to usable storage space in an attic. Several manufacturers offer ready-made folding stairways which can be fitted into a hallway ceiling. They are made from both wood and aluminum, or a combination of these materials. Installation is a two-person job, so enlist a friend to help with putting up the stairway.

Perhaps you're fortunate enough to live in an older home that's complete with a full staircase to the attic. If so, you've probably found that the attic is a great place to store seasonal items and memorabilia. Home owners without easy access to the attic either don't use the space, or are forced to haul out a stepladder when necessary.

However, there is an alternative. A folding attic stairway allows you convenient access to this otherwise unused space without compromising the floor plan below. All that's needed for the job are a few basic tools, some framing lumber and a friend to help out downstairs when you're working up in the attic.

Remember that the ceiling framework in most homes without attic access was designed primarily to support the ceiling only. If you plan to use this space for heavy storage, make sure you place these items above a partition or a load-bearing wall for support.

For our project we installed a pre-made folding stairway. The particular unit used in this example accommodates ceilings up to 105 in. high and fits a rough opening of 22x54 in. While our choice was a stairway with wooden treads and stringers, similar-working units with aluminum stringers and all-aluminum models are available too.

Laying out the opening

The first step in a folding stairway installation project is to inspect the spacing, direction and size of the ceiling joists. Our ceiling was framed with 2x6 joists on 16-in. centers and the stairway unit was to lie parallel with the joists. We only needed to cut away one joist to achieve the required 22-in.-wide rough opening. Installing a folding stairway at right angles to the joists involves a similar operation, but more joists will have to be cut and the framing will be more involved.

When considering the placement of your stairway, keep in mind that besides providing space on the floor below for unfolding the stairs and moving around the unit, you'll need headroom at the top of the stairs.

Once you've decided where the stairway is to be placed, climb into the attic to remove any insulation over and around the intended opening. Remember that the ceiling itself will not support your weight. Step only on the joists. After removing the insulation, tack-nail wide boards or ¾-in. plywood on the joists around the area where you'll be working.

If possible, plan to use an existing joist as one side of the rough opening framework. You'll need to find the position of this joist and mark it on the ceiling of the floor below. Install a ³⁄₁₆-in.-dia. bit in a drill and bore test holes through the ceiling in the rough opening area to locate the joist. Use a straightedge to clearly mark the joist line on the ceiling. Then, lay out the rough opening with a framing square and straightedge.

The term "rough opening" refers to a size ½ in. wider and longer than the unit to be fit. This allows for small errors in laying out and squaring the framework and requires that shims be fit between the unit and the framework before fastening is begun. It's a good idea to double-check the actual size of the folding stairway case to make sure it will actually fit the specified opening.

With the rough opening marked, bore ³⁄₁₆-in.-dia. holes at each corner so you'll be able to find the defined area in the attic.

Framing the ceiling

In any situation where you find that you have to cut through ceiling joists, you'll need to prepare temporary support partitions to carry their load before they're cut. Starting at one end, cut two pieces of 2x4 to a length that spans the two joists on

1 Completed framing includes headers for supporting the cut joist and a trimming joist placed at width of rough opening. Components are joined with metal hangers and nails.

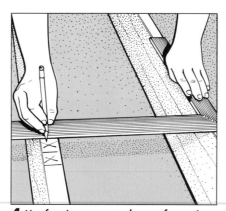

4 Use framing square to lay out for cutting joist. Actual cutline is 3 in. outside rough opening to allow for doubled header.

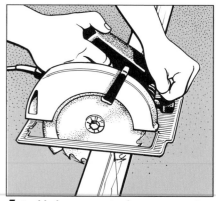

5 Set blade on your circular saw to maximum depth and cut the joist on inside of the line at each end of the opening.

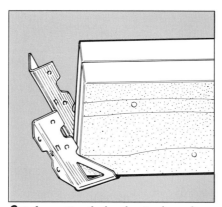

8 Before setting the headers in place, slip double joist hangers on the header ends for fastening to the ceiling joists.

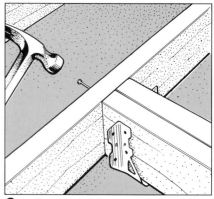

9 Replace headers between joists and nail through to header ends. Install nails in hangers and toenail with 10d nails.

each side of the opening. These serve as a top and bottom plate for the temporary support partition. Then, cut three studs so the combined height of the plates and studs equals the ceiling height. Nail the top plate to the stud ends with 16d common nails. Lift up the top plate and studs so the plate is positioned about 3 to 4 in. away from the opening. Wedge the bot-

tom plate under the studs and tap the assembly in place so that it's plumb. Then, toenail the studs to the bottom plate. After the first partition is in place, install another at the other end of the opening in the same way.

With the temporary supports in place, climb back in the attic and use the holes bored at the layout corners to mark the

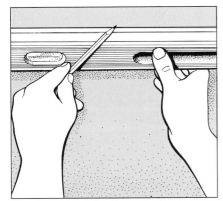

2 *Use a 4-ft. level or long straightedge to mark the side of the rough opening that is aligned with the ceiling joist in the attic.*

3 *Prior to cutting the center joist, erect temporary 2x4 support partitions about 3 in. away from each rough opening end.*

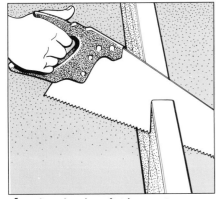

6 *A sharp handsaw finishes cut. Because the cutline is outside the rough opening, make sure you don't cut through ceiling.*

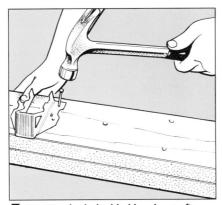

7 *Construct both doubled headers to fit between the joists and install metal hangers to support the ends of the cut joist.*

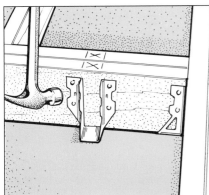

10 *Mark position of trimming joist so its inside face is on the rough opening line. Then, install support hangers on headers.*

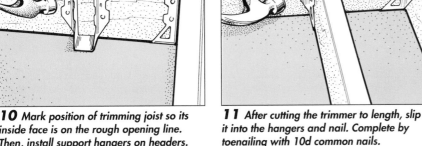

11 *After cutting the trimmer to length, slip it into the hangers and nail. Complete by toenailing with 10d common nails.*

rough opening. Carry the marks squarely up the side of the joist faces and across their top edges. Double-check to be sure your marks are square and properly dimensioned. The section of the joist that runs through the rough opening must be removed and the cut ends supported with headers made of doubled joist stock. To find the correct cutting lines, add 3 in. to the

layout marks at each rough opening end on the joist to be removed. This allows for the thickness of the doubled 2x6. Mark a square line down the face of the joist at these points.

To cut the joist, first set your circular saw blade to maximum depth and carefully cut on the inside edge of each cutoff line. Caution: Carefully read the instruc-

tions that come with your circular saw for safety information and the proper way to use the saw. Wear eye protection to prevent debris from the sawed wood from coming in contact with your eyes. Connect the saw (and all power tools) to a circuit protected by a ground-fault circuit interrupter.

After you have used the circular saw to cut the 2x6 joist, complete each cut with a small handsaw. Try to keep the handsaw from cutting through the ceiling when doing this.

This is a difficult operation especially if the joists are closely spaced. If you do go through the ceiling, simply patch the hole after the stairway is installed. A carefully handled reciprocating saw can also be used for this job. Take the same precautions as for the circular saw if you use a reciprocating saw.

After the cuts are made, remove the joist section and measure the distance between the outer joists at each end of the opening. Cut new joist stock exactly to length for the doubled headers at each end and nail together with 12d common nails. It is important to make sure the ends and edges are flush.

Mark the positions of the cutoff joist ends on the headers and lay out a square line at the mark to indicate the metal hanger placement. Then, install the hangers that support the joist ends. Slip double joist hangers on each end of the headers, but don't nail them in yet. Slide the headers in place and squarely align them with the layout marks and flush with the existing joists. Then, secure them with 16d nails driven through the joists into the header ends. Install hanger nails or 1½-in. roofing nails in the hangers and toenail with 10d common nails.

Because the rough opening is narrower than the width that is left between the remaining joists, the completed framing will include a section called a trimming joist that spans the headers and serves as a long edge of the rough opening frame.

The opening layout indicates the position of the trimming joist. Carry the mark squarely up on the header faces and install hangers to carry the trimming joist. Then, nail the trimming joist in place.

After the framing is completed, you're ready to remove the ceiling. With a helper below to catch the cutout section, cut around the opening with a compass or keyhole saw. Then move downstairs and nail the ceiling around the rough opening to the new framework.

Installing the stairway
First tip the stairway on its side, lift it through the opening into the attic and set it aside. Then install temporary ledgers

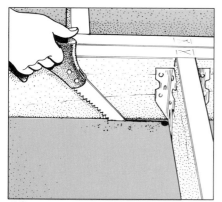

12 *Have a helper on hand in room below when cutting opening with a saw. Then nail the ceiling to the new frame.*

13 *Install temporary ledgers to support folding stairway while it's being attached. Double-headed nails permit easy removal.*

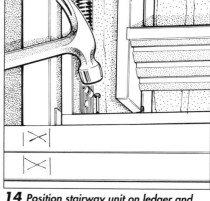

14 *Position stairway unit on ledger and use 8d nails to temporarily secure fixed end. Use shims to square unit, if necessary.*

on both ends of the opening to support the stairway case while it's being positioned and fastened. The unit we installed required the hinge-end ledger to extend ½ in. into the opening and the ledger on the opposite end to extend in ⅞ in. Use 2x4 stock for the ledgers and secure with 16d common nails.

Set the stairway into the opening and let it rest on the ledgers. With the unit still folded, place shims between the stairway case and the headers to straighten and square the unit. Check that the unit is absolutely level and temporarily nail the case ends to the headers with 8d common nails. Leave the nail heads exposed for easy removal.

Have your helper fold the midsection of the stairway down but keep the bottom section folded back. Then bore pilot holes to prevent splitting, and nail through the stairway case to the headers with 16d common nails. Nail through the holes provided in the hinges and complete the fastening by spacing nails 16 in. apart around the entire case. Be sure there's a shim to fill the space between the case and framework where you nail.

Cutting to length

With the unit still partially unfolded, place some weight on the stairs so you're sure the hardware is fully extended. Lay a straightedge along the top of one stringer and slide it down until it touches the floor. Mark the length on the straightedge. Then, line up the straightedge with the back of the stringer, extend it to the floor and mark that length.

Repeat the procedure on the other stringer to ensure that the legs will seat firmly on the floor even if it's not perfectly flat.

Fold the staircase up so you can mark and cut the lengths on the bottom stringers. Unfold the stairway and have your helper stand on the second or third

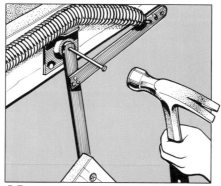

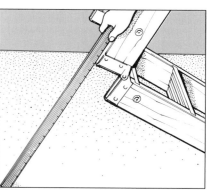

15 *When unit is square and level, drive nails through all appropriate locations. Prebore the holes to prevent splitting.*

16 *Open stair midsection while keeping lower section folded. Use straightedge to measure cutoff length of lower section.*

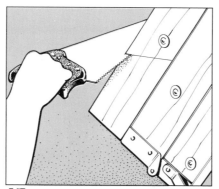

17 *Transfer length to lower section and mark cutoff line. Saw each stringer to the waste side of the line with a handsaw.*

18 *Cut mitered trim for opening and attach to the stair casing with 4d finishing nails and to the headers with 6d nails.*

tread. Check that the stairway sections form a straight line and there are no uneven gaps between them.

Complete the stairway installation by first removing ledgers and temporary support partitions. Install mitered case molding around the opening, leaving a ³⁄₁₆-in. reveal between the stairway case and the molding edge. Use 4d finishing nails to attach the molding to the case, and 6d nails to attach the molding to the frame-

work. Use a nail set to sink the nails, sand with 120-grit sandpaper and prime.

Finally, fill the nail holes with spackling compound or wood filler and paint. Latex paint can be used but oil-based paint works best on woodwork. It dries slowly to a hard surface and comes in four levels of gloss: flat, eggshell, semigloss, and gloss. Patch any damage to the ceiling by following the directions for repairing holes in drywall on Page 111.

DOORS & WINDOWS 4

How to strip
WOODWORK

Degree of difficulty: Hard   Estimated time: 20 hours   Average cost of materials: $75

Of the three methods for stripping woodwork, using chemicals is often the preferred one. However, stripping can also be accomplished using heat and belt sanders. Whatever the method, wear a respirator fitted with appropriate vapor filters, a long-sleeved shirt and gloves.

Removing old paint from woodwork is certainly one of the most time-consuming—and aggravating—tasks anyone can undertake. Of course, the rewards are great, too, especially if you are working on a classic home where the elaborate architectural details have disappeared after years of careless repainting. The crispness of line and subtlety of design are nothing but blurs, only a hint of what they used to be.

There are many different ways to approach this job and you should consider your alternatives carefully before going ahead. You should also factor in how much time you have available, how

much money and how much patience. All of these, of course, depend on the size of the job.

If you are involved in restoring an old house and want to strip all the woodwork bare so it can be covered with stain or a clear finish, you are looking at an incredible amount of work. And the expense is no small matter. Buying chemical remover gallon after gallon for a job like this can break just about anyone's budget. For these reasons, most people will opt for removing all the trim, pulling out the nails from the back side and sending it all to a commercial stripper where the boards are dipped in vats filled with

148

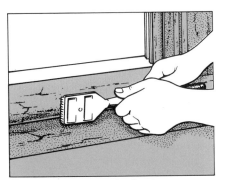

1 If old paint or other finish is loose on surface, first remove flaking areas with a scraper. Hold tool at low angle and pull.

2 Apply semipaste paint remover to horizontal surfaces using an inexpensive paintbrush. Apply in a thick layer.

3 When paint wrinkles, remove by sliding dull-edged putty knife under sludge at low angle. Clean off knife in empty can.

remover. This system works well, but it does have some drawbacks. It can be expensive and when the boards return, they usually require a great deal of sanding, filling and repair to bring the stock into proper condition for a good finish.

On smaller jobs, for instance one or two rooms, the task is much more manageable. But still, you should seriously consider how important a natural finish is to you. Removing the last 10 percent of the old paint from a sash or molded casing can take nearly as much time as the first 90 percent. By repainting a properly prepared surface, the architectural detail will come through as if it were new, and you can save yourself a good deal of effort. It depends on the condition of the old paint.

If you only have a couple of coats on the woodwork and the top coat is simply veiled with grime and some minor flaking, then cleaning, scraping and sanding will normally suffice. But if the old paint has serious defects such as excessive peeling, blistering, alligatoring, or simply too many layers, you will have to go the stripping route.

Stripping methods
There are three basic methods for removing paint. The first is by using remover

for paint and varnish. Available in liquid or semipaste, these chemical formulations soften the paint so it can be scraped, or in the case of water soluble brands, washed off with a stream of water. The second method is by mechanical means. This involves the use of hand scrapers and power sanders.

The third is by using heat. When heat is applied directly to a painted surface, the paint is softened and can be scraped off with a putty knife. For this method, you should use only a flameless heat gun or an electric heat plate. An open flame torch should not be used in any circumstance. It presents a dangerous fire hazard inside the house and it's almost impossible to use without frequently scorching the wood.

Chemical strippers
Of the three methods, the use of a chemical paint remover is generally favored because the procedure requires very little skill and cannot harm the wood, unlike the mechanical or heat methods.

There are two basic types of chemical remover: liquid and semipaste. And among them you can select ones formulated for solvent cleanup, water cleanup or no cleanup. Water-cleanup removers

work well, but their use is often limited to outdoor applications because it's usually impractical to wash off the residue with a jet of water indoors. The no-cleanup removers also work well, but sometimes leave a bit of residue which must be cleaned with a solvent. For general purpose work, the solvent removers are your best bet.

Removers are available in both flammable and nonflammable varieties, and since both kinds perform equally as well, the obvious choice is the latter, particularly for indoor applications.

All removers are highly toxic so every precaution should be taken to protect the skin and eyes, as well as the respiratory system. Be sure to read and observe all label warnings on the product you buy. Also wear gloves, goggles, a long-sleeved shirt and a respirator with appropriate vapor filters—wearing a paper dust mask will not protect you from inhaling the harmful vapors produced by chemical strippers.

The liquid removers are generally fast-acting and are used primarily on horizontal surfaces. The semipaste types work a bit slower but are better suited for vertical surfaces because they will cling without dripping.

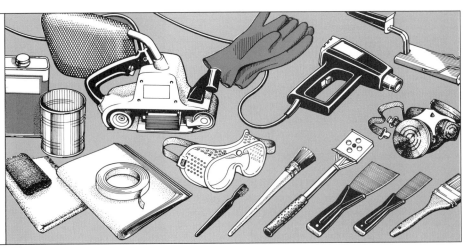

Depending on the stripping techniques you use, here's a sampling of tools (from left to right): paint remover in liquid or semipaste form; empty can for cleaning putty knives; steel wool and rags for final cleanup; newspaper and masking tape to protect surrounding surfaces; belt sander for broad, flat surfaces; gloves and goggles; heat gun or electric heat plate to soften paint; respirator with vapor filters; toothbrush and sash brush for tight spots; scraper; putty knives; and an old paintbrush.

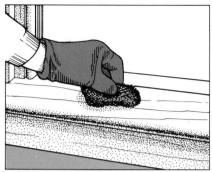

4 *Use steel wool to remove sludge from crevices and depressions where putty knife won't reach. Wear gloves to protect hands.*

5 *Use sash brush—or old toothbrush—to remove sludge from corners or confined areas. Brush can be cleaned with solvent.*

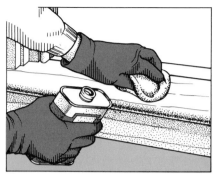

6 *Once residue is removed, thoroughly clean surface with solvent-soaked rag. See container label for appropriate solvent.*

Using a chemical stripper

To strip paint, apply a liberal coat of remover—the thicker the coat the better. Liquid remover can be poured onto a horizontal surface then spread with a brush or spatula. Semipaste remover is poured into a wide-mouth can and then applied with a fully loaded brush. With either type, the aim is to lay on the remover with as little brushing as possible. When applied, a waxy film forms over the surface of the material to retard evaporation, which allows the active ingredients to work into the paint. Too much brushing disturbs this film and thereby weakens the action.

Allow the remover to stand undisturbed for about 20 to 30 minutes or until the surface has wrinkled; this indicates the paint has softened. Then, use a putty knife to lift and slide the sludge off the surface. Hold the knife at a low angle and push it gently in the direction of the grain when possible. The corners of the knife should be rounded slightly in order to prevent gouging. You can either sand or file these corners to take away the edge.

On irregular surfaces, a pad of 2/0 steel wool is used to remove the sludge. For crevices, corners and confined areas, you can use a toothbrush, oval sash brush or even a pointed or flat-ended dowel. If the first application has not completely penetrated and softened extra tough or multiple layers of paint, simply apply a second coat of remover. Small remaining patches of paint can usually be removed with steel wool moistened with remover.

It is best to work no more than 2 or 3 sq. ft. of surface at one time because, if the remover dries before you scrape it off, it will require recoating.

The final step is to remove all residue from the surface. For solvent cleanup removers, this is usually done with paint thinner, but be sure to check the label instructions and use the recommended neutralizer. Saturate clean toweling or burlap and thoroughly cleanse the surface. A once-over will rarely be sufficient, so turn the rag over often or switch to fresh ones as needed to avoid redepositing any of the residue. Any remaining trace on the wood will interfere with adhesion and drying of the new finish when it is applied later.

7 *Remove window sashes from jambs before stripping paint. Otherwise, areas that fall behind sash stop will be inaccessible.*

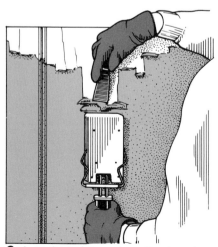

8 *Electric heat plate works well on broad, flat surfaces like doors. It softens paint quickly but has tendency to scorch wood.*

With water-solvent removers, you usually have the option of removing the sludge with a putty knife and following with a brisk water-hose rinse, or you can use the jet of water to remove the sludge. The latter results in a messy runoff that can mar the surroundings, so choose your location with this thought in mind. Also, some water-cleanup removers require no additional treatment, while others call for a final wiping with solvent. Check the label on this score.

When the stripped wood has thoroughly dried, usually overnight, sand it lightly with 120-grit followed by 220-grit paper to prepare it for refinishing. Wood that has been water-washed will require extra sanding because moisture always raises the wood grain. Water can also delaminate thin veneers and weaken non-waterproof glue joints. So remember this when selecting a remover.

Mechanical stripping

A portable belt sander will remove paint fairly quickly from broad, flat surfaces. However, in order to obtain respectable results without marring the surface, proficiency in handling the tool is necessary. This sander cuts aggressively and could easily dig too deeply.

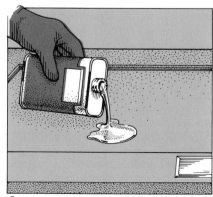

9 *If using a chemical stripper, remove door and lay on horizontal surface. Use liquid type instead of semipaste.*

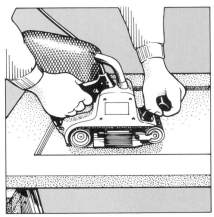

10 *Use belt sander on wide, flat areas that have just a coat or two of paint. Keep sander moving or it will gouge surface.*

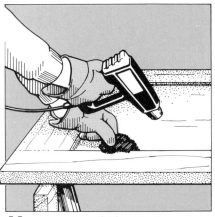

11 *Heat gun is useful for stripping contours and irregular shapes. Soften paint with hot air, then remove with steel wool.*

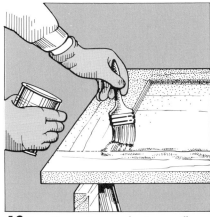

12 *Sometimes not even a heat gun will remove every trace of paint. Follow stubborn areas with a chemical stripper.*

Practice using it on scrap, if necessary, until you acquire a good feel for "landing" the sander on the surface softly and evenly. Once contact is made, the sander must be kept in constant motion, on a level plane and with equal pressure applied to both handles. Make back-and-forth passes within comfortable reach of your arms, releasing the pressure slightly at the end of each pass before making the return trip. This feathers the bite, preventing gouging.

Use an 80-grit open-coat abrasive belt to remove a paint film a couple of layers thick. Then make a few passes with 100- followed by 120-grit belts to smooth out the coarse belt marks. Or you can use a finishing sander for the final smoothing. To strip extra-thick layers, start with a 50- or 60-grit belt.

Small areas of loose paint can be effectively removed with a pull-type paint scraper. This has a square, four-edged reversible blade that allows for plenty of scraping between sharpenings. Two cutting edges are serrated and two are straight. The serrated edge chips the paint faster but leaves grooves in the surface of the wood. The straight edge is used for lighter scraping or to smooth out the marks left by the serrated edge.

This tool functions best when the angle is held close to—but angled slightly away from—the surface. Begin scraping from a broken edge of paint and apply firm pressure as you pull the tool along. You'll know the grip angle is correct when the chips fly with little effort.

Stripping with heat
An electric heat plate rests on the surface of the woodwork and concentrates heat on the paint. This softens a path about 3 in. wide, which is removed with a putty knife. It performs well on wide, flat surfaces and is held on the surface for about four to eight seconds depending on the

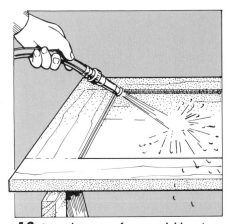

13 *One advantage of water soluble strippers is that the workpiece can be washed off quickly outside with a garden hose.*

thickness of the layer. When the paint has softened, the plate is shifted to the adjacent area. In the meantime, the knife is used to lift and remove the softened paint. Prolonged heating will damage the wood by scorching it.

The heat gun is a good alternative to the heat plate and it's particularly useful for softening paint on narrow or irregular surfaces such as moldings or grooves. Hold the nozzle several inches from the surface and advance it very slowly. As you do this, follow along with steel wool or an appropriately shaped scraper to remove the softened paint. Wear heavy-duty protective gloves and make sure to keep the following hand clear of the hot air stream. These guns can deliver temperatures of 1000° F. With a little practice they are very easy to use.

Safety note
If you have a house built before 1950, you're likely to encounter lead-based paint on your woodwork. Health experts regard it as a serious poison and that's the way you should treat it. Children are

particularly susceptible to poisoning. Keep these points in mind:

■ Do not eat or smoke near the work site. Treat scrapings, dust, chemical residue and cleanup material as toxic waste. Discard them properly and immediately. Note: In many municipalities it is against the law to dispose of toxic waste with normal garbage. You may be required to dispose of toxic waste, such as paint remover, at a designated location or toxic waste dump site. Some communities have toxic waste collection days.

■ Keep children and pets away from the work site. In case of accidental poisoning by chemical strippers, immediately contact your local poison control center for the appropriate steps to take for the particular product ingested. Have the product container with you when you phone. Do not induce vomiting unless otherwise instructed by trained personnel.

■ Immediately wash off any chemical stripper that comes in contact with skin under a stream of cold water from a tap or garden hose.

■ High temperatures can release toxic lead vapor. If you use heat paint removal methods, provide good ventilation and wear a respirator.

■ Sanding and scraping releases lead paint dust into the air. Wear goggles, gloves, a long-sleeved shirt, long pants and a double-cartridge filter mask. Close off the room where you are working, but provide sufficient ventilation. Very fine lead dust will continue to sift down after you are through. Therefore, do not occupy the room for at least two days. Vacuum the room thoroughly before putting it to use. Then wrap the vacuum bag in an airtight plastic bag.

How to fix
A PROBLEM DOOR

Degree of difficulty: Easy   Estimated time: 1 hour   Average cost of materials: $5

While most of us think of a house as a static structure—totally unlike a mechanically functioning object such as a car engine, houses do have moving parts. And, in the same way that an engine needs a periodic tune-up, the moving parts of your house may have fallen out of adjustment and require attention. The doors are the most likely candidates for wear and tear. Changes in humidity cause them to bind against the jamb, and worn or poorly fitted hinges will cause the door to sag. Perhaps it's time to perform a tune-up on your house to get those doors working like new?

Checking the hinges
Hinges should be recessed so the hinge leaves are flush with the door edge and jamb. If a recess is too deep, the door edge can bind against the jamb before the door is completely closed. This condition can eventually loosen the screw fastenings.

Check to make sure the screws are tight by pulling outward slightly on the door. If you see any movement between the hinge and wood, try tightening the screws. If the screw continues to turn when it should be tight, then the screw hole is stripped and needs attention.

The easiest solution to a stripped screw hole is to replace the old screws with longer ones. Because most jambs are ¾ in. thick, installing a 1½-in.- long screw usually will catch the framing beyond the jamb. First, bore a pilot hole through the jamb for the longer screw. Don't over-tighten the new screw to avoid splitting the jamb.

You can also plug a stripped hole with a dowel and then re-fasten the hinge with the original screw. Begin by removing the hinge leaf. If your door is hung on two hinges, you'll have to remove the door completely. Check the holding power of each screw so you can fix all the problem holes at one time. If your door is hung on three hinges you can remove one of them without removing the door.

First, support the door with a couple of wooden shingles or other tapered wooden wedges. Use a claw hammer to tap these two boards under the door until the door's weight is removed from the hinge. Then remove the screws to free the hinge leaf.

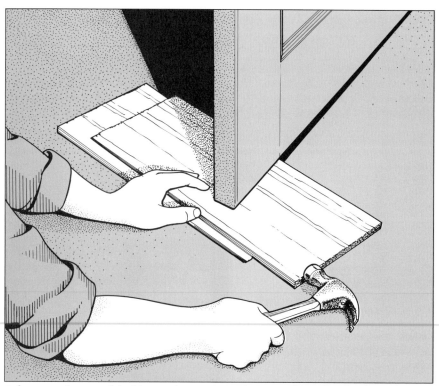

Before removing any of the hinges, place two opposing tapered wooden shingles under the door. Then, take the door weight off the hinges by tapping the shingles together.

Using the old screw hole as a pilot, bore a ⅜-in.-dia. hole taking care not to go completely through the jamb. Cut a plug from a ⅜-in.-dia. fluted dowel pin. Glue the plug in place and let dry before boring the new pilot hole.

If any of the hinge mortises are too deep, shim them before reinstalling the hinges. Trim a thick piece of veneer or mat board to the size of the mortise. Then, place it in the mortise, bore screw holes and install the hinge.

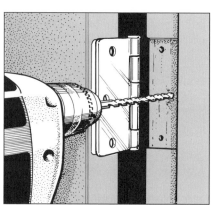

1 Fix stripped screw holes by boring a ⅜-in.-dia. hole and gluing a plug in place. Don't bore completely through the jamb.

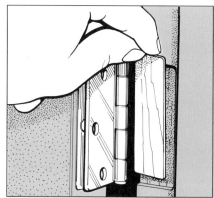

2 If hinge leaf sits below wood surface, the mortise is too deep. Repair by installing shims between leaf and mortise bottom.

152

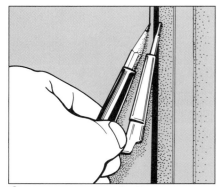

3 *Use a compass to scribe the ⅛- to ⅜-in. clearance line on the latch side and top of door. Leave ³⁄₁₆- to ¼-in. gap at bottom.*

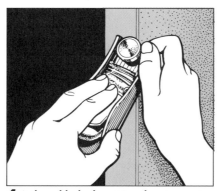

4 *A sharp block plane trims door to exact size. Remove door, and plane in from ends when trimming top and bottom edges.*

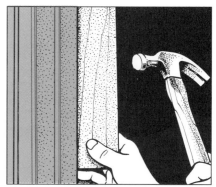

5 *First try adjusting the stop clearance by tapping the stop into position. Then, secure the stop with 4d finishing nails.*

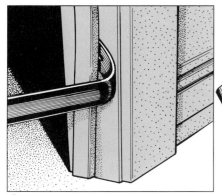

6 *To remove stop, punch bottom nail through and pry the stop off. Pull remaining nails from back with locking pliers.*

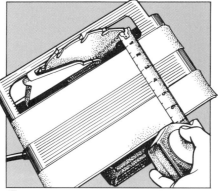

7 *Use a circular saw to remove excessive material. Measure distance from tooth to base edge for positioning cutting guide.*

8 *Clamp cutting guide to door spaced at the correct distance from trim line. Score line with sharp knife to minimize tearing.*

Proper clearance

If the door rubs against the jamb as it closes, it must be trimmed to fit. The top and sides should show a ⅛- to ³⁄₁₆-in. space and a ³⁄₁₆- to ¼-in. gap should appear at the bottom. Set an ordinary compass to the correct clearance. Hold the point on the jamb edge and scribe the trim line around the door.

If you have a small amount of material to remove on the latch edge or outer corner of the top, you can do the job with the door in place using a block plane. You may need to remove the latch set. If so, check that the latch plate is flush with the door edge when reinstalled. If necessary, deepen the mortise with a sharp chisel. Trimming the full length of the top or any part of the bottom requires that the door be removed. First, wedge the door to take the load off the hinges. Then, tap the hinge pins out. Remove the top pin last and be prepared to catch the door when it's free.

The top and bottom are trimmed by planing in from each end to avoid splitting the door stiles. If you need to remove more material than can be planed comfortably, use your circular saw for the job.

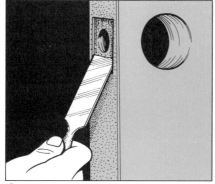

9 *After removing wood near the latch set, check that the plate is still flush with the edge. Adjust the mortise with sharp chisel.*

Use a blade designed for making finished cuts and apply masking tape to the saw base plate to prevent marring the door. Then, measure the distance from the plate edge to a tooth on the blade.

Clamp a straight cutting guide to the door so that the distance between the guide and the cutline is equal to the distance between the blade and the base edge. Scribe the trim line with a sharp knife to minimize tear-out.

Pulling out the stops

If the door contacts the stops before the latch engages, the stops will need to be adjusted. If the contact area is small, try tapping the stop into position with a block of wood and hammer. Once the door closes easily, nail the stop with 4d finishing nails.

If tapping it doesn't work, or the door is simply too tight all around, remove the stops by punching a nail completely through at one end of each piece with a nail set and then prying off each stop. Reinstall by first closing the door and pressing gently until the lock hits the strike.

With the door at this position, the head stop can be installed with a ¹⁄₁₆-in. clearance between the door and the stop. Nail with 4d finishing nails and attach the remaining stops with the same clearance.

In cases where the stop abuts the casing, it's simplest to adjust the clearance by moving the strike plate. Remove it and expand the latch hole. Then, plug the old screw holes and install the strike in the correct position. Fill the remaining gap with wood filler; sand and finish.

How to replace
A SLIDING GLASS DOOR

Degree of difficulty: Hard **Estimated time:** 12 hours **Average cost of materials:** $1200

Although sliding doors are quite expensive propositions for most do-it-yourselfers, they work well and can add visual appeal to an older-style home. Some new sliding doors can be fitted with venetian blinds or pre-assembled wood muntins.

It wasn't so long ago that a sliding glass door, or patio door as many manufacturers call it, was a new idea. They were the darlings of the remodeling trade and quickly became a frequent amenity of any kitchen renovation or room addition. Their list of attributes seemed almost endless: They allowed more natural light into the house, made access to the outside—particularly onto an outdoor deck—easier, and perhaps most important, freshened the appearance of an older home by giving it a contemporary look.

They were so successful that new home builders quickly adopted them as standard equipment on both low-budget and high-ticket homes. Unfortunately, not all these doors were high-quality units and not all were installed in the most sensible location. Both of these shortcomings

1 *Begin by removing fixed door panel from old sliding unit. Usually, it's held by brackets screwed to the door and jamb.*

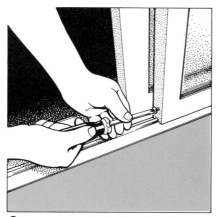

2 *Loosen screw that holds plastic alignment bracket on bottom corner of fixed door. Slide bracket away from sill track.*

3 *Next, loosen the alignment bracket on the top corner of the fixed door and pull bracket down. Door should now be free.*

4 *Grip fixed panel with both hands and lift up into top track until bottom clears lip on lower track. Pull out door bottom.*

were present in the house we chose for the installation described in this example.

The existing aluminum door was installed badly, and as a result worked poorly. But the primary complaint was that the door faced south and was positioned in the main dining area. During the summer months the room was uncomfortably hot and the drapes that covered the doors not only restricted air flow, but also were fighting a losing battle with three active young children.

The replacement choice solved these problems: A brand-name wood and aluminum-clad sliding door. The unit was very well-made and it featured removable glass panes on the inside of both doors. This space, between the inner and outer glazing, was designed to accommodate either the manufacturer's venetian blinds or pre-assembled wood muntins to give the door a traditional look. The unit is available clad in one of several colors: white, dark brown, gray, or tan. While the unit is expensive, running over $1200 without tax, it did solve the home owner's problems well and operated beautifully. If you plan to install a unit different than the one shown here, the basic directions that follow will apply in nearly every way.

Before you begin
One of the most important considerations is the simplest—namely measuring your existing door. You will want to get the closest match possible so you won't have to make structural changes in the house wall. Measure the height and width of the door and draw a sketch of the way it is shaped before you go shopping for a new door. This should give your local dealer all the necessary information.

Do keep in mind that your new door should always be smaller than your existing door because it's easier to close in a

wall opening than it is to increase it. The latter requires removing the existing header and installing a new one to carry the additional weight.

Removing the old door
Begin by removing the casing boards that trim the inside of the door. Be careful when prying these away from the wall because you may be able to use them again on the new door.

Next, remove the screen door—if you have one—and begin removing the fixed panel on the slider. These are always joined to a side jamb with some type of bracket, usually one that clips over a lip on the jamb and is screwed to the stile of the door. On this door there were three such clips. Once these are removed, go to the opposite door edge and loosen the upper and lower alignment brackets as shown in Figs. 2 and 3. These serve to keep the outboard end of the fixed door stable.

When these brackets are loosened, slide the door to one side, enough to grip the edge, then lift up the door so the top slides

completely into the upper channel. This will free the bottom edge of the door so that it can be pulled away from the bottom track. Lower the door away from the track and set it aside.

Follow the same basic procedure to remove the sliding door: Loosen the roller wheels at the bottom corners of the door. Then lift up the door, pull out the bottom, lower the door and set it aside. At this point the doorjamb assembly should be all that's left in the rough opening.

Depending on how the original frame was installed, the exterior trim may or may not cover a flange that surrounds the jambs. In this case, the old door had no such flange. It was simply attached with screws through the jambs to the jack studs on either side of the opening and to the header and the house floor. If you have a flange door, then the exterior trim must be removed first to get at the flange nails that hold the door to the house. Remove the screws or the flange nails and set the frame aside.

Preparing the opening
Once the opening is clear, check the header and floor for level, the jack studs for plumb and the corners for square. It is crucial that all these elements are true. Otherwise, the door will be difficult to install and may operate poorly.

On this job we were fortunate: The opening was in good shape. If yours isn't, then you'll have to shim out the various wooden framing members until everything is right. Generally, this is best accomplished by leveling the floor shims first, then plumbing the stud shims and leveling the ones on the header. Cedar shingles and ¼-in.-thick plywood strips are generally the preferred choice for this job. The shims should be added to both sides equally so the door remains centered in the opening.

5 *Once both doors and the door frame are removed from the opening, check corners of rough opening for square.*

6 *Remove old caulking or other sealant from sill, then check for level. If sill is not level, new door must be shimmed to level.*

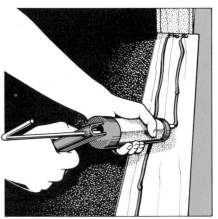

7 *Apply two heavy beads of caulk to sill to prevent air and moisture penetration after new door is installed.*

Assembling the new door

Depending on the manufacturer—and the way your supplier sells the door—the fixed panel may or may not come attached to the door frame. On this job, the fixed door was already in place. But many other sliding doors come with the door separate and the frame (jambs and sill) unassembled as well. Because joining these parts is different, depending on the manufacturer, be sure to follow the assembly directions that come with the door carefully.

Note: Unless the manufacturer recommends something to the contrary, it's a good idea to install the fixed panel before installing the frame. With the panel in place, the frame will be more rigid and therefore easier to handle. And, the fixed panel will serve to keep the whole assembly square, which makes the installation much easier.

After the frame is assembled, apply two heavy beads of silicone caulk to the area of the floor that will be covered by the door. This will keep moisture, insects and air infiltration from coming in under the new door.

Next, get some help so there's a person on each end of the frame and lift it into place. Keep the assembly at least 6 in. off the caulk until you have pushed the frame into the opening. Once the new flange is bearing on the outside of the sheathing, lower the frame sill into the caulk and push the top in against the header. If you simply slide the unit into place, bottom first, the caulk will be scraped from the floor and the seal will be destroyed. Have your helper hold the assembly while you check the edges of the jambs for plumb, level and square. Once satisfied, attach the door to the house wall by driving 2½-in.-long roofing nails through the flange and into the studs and header that surround the frame.

Installing the sliding door

Again, depending on the brand of door, the sliding panel may be installed and adjusted differently. In this case, the door was simply lifted up into the top track, pushed in at the bottom, then lowered onto the rib that acts as a guide for the built-in rollers at the bottom of the door. Read the directions for your brand carefully before proceeding.

Next, install the door handle, catch and lock mechanism on the sliding door, and the strike plate in the jamb. At this point, roll the door back and forth and check how it meets the jamb. For the door to roll properly, for the catch and lock to work and for the weather stripping to be effective, the door stile must be absolutely parallel to the jamb. If it isn't, then the rollers at the bottom of the door must be adjusted properly.

Next, install the trim around the outside of the jambs. In this case, we used 1x4 pine boards ripped to fit between the jambs and the siding. This was an easy "fix" and it closely matched the existing trim on the house. If you have different trim, for instance brick molding or 1x6s, then you'll either have to fill in some siding, or cut some more away until the space is the right size for the stock that matches the rest of your house. In any case, keep in mind that the trim should be nailed directly on the sheathing, not onto the siding. Once the boards are installed, caulk around the perimeter of each and fill the casing nail holes with wood putty.

Trimming the inside of the door

Before applying the interior trim boards, make sure that you fill the void between the new doorjambs and the studs on either side with insulation. You can either slide in small amounts of fiberglass insulation or use a foam type as we did.

If you opt for the fiberglass, be careful not to compress it too much because this drastically reduces its effectiveness. Generally speaking, the foam insulation works better and quicker. It's available in spray cans at hardware stores, lumberyards and home centers. To use it, simply turn the spray can upside down and

8 *Lift new door frame into opening so sill comes down flat on caulk. Push top against wall. Don't slide bottom over caulk.*

9 *Check door frame for square, plumb and level. Attach by nailing through perimeter flange with galvanized roofing nails.*

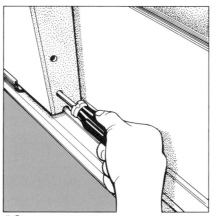

10 *Install sliding door, then adjust rollers at bottom corners through access holes. Door must slide smoothly and hit the jamb flush.*

11 *Cover perimeter flange with wood trim that fits between new doorjambs and siding. Set and fill casing nail heads.*

squeeze the nozzle. The foam will come out through an extension tube.

Some foams expand over twice their volume once they are in the cavity. If you fill the whole space when the foam is wet, it will continue to expand and you'll have to cut the excess away later when it's dry. So be sure to read the product's label directions for correct application.

Extension jambs

For casing trim to look right around any opening, the inside edge of your jambs must align perfectly with the surface of your room wall. Because of this, many doors—and windows for that matter—have jambs that are slightly narrower than what's required. The idea here is that the manufacturer has no way of knowing what your wall finish is—drywall, lath and plaster paneling, and so forth. Because all these can vary in thickness, jambs are designed to receive another strip of wood to bring them out flush with the wall. These are called extension jambs and are wedged between the jambs and the wall.

13 *Nail extension jambs to doorjambs so frame is flush with wall surface. Set and fill nail holes, then nail on casing boards.*

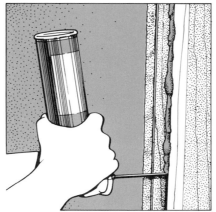

12 *Working from inside, install insulation around perimeter of new door frame. We sprayed in aerosol foam insulation.*

To install them, simply measure the distance from the edge of the jamb to the wall surface and rip the extension jambs to match. Then nail them over the standard jambs. Once these are in place, apply the casing boards.

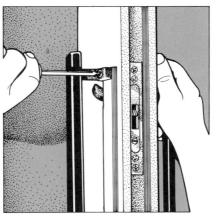

14 *Inside and outside door pulls are attached with same two machine screws. Screws slide through pre-bored holes.*

Finishing up

Install the screen door with its latch, lock, handle and strike plate and adjust its rollers so it closes against the jamb tightly. On the door we installed, the screen was designed to be retractable. It had a spring mounted along its top edge that conveniently pulled the door closed after it was released.

Another feature of this door, as mentioned before, was a venetian blind assembly installed between the double glazing on both door panels. To install them, all that's required is removing the inside glass panels on both doors, hanging the blinds inside and then attaching a small control knob in the lower right-hand corner. The glass panels that cover the blinds have a hole bored through that provides access to the control from inside the room.

Maintenance

Routine maintenance can help keep sliding glass doors gliding freely in their tracks. Trouble-free operation depends on simply vacuuming out and cleaning tracks and rails on a regular basis to remove obstructions and grime that accumulate on the track where the door slides. To maintain sliding doors, use a cloth dampened with a solution of mild household detergent and water. Also, use a silicone spray to lubricate the tracks, locks, latches and other moving parts on the door. Inspect rollers and plastic glides for wear and replace them if necessary. Most sliding door parts can be purchased from the window dealer or directly from the manufacturer.

Regular window washing will keep the panes crystal clear—but remember, sometimes cleaning the windows can make them invisible to passersby and playing children. A decal affixed in the middle of a large sliding door windowpane can prevent injury.

How to repair
A PATIO SCREEN DOOR

Degree of difficulty: Easy **Estimated time:** 3 hours **Average cost of materials:** $15

Holes in screen doors are an open invitation to insects. And since screen repairs are easy, there's no excuse for putting up with insects indoors.

Many homes feature sliding patio doors as an efficient and attractive way to connect indoor space with the backyard, deck or balcony. As with most parts of the home, these doors require periodic maintenance. And, like most maintenance, the hardest part is getting around to the job. Usually, the job involves repairing or replacing damaged screen and cleaning the rollers and tracks for smooth sliding.

Patio doors glide on hidden rollers which run on metal tracks. Bad sliding, however, is rarely due to damaged rollers. Instead, the problem is usually caused by debris on the tracks or around the rollers. Therefore, your first job is to inspect the

tracks and clean them if necessary. But if rough sliding persists, you'll have to examine and clean the rollers.

Typical sliding screen doors have four spring-held adjustable rollers, two on the top and two on the bottom. Each roller has an adjustment screw. To remove the door, first back off the adjustment screws. Then, slide a piece of thin cardboard between each bottom roller and the track to lift the rollers off the track. Remove the door by pulling the bottom out toward you.

The rollers in the screen door can be removed by prying them out with a screwdriver. Soak the rollers in mineral spirits and clean them with a brush. Then

1 *Most trouble starts with dirty tracks. The best way to maintain your sliding patio doors is periodic cleaning.*

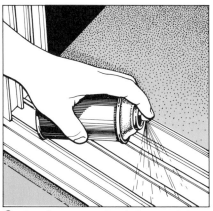

2 *After cleaning, apply a light spray lubricant to discourage dirt buildup and help keep the rollers moving smoothly.*

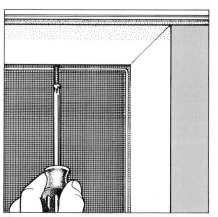

3 *To remove the sliding screen door, first release the tension on the door rollers by retracting the adjusting screws.*

wipe them dry and lubricate with light oil. You can get replacements for damaged rollers at glazing shops, home centers or direct from the manufacturer.

Removing a fixed door

The rollers in the glass door should be checked also. Unlike the screen door, the glass door has only two rollers, both at the bottom. To remove the sliding glass door, first remove the fixed door which is secured to the jamb with retaining brackets. Remove the brackets and slide the fixed door about halfway open. Then lift it into the top track and pull the bottom out. The sliding glass door can now be removed in the same way. Lift and then pull the bottom out toward you. The sliding glass door rollers are held in place with retaining screws. Remove these screws to free the rollers.

Fixing small holes

Inspect the screen for small punctures. Holes about ¼ in. in dia. or less can be repaired by applying a dab of household cement or quick-setting epoxy as shown in Fig. 8. Holes or tears up to about 1 in.

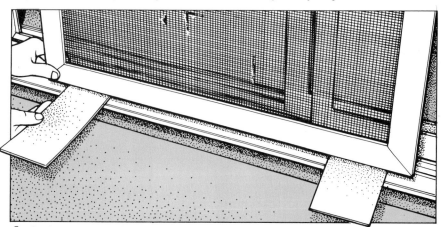

4 *After loosening the roller adjustment screws, slip a piece of cardboard under each of the bottom rollers to clear them from the track. Then, pull out the bottom.*

can be repaired with screen patches available at hardware stores. These are small squares of screening that have hooked ends that lock into the screen when pressed against it.

Replacing an entire screen

For larger damage, you must replace the entire screen. You'll need an inexpensive screen installation tool which is available at hardware stores where screening and replacement spline is sold. It comes with two rollers: one with a convex-edge profile for pressing the screen into the groove of the door frame, and one with a concave profile for installing the retaining spline. This tool comes in various roller thicknesses, so make sure you get the one

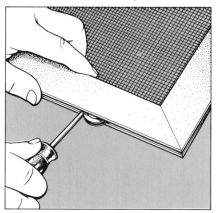

5 *After the screen door has been removed, the rollers can usually be extracted by prying them out with a screwdriver.*

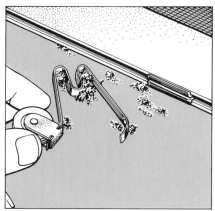

6 *Dirt and debris on the tracks eventually collect in the rollers. This can cause rough operation or lock up the rollers.*

7 *Thoroughly wash the rollers in mineral spirits. After wiping them dry, lubricate with a light oil for smooth running.*

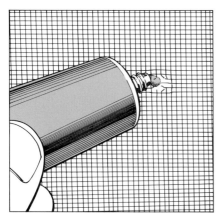

8 *A dab of fast-drying cement or epoxy will plug a small hole in screening. For larger holes—¼ to 1 in.—use a patch.*

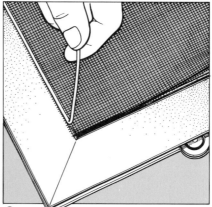

9 *To remove the old screen, pry up an end of the spline and pull it out. If the spline's not old and brittle, you can reuse it.*

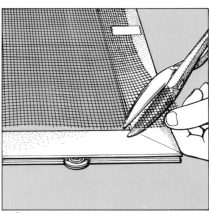

10 *Cut the new screen so it extends about 1 in. beyond the frame groove on all sides. Trim the corners to avoid bunching.*

that corresponds to the groove size in your screen door.

Remove the screen by prying out the old retaining spline which is pressed in the frame groove. If the old spline is still flexible, you can reuse it. Otherwise, purchase new plastic spline of the same size. Lay the new screening over the frame and trim it about 2 in. longer and wider than its finished size. Then, temporarily fasten the screen to the frame with masking tape at a few points along each edge to keep it from shifting. To avoid bunching up at the corners when forming the screen groove, make a diagonal cut across the corner of the screen up to the groove corner. Next, remove the tape along one long edge and use the convex roller on the screen tool to press the screening into the groove. Use moderate pressure, making several passes until reaching the required depth. Remove the tape from the opposite side as you go to prevent overstretching the screen. Then, move to the other side, do the same thing, and finish up with the shorter ends.

After the screen is in place, install the retaining spline. Using the concave roller,

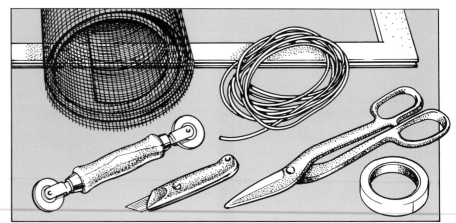

11 *Screen-repair materials and equipment include replacement screen and spline, installation tool with concave and convex roller, utility knife, tin snips and tape.*

firmly press the spline over the screen and into the groove. Use a screwdriver to push the spline in at the corners.

Depending on how old your doors are, screening can be made from either aluminum or fiberglass. If you use fiberglass screen, you do not have to make a crease with the convex wheel on the installation tool (Fig. 12). Install it by using only the

concave roller on the installation tool (Fig 13). Complete the job by trimming the excess screen with a sharp utility knife. Using moderate pressure, run the blade along the top of the spline so the screen is trimmed neatly to the groove edge; then you can reinstall the doors by reversing the procedure you followed for removing them.

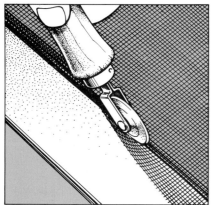

12 *Use the convex roller to force the screen into the frame groove. Make several light passes rather than one heavy pass.*

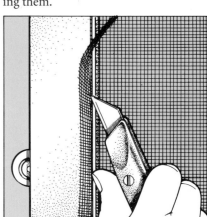

13 *The retaining spline is pressed into the groove with the concave roller. Use a screwdriver to handle the corners.*

14 *Remove screen excess with a utility knife. Using minimum pressure, cut along the groove slightly above the spline.*

How to replace
A LOCKSET

Degree of difficulty: Easy **Estimated time:** 2 hours **Average cost of materials:** $20

Worn-out locksets can be a major aggravation. But they're not hard to replace with common household tools.

To remove the inside handle, first examine the sleeve for either a small opening or a clip that protrudes through a slot. If the sleeve on your lockset shows a protruding clip, press it with a screwdriver and pull off the handle. If there's a small hole, you should push an awl or nail through it to depress the clip.

The cover plate or rose snaps off by means of a slotted clip, or by turning it past a number of grooves in the rose flange. If your lockset has a slotted clip, depress it and pry the rose free. If the rose is the grooved-flange type, look for an opening and pry off the rose with a screwdriver.

If you don't find a screwdriver slot, use pliers to turn the rose until the grooves line up with the gaps in the mounting plate, and then you can remove the rose. Next, separate the lock halves by removing the two long screws that hold them together, and remove the lock from the door. Then you should take out the bolt by removing the two small wood screws that fasten the bolt plate on the door edge.

To install your new lockset, first install the new bolt. If you're lucky, the new bolt plate will be the same size as the old one. If it's larger, extend the recess in the door with a chisel. If the recess is too big, install the bolt and fill the excess with wood filler to be finished later. Then slide the lock cylinder through the door from the out-

side. Make sure that the bolt catches in the slot of the lock. Assemble the lock halves with the two long screws.

To install the rose and handle, simply snap them over the clips. If your rose needs to be twisted on, press it firmly against the door and turn it until the grooves in the flange catch on the mounting plate. Then check to see if the old strike plate works with the new lock. If so, and the finish is an appropriate match, the job is done. Otherwise, you should remove the old strike plate and install the new one. To measure the exact location, close the door and mark the correct bolt position. Align the new plate and adjust the recess as necessary as with the bolt plate.

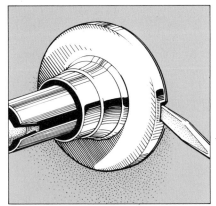

1 To remove the handle, find the clip on the sleeve and press. Use an awl if the clip is reached through a small hole.

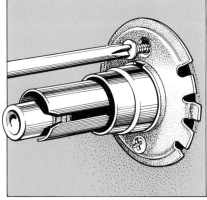

2 After the handle is removed, pry off the rose with a screwdriver to gain access to the main lock screws underneath.

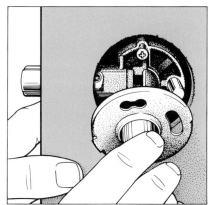

3 Two long screws extend through the door and hold lock halves together. Remove these and lock will come apart.

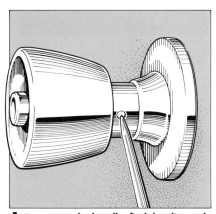

4 Take out the bolt by removing the two small screws that attach the plate to the door edge. Pry out the bolt if it's stuck.

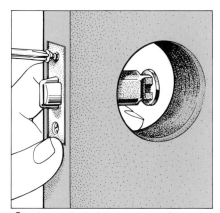

5 After installing the new bolt, slide the lock cylinder in place and check that it engages properly with the bolt.

6 Reassemble the lock with the two long screws. Snap the new rose and handle in place and then install the strike plate.

How to install
A DEADBOLT LOCK

Degree of difficulty: Medium   **Estimated time:** 3 hours   **Average cost of materials:** $25

It seems that all of us are more security conscious than we used to be. New high-end electronic security systems seem to be springing up everywhere these days. And while many of these boast truly remarkable capabilities, it's important to remember that any good security system should start out with the installation of deadbolt locks on all your exterior doors. With a little care and the right tools, you can install them yourself and save a substantial amount of money in the process.

Deadbolts come in two basic styles. One requires a key to lock and unlock the door from both sides. The other requires a key on the outside, but is easily operated with a turn unit knob from the inside. The type of deadbolt you choose will depend on the type of doors you have and on fire-safety factors. Always make sure that if a fire does break out, you can escape easily without fumbling for keys in a possibly dark, smoky situation. Where you need a key to unlock the door on both sides, at least have an accessible place on the inside where you can store a spare in case of emergency.

If you have a door with a glass panel in it, then an inside key lock offers more protection from an intruder who might be able to reach the turn units by breaking the glass. If your doors have no glass, then locks with inside turn units will work fine. The added advantage of a lock that has a turn unit on the inside is that you

Installing a deadbolt lock on your exterior door is the first step in improving the security of your home. Several kinds are available, depending on the type of door and safety factors. The job requires just a few tools and a few hours.

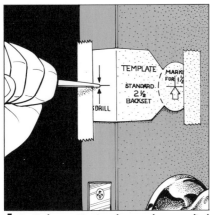

1 *Begin by positioning the template supplied with your lock on the edge of your door. Use an awl to mark hole locations.*

2 *Bore lockset hole first using hole saw. Bore until pilot bit breaks through other side, then complete hole from other side.*

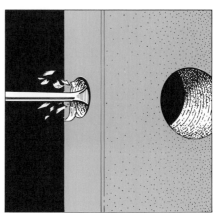

3 *Bore bolt hole next, making sure to keep bit aligned vertically and horizontally. Accuracy is crucial on this job.*

don't need a key to get out in the event of a fire.

The choice is yours. The installation is virtually the same.

Start by deciding where you want the lock to be. If you have a hollow-core door, stay just above the lockset that is already on your door. Hollow-core doors are reinforced near this lockset and, therefore, are strongest at doorknob level. Even if you have solid-core doors, stay as close to the lockset as possible for the greatest amount of strength.

When you buy your deadbolt, you will find directions that include the exact drill bit sizes you will need. Make sure you have all the bits to meet those requirements. Inexpensive, adjustable hole saws work really well. You will also find a paper template to help you mark the exact hole locations.

Getting down to work

The hole for the lock cylinder should be bored first. While you bore the hole, pay close attention to the angle of your drill and make sure that you bore straight in.

Don't drift to the left or right. If you are working alone, block the door so that it remains steady and concentrate on a straight hole through the door. When the larger hole for the lock cylinder is finished, bore the smaller bolt hole. Use the same procedure.

When the holes are bored, press the bolt in place and mark around the plate with a sharp knife. Then, chisel out the plate area according to the manufacturer's recommended depth. Next, press the lock cylinder into its opening from the outside and make sure that it catches the bolt. Installing a strike plate for a deadbolt is a little more involved than for a regular lockset.

Many deadbolts come with a reinforcing box to give the door frame added strength. Measuring for this box is critical. Because doors often warp when in place, simply measuring from the bolt to the edge of the door and transferring those measurements to the doorjamb does not always work. A better way is to paint the edge of the bolt with lipstick and then, after closing the door, turn the

bolt against the door frame. The lipstick marks the exact spot where the bolt will strike the frame. There's no going wrong with this tip.

Determine the exact center of the lipstick mark and take all measurements off of this point. When installing a reinforcing box, you will need to bore two holes and then trim them into a square hole for the box.

Chisel must be sharp

Even if no reinforcing box is included, you will have to chisel out a recessed area to accept the strike plate and a heavier, brass reinforcing plate. The total depth of these two plates will be near ¼ in.

When the door frame is ready for the strike plate, reinforcing plate and/or reinforcing box, bore the screw holes. The reinforcing plate will come with heavy screws at least 3 in. long that will extend through the door frame and into the exterior wall studs. Install these and the screws for the strike plate and the job is complete. Repair door problems by following the directions on Page 152.

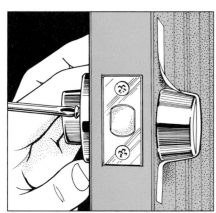

4 Trace bolt plate on edge of door, then mortise out door edge so plate will sit flush. Be sure to use a very sharp chisel.

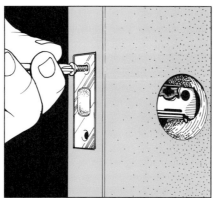

5 Slide bolt into hole and make sure it fits flush on door edge. Pre-bore screw clearance holes, then attach with screws.

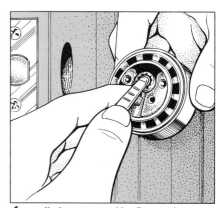

6 Deadbolt is activated by flat pin that joins both sides of lockset. Pin length can be adjusted to match door thickness.

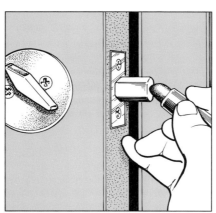

7 Slide lockset and pin through deadbolt mechanism, then tape to door. Slide other half of lockset into place and attach.

8 Test bolt for proper operation, then when satisfied, coat end of bolt with lipstick, close door and slide bolt onto jamb.

9 Using lipstick mark as guide, mortise jamb to receive deadbolt hardware. When hole is complete, attach plates with screws.

How to install
A STORM DOOR

Degree of difficulty: Medium **Estimated time:** 2 hours **Average cost of materials:** $250

As the long shadows of summer fade and cooler weather approaches, it's time to think about the upcoming heating season and ways to improve the energy efficiency of your home. Or, stated more simply, how to reduce heating costs and save money.

Creating a formidable first line of defense—blocking cold air before it can enter the house—is a key step in defeating Old Man Winter. One of the major culprits of heat loss is a home's front door. Each time the door is opened and closed, a blast of cold air steals some warmth. The traditional way to deal with this problem is still the best way—install a snug-fitting storm door.

A storm door is more than simply another barrier against the cold. A properly installed storm door forms a buffer of air between the two doors to insulate and protect the house from extremely cold, windy conditions. A storm door also allows you to open the front door from inside without inviting in snow, rain or the most recent northerly cold front. Many of today's storm doors come with screens and removable windows for year-round use. Some home owners prefer to remove the storm door each spring and install a screen door for use during spring and summer only.

Storm doors are available in a wide variety of sizes and styles to fit your home and budget. A prehung unit is the easiest to install since it comes with the hinge and outside mounting flange attached to the door. Choose from doors made of wood, aluminum and new tough plastics.

Before you go shopping for a door, measure the inside dimension between the doorjambs on the front doorway. Also, measure the height of the door opening.

The prehung door installed here is made of tough polypropylene and is guaranteed not to rust, crack, dent, split or rot. It features the latest energy-saving design and easy do-it-yourself installation. In fact, the entire installation took less than two hours. One of its best features is the self-storing window and screen that slide down into the bottom half of the door for safe, convenient storage. The 36-in.-wide x 80-in.-high door costs about $250. A 32-in.-wide model is also offered.

To install a new storm door, first prepare the opening by removing any trim that might get in the way. Storm doors are available in different materials, including aluminum, wood and specially made plastics. For ease of installation and reliability, purchase a prehung unit at a home center or hardware store.

Prepare the opening
The first step is to prepare the opening to accept the new storm door. Remove the old storm door, if necessary, and any ornate trim or molding that will interfere with installing the new door. Next, hold the door in the opening and check the fit.

It may be necessary to add a thin wood strip to reduce the opening (Fig. 1). Now's

a good time to repaint and touch up, if necessary.

Once the door opening is prepared, check the installation instructions for the height where the rain cap that fits over the door should be installed. For the door shown, the rain cap was positioned 80⅜ in. above the sill. Attach the rain cap with just one screw at this time. Next, take the

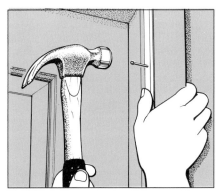

1 If the door opening is a little too wide for the door, fasten a thin wood strip to the inside of the doorjamb with finishing nails.

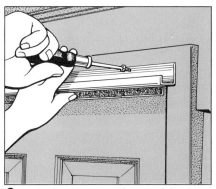

2 Screw the rain cap to the top of the door opening. The extruded aluminium cap helps divert rain water away from the opening.

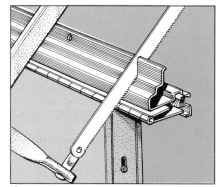

3 A prehung unit comes with hinge and mounting flange attached to door. Cut off oversized hinge to fit opening exactly.

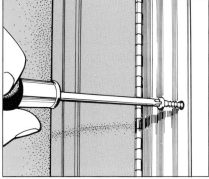

4 Drive screws through predrilled holes In the mounting flange to secure door. Check flange with a level to be sure it's plumb.

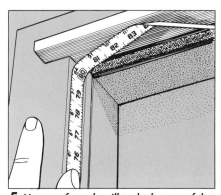

5 Measure from the sill to the bottom of the rain cap to determine length of latch-side mounting flange, also called a Z-bar.

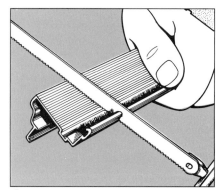

6 Cut extruded aluminium flange to length with a hacksaw. Be careful not to pull out factory-installed weather stripping.

distance from the sill to the underside of the rain cap and subtract ⅛ in. In our case, this comes to 80¼ in. This measurement determines the length of the hinge-side mounting flange, also called the Z-bar. Note that the flange is several inches longer than necessary so that you can cut it to fit your door opening exactly. Support the door and use a hacksaw to cut the flange to length (Fig. 3).

Run a bead of latex caulk down the back of the mounting flange. Tilt the door into the opening and align the top, out-side edge of the flange with the end of the rain cap. Drive one screw through the uppermost screw hole on the flange to hold the door in place. Next, hold a lev-el against the flange to make sure that it's plumb, then drive in the remaining screws (Fig. 4). Remove the one screw holding the rain cap in place and apply a bead of caulk to the back of the rain cap. Reinstall the rain cap with even space along the top of the door, and drive in the remaining mounting screws.

Now, measure from the sill to the under-side of the rain cap on the latch side of the door to determine the length of the latch-side mounting flange (Fig. 5). Cut the flange to length with a hacksaw, apply a

bead of caulk to its back surface and install it with screws (Fig. 7). Be sure that there's an even space between the flange and the edge of the closed door. Also, check the installation instructions to see if it's necessary to leave space between the door and flange for expansion and con-traction. This will be the case for most plastic (PVC or polypropylene) doors since they react to temperatures more dramatically than aluminum storm doors.

The required space will depend on the air temperature when the door is installed.

Installing the hardware
Most doors come with some sort of weather strip for the bottom of the door. The unit shown here has an easy-to-install door sweep that slips over the door bot-tom (Fig. 8). Adjust the height of the door sweep to ensure it forms a tight seal against the sill when the door is closed completely.

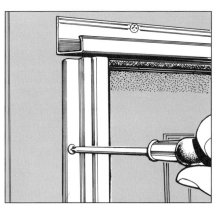

7 Fasten the latch-side mounting flange with screws. Check space between the flange and door before driving screws.

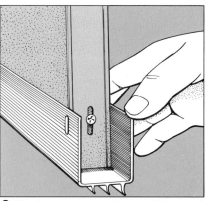

8 Slip door sweep over bottom of door and adjust it so that it forms a tight seal against sill. Fasten sweep with screws.

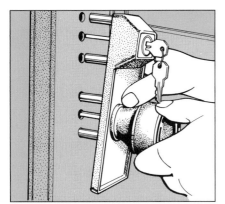

9 *Easy-to-install doorknob and lock assembly mounts to the outside of the 1½ in.-thick door through six pre-bored holes.*

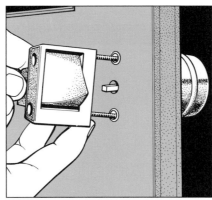

10 *Mount finger-latch mechanism to inside of door, opposite the doorknob. Secure the latch with two machine screws.*

attach the closer with simple drop-in pins (Fig. 14). A small setscrew on the end of the closer cylinder allows you to adjust the speed at which the door closes. Turn the screw clockwise to slow the door; counterclockwise for faster closing. Open the door all the way and allow it to close. Make adjustments to keep the door from slamming shut or to ensure that it closes completely.

Maintenance

Since most storm doors are on the first line of defense against the elements, routine maintenance and cleaning are important for continued reliability. Periodically inspect the channels for damage and repair them as soon as possible, either by replacing the damaged part on a plastic door, or using pliers to bend damaged parts back into shape on aluminum doors. A wooden storm door will eventually require a fresh coat of paint or some other finish to protect it from the ravages of the elements. And the closers on all types of storm doors will need lubrication. Use a spray-on silicone-based lubricant for the job.

Doorknobs, locks and closers

Most storm doors come with pre-bored holes so that installing the knob and lock assembly is quick and easy. If yours doesn't, you'll have to drill holes for the door hardware using an electric drill fitted with a bit designed to bore metal, wood or plastic. Simply follow the manufacturer's instructions. Note that the

door installed here also has a key-operated deadbolt for added security (Fig. 11). Another good feature to look for when purchasing a storm door is one equipped with two automatic closers.

To install the automatic closers, first attach the jamb bracket to the hinge-side doorjamb (Fig. 13). Next, fasten the door bracket to the inside of the door and

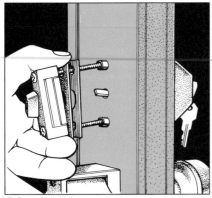

11 *Install the deadbolt opposite the key lock. Be sure that the flat spindle is seated properly in the center of the bolt assembly.*

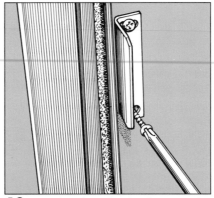

12 *A simple L-shaped strike plate is used to engage the latch and hold the door closed. Screw strike plate to doorjamb.*

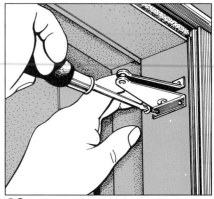

13 *Screw the jamb bracket in place, as shown, to support the automatic door closer. Fasten it with four 1½-in. No. 12 screws.*

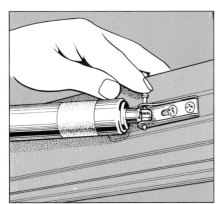

14 *After screwing the door bracket to the inside of the door, attach the closer by inserting a locking pin through the bracket.*

15 *Door features an adjustable window that locks at several positions. Window can be lowered and stored in bottom of door.*

16 *Fiberglass screen stores in bottom, too. Pull up screen when needed. Window and screen can be used simultaneously.*

How to repair
GARAGE DOORS

Degree of difficulty: Easy **Estimated time:** 4 hours **Average cost of materials:** N/A

Lifting and lowering a heavy sectional overhead garage door should normally be an easy task because of built-in mechanical advantages: rollers, pulleys and counterbalance springs. But over time, this job can become very difficult due to neglect of simple maintenance, or because some parts are broken, worn or misaligned. The job doesn't take much time and only a few simple tools are needed to get your garage door into tip-top shape once again.

The most common cause for a door to move sluggishly is lack of lubrication—coupled with the accumulation of dirt and grime—in the roller bearings. Another possible source of friction can be traced to grime-caked or rusted roller shafts which prevent the roller hinges from pivoting freely as the door moves through its tracks.

Periodic oiling of the rollers and hinges, as well as the pulleys and the insides of the tracks, will help keep the door working. But keep in mind that oiled tracks tend to collect dirt so don't overdo your lubrication. Just apply a thin film of lightweight oil to the rollers and occasionally wipe the tracks clean with an oil-dampened cloth.

Removing rollers
Severely neglected roller assemblies may well call for removal in order to do a thorough job of cleaning and lubrication. If you have to go this route, be sure to remove only one roller assembly at a time and replace it before removing another.

When replacing the hinge, attach the bottom leaf first, then insert a thin cardboard shim between the adjacent door panels before tightening the nuts on the upper leaf. This will prevent the door panels from binding when the door is closed.

Although the rollers are designed to function in the tracks with a fair amount of play, loose hinges will invariably cause the rollers to move out of alignment and bind. So get into the habit of inspecting the hinges periodically to make sure they are securely tightened in place.

Track alignment
Another trouble spot to check when the door is balky and functioning poorly is the track alignment. Hard use and abuse

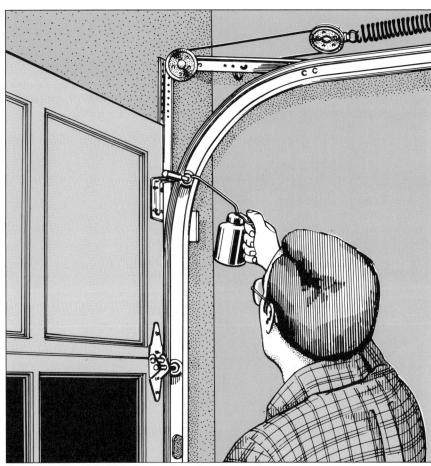

1 Remove any accumulated grime from the rollers and tracks using an oil-dampened rag. Once they're clean, periodically lubricate the rollers with a touch of lightweight oil.

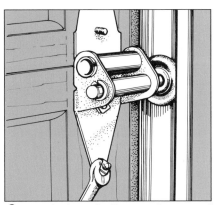

2 Severely clogged rollers must be removed from the door by backing off retaining nuts. Be sure to remove one roller at a time.

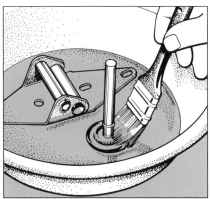

3 Once roller and hinge are removed, wash both in kerosene until thoroughly cleaned. Use an old paintbrush or toothbrush.

167

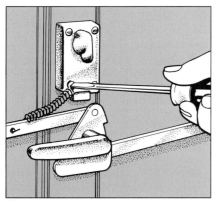

4 *If return spring on lock bar has lost tension, replace it. One end of spring is hooked on bar, other is screwed to lock.*

5 *The lockset should be lubricated from outside the door using graphite—in dry or liquid form. Do not use oil on the lock.*

6 *If lock bar doesn't slide into strike opening in the track, then loosen guide bracket screws and adjust bracket up or down.*

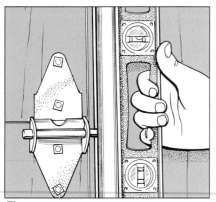

7 *If severe binding between roller and track occurs, then track is probably out of alignment. Check for plumb using a level.*

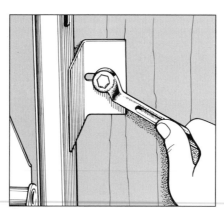

8 *If track is out of plumb, loosen mounting-bracket lag screws so it moves. Three or four brackets per track are common.*

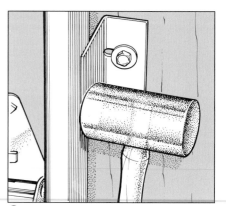

9 *To adjust track, drive it in the appropriate direction using a soft-faced mallet. Once track is plumb, retighten lag screws.*

in operating the door, as well as normal settling of the garage structure, can cause the tracks to become misaligned. Visual observation of the rollers in the tracks and checking for plumb with a spirit level will indicate whether an adjustment of one or both tracks is required.

Another situation that results from settling is the gradual misalignment of the lock bars. Eventually the bars can start to rub against the strike opening and in the worst cases, miss the hole completely.

The problem can usually be solved by adjusting the slotted bar guides on both ends of the door. In extreme cases it may even be necessary to enlarge the opening with a metal file to allow free movement of the bar.

Counterbalance springs
The counterbalance springs on the typical door shown here have no built-in adjustment mechanism like some of the older doors had. The only way to adjust the springs on these newer doors is to increase or reduce the tension by tightening or loosening the connecting lift cable. If the spring has lost its tension, it

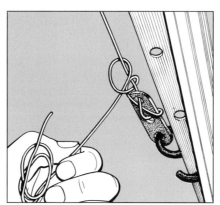

10 *To change tension on counterbalance spring, open door completely; then tighten or loosen support cable in its bracket.*

should be replaced. This is indicated when the spring, under no tension, does not close tightly and shows spaces between the coils. This determination, as well as the adjustment or removal of the springs, must be done with the door in the fully opened—raised—position.

Some experimentation is required to adjust the counterbalance springs. If your

door is sluggish, tighten the spring slightly by pulling more cable through the locking bracket as shown in Fig. 10. If the door lifts too quickly, loosen the cable. In either case be sure to reattach the cable to its locking bracket as shown.

In addition to these simple maintenance chores, also be on the lookout for failing paint on the exterior of a wood door. Keep it well painted to seal out moisture. And occasionally check the weather-stripping seal at the bottom of the door. Replace it if it has lost its flexibility or has become misshapen.

Safety
If your garage door has torsion springs, which are located directly over the top of a closed door, do not attempt to adjust or replace these springs. Instead, call in a professional who is equipped with the appropriate tools and expertise to handle the job. Remember, any garage door can be attached to an automatic garage door opener, so also check and maintain the trolley and rail that connect the opener to the garage door, and any other mechanical parts.

How to install
A GARAGE DOOR OPENER

Degree of difficulty: Medium   **Estimated time:** 5 hours   **Average cost of materials:** $150

Automatic openers can add convenience and ease of operation to otherwise unwieldy garage doors. Purchase a model that offers a well-illustrated instruction manual and a phone-in customer support line which will provide answers to installation questions.

If you've lived for years without a garage door opener, your attitude toward installing one is probably pretty typical: Sure it would be convenient, but it's just not a necessity. Still, it seems that everyone who has a garage door opener swears he or she couldn't live without it. So, with visions of the door gliding open at the push of a button, you might reconsider the installation of an automatic garage door opener.

There are basically three types of home garage door openers: chain-driven, screw-driven and those raised by a nylon tape. All three are capable of opening a standard garage door. For the installation described here we opted for a typical chain-driven opener based on its reputation for durability, safety and ease of installation. The one shown here costs about $150, while the range of six other models cost from $95 to $165.

Note: Other garage door openers are installed in a similar manner. Of course, follow the manufacturer's directions for your particular model.

Powered by a ½-hp motor, the opener can lift a door up to 7½-ft.-high x 18-ft.-wide. This extra power is more than enough to open a typical one-car garage door that measures 7½-ft.-high x 9-ft.-wide. It also opens sectional doors and one-piece, tilt-up doors. This model's other features include a time-delay light which stays on 4½ minutes after the door is activated, an ON/OFF pull-cord that lets you use the light as an overhead work light, programmable transmitter codes that have over a thousand changeable combinations, a vacation switch that shuts off the opener while you're away, and an exclusive security feature that prevents others from activating the opener with a similar remote control.

The battery-powered, hand-held transmitter has two push buttons. One of the push buttons opens and closes the door, the other activates the special safety feature that prevents stray radio signals from opening the door—a problem with many older openers.

Installing openers should require no special tools and should take about 3 to 5 hours to complete. When shopping for an opener look for a detailed owner's manual which provides clear instructions and plenty of helpful illustrations. Some manufacturers may even offer a how-to videotape along with their openers showing an actual installation. Also ask if the manufacturer of the opener you plan to install has a toll-free customer support line that you can call.

Assembly

Begin by joining the four sections of tubing with the 6-in.-long inserts (Fig. 1). Press the inserts into the tubing ends as far as possible. Next, press the plug button into one end of the tubing (Fig. 2). Then, insert the tubing end with the plug button into the tube support on top of the power unit (Fig. 3). Slide the traveler onto the tube assembly so the arrow on the traveler points toward the garage door (Fig. 4). Push the idler assembly onto the end of the

tubing (Fig. 5). Next, position the traveler 44 in. from the front edge of the tube support. Accurately mark the tubing for future reference (Fig. 6). Then attach the loose end of the chain to the traveler using a screwdriver to push the master chain link's retaining clip into position (Fig. 7). Carefully unroll the chain and wrap it around the drive sprocket which is located on top of the power unit (Fig. 8). Thread the cable at the end of the chain through the idler assembly (Fig. 9). Check that the traveler hasn't moved from the 44-in. mark. Attach the loose end of the cable to the traveler with a master chain link (Fig. 10).

Next, adjust the chain by tightening the adjustment bolt on top of the power unit (Fig. 11). Turn the bolt until the chain sags about ½ in. below the midpoint of the tubing assembly. Finally, tie the manual disconnect cord to the latch on the traveler (Fig. 12). This safety feature allows you to disconnect the traveler and raise the door by hand.

Installation

First mark the centerline of the garage door at its top. Use a level to transfer this line to the header joist above the door

1 The first step is to join together the sections of 1¼-in.-dia. steel tubing using the 6-in.-long insert tubes.

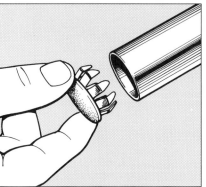

2 At one end of the assembled length of tubing (it doesn't matter which end), push in plug button until it's fully seated.

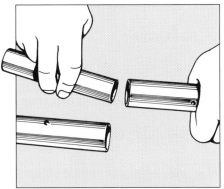

3 Slide the tubing end with the plug button into the tube support housing on top of the door opener power unit.

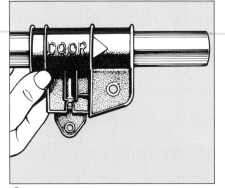

4 Slide the traveler onto the tubing so the arrow on the traveler points toward the door and away from the power unit.

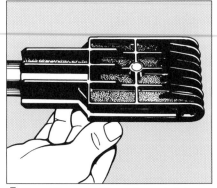

5 Place idler assembly on the end of the tubing. The idler assembly houses a free-spinning pulley that guides the cable.

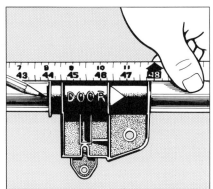

6 Place traveler 44 in. from front edge of tube support on power unit. Mark 44-in. dimension on tubing for later reference.

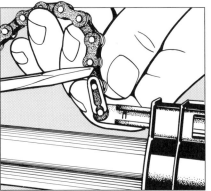

7 Attach chain to traveler using a master chain link. Use a screwdriver to push on retaining clip that secures the link.

8 Run the chain from the traveler back to the power unit. Then, loop the chain around power unit's drive sprocket.

(Fig. 13). Have someone raise the door to its highest point. Use a tape measure to determine the distance from the floor to the door's top edge (Fig. 14).

Next, add 2 in. to this high-rise dimension, and mark this new dimension on the header. Align the bottom edge of the header bracket with this mark, and fasten it with two lag screws (Fig. 15). With the power unit on the floor, lift the tubing end and secure the idler assembly to the header bracket with a clevis pin. Pass the pin through the bracket and idler and secure the assembly in place with a lock clip (Fig. 16).

With the tubing end secured to the header bracket, carefully lift the power unit and set it on top of a ladder. Prepare to hang the unit from the ceiling joists. Position the unit so the tube assembly slopes up gently toward the header bracket. However, it's more important that the door open freely than to maintain this slope. Hold the unit in place and have a helper raise the door slowly to check the door's clearance.

For an open-frame ceiling, simply secure the mounting straps to an exposed joist with lag screws (Fig. 17). If the garage has a finished ceiling, screw a 1x6 through

the drywall into the ceiling joists. Then, screw an angle iron to the 1x6, and bolt the mounting straps to the angle iron.

Next, attach the straight steel bar link to the traveler with a clevis pin and lock clip. Then, bolt the L-shaped steel arm to the bar link (Fig. 18). Bolt the door bracket to the end of the L-shaped arm (Fig. 19). Now, tug on the disconnect cord, and slide the traveler up to the closed door. Hold the bracket against the door so that the center of the bracket is between 3 in.

and 6 in. from the door's top edge. The exact position is not critical as long as it's within this area. Mount the bracket to the door with two carriage bolts (Fig. 20) that are installed through the door with their heads on the outside.

The last step of the installation is wiring the push-button wall switch to the power unit. Attach the wire leads to the switch and mount the switch to the garage wall (Fig. 21). The switch should be at a convenient height, and a person standing by

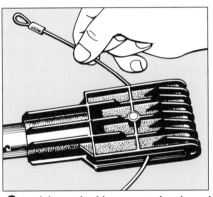

9 Feed the steel cable, connected at the end of the drive chain, around the pulley housed in the idler assembly.

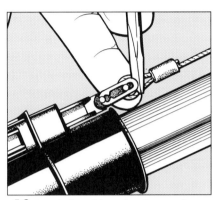

10 Attach the cable end to the traveler with a master chain link. As before, secure the cable with a retaining clip.

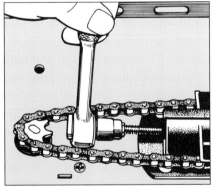

11 To adjust chain tension, tighten the adjustment screw on top of the power unit. Chain should sag about ½ in.

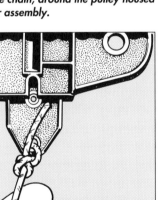

12 Tie the disconnect cord to the latch on traveler. Pull cord to disengage traveler so garage door can be lifted manually.

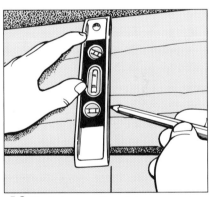

13 Mark the centerline of the garage door. Then, with a level, transfer this line to the header just above the door.

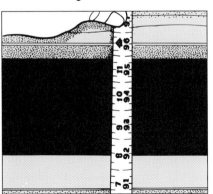

14 Find the highest point the door reaches by measuring from the floor as a helper lifts door. A typical height is 92 in.

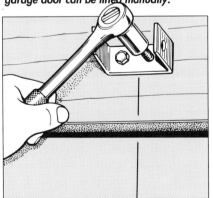

15 Fasten header bracket above door with two lag screws. Place bottom edge 2 in. above door's high-rise dimension.

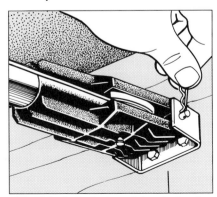

16 Slide clevis pin through header bracket to fasten idler pulley in place. Secure assembly with pin passed through lock clip.

it should have an unobstructed view of the door. Run the switch wire to the power unit and connect it to the terminals on its back (Fig. 22).

Adjustments

The final adjustments to an automatic garage door opener are very important steps toward permitting smooth and safe operation.

Begin by setting the same frequency code on the transmitter and the power unit. This is done by pushing the tiny rocker switches located inside the transmitter and on the back of the power unit (Figs. 23 and 24). Use a sharpened pencil to set the switches randomly.

Next, plug the unit's power cord into an electrical outlet. If an outlet isn't within reach, have a licensed electrician install one near the unit.

Now, test the reverse force adjustment. Press the transmitter button to close the door. While it's closing, use both hands to hold the door until it reverses automatically. If the door reverses when it is barely touched (or before you touch it), then twist the large knob on the power unit's underside clockwise a quarter-turn to decrease its sensitivity. If the door is difficult to stop by hand, turn the knob counterclockwise to increase the closing sensitivity.

Next, adjust the fully opened and closed positions of the door. Adjust the closed limit first. Push the transmitter button to close the door. It will stop a foot or two above the floor. Then, slowly rotate the small black knob on the underside of the power unit until the door is closed.

Now, press the transmitter button to open the door. This time, rotate the small white button on the underside of the power unit to adjust the door to the fully opened position.

Next, try the safety reverse adjustment. Place a 1-in.-thick board on the floor across the threshold. Then, push the transmitter button to close the door. The door should reverse after coming in contact with the block. If it doesn't, adjust the close-limit knob. This is a critically important adjustment, so make sure it is done properly.

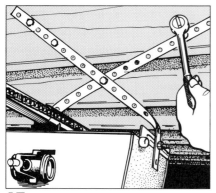

17 Hang power unit from ceiling joists with metal mounting straps. Bolt straps to unit and secure to joists with lag screws.

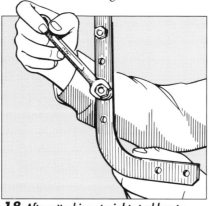

18 After attaching straight steel bar to traveler, bolt on L-shaped arm. The mounting holes in the bar permit adjustments.

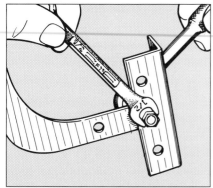

19 Bolt right-angle door bracket to the L-shaped arm. A special shoulder bolt permits the bracket to pivot freely.

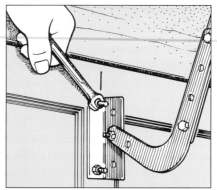

20 Fasten bracket with carriage bolts. Bore bolt-shank clearance holes through door and insert two bolts from outside.

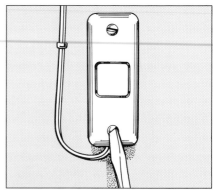

21 Install push-button switch inside garage. Place switch above reach of children and within sight of garage door.

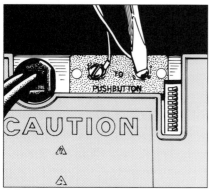

22 Run wire from push-button switch to terminals on power unit. Strip insulation and secure wires under the terminals.

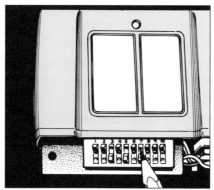

23 Remove cover on transmitter to reveal 10 tiny rocker switches. Use a sharpened pencil to set the frequency code.

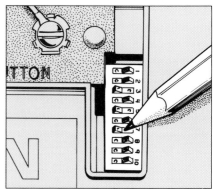

24 Repeat procedure on rocker switches at rear of power unit. Frequency code should be identical to that on transmitter.

How to maintain
A DOUBLE-HUNG WINDOW

Degree of difficulty: Easy **Estimated time:** 2 hours **Average cost of materials:** $25

The wood double-hung window with counterbalanced weights—a traditional style for many years—consists of an upper and lower sash, each of which slides up and down in its respective channel. The weights, connected to the sash with a cord and pulley arrangement, control its movement, allowing it to be lifted effortlessly or held in any position.

In recent years aluminum and vinyl components together with spring-lift mechanisms have been gradually substituting for wood-and-weight type windows. These newer type double-hung windows rarely need more than a cleaning and lubrication of the channels to keep functioning properly.

But not so with wood windows. As they get older they may occasionally develop annoying sticking problems resulting from paint or dirt accumulation, swelling and warping due to high humidity or direct water seepage under the paint film. And a broken sash cord will cause either jamming during movement or a failure of the upper sash to remain closed or lower sash to remain open.

Typical window problems and solutions are shown in the drawings here. More often than not, the simple remedies can get the window back to working order fairly easily. If not, it may be necessary to remove the inside stops, parting strips and sashes to make the corrections. Although these measures are involved, they're not difficult.

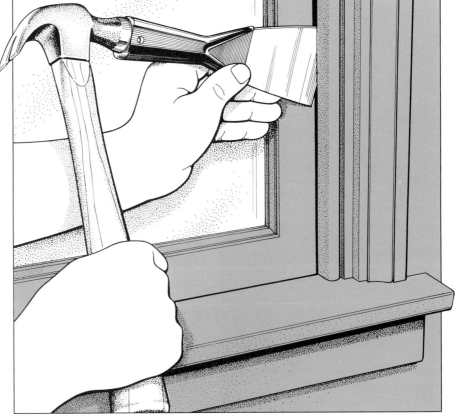

1 *A problem with a sluggish window can often be traced to paint buildup. To free a stuck sash, gently tap a wide-blade putty knife between the sash and stop to break the paint seal. Do this all around if necessary. Avoid using excessive force, which could damage the window.*

2 *Move outside and force a pry bar between the sash and sill and pry up the sash. Scrap wood pad protects sill.*

3 *Use a wide chisel to shave off dried paint lumps or dirt accumulations from inside the sash channels, stops and parting strips.*

4 *To create a smoother sash channel, wrap sandpaper around a wood block and sand the edges of the stops and parting strips.*

Freeing a stubborn sash

When a window is stuck fast, examine it carefully to determine the cause and exact location of the problem before attempting the solution. If a paint seal is the cause of the trouble, one of the methods shown in this example will usually free the sash. In any case, avoid using brute force, which could result in damage to the sash or the frame. Gentle prying or nudging will usually do the trick.

The problem of a sluggish window can usually be traced to paint-layer buildup. This reduces the gap between the sash and frame members which is necessary for free movement. This problem can be avoided by taking care to sand the old coating before repainting. Pay particular attention to runs and sags which should be leveled off either by sanding or scraping. Light sanding or scraping will also serve to remove built-up grime and to widen the gap when moisture has caused a stop or parting strip to swell or warp.

Sash removal

If the previous measures do not solve the problem, it may be necessary to remove the upper or lower sash, or both. This will allow access for planing, or for other work such as replacing the weight cords, repairing or replacing stops or for installing replacement window channels.

To remove the lower sash, it's necessary to remove the front stop only. This is usually held in place with a few finishing nails, but paint along the joint lines has the same effect as glue. Use a sharp utility knife to neatly score cut the paint on the joint line before prying the stop molding loose.

Removal of the upper sash necessitates removal of the parting strip. This, too, is

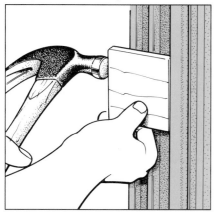

5 A lightly binding sash can be helped by gently tapping a wood block along the stops to widen the channels slightly.

6 Rub a candle or paraffin stick on the edges of the inside stop, parting strip and outside stop to get sash to slide smoothly.

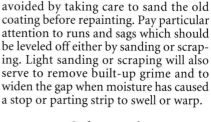

7 To remove inside stop, score paint on joint line with utility knife; use chisel to pry off. Start at bottom of stop, not at top.

8 Once the stop is removed, grip lower sash, then lift it slightly to clear stool trim and swing it out. Stool is attached to sill.

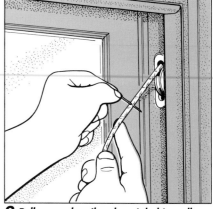

9 Pull on cord until sash weight hits pulley; then slip nail through cord. This keeps sash from being pulled back into jamb.

10 Brace sash in place, pull cord knot from containment hole. Undo the knot, free the cord and repeat operation for other side.

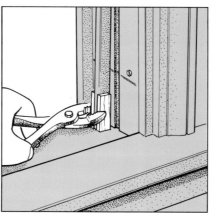

11 Use pliers to pull the parting strip out of its groove so you can remove upper sash. Protective wood strips prevent damage.

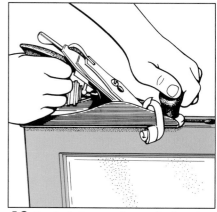

12 Hand planing may be required to trim sides of sash for better fit. Planing of inside stops and parting strips may be needed.

secured with finishing nails, but since it's recessed in a shallow groove in the side jamb, it's not removed by prying. Instead, carefully pull it out with pliers. Keep in mind that the blind stop at the rear of the window—facing the outside—is captive and can't be removed to free a sash.

Replacing sash cords

When a sash weight cord needs to be replaced, due to breakage, it's best to replace all the cords in the window at the same time. Otherwise the whole process will have to be repeated when another of the old cords breaks, which is a likely possibility. However, instead of using cord, the replacement should be made with long-lasting, durable chain. Although weight-balanced windows are no longer mass-produced, sash chain, together with its companion coil and clip-fastening fixtures, is generally available at hardware stores and lumberyards.

The typical weight counterbalance system has sash weight access panels at the base of the jambs. If your windows don't have these panels, then you'll have to

remove the inside casing trim to gain access to weights.

If your windows are equipped with the more modern spring-type lifting devices, the maintenance required usually involves merely adjusting the tension of the spring which is encased in a metal tube. The adjustment is made by detaching the

spring case from the jamb, then winding or unwinding the spring, as required, to increase or decrease the tension.

If you care to invest the moderate cost, you can upgrade your double-hung windows with replacement window channels which are designed to replace cord and pulley and spring lift systems.

13 *Windows with sash weight pocket panels make for easy access. Remove the screws on covering panel to get to weight.*

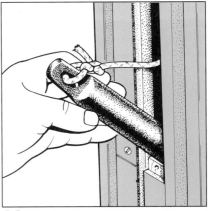

14 *Lift weight from opening to replace cord with chain. With some windows, casing trim must be removed to gain access.*

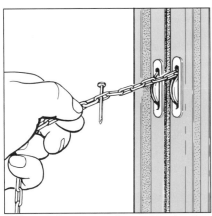

15 *Feed chain over pulley until lead end can be pulled from access hole. Insert nail through link to keep the chain from falling.*

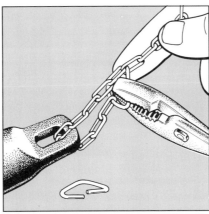

16 *Loop the chain through the hole in sash weight. Then secure it with a chain clip (shown) or with a short length of wire.*

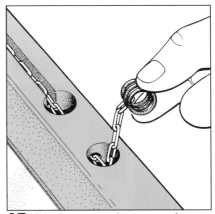

17 *Slide chain into sash groove and out containment hole; then attach end. Push retainer into hole and lift sash in place.*

18 *Aluminum replacement channels are available for standard-size windows. To install, channels are first fitted to both sashes.*

19 *Discard window weights, pulleys and parting strips; slide channels and sashes in place, bottom first. Reinstall sash stops.*

20 *Use silicone spray lubricant to keep sash channels clean and smooth. It works on both wood and metal channels.*

How to fix
BROKEN WINDOWS

Degree of difficulty: Easy   **Estimated time:** 2 hours   **Average cost of materials:** $10

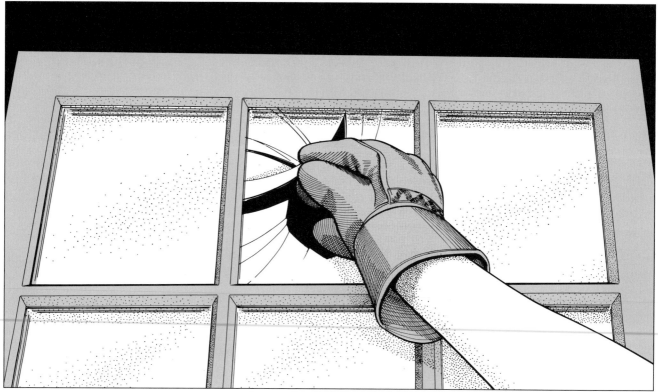

An errant baseball or a Frisbee is often the culprit behind a broken windowpane. Luckily, reglazing is an easy task and repairing the damage takes a minimal amount of time.

Replacing a broken pane of window glass is a relatively simple task and, for most home owners, an inevitable one. However, if it's performed carelessly, it can result in serious injury. Follow the shop-tested, step-by-step instructions presented here to repair shattered windows like a pro—safely and easily.

To make the job easier, it's advisable to remove the window sash from the frame and repair it on a workbench. Lay the sash on the bench with the exterior side of the window facing up. While wearing heavy-duty leather work gloves and safety goggles, pull free any loose shards of glass from the wood sash and muntins.

Next, remove the old putty from around the sash and muntins. If the putty hasn't become too hard, you can pry it off with an old chisel or rigid-blade putty knife. Otherwise, you'll have to soften the putty first with a heat gun and then scrape it off (Fig. 1). Also, remove the glazier's points that you'll find under the

old putty stuck into the wood sash and muntins. The small metal points secure the window glass to the sash.

After removing the old putty, pull free all of the remaining broken glass. Now scrape down the sash and muntin rabbets to the bare wood using a chisel held perpendicular to the surface (Fig. 2). Try to avoid digging into and gouging the wood.

Next, apply a liberal coat of linseed oil to the clean rabbets with a small brush. The linseed oil will prevent the bare wood from absorbing any oil out of the new glazing putty. Oil in the glazing putty helps to keep the putty flexible and crack-free longer.

Installing a new pane

While the linseed oil is soaking into the wood, cut the replacement glass pane. Cut the pane from single-strength glass with a standard glass cutter, available at most home centers and hardware stores.

Measure the opening and subtract ⅛ in. from the overall width and length.

Next, nail a straight-edged board to the workbench and butt the replacement glass against it. Lubricate the cutline with kerosene and, while using a framing square as a guide, score the glass with the cutter (Fig. 4).

While wearing gloves and goggles, hold the glass with the cutline on the edge of the bench. Push down firmly and the glass will break cleanly on the line. Although glass cutting is very easy, if you'd rather, you can custom-order precut glass from most hardware stores and glass shops.

Next, apply a ⅛-in.-thick bead of glazing compound (not putty) in the rabbets around the opening (Fig. 5). Compound is preferred for window repairs over putty because it doesn't become brittle when it dries, and it also resists cracking and shrinking.

While wearing gloves, position the glass pane in the opening and press down gen-

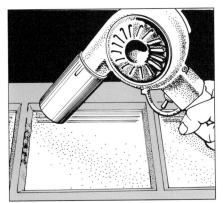

1 *Use a flameless heat gun to soften old, brittle putty. Heat the putty (be careful not to char the wood) and then scrape it off.*

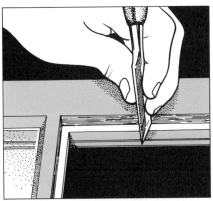

2 *Scrape clean sash and muntin rabbets with a sharp chisel. Hold chisel perpendicularly and scrape down to bare wood.*

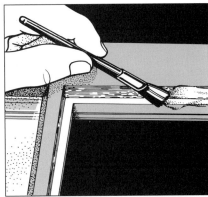

3 *Apply a coat of linseed oil to the clean rabbets. This prevents bare wood from absorbing oil out of the new compound.*

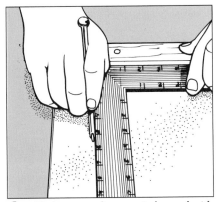

4 *Hold glass cutter between index and middle fingers and score glass. Use square and board, nailed to bench, as guides.*

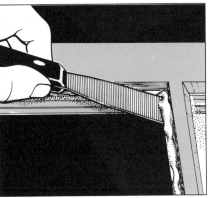

5 *Use a flexible-blade putty knife to apply a ⅛-in.-thick bead of glazing compound in the four rabbets around the opening.*

6 *Place new pane into the opening and press down gently. Squeeze out air pockets trapped in compound for a good seal.*

7 *Install push-point glazier's points with a rigid-blade putty knife. Force the points into the wood to hold the glass securely.*

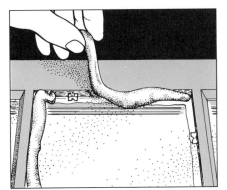

8 *Roll glazing compound between your palms to form ⅜-in.-dia. ropes. Lay these ropes around the perimeter of the glass.*

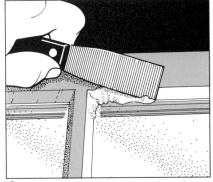

9 *Hold the putty knife at an angle and press the compound into the rabbets to form a smooth, triangular-shaped bead.*

tly to eliminate any air pockets that may appear in the compound.

Then, using a rigid-blade putty knife, push glazier's points in the rabbets to secure the glass (Fig. 7). Space the points about 4 in. apart.

Note that there are two basic types of glazier's points: there's the flat, triangular style, and there are the push points. Push points, as shown in Fig. 7, have two turned-up tabs that make them much easier to install than the flat triangular points.

Roll glazing compound between your hands to form ⅜-in.-dia. ropes. Lay the ropes around the edges of the pane (Fig. 8) and press them into place with your fingers. Make sure to conceal all of the glazier's points.

Now, using a flexible-blade putty knife, compress the compound to form a smooth, triangular-shaped bead (Fig. 9). Clean off the excess compound from both sides of the glass.

Allow the compound to dry for about a week before painting it. Then, apply the paint so that it extends about 1/16-in. onto the glass to form a moisture seal. This little trick will help to protect the compound while helping to seal the glass from excessive moisture.

How to install
WINDOW SHUTTERS

Degree of difficulty: Medium   **Estimated time:** 3 hours   **Average cost of materials:** $80

Shutters are available at lumberyards and home centers. They are an affordable way to spruce up tired-looking windows while offering a way to control light and privacy.

Dressing up your windows with wood shutters is a great way to add an exciting visual accent to the decor of your home. Installing shutters, however, is not simply window dressing. You can swing aside these fully functional accessories for maximum light and visibility, or adjust the louvers for just the right combination of sun and privacy.

In addition to the traditional adjustable-louver variety, shutters are also available in fixed-louver and non-louver, fabric-covered versions. Whatever style you choose, however, the installation procedure is the same.

Tools and types
While installing interior wood shutters isn't a difficult job, it does require careful measuring and trimming. To get the job done you'll need a few basic tools. A tape

measure, saw, plane, awl, chisel, drill and screwdriver are the essentials.

Wood shutters are available at home centers and lumber dealers in single panel sizes ranging from 6 x 16 in. through 12 x 36 in. In addition to being sold as individual panels, you'll also find them in sets of four.

Shutter hardware is sold in a separate kit that includes everything you'll need for a four-panel installation. Also available is a hanging-strip hardware kit that permits vertical and horizontal shutter adjustments.

Don't forget to consider the style of the installation. As an alternative to a full-window installation, cafe style features a row of shutters along the bottom half of the window leaving the top open. In a tier-on-tier installation, a set of shutters is hung above another. One of these alter-

nates is a good solution if your window height is greater than the tallest available shutter (Fig. 1).

Measuring the window
First, decide whether you'll be mounting the shutters on the inside of the window (jamb), or outside the jamb on the trim (casing). Installing the shutters on the casing is accomplished with a hanging-strip kit, and shutter fitting is somewhat easier.

Our instructions describe inside mounting, but the general procedure for installing the shutters on the casing is similar.

Measure the height and width of the area to be covered by the shutters. Because the jambs or casings may not be parallel, measure at several locations and take note of the shortest height and narrowest width

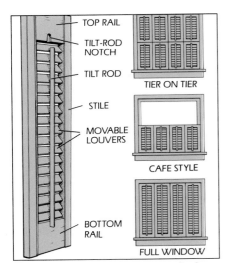
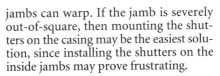

1 *While their components are standard, shutters are offered in a range of sizes and can be installed in three basic ways.*

measurements (Fig. 2). Jot the measurements down and take them with you when you go to purchase the shutters.

Using a large steel square, check that the window jamb is square (Fig. 3). Over time, with constant exposure to moisture and changing temperatures, window

3 *Check the window jambs for square. Severely out-of-square jambs make an outside, casing installation a better idea.*

jambs can warp. If the jamb is severely out-of-square, then mounting the shutters on the casing may be the easiest solution, since installing the shutters on the inside jambs may prove frustrating.

Trimming the shutters

Check the instructions supplied with the shutters to determine the amount of stock that can be trimmed safely. Then, lay out the shutters in the positions that they'll be hung. The tilt rods should be face up with the wide rails at the bottom. Place 1/32-in. clearance shims between the shutters and allow for 1/16-in. clearance where the shutters meet the jamb (Fig. 4).

Unless the amount of wood to be removed is very slight, it's best t o divide the excess among all the shutters and trim both sides of each to reach the desired dimension. Use a hand plane to trim the shutters to width (Fig. 5).

If the window jamb is slightly out-of-square, hold one shutter against a jamb and lean it so the top can be held against the top of the window opening. Then, scribe the cutting angle with a compass fitted with a pencil (Fig. 6).

Lay out the top and bottom cutting lines allowing 1/8 in. for clearance. If you're installing the shutters in a tier-on-tier configuration, allow for a 1/16-in. clearance between the shutter rows. Use a sharp, fine-tooth crosscut saw to cut the shutters to length (Fig. 7).

Installing hinges

Fixed-pin butt hinges are used between shutters, and loose-pin angled-leaf hinges are used to connect the end shutters to the window jambs.

The shutter-to-jamb hinges are usually installed in recesses cut in the shutter stiles. First, lay out the hinge positions. Cut each hinge recess by making a series of cuts with a backsaw (Fig. 8). Then

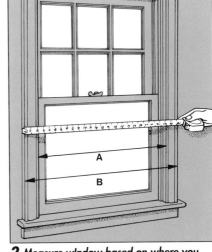

2 *Measure window based on where you want the shutters installed: between the jambs (A) or overlapping the casing (B).*

remove the waste with a chisel (Fig. 9). If you prefer, you can omit the recess. In this case, you'll have to increase the clearance between the shutters and jamb.

Use an awl to mark the screw locations, bore the screw pilot holes and then install the hinges.

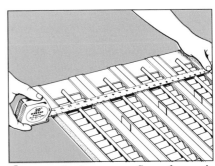

4 *Lay out the shutters on a flat surface and place 1/32-in. shims in between. Then determine amount to be trimmed from edges.*

5 *A sharp hand plane removes stock when trimming. Remove an equal amount from all shutters for uniform appearance.*

6 *Shutters for slightly out-of-square windows can be cut to fit. Scribe line with compass while holding shutter in place.*

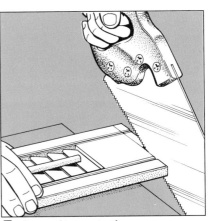

7 *After marking cutting lines, remove excess length from shutters with a sharp, fine-tooth crosscut saw. Sand edges smooth.*

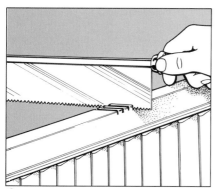

8 *To recess loose pin hinges in shutter edge, first make saw cuts. Cut only as deep as the thickness of the hinge leaf.*

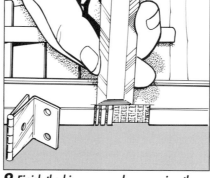

9 *Finish the hinge recess by removing the waste with a chisel. Then, mark screw positions, bore pilot holes and secure hinges.*

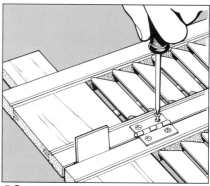

10 *Mount fixed-pin hinges by first laying out shutters with shims for clearance. Shutters rest on wood strips to protect tilt rod.*

11 *Temporarily position shutters in opening and shim for appropriate clearance. Carefully mark hinge locations on jamb.*

Securing to the window

After the hinges have been installed, place ¹⁄₁₆-in. shims on the windowsill and position the shutters in the opening. Then, mark the hinge locations on the window (Fig. 11). Remove the shutters and lift out the loose pins. Screw the four hinge halves to the window (Fig. 12).

Finally, align the knuckles of the hinge halves on the shutters and window, and insert the pins.

If you're mounting the shutters on hanging strips, first bolt the loose-pin hinges to the strips by passing the bolts through the slotted holes (Fig. 13). Center the bolts in the slots and temporarily tighten. Then, align the shutters with the strips and mark the hinge locations on the shutter edges. Remove the loose pins and install the hinge halves on the shutters. Then screw the strips to the window and hang the shutters. Loosen the bolts and adjust for correct clearance. Tighten the bolts and install the remaining screws.

12 *After boring the screw pilot holes, secure hinge halves to the jamb with the supplied screws. Align and install shutters.*

Although shutters are available prefinished, a spray stain or paint is an easy way to top off the unfinished type. Tape newspaper over surrounding areas. Coat the backs of the shutters first, allow them to dry, and then coat the fronts.

To install the shutter-to-shutter hinges, place the shutters facedown. Place ¹⁄₃₂-in. shims in between the shutters to separate them. Then mark the pilot holes with a pencil and use a drill to bore the pilot holes. Secure the hinges in place (Fig. 10).

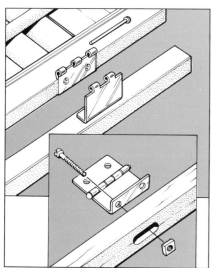

13 *Hanging kit has strips with slotted holes for adjustment. After bolting hinge, mark shutter hinge location and install.*

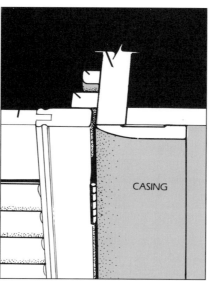

CASING

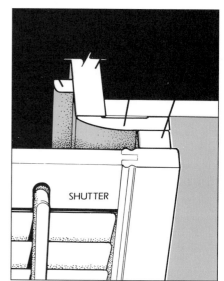

SHUTTER

14 *A hanging-strip kit can be used for inside window mountings (left) or securing shutters to casing (right). Secure strips to window, engage hinges and insert loose pins.*

AROUND THE HOUSE 5

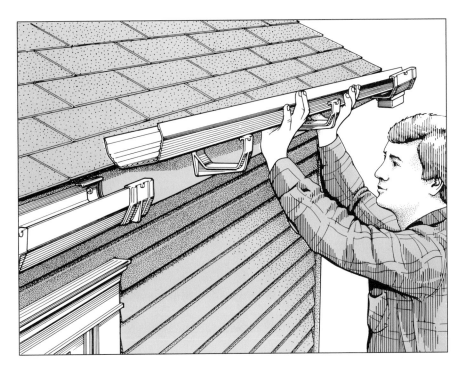

How to install
VINYL GUTTERS

Degree of difficulty: Medium   **Estimated time:** 6 hours   **Average cost of materials:** $100

Gutters may be made from aluminum or wood. For durability, however, new vinyl gutter systems are recommended for replacement installations.

Like most people, you've put it off too long already. The old aluminum gutters and downspouts in this example are probably similar to yours. Although the system had stood up well over the years, it was now a leaky, corroding, dented eyesore. Among the variety of replacement gutter systems available are several kinds made of plastic (vinyl).

Vinyl gutters have been available to home owners for many years now. However, only recently have they become popular due to newly designed systems that stress easy, do-it-yourself installation and new features, colors and styles. Vinyl seems to be a near-perfect material for gutters and downspouts. It won't dent, rust, chip, peel or corrode. It's resilient enough to bounce back from the blow of an errant baseball, and vinyl never needs painting. Although, you can paint it, if

desired, to match existing trimwork or siding. Vinyl gutters are available in white, brown and gray, with more colors to come in the near future.

But best of all, vinyl gutters are a pleasure to work with. Vinyl is lightweight, smooth-surfaced with no sharp edges or corners and it cuts easily with any fine-tooth handsaw. One problem with vinyl is that on very cold days it becomes brittle and it will crack if struck sharply.

The major differences between the various vinyl gutter systems are the shape and size of the gutters and downspouts and the method used to join the parts. Gutters range in size from 4 to 5 in. wide and in lengths from 10 to 32 ft. long. They come in three basic shapes: a modified U-shape (as shown in the drawings), a half-round, and a K-shape that resembles a standard aluminum gutter.

1 Snap a chalk line on the fascia. Be sure line slopes toward a downspout. Highest point of line is ¾ in. below roof shingles.

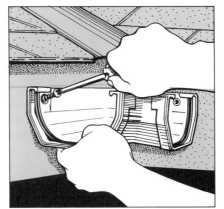

2 Attach inside corner fitting with its top edge on the chalk line. Avoid overtightening the screws which could crack the fitting.

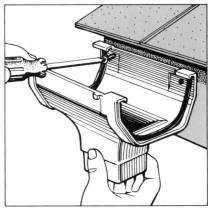

3 Secure the drop outlet to the fascia with two screws. Be sure outlet extends beyond shingles to catch rain runoff.

Downspouts come in square, round and rectangular shapes.

More important than the size or shape of the gutters is how the vinyl parts are joined together. The two popular methods used are solvent weld and snap-together parts with gasket seals. Since snap-together systems are easier and quicker to install, and more forgiving—they allow adjustments and reassembly—the choice is easy.

In this example we installed a solid PVC, snap-together system. The system consists of 44½-in.-wide x 10-ft.-long modified U-shaped gutters and 2½-in-wide x 10-ft.-long square downspouts.

The downspout system installed used an ingenious system of fittings, brackets, strap hangers, galvanized clips, drip edging, couplers and wedge-shaped vinyl shims to make gutters and downspouts adaptable to virtually any building.

The drawings here show the most typical situation: installing gutters on a vertical fascia. As well, you can install the system on a sloping fascia and directly to

exposed rafter tails. If the house has no fascia or rafter tails, use special strap hangers that attach to the roof. The gutter also offers some unique features to combat a problem that plagues all gutter systems: the accumulation of wet leaves and debris. The interior surface of each gutter is lined with triangular-shaped ridges that permit water to pass under the leaves to carry them away.

Besides featuring a standard drop outlet, the fitting that joins the gutter to the downspout, the gutter also has a high-flow outlet that has a larger opening with curved sides to draw and flush out more water more rapidly.

Use a high-flow drop outlet to move excessive amounts of rainwater or when you'd like to reduce the number of downspouts. One high-flow outlet will serve up to 1,200 sq. ft. of roof area as compared to 700 sq. ft. per standard outlet. For areas that collect lots of leaves, install a leaf separator to the drop outlet (Fig. 13). This unique fitting has an angled screen that rejects leaves, twigs,

acorns and other debris while water passes through to the downspout.

At the end of each downspout install a flip-up splashblock (Fig. 16) to carry water away from the foundation. Lift the splashblock out of the way when mowing and trimming the lawn.

Also, vinyl downspouts are adaptable to most other types of gutter systems. If your aluminum gutters are in good condition, but the downspouts need replacing, then install new vinyl downspouts to the existing gutters by using a special adapter fitting.

Cost considerations

Okay, it's agreed: Vinyl gutters are easy-to-install and virtually maintenance-free. The next question is obvious: How much do they cost? Generally, vinyl gutters are comparable in price to painted, heavy-gauge aluminum gutters. A typical 40-ft. vinyl gutter run with two downspouts, using standard fittings, costs about $90 to $120. A 10-ft. gutter costs about $8; a 10-ft. downspout about $9. Prices vary

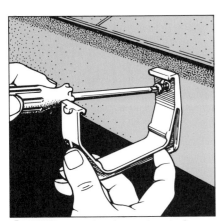

4 Install a gutter bracket, with a single screw, every 30 in. Be sure to keep the top edge of each bracket on the chalk line.

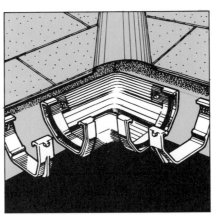

5 Attach a gutter bracket about 2 in. from each side of the inside corner to provide additional support for the gutter ends.

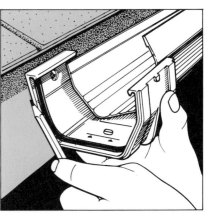

6 Here's a quick way to position slip-joint fittings: Align gutter end with insertion mark in fitting and pencil a line on fascia.

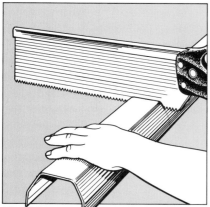

7 *Hold gutter upside-down and cut it to length with either a fine-tooth handsaw, radial-arm saw or power miter saw.*

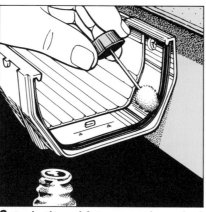

8 *Apply silicone lubricant to gasket seals of slip-joints to promote smooth sliding action as the gutters expand and contract.*

9 *The high end of a gutter run doesn't require a drop outlet. In such a case, install an end cap with gasket over gutter.*

around the country. Keep in mind that a complex job requires more fittings and is, therefore, more expensive. Vinyl gutter systems are sold at hardware stores, home centers and lumberyards.

Gutter installation

The first few steps taken are exactly the same regardless of the type of gutter system being installed including vinyl aluminum or steel. Start by drawing a rough sketch of the house showing all gutter and downspout locations. Measure the house and add these dimensions to the sketch. Using the sketch as a guide, list all the vinyl parts needed to complete the system. Most manufacturers offer a parts booklet that makes it easy to order the right components for your particular installation needs.

Next, take down the old gutters and downspouts. Pull the gutter spikes and cut strap hangers to free the gutters. Use a flat pry bar to remove the straps that hold the downspouts to the house. This is a good time to repair and repaint the fascia, if necessary.

Now prepare to snap a chalk line to establish a reference mark for installing the drop outlets and gutter brackets. Be sure the line slopes slightly toward the downspout to drain water from the gutters. If the gutter run has a downspout at each end, start at the center and snap a line that slopes toward each downspout. The recommended slope to drain water properly is between ¼ in. and ½ in. for every 10 ft. of gutter. Therefore, a 40-ft. gutter run will slope about 1 to 2 in. Position the highest point of the chalk line about ¾ in. below the roof shingles. Once the chalk lines are snapped, attach the drop outlets, gutter brackets and corner fittings with the rust-resistant, Phillips-head screws provided. Space the gutter brackets about 30 in. apart (24 in. apart in heavy snow regions). However, skip a bracket every 10 ft., or wherever two gutter ends meet, to leave a space for installing a gutter slip-joint. Be sure that the top edge of each fitting is on the chalk line to maintain the proper slope.

The inside surface of each drop outlet, corner fitting and slip-joint has insertion

marks that indicate how far into the fitting the gutter should enter. It's important to align the gutter ends with the insertion marks to ensure proper spacing; this allows the gutters to expand and contract freely without buckling. Starting at a corner fitting or drop outlet, lay a gutter section across the gutter brackets, but don't snap it into place yet.

Place the gutter end on the insertion mark in the corner or drop outlet and move to the other gutter end to position a slip-joint fitting. Align the gutter end with the mark on the slip joint and draw a pencil line on the fascia to indicate the fitting's position (Fig. 6). Screw the slip-joint to the fascia and apply silicone lubricant liberally to the gasket seals. The silicone maintains smooth sliding action between the gutters and the flexible neoprene seals.

Also, apply silicone to the seals of the corner fitting or drop outlet. Align the gutter section with the insertion marks and slip the rear gutter edge under the back lips of each fitting and bracket. Now rotate the gutter down and in to snap its

13 *Optional leaf separator has an angled screen that allows water to pass through to downspout while rejecting leaves.*

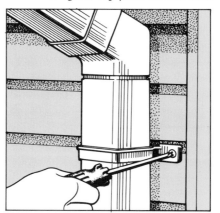

14 *Secure downspout with brackets. Note that a ¼-in. space between elbow and downspout is required for expansion.*

15 *Attach elbow to bottom of downspout with a sheet-metal screw or solvent-weld the parts with PVC cement.*

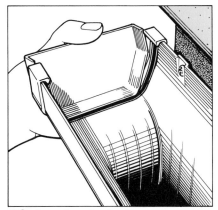

10 *The end cap for the drop outlet fits inside of the outlet. The gasket on the drop outlet creates a watertight joint.*

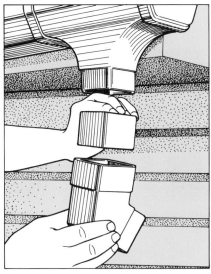

11 *Connect elbow to drop outlet with 2-in. sleeve cut from a length of downspout. Sleeve fits inside elbow and over outlet.*

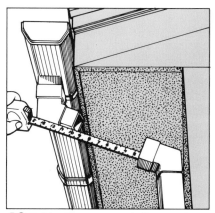

12 *Hold a downspout and elbow against the wall and measure between the two elbows. Cut downspout to match.*

front edge under the front lips of the fittings and brackets. Use your thumbs to apply upward pressure on the front lip of each gutter bracket to compress the seal and snap the gutter in place. Continue positioning slip-joints and installing gutter sections to complete the run. When you must cut a gutter or downspout length, use any fine-tooth hand or power saw. For the cleanest, quickest cuts, use a radial-arm saw or power miter saw. Finally install end caps to the drop outlets or gutter ends (Figs. 9 and 10).

Downspout installation

Start at each drop outlet and work down, piece by piece, toward the splashblock. Most gutter installations will require an offset to reach from the drop outlet back under the house eaves to the house wall. Make the offset using two elbows connected by a short section of downspout. Note that a 2-in. sleeve, cut from a piece of downspout, is needed to join the first elbow to the drop outlet (Fig. 11). To determine the length of the offset, put an elbow on a length of downspout, slip two downspout brackets onto the downspout and hold this assembly against the house. Now measure the distance between the two elbows (Fig. 12) and cut a section of downspout to match.

Next, install the vertical downspout to the house wall with downspout brackets. Two or three brackets are sufficient for a typical 8- to 10-ft. downspout. Be sure to leave about a ¼-in. space for every 10 ft. of downspout to permit expansion. Position the ¼-in. space just below the second elbow at the top end of the downspout (Fig. 14). Now fasten the third, or lowermost, elbow to the bottom of the downspout with a ½-in. No. 6 sheet-metal screw. You could also solvent-weld the parts together with PVC cement. Ask for instructions where you buy downspouts.

Then, join the splashblock to the elbow with a 2-in. sleeve. Again, fasten the parts together with a sheet-metal screw or PVC cement. To carry rainwater farther from the house, replace the sleeve with a longer section of downspout. A special adapter is available if you want to connect the downspout directly to a 4-in.-dia. sewer drainage pipe.

Although we've shown a typical installation, remember that vinyl gutters and downspouts are adaptable to work efficiently on virtually any type of building imaginable.

Ladders

When working on downspouts, make sure to use a sturdy ladder for any work that takes you close to the roof. Ladders are rated according to their strength, which is indicated on a label usually

16 *Swing-up splashblock makes it easy to mow around downspouts. It's 3 ft. long to carry rainwater from foundation.*

affixed to a rail. Typically, a Type II ladder is sufficient for most jobs around the house. Better yet, or if you plan to do any extensive work on your roof in the future, purchase a Type I ladder—designed for industrial use. Common sense should tell you never to use a ladder with loose parts or one that has not been maintained. At the end of each day inspect the ladder for signs of potential trouble. Store wooden ladders in a cool, dry place to discourage warping. Straight ladders are available in 4- to 12-ft. lengths. Extension ladders are available in lengths ranging from 16 to 40 ft. when fully extended.

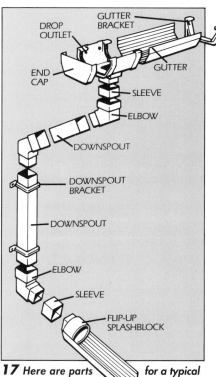

17 *Here are parts for a typical gutter and downspout. This variety of snap-together parts speeds installation.*

How to repair
A PORCH

Degree of difficulty: Medium   Estimated time: 18 hours   Average cost of materials: $350

Repairing a porch can mean a major overhaul or simply tearing up old, worn flooring and replacing it with new boards. Whatever the job, repairs can be accomplished without disrupting any structural components.

Because the porch is generally not built as an integral part of the main house, repairing or replacing it is well within the realm of the competent home do-it-yourselfer. The porch rebuilt in this example was set into the corner of the building. Other types include those that are open at both ends, and those supported by the building on three sides.

Before you begin work, make a preliminary inspection to determine the scope of the project. Inspect the deck, railings, posts and related woodwork for deterioration. To check for decay, probe the wood with an awl or screwdriver in several places. Bad flooring may be all that needs to be repaired, but this often suggests that more serious problems may lurk underneath.

Frequently, newel posts (the posts that terminate the railing at steps and do not connect to the roof) are poorly secured to the porch floor. These should be replaced or refitted for safety. Also check the condition of the roof support columns, which are prone to deterioration at their bases.

Next, inspect the porch for sags that may indicate frame deterioration. Hold a level against the roof support beam. If it's not level, determine whether the foundation piers or framework are at fault. If the piers are plumb and sound, they may simply need repointing. If not, you'll have

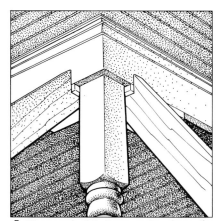

1 *Place notched 2x6s up against the roof beam to support the rod temporarily. Secure them near each porch column.*

2 *Toenail the base of the 2x6 supports to a short slab, and take up the roof load by driving tapered stakes into the ground.*

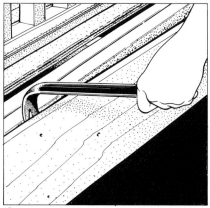

3 *Pry away the molding and fascia around the deck framework and inspect the rim joists for signs of deterioration.*

to replace them. Be sure to dig below the frost line and position them plumb. They can be built with concrete block or brick, and mortar. Poured concrete can also be used. Construct square forms or buy tubes specially made for this purpose. If you can, crawl under the porch to inspect the structure. Problems in the framework indicate that a more complete rebuild is necessary.

Steps, newels and railings

The steps that lead up to the porch are a common source of trouble. In the example shown here, the steps were fairly new and were manufactured as a separate unit, so removing them was simple. For older steps, you must remove the nails holding the stringers to the frame. If they need to be rebuilt, save a stringer to use as a pattern.

If the railings are in good condition you may be able to leave them in place and work around them. Otherwise, remove them by driving the nails that fasten them to the posts through with a drift punch. If you're not going to reuse them, it's sim-

plest to saw through the rails near the posts or walls and pry away the remaining pieces.

If you're going to replace the entire framework, make construction notes before you start. Record the distance of the outside rim joist from the building and also note the direction of the interior joists.

Supporting the roof

If you've decided to replace the flooring or are going for a complete rebuild, you'll first need to support the roof so it no longer rests on the floor structure. For our corner porch, we installed two temporary support posts, 90° to each other, at the porch corner. On porches with two open ends, it's usually only necessary to support the roof on the long front face. Place a support wherever there's a foundation pier.

Each support should be made from a length of 2x6 about 3 ft. longer than the height of the roof beam above the ground. The upper end of each temporary sup-

port must have a notch cut out so it will fit against the beam, and the bottom end must be cut off parallel with the ground line. Gauge this trimming angle by leaning a piece of the support stock against the roof beam on edge. Hold a level against the face and mark the angle. Transfer the angle to the bottom end and trim to the line. At the top end, mark a square notch about 3 x 3 in. at the same angle and cut away the waste. Then cut two 24-in. tapered stakes from a scrap 2x4 and two pieces of 2x6 about 15 in. long for platforms. Place the notched end of the support against the bottom of the roof beam, and then place the platform underneath the bottom of the support on the ground. Toenail the support to the platform. Then drive the tapered stake into the ground behind the platform until the support takes the roof load off the porch columns. When all of the temporary supports are in place and you're sure they're carrying the load, you can begin to remove the flooring and begin to disassemble the frame.

4 *Remove the rails with a pry bar and wedge. If you plan to reuse them, drive the nails through with a drift punch.*

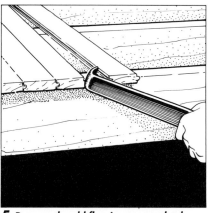

5 *Remove the old flooring to completely expose the underlying structure. Inspect the framework for structural soundness.*

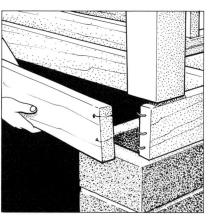

6 *With the roof temporarily supported, disassemble the framework. Begin by removing the end rim joists.*

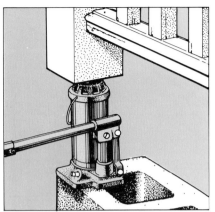

7 *Place a hydraulic jack between a foundation pier and porch post to adjust the roof to its correct height.*

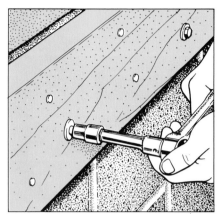

8 *Lag bolt a joist to the house, allowing for a space between it and the siding equal to the deck thickness, plus ⅛ in.*

Removing framework

Next, remove the deck framework molding and fascia. Carefully cut the caulk line between the siding and the deck with a sharp knife. Remove the decking with a pry bar and examine the joists for decay. If there are signs of rot, sometimes you can reinforce the existing joists by simply nailing new ones into the sides of the old ones. Often, though, it's more practical to replace them. To do this, remove the nails that fasten the joists to the rim joists at both ends. Cut new joists to the same size and nail them in place. Be sure to keep the top of the new joists flush with the top of the rim joists. If the whole deck framework is rotted, remove all the joists and start from scratch.

Removing porch columns

With the old framework out of the way, and the roof temporarily supported by the 2x6s, you can remove any porch columns that may need to be replaced. Columns that are left should be connected temporarily to the roof beam with lengths of scrap wood. These posts were

never intended to hang from the roof and, depending on how they're fastened, are liable to simply fall off.

Place a hydraulic jack between a foundation pier and porch post and slowly lift the roof. Raise the roof to its correct height, plus about ¼ in. for clearance. Adjust the temporary supports as you go. If the porch posts have been removed, you can nail two 2x4s together for a jack post. Be sure it's plumb, and toenail the top end to the roof beam so it doesn't slip.

Rebuilding the porch

The first step in rebuilding your porch is to construct the outside of the framework, or box. Begin by selecting a piece of joist stock to install on the building. It's rare to find perfectly straight framing lumber. Most boards have a crown which must be marked before you use it for framing. Sight down the length on one edge and mark the edge of the board that has the convex crown. The joist should be installed "crown up" so that the weight of the floor will tend to straighten the board over time. If the joist is severely crowned—more than ½ in.—strike a chalk line along its length and saw or plane to this line.

Next, determine the height of the joist that's fastened to the house. Measure the thickness of the new flooring, and add ⅛ in. for clearance. Then, make a mark on the house wall at this point and strike a reference chalk line. Cut the joist to length, taking into account the thickness of the

joists that will meet at corners. Use 16d galvanized nails followed by ⅜-in.-dia. x 3½-in. lag bolts to fasten the first rim joist to the building. Next, attach the perpendicular rim joists and the remaining outer rim joist. Double those rim joists that carry the internal joists, span long distances or support posts that hold up the roof. On our job, though the porch was a small one, we doubled the rim joists around the perimeter. Liberally nail these doublers with 16d nails.

Setting the slope

The porch should be pitched away from the building about ¼ in. over 4 ft. to allow for water runoff. Set this slope before the internal joists are placed. Place a 4-ft. level on one of the rim joists that extend out from the building. Insert a ¼-in. shim between the outer end of the level and the joist and raise or lower the box until the bubble centers. Install cedar shims under the frame to fix this height, or notch the joists if the frame is too high. Make this check on each side of the porch.

Next, lay out the positions of the interior joists. Minimum spacing for the floor joists should be 16 in. on center for good structural support. If your porch is small you can divide up the length into equal spaces that come as close to 16 in. as possible. Mark the joist positions with a square line down the inside faces of the rim joists that they hang on. Place an "X" to indicate on which side of the line the joists are hung.

Mark the crown on the lumber to be used for the joists and check that they're all the same width. Occasionally, sizes will vary slightly and this should be taken into consideration when positioning the joist hangers so the tops of all the joists will be flush. Set the joist hangers at the proper height and nail them in place using the special nails provided.

Measure the joist length across the box at both ends and cut the joists to fit. Slip them in place and nail through the hanger holes using the joist hanger nails. Then toenail the interior joists to the rim joists using 16d nails. Two nails per end are adequate.

Preparing framing for the newel post

Next, prepare the framing to accept the newel post. On this job, we found that the post was not fastened directly to the frame, but was held in place with angle brackets screwed to the floor. Since the post was basically sound and architecturally attractive, we decided to use it as part of the new structure. In order to attach it properly, we notched the end to receive a poplar splice that would extend below the floor and attach to the frame.

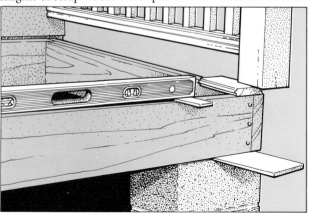

9 *For good drainage, slope the deck away from the house about ¼ in. over 4 ft. Use a 4-ft. level with a ¼-in. shim under one end. Adjust the frame until the bubble centers.*

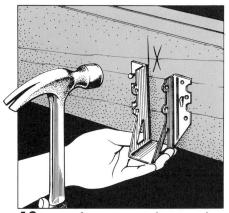

10 *Using a framing square, lay out and mark interior joist positions on rim joists. Nail the joist hangers to correct height.*

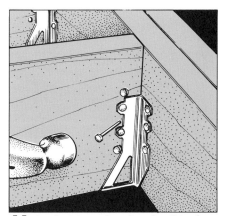

11 *Cut the joists to length and nail in place with joist hanger nails. Complete the nailing with 16d toenails, two per end.*

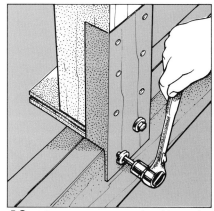

12 *Splice an extension on the old newel post to fasten it to the frame. Box in around the post for flooring support.*

We cut out the inside piece of the doubled rim joist so that the poplar extension fit it snugly and lag-bolted the post to the frame. Then we fit 2x4 blocking across the joint. This blocking supports the floorboards around the post. If you're replacing your post with a new one, extend it into the framework and box it in.

Making porch posts
Porch posts, both the posts that support the roof and the newel posts, can be made if necessary. Design details of these posts give character to the house and attention should be paid to building posts that are in keeping with the house design. Round posts are made on a lathe. If the post is longer than the capacity of your lathe, you can make it in sections. Turn a tenon in the end of each section that will fit a corresponding hole bored in the adjacent piece. Assemble the sections with waterproof glue. Square posts can be solid or hollow. Hollow ones allow you to create a wider post without the unnecessary weight of solid wood. They are built up

with boards butt-joined at the corners, and can be made in sections with sides that are parallel or tapered. Square posts are ornamented with base and crown moldings in keeping with the style of the house. Both solid and built-up square newel posts should have a cap, usually with beveled edges, to protect the end grain of a solid post, or to close off the open end of a hollow post.

To deck over our porch, we used tongue-and-groove clear fir, which is standard for porch floors. Face-nail the first piece in place using 8d galvanized finish nails, tongue edge out. If the groove edge of the first piece is exposed, rip or plane this edge to remove the groove. Nail the succeeding pieces by driving the nails diagonally through the tongues. Use a nail set to finish driving the nails and avoid marring the wood. If you have trouble fitting the boards, avoid hitting them in place with your hammer. Instead, cut a scrap of flooring to use as a tapping block. For badly bowed boards, face-nail and toenail a portion of the board that you can get to fit, and use a pry bar to pull the

rest of the piece into place. Let the ends run wild, to be trimmed when the floor is completed.

After the flooring is installed, you can remove the roof supports and allow the posts to rest in place on the deck. If you're replacing any posts, install them now. Toenail the posts in place with 8d galvanized nails. Snap a chalk line along the uncut floorboards to the desired deck overhang and cut to the line. When figuring the overhang, be sure to take into account the fascia and molding that will be applied and add an additional ½ in. to 1 in. to the overhang for a reveal. If you're reusing the old railing, toenail it back in place with 8d finishing nails. You can also purchase ready-made railing and baluster parts at some lumberyards, or make your own.

Making railings
To make the railings, select weather-resistant 2x4 stock such as cedar, redwood or pressure-treated lumber. Use a router or table saw to shape the top of the rail to the desired profile. We used a

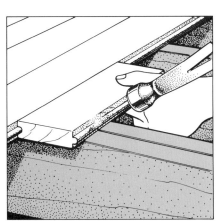

13 *Use a tapping block to tighten up the joints in the flooring. This saves marring the tongue-and-groove boards.*

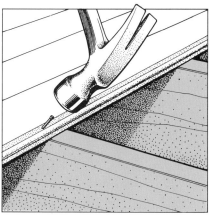

14 *Drive 8d galvanized finishing nails diagonally through the tongue. Finish driving the nails with a nail set.*

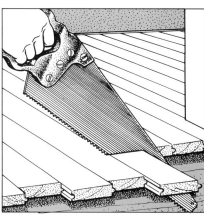

15 *It's quicker to trim the flooring after it's all installed. Strike a chalk line, taking into account necessary overhang.*

189

16 *Fascia boards are installed over the rim joists. Miter the corner and fasten with 8d galvanized finishing nails.*

17 *Install the decorative molding under the flooring overhang. Leave a ½-in. to 1-in. deck overhang beyond the molding.*

table saw to cut a simple 45° bevel along the top edges of the top and bottom rail. Then set up the table saw with a dado blade and cut a 1½-in.-wide x ½-in.-deep groove in the bottom of the top rail, and the top of the bottom rail. Caution: When working outdoors, always connect elec-

trical power tools to a circuit protected by a ground-fault circuit interrupter (GFCI). Also consult the owner's manual accompanying any power tool for the correct and safe way to operate it. Wear eye protection—and a respirator when sawing weather-resistant lumber. Rip two

strips to fit flush inside these grooves the full length of the rail. Cut the balusters 1½ in. square and to finished length. Measure the distance between the posts and cut the rails and strips to exact length.

To figure the baluster spacing, first estimate how many balusters you think you need for a run of railing. Divide the total rail length by the number of balusters desired plus 1 to get the approximate baluster spacing. Then multiply the number of balusters by their width (1½-in.) and subtract this from the total rail length. Divide this amount by the number of balusters plus 1 to get the exact spacing between each baluster.

Mark off the strips with the correct spacing. Nail the 1½-in. strip to the ends of the balusters at the marks and keep the edges flush. Repeat this on the other ends of the balusters. Place the assembly in the groove of the bottom rail and nail through the strip. Then turn over the unit and repeat the procedure with the top rail. Place the assembled railing in position and toenail it to the posts with 8d galvanized finishing nails. Use a nail set to finish driving the nails.

The frame is then covered with 1-in. fascia boards of the same width as the joist stock and mitered at the corners. Apply this fascia to the box with 8d galvanized finish nails. Because the porch is sloped, the line for the miter cut on the end fascia boards will not be precisely square to the edge of the board. Mark the appropriate cutting line by holding the uncut fascia in place and tracing the frame corner on it. Follow this line when cutting the 45° miter. Don't forget that it represents the inside line of the miter. After applying the fascia, install the molding with 4d galvanized nails.

Finally, caulk around the edge of the deck where it meets the siding to seal the corner and protect the house and porch framework from moisture. Reattach the steps using 16d nails. Then prime your porch and paint it with a good quality oil-based enamel.

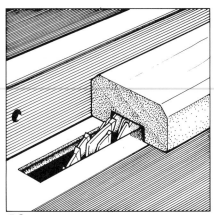

18 *Use a dado blade in the table saw to plough the 1½-in. x ½-in. groove in the rails for the baluster assembly.*

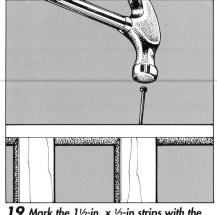

19 *Mark the 1½-in. x ½-in strips with the baluster spacing and nail to the baluster ends. Keep the edges flush.*

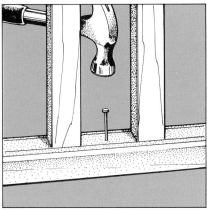

20 *Attach the completed baluster assembly to the top and bottom rails by nailing through strips with 6d galvanized nails.*

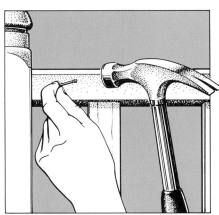

21 *Install the railing by toenailing it to the posts with galvanized nails. Finish driving the nails with a nail set.*

Dealing with specially treated wood

Wood that is specially treated for outdoor use, and which is often used in porch and deck construction, can be toxic if handled improperly. Such weather-resistant lumber, also called wolmanized and pressure-treated lumber, may be treated with chemicals that can be harmful if its sawdust is inhaled, or after prolonged exposure to the skin. Always wear a respirator when sawing this wood, and never burn any scraps in a fireplace. Some municipalities ban the disposal of chemically treated wood and sawdust along with ordinary household garbage.

How to install
A BRICK-IN-SAND PATIO

Degree of difficulty: Easy   **Estimated time:** 5 hours   **Average cost of materials:** $200

A brick-in-sand patio, also known as a mortarless patio, is a simple way to dress up a backyard. Bricks can be arranged in a simple or more complicated pattern.

The brick-in-sand patio, also known as the mortarless patio, will add lasting value and utility to your home. The color and texture of the bricks are pleasing and they bring a welcome relief from the monotony of a typical concrete patio or walk.

Also, the construction of a brick-in-sand patio requires less physical effort than its concrete counterpart, and it's more forgiving. Once concrete is poured, it's poured. With sand, if you make a mistake with a few bricks, all you have to do is take them out and replace them.

Most of the tools needed can be found in any home's garage or basement. The only special items needed are a mason's hammer, brick chisel or wide-blade cold chisel, line level and a masonry blade for a circular saw.

Planning the patio

Start by surveying your yard for its best and worst features. Consider whether your goal is privacy, relaxation in the sun or shade, or enjoying a view. Also keep in mind that you should not feel restricted to a simple geometric brick pattern if something else complements the surroundings better.

To help choose the overall size of your patio, roughly stake out the best area. Then check to see if it will comfortably accommodate what you'd like to do there: Is there enough room for a table, lounge chairs, a barbecue and so forth? Once you've determined where and how big the patio is going to be, you'll have to choose an edging.

One option is a border of bricks placed on their ends, instead of flat on their sides.

1 Lay out patio side nearest house first. Drive stake 1 ft. past both ends, then attach string and level it using line level.

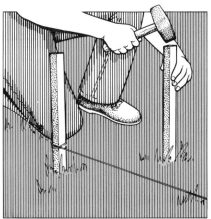

2 Drive stakes for adjacent sides at corners of patio. Hang string on stakes and, again, level it in place using line level.

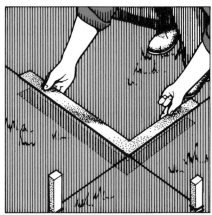

3 After all stakes and strings are in place, check each corner for square using framing square or by comparing diagonal measure.

These are called soldiers and are especially suited to circular or gently curving applications. They require a deeper trench underneath because they must line up with the surface of the flat bricks.

If your soil has a good deal of clay in it, which leads to bad drainage, soldier bricks should rest on a 6-in.-deep bed of gravel. Otherwise they will heave when the ground freezes.

Another possibility is making a concrete curb. This edging generally is poured in 6-in.-wide forms and requires the laborious mixing and handling of concrete. In our view this undermines the simplicity of the brick-in-sand construction and therefore is less appealing. Also, in cold climates the curbs will heave unless they are poured below the frost line, which can be over 4 ft. deep.

We feel the most practical edging is wood timbers, commonly 4x4, 4x6 or 6x6 pressure-treated stock, redwood or cedar. The pressure-treated stock should be approved for ground contact and graded for .40 retention. The redwood and cedar come in a variety of grades and prices, so when shopping explain to the salesperson what you have in mind for the wood. Another choice in timber edging is the standard railroad tie. True railroad ties are long-lasting and can be economical, especially if a railroad in your area is doing extensive track work. For this patio we used 4x6 pressure-treated timbers with an actual dimension of 3½ x 5½ in. for edging.

No matter what type of edging you choose when designing your patio, plan to use as many full-length timbers as possible. Full-length sides hold the bricks together better, look more uniform and, if straight, require less alignment. But if you want a large patio, simply butt the timbers together and just try to avoid very short lengths.

Selecting the brick

With the edging chosen and the patio size and shape roughed out, select your brick. We recommend brick that was manufactured as a paver, that is, a hard-fired brick with a severe weather (SW) rating. This is especially important in cold climates where freeze- and thaw-cycles will cause soft brick to crack and spall. Bricks are available in various geometric and interlocking shapes, but the most common are the standard and modular types.

A standard paver is 2¼ x 4 x 8 in., with 4½ bricks equaling 1 sq. ft. Modular brick measures 2¼ x 3⅝ x 7⅝ in. and it also takes 4½ bricks to cover 1 sq. ft. Because of the uneven square footage of modular bricks, they can be a bit more difficult to lay in a uniform pattern. But if you've chosen a design that is not geometric, you won't have any problems. We opted for standard brick with a rough face for good footing. But no matter what you choose, order enough brick to cover your square footage, plus about 5 percent more to replace any bricks you break.

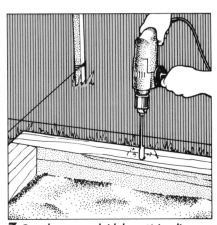

7 Once beams are laid, bore ⅝-in.-dia. hole through beams at 2-ft. intervals. Use spade bit in drill or auger in bit brace.

Site preparation

Preparing the site requires a shovel and pick (for stubborn areas), a few wooden stakes, nylon mason's string, a line level and a tape measure. Once your general area is staked out, choose one side as a starting point, usually the side nearest the house. Keep in mind that you want the patio to slope slightly away from the house so water will not drain toward the foundation wall.

The finished surface of your patio will only be as uniform as the excavation underneath it. Soil must be removed so the resulting surface is as flat (not level) as possible and so it slopes uniformly away from the house. Begin by driving a stake 1 ft. beyond each end of your reference side. These stakes should be equidistant from the house wall and should align with the outer edge of the patio, including the edging timbers. Level a mason's string about 4 in. above the ground using a line level and mark both stakes where the string intersects. Next, measure down to the soil. If you want the patio to be rough-

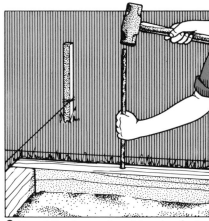

8 To stabilize beams, install lengths of reinforcing bar in each hole using a sledge hammer. Drive rebar flush to surface.

4 *Remove soil from patio area with shovel and pick for stubborn spots. Measure to strings frequently to check progress.*

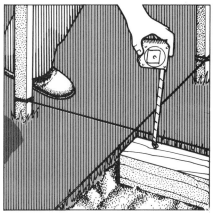

5 *Lay timber within perimeter of excavation. Then measure to string to determine depth of trench required under beam.*

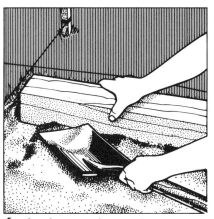

6 *Adjust beams—relative to the string—by adding or removing sand from underneath. Make sure beams do not rock.*

ly flush with the surrounding ground, then this point will represent the surface of the brick. However, if the ground already slopes slightly away from the house—which is a fairly standard building practice to help divert water away from the foundation—then you may want to keep the bricks at the high end slightly above grade. Two inches would be a good starting point.

Once the measurement from the string to the finished brick surface is established, add to this figure 2¼ in. for the brick and 2 in. for the sand underneath. This determines the depth of your excavation below the string.

Next, drive stakes and set up lines for the two adjacent sides. Level both lines in place and check where they meet the first line for square using a framing square. Both lines should slope away the same amount from the reference line, about 1 in. for every 10 ft. of patio. Measure down the same amount on the outboard stakes for both these lines, to establish the proper slope. Then lower the

strings to these marks. Add the layout string for the last side of the patio and check where it intersects the sides for square. This completes the layout, and because all the strings are on the outside of the finished patio, you can excavate without removing them.

Excavation
Begin digging at the perimeter of the patio. Check measurements to the line frequently to maintain proper depth. Then move toward the middle area. Always try to slide the shovel into the surface at a low angle instead of digging straight down. This will create a smoother, more compact surface for the sand and bricks above. For additional reference points in the middle of a large excavation, install a few temporary strings—that span the area—at the same height as your layout strings.

Once the excavation for the brick is complete, you'll have to remove more soil from the perimeter for the edging timbers. Because we used 4x6s with their wide

sides aligned vertically, this meant digging an extra trench that was approximately 4 in. wide and 1½ in. deeper than the rest of the excavation. Cover the bottom of these trenches with a thin layer of sand for adjusting the timbers. Slide the timbers into place and again measure to the string frequently to check for alignment.

When the timbers are installed, they should be stabilized with either wooden stakes or steel reinforcing bar (rebar). If your ground is soft, use 2x2 pressure-treated stakes at least 24 in. long. Drive these every 3 ft. around the perimeter of the timbers to a depth 1½ in. below the top of the timbers. Nail the stakes to the timbers with 16d galvanized nails. If your ground is rocky, it's a better idea to stabilize the timbers with rebar. To install, simply bore a ⅝-in.-dia. hole through the timbers at 3-ft. intervals. Then drive a 3- or 4-ft. length of rebar into each hole. You can buy the rebar at most building supply outlets. It's easily cut to length with a hacksaw or bolt cutters.

Laying the base
With the edging now in place, smooth out the interior as much as possible using a garden rake. Then cover the ground with 4-mil.-thick black polyethylene plastic, overlapping the rows about 6 in. This plastic greatly reduces the likelihood of grass and other plants taking root between the bricks.

Cover the plastic with sand. Builder's fill-sand is often used for patios like this. It's inexpensive and works fine. But we decided to use No. 10 limestone screenings instead. We felt the latter forms a superior base because the particles tend to "lock up" better once they are compacted. But if these screenings cost more in your area, stick with the fill sand. Your building supply outlet will know how much you need based on the size of your patio.

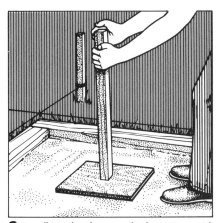

9 *Install sand, rake smooth, then spray with water. Compact sand with tamper made of ¾-in. plywood and 2x2 handle.*

10 *Rest screed on beams and move back and forth to smooth sand. Remove high areas with trowel, add sand to low areas.*

11 *Begin laying brick in one corner. Work from plywood panel, and use rubber mallet to adjust brick alignment.*

12 *Cut brick to size using brick chisel and maul. Score cutline on all four sides of brick, then strike with maul to break.*

13 *For cleanest cuts, use masonry blade in saw. Build jig from 2x4, 1x4 and 1x2 stock nailed to surface of plywood panel.*

Distribute the sand with a rake to the approximate depth, then use a pitch fork to pierce the plastic every 12 in. or so to allow for water drainage. Rake the sand as smooth as possible, then soak the whole area with water. Use a wide, soft spray on your hose nozzle to prevent washing the sand away.

As the sand is drying, make a screed board from a straight 2x4 or 2x6 that spans the width of your patio. The sand must be smoothed and tamped to a uniform depth of ¼ in. to match the thickness of the brick, so cut a notch on both ends of the screed board about 6 in. long and 2¼ in. deep.

Build a tamper like the one shown in Fig. 9, then tamp the sand in the whole patio. Make sure it forms a firm base, but don't worry at this point about slight mounds or depressions. Next, set the screed on top of the timbers and use a back-and-forth sawing action to move it across the sand. Stop and tamp the base ahead of the screed as it builds up. If the sand compresses so much that it no longer reaches the bottom of the screed, add more sand, tamp again and screed again. The result of your work should be a smooth, firm surface. Keep in mind that screeding areas wider than 10 or 12 ft. will require the aid of two helpers—one on each side of the screed, while you work the tamper and trowel.

Setting the brick

Stack all your bricks around the perimeter of the patio, then lay a sheet of ⅜-in. plywood on the sand near one corner of the timbers. The plywood will distribute your weight over a larger area and therefore will not distort the smooth sand base.

Begin laying the bricks at one corner. Start your pattern and move out from the corner, repeating the design as you go. For the tightest fit, set each in place by

abutting the adjacent bricks near the top, and then pushing the new brick down onto the sand. If you place it on the sand, then push it over, sand will pile up between the bricks and your pattern will be loose.

Do not stand or kneel on the bricks at this point because your weight will distort the pattern. Besides, working off the plywood will give a good vantage point for checking the bricks for poor alignment. If your pattern is geometric, check for alignment every few rows by holding a string or straight board across the entire patio. Have a trowel and some extra sand handy for elevating the bricks that are thinner. For those that are thicker, a few sharp blows with a rubber-faced mallet should bring them flush.

Cutting brick to size

If your pattern requires cutting some bricks, you have several options. You can use the straight claw end of a mason's hammer to score the cutline. Then simply strike the waste with the face of the ham-

14 *Once bricks are installed, spread sand over them and sweep to drive sand between cracks. Then, spray with water.*

mer and it should break on the line. But unless you are familiar with this method, it can be a little imprecise. A better approach for the beginner is to use a brick chisel or wide-blade cold chisel to score the brick first. If, however, you need a perfectly smooth cut, the best way is with a masonry blade in a circular saw. A simple jig for holding the brick and aligning the saw is shown in Fig. 13.

Cut into both sides first to a depth of about ¾ in. Make each of these cuts in three successively deeper passes. Once both side cuts are made, simply break the brick with a hammer and chisel. No matter how you choose to cut the brick be sure to wear safety goggles to shield your eyes from flying chips.

Once all the bricks are laid, spread some sand over the patio and sweep it in several different directions to force sand between the bricks. Spray the entire surface with water, let it dry and sweep off any excess sand.

Maintenance

Over time, a mortarless patio will show signs of age. Weeds may grow up between joints and individual bricks may crack and spall. Weeds can be plucked from between the joints and coated with a commercially available herbicide. Follow package directions for proper and safe use of the herbicide. Once the joints between the paver have been cleared of weeds, sprinkle sand over the bricks and then spray the area with water as you did when the bricks were first installed (Fig. 14). Once installed, bricks that get damaged can be pried up using an old screwdriver. For interlocking bricks, it may be necessary to use two screwdrivers to extract them. Add sand where the bricks were removed, replace the bricks and then use a tamper to bring them to level with the other bricks.

How to maintain
AN ASPHALT DRIVEWAY

Degree of difficulty: Easy   **Estimated time:** 2 hours   **Average cost of materials:** $20

Sealing a driveway extends its life and improves its appearance. It's important to prepare it for sealing. Clean it, patch its potholes and fill its cracks; then apply sealer.

1 *Clean oil and grease stains with driveway cleaner and scrub brush. Or use a solution of warm water and household detergent.*

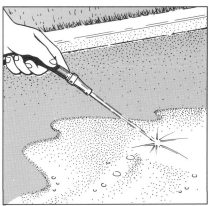

2 *To remove cleaner and residue, thoroughly rinse off the scrubbed areas using a garden hose with a spray nozzle.*

Your driveway, like your house, can easily become an eyesore if you neglect it. But it doesn't take much effort or money to keep an asphalt driveway in top shape and looking almost like the day it was installed. Also, routine driveway maintenance will keep small problems from becoming big ones and postpone the major expense of replacement.

Proper installation
All a driveway needs is periodic attention, like filling cracks and potholes and applying a couple of coats of sealer.

If your driveway was installed by a good paving contractor, it's about 4 in. thick and was well-rolled on a substantial subbase. If so, it has probably stood up well and all it may need is occasional sealing for cosmetic purposes.

If, however, your driveway was installed by an unscrupulous paver, and is only an inch or so thick, then it's probably already falling apart. Sealing and patching will help its appearance, but they only postpone its inevitable deterioration.

Several forces act against even the best driveways, and here's what typically happens. Temperature cycles, especially freezing and thawing, cause the driveway to expand and contract over time. Although flexible, a driveway has a limit to how

3 *To prepare small holes for filling with patching compound, clean out crumbling pavement and dirt using a stiff wire brush.*

4 *Loose debris can be removed from narrow holes and wide cracks using a crevice nozzle and a shop vacuum.*

5 *Mound patching compound in holes using a small trowel. Patch should be about ½ in. higher than the surrounding surface.*

6 *Tamp down patch even with rest of driveway using a small piece of 2x4. Pack down patch as tightly as possible.*

7 *Complete packing of dish-shaped potholes by placing a board facedown and pounding on it with a heavy hammer.*

8 *Smooth patching compound with a trowel and work it to a feather edge. This compound is ideal for repairs against curbs.*

many expansion and contraction cycles it can take. Eventually, small cracks open in its surface and water seeps through to the sub-base. Periodic wettings compact and settle the soil, creating a sizable void under the pavement. Ultimately, the weight of an automobile will crush through that spot, causing a pothole.

Or, water trapped in cracks below the surface turns to ice during a freeze. Water expands when frozen and enlarges the cracks. Gas, grease and oil drippings act as solvents and damage the pavement by dissolving the asphalt, particularly during hot weather.

Surface preparation

It's important to prepare your driveway's surface before sealing it. Like any coating, sealer bonds better when applied over a clean surface. Also, patches and repairs last longer if they are made first, then protected by two coats of sealer.

Begin by using a shovel or ice scraper to scrape off lumps of grease and dirt. Pull grass or weeds out of cracks, trying to remove their roots as well. Otherwise, scrape them off flush to the surface and

apply a commercially available herbicide. Follow package directions for correct and safe use. Use a knife or trowel to dig out the roots and dirt, and enlarge the hole to provide a suitable cavity for the patching material.

Use a stiff broom to sweep clean the driveway and check for areas where grease, oil or gas drippings have marred and softened the surface. Scrub these spots with a driveway cleaning solution, or with warm water and household detergent. Use a stiff scrub brush and spray rinse the area with a garden hose.

Patching

Small holes and depressions are repaired with asphalt driveway patching compound. This pastelike material contains small aggregate (gravel). For a small hole, chip out all broken blacktop material around the edges to about 2 in. deep. Brush out or vacuum up loose material and fill the hole with compound to about ½ in. higher than the surrounding pavement. Use the end of a short length of 2x4 as a tamp to compact the compound until it's level with the pavement.

If the hole is shallow and dish-shaped, complete the packing by placing a board facedown on the compound and hitting its face with a heavy hammer. Finish off the repair by tapering the patching compound to a featheredge using a trowel. This compound is ideal for repairs that are needed near curbs.

The relatively fine consistency of the patching compound makes it easy to level, but since the featheredge is worked over the surrounding pavement, it's important that the pavement surrounding the hole be cleaned thoroughly to ensure the compound will adhere properly to the surface.

Cracks

Blacktop driveway crack filler comes in a cartridge and is used for cracks up to as much as ¼ in. wide. Brush or vacuum loose material out of the crack, then lay in a continuous bead of filler. Allow it to set for about 10 minutes, then stroke over it with a putty knife to level and firm the bead to the crack's edges. Read package instructions for the exact setting time. If the crack is more than ½ in. deep, it should first be packed with sand to within ¼ in. of the surface.

Potholes

A large pothole in the driveway is repaired with cold-mix, an asphalt-based filler that has larger aggregate than driveway patching compound. Typically, it comes in a large bag.

Use a cold chisel and hammer to chop out crumbling pavement until the pothole is rimmed with a clean, firm edge. If possible, undercut the hole slightly to lock the patch in place. Dig down until you get to a solid surface and remove loose debris from the hole's bottom. Shovel the mix into the hole, mounding it so it's about ½ in. higher than the surrounding surface. Compact the mound by tamping with a block of 2x4.

You can also pack the cold-mix by placing a scrap piece of plywood over the mound and driving back and forth over it with the front wheel of your car. Deep potholes should be filled and tamped in layers. Add some mix, tamp, then add more mix and tamp. Continue until the cold-mix can no longer be compressed.

Sealing

A coat of waterproof blacktop sealer, applied every two or three years, will protect the driveway from the sun, rain and snow, and will improve the driveway's overall appearance.

The sealer comes in 5-gal. cans and usually needs only to be stirred before use. Read the product label to determine how much area it will cover. Usually this ranges between 200 and 300 sq. ft., depending on the porosity of the surface. Apply the sealer with a long-handled applicator that has a squeegee blade on one side and a brush on the other.

First, pour enough sealer from the can to work a 3- or 4-ft.-wide strip across the driveway. Using the squeegee side of the applicator, spread the sealer across the driveway, working it into all tiny cracks and crevices. When the strip has been covered, flip over to the brush side and use it to level the coating and smooth ridges left by the squeegee. Work the brush at right angles to the path worked by the squeegee. (Roller applicators are also available and can be used as a driveway sealer applicator instead of a squeegee/brush.) Also make sure to don old running shoes and work clothes for this job—and avoid tracking sealer into the house; sealer is very messy and difficult to clean off surfaces it comes in contact with.

When applying the sealer to the driveway, don't leave puddles of sealer and don't spread it too thin. It's best to apply two coats. Read the label instructions to determine how long to allow the sealer to dry before recoating—typically about 36 hours between coats.

Supplies

Home centers sell a variety of driveway maintenance products, including driveway/garage floor cleaner in 1-qt. containers, patching compound in 1-gal. packages and crack filler in 10½-oz. cartridges. Cold-mix patching compound is available in 60- to 70-lb. bags. Do not attempt to reseal or patch asphalt if the temperature falls below 40° F. In the event that cold weather has caused cold-mix patching compound to harden, place the bag in a warm room for several hours to soften the material before working.

9 *Driveway crack filler is used on cracks up to ¼ in. wide. Fill deep cracks with sand before applying filler.*

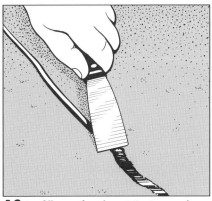

10 *Let filler set for about 10 minutes, then smooth and compact it with a putty knife. Apply a second bead if necessary.*

11 *Remove loose pavement around large potholes by chopping it out with a cold chisel and a hammer. Trowel in cold patch.*

12 *Cold patch must be thoroughly packed down. One method is to place plywood on patch and drive a car onto the plywood.*

13 *Apply two coats of sealer with squeegee/brush or a roller applicator. Spread the sealer first with squeegee blade.*

14 *After sealer is evenly spread, brush at right angle to direction taken with squeegee. Work the sealer into the surface.*

How to maintain
GARDEN TOOLS

Degree of difficulty: Easy   **Estimated time:** 1 hour   **Average cost of materials:** $15

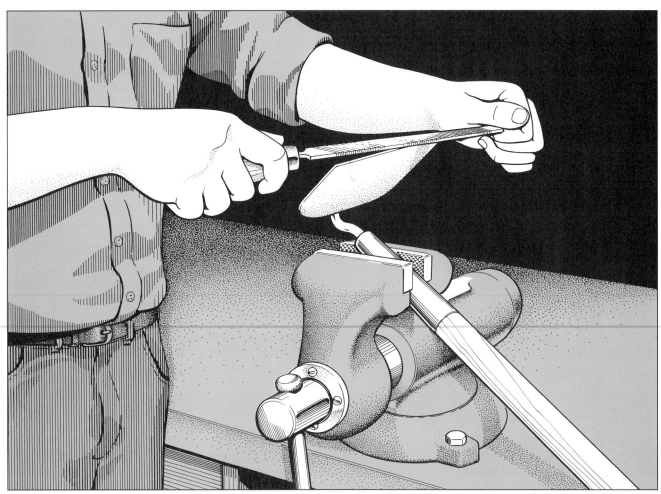

When comparing the cost of purchasing new tools to the minimal effort required to maintain the ones you already own, sharpening blades and replacing handles will seem like a bargain. Some files, sharpening stones and lubricating oil are often the only things needed.

As February melts into March and Old Man Winter's chilly grip begins to loosen and slide away, our thoughts turn to springtime, warmer weather and outdoor activities. To millions of home owners, spring also means gardening, landscaping and lawn care.

To some, these chores are considered a hobby and a cause for excitement and anticipation. To others, they are simply just that, chores. However you look at it, it makes sense to keep lawn and garden hand tools in tip-top shape. Simple routine maintenance will pay off in safe, effective and long-lasting tools. If this isn't incentive enough, check out the cost of

new garden tools during your next trip to the hardware store. You may be surprised at just how much a good shovel or garden rake costs these days.

Here, we show how to maintain and repair twelve different lawn and garden hand tools. Also, how to repair or, if necessary, replace a wooden handle. Plus, for those who own an old reel-type push lawn mower, we show an easy way to sharpen the blades.

Of files and stones

For most sharpening jobs, a fine or medium-fine, single-cut file will suffice. A coarser double-cut file can be used when

heavy stock removal is required. If an edge is badly nicked or damaged, use a bench grinder to reshape the edge. Then, sharpen the cutting edge with a file or stone. Regardless of the sharpening method you use, be sure to maintain the tool's original, factory-ground bevel angle.

The proper filing technique is a job for two hands, as shown here. Apply pressure on the forward stroke only. Lift the file on the return stroke. Use a file card or wire brush to clean the file.

Sharpening stones come in various shapes and sizes and in fine, medium and coarse grits. Stones may be used instead of a file or in conjunction with one. Always

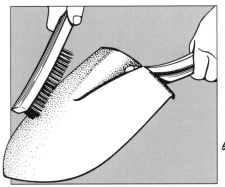

1 *Extend the useful life of tools by removing rust immediately. Use a wire brush or steel wool to expose clean, bare metal.*

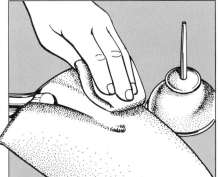

2 *Wash off caked-on dirt and mud. Then use a soft, clean cloth to apply a light coat of oil to protect the metal blade from rust.*

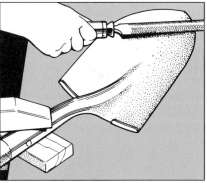

3 *Clamp shovel to a bench, for sharpening. Start with double-cut file to reestablish bevel. Sharpen edge with a single-cut file.*

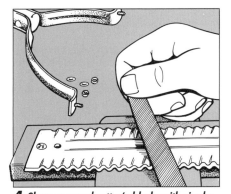

4 *Sharpen weed cutter's blade with single-cut file. Screw blade to wood block with edge overhanging. File on upstroke.*

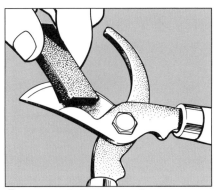

5 *Use a small, flat stone to sharpen pruning shears. Hold stone at original bevel angle and make several sweeping strokes.*

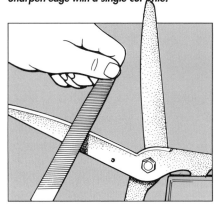

6 *Sharpen hedge clippers with a fine, single-cut file. Secure clippers in vise and make straight, in-line strokes across the blade.*

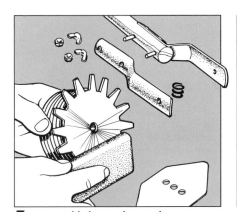

7 *Disassemble lawn edger and remove burrs from circular blade with a flat stone. Sharpen the teeth with a fine file or stone.*

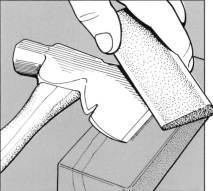

8 *Use coarse stone to reshape cutting bevel on a hatchet. Then, hone edge with a fine stone. Rest hatchet on a wood block.*

use lubricating oil on a stone to float away metal particles.

Sharpening edges

■ **Hoe**—A hoe's cutting bevel is located on the outside surface of the blade. Secure the hoe in a vise and, using a single-cut file, such as a mill bastard file, sharpen the edge. Be certain to maintain the original bevel angle. Also, advance the file forward and laterally simultaneously so that each stroke files across the entire edge.

■ **Shovel**—Before sharpening a shovel, inspect the blade for rust. Remove rust down to bare metal using steel wool or a wire brush (Fig. 1). To deter further rusting, apply a thin protective coat of oil to the blade with a soft cloth (Fig. 2).

Since a shovel blade often has a damaged digging edge (due to surprise encounters with buried rocks), it may be necessary to start filing with a coarse double-cut file (Fig. 3). Continue filing until all nicks and damaged spots are removed. Then, select a medium-fine, single-cut file to sharpen the digging edge.

■ **Grass/weed cutter**—The easiest way to sharpen the corrugated blade of a grass/weed cutter, also known as a grass whip, is to remove the blade from the

handle and screw it to a wood block. Fasten the blade so that one edge overhangs the block slightly. Then, clamp the block in a vise. Sharpen the edge with a stone or single-cut file. Advance stone or file on the upstroke, as shown in Fig. 4.

■ **Pruning shear**—The small, curved jaw of a pruning shear is best sharpened with a small stone (Fig. 5). Stroke the beveled edge in continuous sweeps. If a wire edge (burr) happens to form on the back of

the jaw, hold a stone flat against the jaw and rub lightly.

■ **Hedge clippers**—Sharpen hedge clippers with a fine, single-cut file. The secret is to file in straight strokes across the cutting edge while holding the file perpendicular to the blade (Fig. 6). Don't slide the file laterally. This straight-stroking technique forms tiny serrations on the cutting edge that help prevent such things as twigs and branches from sliding out from between the blades as the handles close together.

■ **Lawn edger**—To sharpen a lawn edger, first disassemble the tool's head. A typical edger has two blades: one rotating circular blade with deep teeth, and a stationary diamond-shaped blade. The teeth of the circular blade often have burrs due to contact with a sidewalk or curb.

Hold a sharpening stone flat against the blade and rub lightly to remove the burrs (Fig. 7). Sharpen the bevels on each tooth with a small, narrow stone or fine file. Sharpen the stationary blade in the same manner.

■ **Hatchet**—Sharpen a hatchet first with a coarse stone to redefine the cutting bevel. Then, hone the edge with a fine-grit

stone. Hold the hatchet against a wood block during sharpening to stabilize it (Fig. 8). If the head is loose, drive a steel wedge (sold at hardware stores) into the end of the handle, as shown in Fig. 20.

■ **Bow saw**—Cutting green wood causes the teeth of a bow saw to lose their set which, in turn, reduces the saw's effectiveness. Using a saw set, reset the crosscut teeth (Fig. 9). Note that the raker teeth—the double-pointed teeth—are not set. To sharpen the teeth, clamp the saw blade in a vise and use a triangular file to sharpen bevels on each crosscut tooth (Fig. 10). The raker teeth aren't beveled. File them straight across.

Handle repair

It's very important that all tool handles fit securely. Never use a tool with a loose, split or cracked handle. Note that some minor splits can be repaired, as shown, while in other cases, the handle must be replaced completely.

There are two major exceptions: Always replace a damaged handle of a striking tool such as a hatchet or sledge hammer. Makeshift repairs on these tools can be

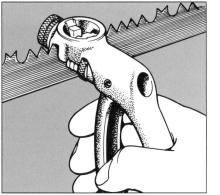

9 Crosscut teeth of a timber-cutting bow saw are set. They're bent alternately to left and right. Use a saw set to reset the teeth.

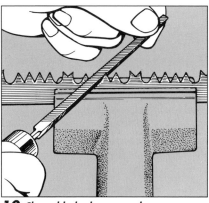

10 Clamp blade close to teeth to prevent chattering. Using a triangular file, sharpen crosscut teeth to match the original bevel.

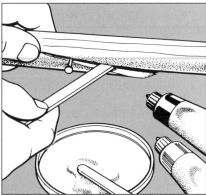

11 Repair splits with epoxy adhesive. Wedge open spilt with a nail. Mix two-part glue and spread it in split with a stick.

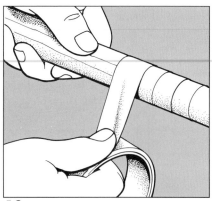

12 Hold glued-up split closed with tape. Be careful not to squeeze out too much glue. Leave the tape until the glue is cured.

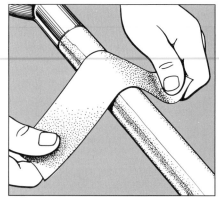

13 Smooth rough spots on handles to reduce the chance of getting splinters. Work sandpaper strip back and forth.

14 Using a cloth, rub boiled linseed oil into the handle to make the wood weather resistant. Repeat this treatment annually.

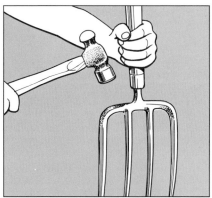

15 Broken handles are beyond repair and must be replaced. Use a ball-peen hammer to separate fork tang from handle sleeve.

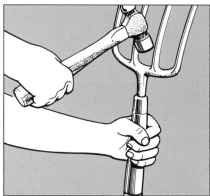

16 Using a ball-peen hammer, drive the fork onto a new handle. Be sure to hold the handle off the floor while hammering.

dangerous—a heavy piece of metal could fly off a repaired handle and cause serious injury. Epoxy is not strong enough to withstand forces exerted on these tools.

Repair a split handle with epoxy adhesive. Wedge open the split with a nail and spread the glue with a stick (Fig. 11). Pull out the nail and tape the split closed (Fig. 12). After the glue dries, sand the entire handle smooth to prevent splinters (Fig. 13). Finally, rub the handle with boiled linseed oil to help protect the wood (Fig. 14).

Sharpening a reel mower

Reel-type lawn mowers have spiral-shaped blades that make sharpening them quite tricky. However, an easy way to touch up the cutting edges is with automotive grinding compound, also called lapping and grinding compound. It consists of abrasive grit suspended in heavy grease.

First, slide a flat sharpening stone back and forth along the mower's bed knife to dress the edge (Fig. 22). Next, adjust the bed knife so that it barely touches the blades as the reel is rotated by hand. Then,

apply a bead of compound along the edge of the bed knife (Fig. 23). Finally, slowly rotate the reel backward about four complete revolutions (Fig. 24). Wipe off the compound with paint thinner and test the mower. If necessary, readjust the bed knife for clean cuts.

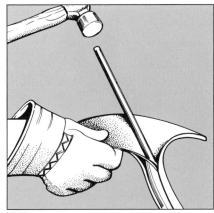

17 *To replace a spade's handle, remove the rivet holding the handle. Then, use a steel rod and hammer to drive out handle.*

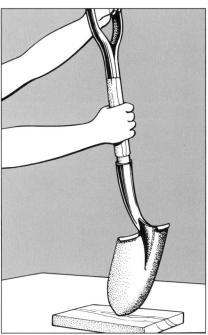

18 *Force new handle into socket and strike against wood block to seat it fully. If necessary, trim handle slightly.*

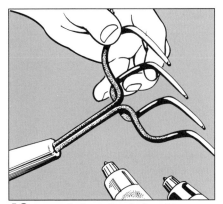

19 *Secure the loose head of a cultivator by filling socket with epoxy adhesive. Five-minute epoxy is ideal for quick repairs.*

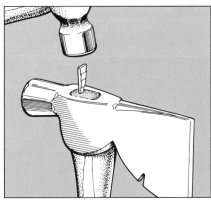

20 *To ensure a tight-fitting hatchet, drive a steel wedge into the top end of the handle. Position wedge at 90° to hatchet head.*

21 *Some garden sprayers have a leather washer attached to plunger end. Apply oil to washer to keep leather from drying out.*

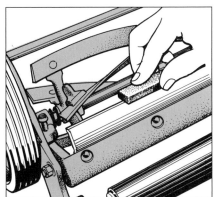

22 *Turn a reel-type mower upside down for sharpening. First, slide a flat sharpening stone back and forth across the bed knife.*

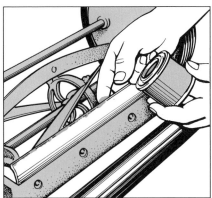

23 *Adjust bed knife so each blade barely touches it. Then, apply a bead of automotive grinding compound to bed knife.*

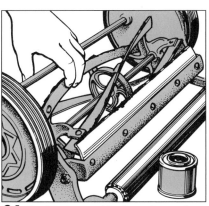

24 *Slowly rotate reel backward so each blade makes light contact with bed knife. Make four complete revolutions.*

How to repair
A GARDEN HOSE

Degree of difficulty: Easy   Estimated time: 1 hour   Average cost of materials: $5

1 *When repairing a hose, use a sharp utility knife to cut out damaged section. Be sure to trim the end as square as possible.*

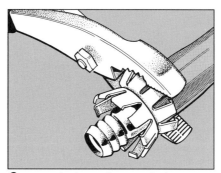

2 *Secure clinch-type fitting with pliers. Squeeze metal fingers around hose. Attach mating hose to the remaining fitting end.*

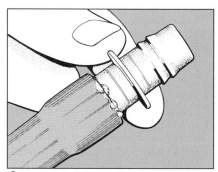

3 *Force ribbed sleeve into hose until collar butts against hose end. If fit is too tight, lubricate sleeve by rubbing it with soap.*

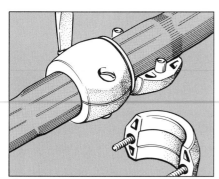

4 *After attaching mating hose section, screw plastic clamps to either side of repair. This fitting can be removed and reused.*

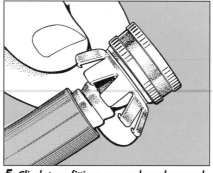

5 *Clinch-type fittings can replace damaged threaded fittings at hose ends. Here, a brass female fitting is inserted into end.*

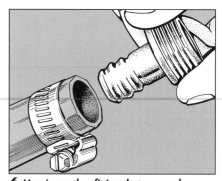

6 *Here's another fitting that can replace threaded fittings. Slip on hose clamp, insert fitting and tighten clamp with screwdriver.*

H as your garden hose sprung a leak? Are the hose fittings damaged or corroded? If so, you don't need to buy a new hose. Simply repair the one you've already got.

Repairs to hoses are simple and inexpensive—hose replacement parts and repair kits are readily available at hardware stores, home centers and garden supply shops. However, before we get into the actual repair steps, let's discuss briefly how to avoid damaging a hose in the first place. Don't fold over and pinch the hose to cut off the water, or store it with sharp kinks in it. Be careful not to drive over a hose with a car or strike it with sharp-garden tools, especially in cold weather. Don't yank on a hose when it's connected to the sill cock (exterior faucet). You can damage the hose and the threaded fittings. Also, never allow water to freeze in the hose. At the first sign of cold weather, bring all gardening supplies indoors.

Repairing a damaged hose
First, use a sharp utility knife to cut the hose and remove damaged sections. Try to cut the hose ends as square and straight as possible (Fig. 1). There are two common hose repair kits sold. One is a metal clinch-type, as shown in Fig. 2. The other is a plastic screw-together clamp (Figs. 3 and 4).

To install the one-piece clinch-type fitting, force the ribbed end of the metal fitting into the hose. If the fit is tight, soak the hose end in hot water. Once the fitting end is pushed into the hose, use pliers to squeeze down the individual metal fingers that surround the hose. Repeat this procedure to attach the mating length of hose to the remaining end of the fitting.

To install a screw-together clamp, first push the ribbed sleeve into the hose end (Fig. 3). If necessary, rub soap on the fitting to act as a lubricant. Next, push the mating hose length onto the other end.

Then, place clamps on each side of the splice and tighten the screws (Fig. 4).

Replacing a fitting
The threaded brass fittings at the end of a hose must be replaced when damaged. When purchasing a replacement part, be sure to get the right fitting—either male or female.

Metal clinch-type fittings are available for hose ends, too (Fig. 5). Force the fitting into the hose end and use pliers to bend down the metal fingers.

Push-in fittings and small hose clamps can also replace threaded fittings. Slip the hose clamp over the hose and force the replacement fitting into the hose end (Fig. 6). Using a screwdriver, tighten the clamp over the hose.

If your garden hose is beyond repair, purchase another made of either plastic, reinforced plastic or rubber. Plain plastic is the cheapest and the least durable.

How to replace
A LAWN MOWER PULL-ROPE

Degree of difficulty: Easy   Estimated time: 1 hour   Average cost of materials: $10

Let's face it. Without that pull-rope wound and waiting, even the best maintained small engine becomes a useless lawn ornament. And don't think that electric-start engines are immune. If this system fails, you must rely on the pull-rope to get the job done.

All ropes wear out eventually. The wise home owner will keep an eye on the condition of the pull-rope so it can be replaced before it breaks. The following rope replacement procedures cover most of the pull-rope starters found on Briggs & Stratton and Tecumseh engines.

Varying engines and applications require different length ropes, so make sure you get an exact replacement. To protect against unraveling, burn both ends of the new rope and use a cloth to wipe them smooth while they're still hot. Avoid working on a lawn mower that is still warm from use.

Briggs & Stratton starters

First, disconnect the spark plug cable from the plug. Use a jumper cable with alligator clips on each end to ground the cable to a metal part of the engine. This is a precaution against accidental starting.

Next, unscrew the securing clip that holds the throttle cable to the housing. Remove the housing bolts and remove the housing (Fig. 1). On the underside of the housing you'll be able to find the starter assembly.

Cut the rope near the handle, pry out the metal rope retaining pin and remove the old rope (Fig. 2). Pull the remaining rope out of the starter as far as it will go. Then, while holding the pulley in place with your thumb, pry the knotted end out of the pulley and cut off the knot (Fig. 3). Remove the rope and then slowly allow the pulley to return to its unwound position.

Tie a knot in one end of the new rope. Turn the pulley counterclockwise as far as it will go, back it off two turns and thread the unknotted end through the hole in the pulley while holding the pulley in place with your thumb (Fig. 4). Then, pull the rope through the hole in the housing. Stretch the rope tight to engage the knotted end and slowly allow the pulley to rewind the rope (Fig. 5). Thread the other end of the rope through

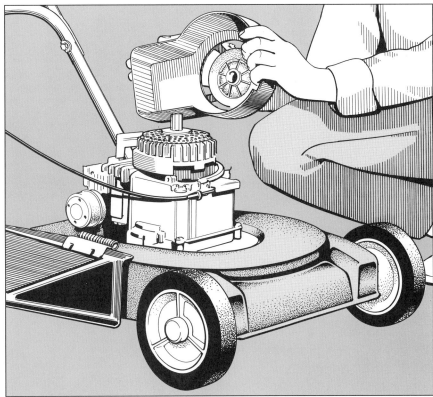

1 To reach the starter mechanism on Briggs & Stratton engines, first remove the throttle cable clip on the housing. Then, ground the spark plug and remove the housing.

the pull-rope handle and tie it securely to the rope's retaining pin.

Tecumseh pull-starters

Many Tecumseh engines feature a starter that's similar to the type found on Briggs & Stratton engines. You can use the above procedure as a guide for replacing the rope on these models.

Other Tecumseh engines make use of side-mounted, vertical-pull starters. The following instructions describe the procedure for the most common side-mounted starters manufactured over the past 8 to 10 years.

Ground the spark plug cable using the same method described for the Briggs & Stratton engine—first disconnect the spark plug cable from the plug and then use a jumper cable with alligator clips on each end to ground the cable to a metal part of the engine. Now you will be able to remove the gas tank by prying back the

retaining clips and sliding the tank upward. Unbolt the air filter and remove the housing (Fig. 6).

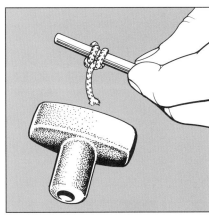

2 Cut the pull-rope near the handle, pry out the metal retaining pin that secures the rope. Untie and throw away the rope end.

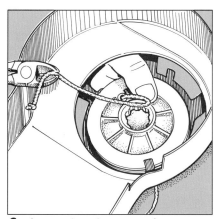

3 *After stretching the rope out from starter, hold spring in place. Pry out the end and cut off the knot. Remove the old rope.*

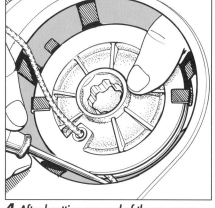

4 *After knotting one end of the new rope, hold pulley with spring tensioned and thread rope through hole in the pulley.*

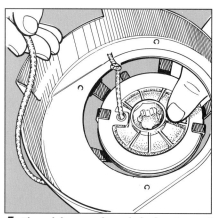

5 *Thread the rope through the housing and stretch it tight. Then, slowly allow the pulley to wind up and resecure the handle.*

You'll see the starter assembly mounted in a bracket that's secured to the engine side (Fig. 7). Check the bracket for a notch in the center of the upper edge. This notch facilitates removing the old rope without disassembling the starter. If your unit lacks this feature, simply shape an approx-imately ¼-in.-deep x ½-in.-wide notch by carefully breaking away the bracket material with a pair of pliers.

Next, pull up on the rope until the sta-ple that secures it to the pulley is centered in the notch. Hold the pulley in position and use a narrow-blade screwdriver to

pry the staple out (Fig. 8). Then, pull out the remaining rope. Hold on to the pul-ley when unwinding the rope. When it's free, wedge a large screwdriver between the bracket and pulley to hold the pulley in place with the spring tensioned.

Remove the rope from the handle by prying out the staple in the handle stem. Thread the new rope through the handle, tie a knot in the end and pull it tight to seat the rope in the handle (Fig. 9).

Feed the other end through the hous-ing. Turn the pulley as tight as it will go. Then, back it off while looking down into the pulley until you see the rope hole. It should be about 180° from the old staple position. Line this hole up with the notch and wedge the pulley in place. Thread the rope under the wire rope clip, through the hole and out the side of the pulley (Fig. 10). Tie a knot in the rope end, pull it tight into the pulley cavity and let the rope wind onto the pulley. Reconnect the spark plug and reassemble the lawn mow-er. Then test the job by starting the engine with the pull-rope.

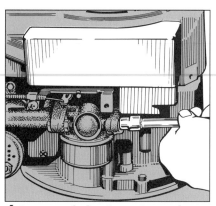

6 *To remove the housing on Tecumseh en-gines, first unbolt the air filter and slide off the gas tank. Then remove housing bolts.*

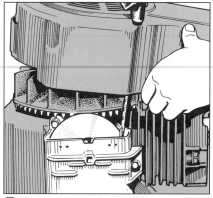

7 *Lift the housing off the engine, pull out rope and set housing aside. The starter assembly is mounted on the engine side.*

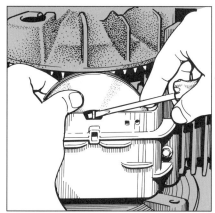

8 *Turn pulley until staple appears in notch on mounting bracket. Remove staple with narrow-tip screwdriver or awl.*

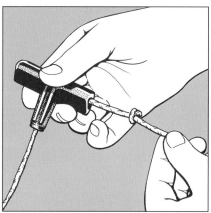

9 *After removing old rope from the handle, thread new rope through, knot the end and pull tight to seat rope in handle.*

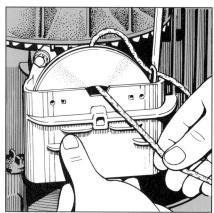

10 *With spring tensioned, pass rope through housing, under clip and through hole in pulley. Knot end and pull snugly.*

How to paint
A HOUSE EXTERIOR

Degree of difficulty: Hard   Estimated time: 20 hours   Average cost of materials: $350

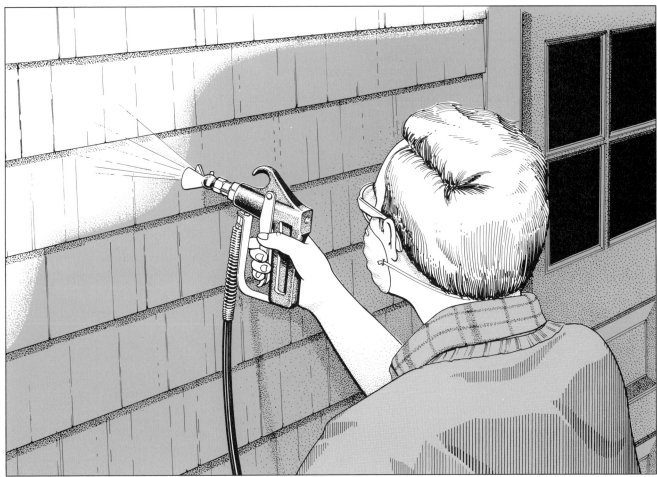

An airless paint sprayer is a great time-saver when it comes to exterior painting. One can be rented, but if you plan to use the sprayer for other projects in the future, it may be worthwhile to purchase your own. Work on calm days and cover unprotected surfaces.

E xterior painting has always been a chore that most people dread. The problem with it has very little to do with painting itself. The simple application of the paint is pretty easy. But the preparation is an entirely different matter. It takes a lot of time, energy and a willingness to work off ladders for long periods. And, it often involves battles with wasps, bees and other annoying creatures. In the hopes of finding new ways to make this necessary chore easier, we contacted the folks at the Paint Quality Institute and asked their advice about proper preparation techniques and the best kind of paint for the job at hand.

Because our building was in such bad shape, we knew that hand scraping would be a tremendous chore. And, we didn't want to use heat removal techniques

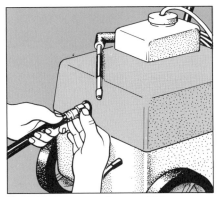

1 Electric power washer uses high-pressure stream of water to remove paint. Attach to water supply with garden hose.

2 Washer units require ground-fault circuit interrupters. This model has handy TEST and RESET buttons built into electrical cord.

205

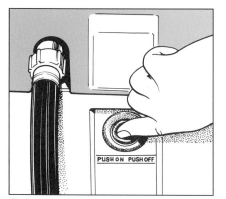

3 *Power switch is usually located directly on washer. Hold spray wand in safe direction every time power switch is turned on.*

4 *Beginning at top of building, wash all the siding and trim with power washer. Keep wand moving to prevent surface damage.*

5 *Once house is washed, make necessary repairs, especially to windows. If old glazing putty is loose, remove it with knife.*

because of the fire danger. So we decided to go the power route. To this end, we obtained a power washer and a clever grinder designed specifically for removing paint. Then we threw in a simple palm sander and a portable drill outfitted with an assortment of abrasive wheels. We rounded out our tool selection with a couple of hand scrapers, wire brushes, sandpaper galore and an airless power painter for spraying the building once the

surface was prepared. With all these tools ready, the input of the Paint Quality Institute in mind, a generous supply of 100 percent acrylic primer and paint on hand, and a can of insecticide spray within easy reach, we flew into action.

The drawings here show the sequence that seemed to work best for us. We were, however, working on grooved cedar shingles. If you have clapboard, board-and-batten or other types of smooth siding,

your work should be easier and go faster. As always, there are no good substitutes for patience and hard work, but power equipment like the units featured here can make the job of exterior painting considerably more enjoyable.

Power washer
It's always a good idea to wash the exterior of a building before painting to remove any residue that may have col-

6 *On broken windows, remove any glass fragments and old putty. Then coat sash— where glass will go—with mineral spirits.*

7 *Roll out thin rope of glazing putty, then press into sash. Mineral spirits keep wood moist so putty won't dry out too quickly.*

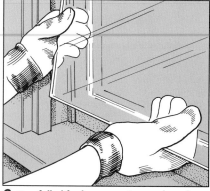

8 *Carefully lift glass pane into sash and press into putty. Make sure putty seals entire perimeter of back side of glass.*

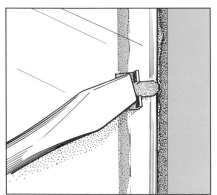

9 *Install glazing points every 10 or 12 in. around perimeter of glass. To install this type of point, use a flat-blade screwdriver.*

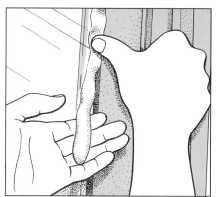

10 *For outside perimeter of glass, roll out thicker rope and press into corner between sash and glass. Slightly overfill corner.*

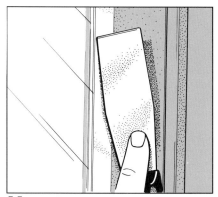

11 *Smooth putty in place using stiff putty knife. Dip knife in mineral spirits before each stroke to get smoothest finish.*

12 *Once windows are repaired, return to siding and hand scrape any loose paint that was too stubborn for power washer.*

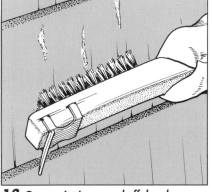

13 *Once paint is scraped off, brush exposed areas with wire brush. Brushing loosens paint that scraper blade missed.*

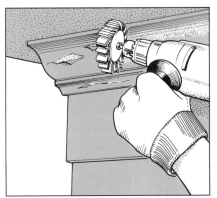

14 *On curved surfaces, flat scraper blade doesn't work well. Drill-mounted abrasive flap sander works better.*

lected on the surface. Of course you can do this by hand. But a power washer will not only clean the surface, it can also remove a great deal of loose, chipped paint in the process.

For this job we used a power washer. The hookup was straightforward and the operation simple. You just attach a garden hose to one end of the unit, plug in the ground-fault protected power cord and turn on the machine. It immediately starts

pumping a stream of water that you direct with a hand-held wand. Generally speaking, power washers are rated by the pressure they deliver. The model used here was listed at 750 psi, which seemed to be the minimum pressure you'd want to handle any paint removal chores. Most experts suggest a washer in the 900- to 1,200-psi range to remove paint, but we opted for less pressure because cedar shingles are so soft.

Though power washers are easily rented, if you'd like to have one for other chores around the house, a painting project could help you amortize the cost of buying instead of renting. The particular unit we used worked very well and sells for about $450.

Grinder
Even though our power washer did remove the bulk of the loose paint, some

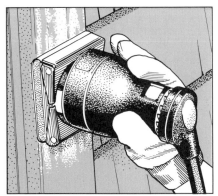

15 *On surfaces where lots of paint has been removed and exposed wood is rough, sand surface smooth with palm sander.*

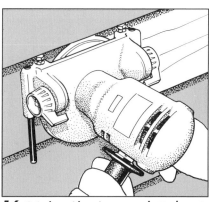

16 *Grinder with paint removal attachment was designed primarily for clapboards but is great on flat surfaces, too.*

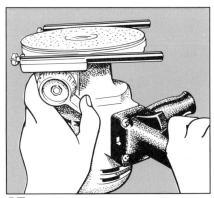

17 *Grinder removes paint smoothly because one side of disc is higher. Side knobs raise and lower side support bars.*

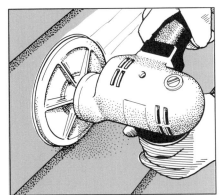

18 *With practice and care, tool can be used without guard. This is especially helpful on large flat surfaces like door panels.*

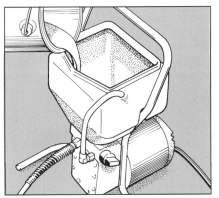

19 *For big jobs, reservoir on power unit is more convenient. It holds more paint and reduces weight at spray head.*

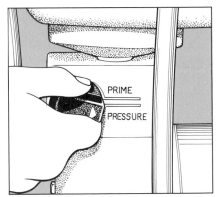

20 *Painter must be primed before work begins. Once priming is complete, pressure is increased for spraying.*

207

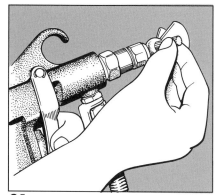

21 *Turn adjusting screw on spray head to select spray pattern. For best results, spray pattern should be no more than 10 in.*

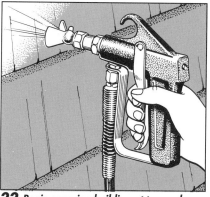

22 *Begin spraying building at top and moving across and down. Keep spray head perpendicular to surface at all times.*

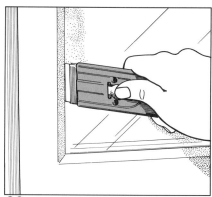

23 *After primer is sprayed, scrape off any splatters from glass before they dry completely. If dry, they're harder to remove.*

blistered and cracked areas remained—especially on flat surfaces—that weren't loose enough to wash off. On these areas we used a grinder with a paint remover attachment. This attachment consists of a rubber-faced metal backer disc surrounded by a sturdy guard. The backer disc accepts flat aluminum abrasive discs that have carbide chips bonded to the surface. These discs come in coarse, medium and fine grits, and though they cost about $6 each, in the long run they are much cheaper to use than standard abrasive discs.

The guard features two adjustable support bars, one on each side of the disc. By setting one bar lower than the other, the leading edge of the disc rides above the paint, while the following edge grinds off the paint. The tool does take some getting used to. But once we mastered it, it removed paint beautifully and left a very smooth surface. The paint does tend to clog the abrasive. But we found that by using two discs, we could put the clogged one in some paint remover while we were using the other. By the time the second one was clogged, the first was ready to use again.

This tool is designed primarily to remove paint from clapboards, so we tried it on another building. The results were excellent. As you'll see in Fig. 18, we even removed the guard and used the tool free-hand. This allows you to work on flat but narrow surfaces where the guard would get in the way. The grinder with the paint removal attachment lists for about $340 but can usually be purchased for much less from mail-order tool discounters. If you do try out this tool, remember to always wear eye protection, a dust mask and heavy gloves when grinding off paint.

Power painter
The last major piece of power equipment we used had nothing at all to do with preparation. It was an airless paint spray system. Though our building was small, it was in such bad shape that it needed four coats of paint: two coats of primer and two top coats. Spraying all this paint certainly made the job go faster, and it required practically no effort, though it did demand a couple of calm days.

An airless sprayer, as its name suggests, doesn't use compressed air to transport the paint. Instead, it simply forces the

paint through a nozzle which atomizes it. Generally speaking, airless sprayers come in two different configurations. The first is the one-piece version that has the power unit, paint reservoir and spray head all together. These painters tend to be heavy and somewhat difficult to maneuver. The second type is designed like the one shown here. The spray head is separate from the power unit and paint reservoir—it's simply connected by a length of hose. In this design, the spray head is much lighter and more maneuverable, and the paint reservoir usually has a much larger capacity. This unit surprisingly easy to use. The spray pattern was very controllable, and all the coats were uniform. One shortcoming with any spray painter is spraying too much and having paint fall on something you don't want painted, for example your neighbor's house or car. For this reason, always work on a calm day and use lots of drop cloths.

Like power washers, power painters can be rented. But you may want to purchase one if you have a large house to paint. It, and others like it, costs about $350 and comes with a roller attachment for interior painting.

24 *Fill cracks in siding, trim, doors and windows with caulk. For best results, apply after surface is primed, but before painting.*

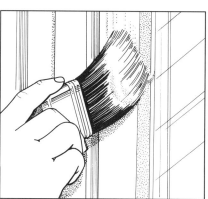

25 *Begin painting windows at sash. Be sure to completely cover new glazing putty, allowing paint just onto glass.*

26 *Once sash is painted, coat jamb and window trim. After all windows, doors and trim are painted, spray rest of siding.*

How to maintain your CHAIN SAW

Degree of difficulty: Easy   Estimated time: 2 hours   Average cost of materials: $15

Follow the general directions given here for properly maintaining and cleaning your chain saw. You can also apply the same directions to maintain other two-cycle machines. As a safety precaution, always keep an appropriately rated fire extinguisher on hand when working around gasoline.

There was a time when chain saws were the province of professional loggers, tree surgeons and landscape architects. But over the past few years, millions have been sold to average consumers who quickly appreciated the usefulness of these tools. Not only are they indispensable for cutting firewood, but they are also the tool of choice for routine tree pruning and cleaning up storm-damaged limbs. Like any piece of power equipment, however, these saws must be well-maintained to work properly and safely. So, to help you get your saw in shape for spring cleanup, we contacted several experts to outline some basic maintenance procedures for chain saws.

These are some general guidelines, but be sure to consult the owner's manual for specific directions on maintaining, cleaning and sharpening the chain blades.

First things first

Depending on the particular saw, the tool may come equipped with a chain brake, automatic chain oiler and other special features.

Because of these differences, you should also read your owner's manual carefully to find out what special features your saw has; the manual will also include a concise troubleshooting guide that will help you diagnose poor performance problems. If your manual has been misplaced, you can get another copy from the manufacturer or where the chain saw was purchased originally. Also keep in mind that even though the repairs described here deal

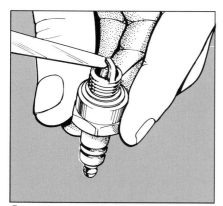

1 *Remove spark plug and clean thoroughly. Check for correct gap with gauge and adjust if necessary. Replace plug yearly.*

only with chain saws, most of the techniques apply to any small two-cycle engine, including those found on string trimmers, leaf blowers, garden sprayers, and even some lawn mowers and snowblowers.

All chain saws are basically similar. They comprise a small two-cycle engine with a long, round-nose bar attached to the side. The cutting chain slides along a groove in the bar and is driven by a sprocket which comes off the engine crankshaft.

Spark plug

Begin by draining the oil and gas fuel mixture from the fuel tank, or by running the engine until the tank is dry. If your saw has been sitting for a couple of months, it's a good idea to flush the empty tank with a little fresh gas to remove any oil sediment.

Next, remove the spark plug and check its electrodes for dirt, oil and corrosion. A fouled plug indicates several possible problems: improper carburetor adjustments, the wrong gas-to-oil fuel mixture and, in some cases, excessive flooding when starting the engine.

We'll talk about carburetor adjustments later, but the other two problems are easy to correct. Simply follow the manufacturer's fuel mixture requirements as well as the directions for the proper starting technique.

If your plug is fouled, clean it thoroughly with emery paper and shake out or blow away any debris. It's also a good idea to wash the plug in gas, using an old toothbrush. After the plug is dry, closely inspect the center and curved electrode for pitting. If either is pitted or rounded over, file both until they are smooth and flat, then gap the plug to match manufacturer's specifications (Fig. 1).

Frequent users should install a new plug every 100 hours of engine use. A ball-

park figure for occasional users is to replace the plug every year.

Air filter

Your engine will only run well if the proper amount of fuel and air are mixed in the carburetor. Because of this, it's essential that you keep your air filter clean at all times.

To check your air filter, begin by brushing away dirt and debris from around the filter cover (Fig. 2). Then press the CHOKE button to close off the carburetor port. This will prevent any debris from falling into the carburetor when you remove the filter. (Note: On some saws, the choke is simply a flapper built into the carburetor cover. Once the cover is removed, the carburetor port is exposed. On such saws, be extremely careful when removing the cover to avoid debris falling into the port.) Remove the filter cover, take it out and brush clean (Fig. 3).

Wash the filter according to manufacturer's recommendations. You can use soap and water and blow dry the filter with compressed air. Some manufacturers suggest other solvents. No matter what your situation, replace the filter if it is torn or still dirty after cleaning it.

Fuel filter

The fuel filter is designed to keep debris from entering the fuel line and fouling

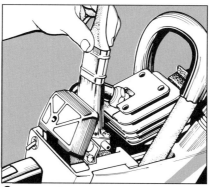

2 *Remove dust and dirt from around the carburetor and air filter. Use either a stiff paintbrush or a shop vacuum to do the job.*

the carburetor. On most saws it's located at the end of the fuel line, inside the fuel tank. To inspect this filter, fish it out of the tank using a wire coat hanger with a loop bent in the end (Fig. 4). Guide the wire into the fuel tank using a flashlight and hook it over the plastic fuel line. Gently pull the line until the filter pops out of the hole. If you pull too hard, you run the risk of tearing the fuel line.

Once the filter is out, check to see if it is clogged with debris. If it is, pull the filter off the end of the line and wash it with

3 *Remove the air filter and, again, brush off the debris. Then wash the filter with soap and water, rinse clean and let it dry.*

gas and a toothbrush, or blow it out with compressed air. If neither cleans the filter completely, get a new one.

Reinstall the filter on the end of the line and then push everything back into the fuel tank.

Make sure the filter goes to the bottom of the tank; otherwise, you won't utilize the complete fuel capacity.

Pull-rope starter

At least once a year it's a good idea to remove the starter housing assembly, even if the pull-rope has been working well (Fig. 5). This gives you the chance to clean the vent slots thoroughly and check for worn parts that may need replacement. If your pull-rope is broken, then follow the manufacturer's directions on how to replace it—different saws require different techniques and tools. If the starter itself is broken, take the saw to your dealer for repair.

Muffler and spark arrestor

The muffler has two basic purposes: to quiet engine sound and to direct harmful exhaust gases away from the user. If it is

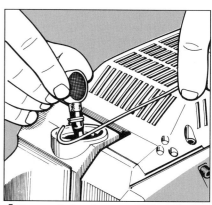

4 *Remove fuel tank cap and fish out fuel pickup line with a bent coat hanger. Make sure line's filter is clean. If not, replace it.*

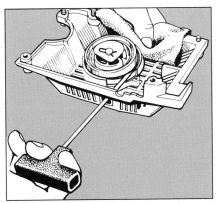

5 *Remove the starter housing assembly and brush debris from entire unit, particularly air vents. Inspect all parts for wear.*

loose and/or corroded, it will fail to do both jobs. So, it's a good idea to inspect it periodically.

To do this job, you first have to remove the covering panel that prevents you from touching the very hot muffler during operation. This is usually part of the chain sprocket housing. Then wiggle the muffler to make sure it's tight (Fig. 6). If it isn't, tighten the bolts to the torque specifications given in your owner's manual. If the muffler is corroded, replace it.

Depending on the age and make of your saw, it may not come equipped with a spark arrestor. This device is simply a fine metal screen that prevents red-hot exhaust particles from leaving the muffler and possibly causing a fire. For this reason, you are prohibited from using a chain saw to cut wood on most public lands unless your saw is equipped with an arrestor.

On the saw shown here, this screen was located just below the exhaust deflector fins. By unscrewing the fin plate (Fig. 7), the arrestor could be lifted out and washed with soapy water and a tooth-

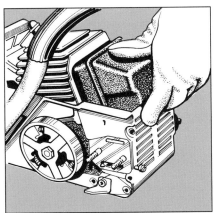

6 *Grasp the muffler assembly and wiggle to make sure it's not loose. Also check for rust. If muffler is damaged, replace it.*

brush. Compressed air also works well to clean this screen. Because the arrestor is exposed to such intense heat, holes are frequently burned in the screen. When this happens, the arrestor should be replaced. In any case, you should inspect the arrestor every time you use the saw to make sure it's in good shape.

On some saws, particularly older ones, this arrestor can be screwed to the inside of the muffler. In these cases the muffler has to be completely disassembled to reach it. Consult your owner's manual

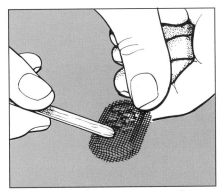

7 *Remove spark arrestor screen and remove debris with a brush. For stubborn spots scrape with small wood stick.*

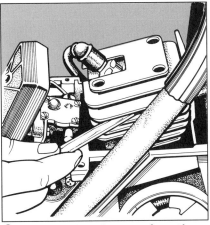

8 *Thoroughly clean the engine fins with a thin wood stick, followed by a stiff paintbrush. Be sure to vacuum up all the debris.*

for directions on how to carry out this more involved procedure. Otherwise, contact your dealer.

Now that the muffler and engine fins are exposed, brush away and vacuum up any debris (Fig. 8). Be especially careful to remove the debris from around the engine's cooling fins. Because the small engines on chain saws and other two-cycle machines are air-cooled, such debris may reduce the air allowed to circulate around the engine which, over time, can cause overheating and damage

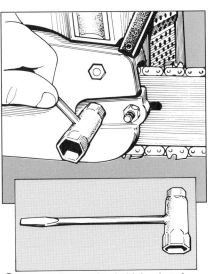

9 *Remove the nuts that hold the chain bar and sprocket housing using a socket wrench or tool (inset) supplied with saw.*

Chain bar

To free up the chain bar—and the chain for that matter—loosen the chain tensioning screw at the front of the saw. Then remove the sprocket housing on the side of the saw using either a socket wrench or the combination tool usually sold with the saw (Fig. 9). Once the chain is loose and the cover is off, lift the chain from the bar groove, and set it to one side. Then remove the bar (Fig. 10).

Thoroughly clean the debris from around the drive sprocket and clutch assembly. Compressed air works well for this. But if the wood chips and dust are caked on, a liberal dose of cleaner/ lubricant and a stiff toothbrush will do the trick. Wipe the saw dry with a rag and complete a visual check of the sprocket assembly. If you detect any worn parts, have them replaced.

Next, clamp the chain bar in a vise—preferably one with protected jaws—and

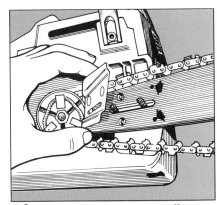

10 *Once the sprocket housing is off, remove the outer bar plate. Then lift chain off sprocket and remove chain bar.*

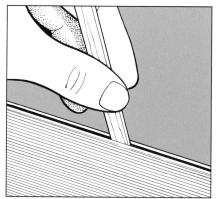

11 *Using a thin wood stick, clean the oil-soaked debris from chain groove on the bar. Use a small nail for stubborn spots.*

remove any dirt and debris from the bar groove. You can use a piece of scrap wood for this job, shaving the end until it slides easily in the groove (Fig. 11). Remember that the bar does wear unevenly—more stress is exerted on the cutting side. Because of this, manufacturers suggest that you turn the bar over before every heavy work session to equalize the wear.

Once the groove is free of debris, clean the oil holes on the side of the bar. These holes allow the chain oil to flow along the chain groove. If they are clogged, the oil won't be able to do its job and both the chain and bar will be short-lived.

Next, inspect the groove rails for wear. Over time, the movement of the chain will create small, metal burrs along these rails. File these surfaces flat and smooth. If the bar groove is distorted or bent, it's time to replace the bar.

Chain

After giving the chain a thorough cleaning with the solvent and a toothbrush, reinstall the bar, chain and sprocket housing. Then tighten the chain-tensioning

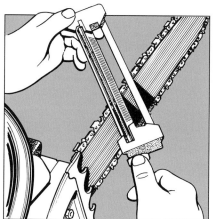

12 *Reinstall the bar, chain, plate and housing, then tighten chain. Sharpen teeth with a combination file guide.*

screw until the chain is nearly as tight as possible. This will keep the chain stable as you sharpen it.

The sharpening techniques required will depend on the type of chain that's on

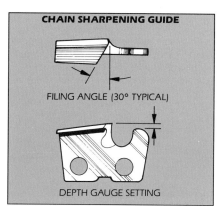

CHAIN SHARPENING GUIDE

FILING ANGLE (30° TYPICAL)

DEPTH GAUGE SETTING

13 *Sharpening angles vary depending on type of chain and manufacturer. The filing angle above is a general guideline.*

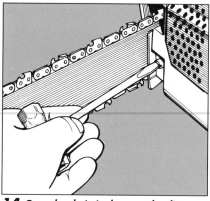

14 *Once the chain is sharpened, adjust tensioning screw with saw tool to match manufacturer's recommended tolerance.*

your saw. Consult your owner's manual for specific directions. However, most saws are sold with what is called a standard chain. This is made of cutting teeth joined by drive links that run in the bar groove. The cutting teeth have a top plate, side plate and depth gauge (sometimes called a raker). You must sharpen all three of these surfaces whenever the chain is dull.

Many people use a special round file for the top and side plates and a separate flat file for the depth gauge. (The manufacturer stipulates which files to use.) But a better idea—especially for the novice sharpener—is to use a combination filing guide like the one we show in Fig. 12. This tool files all three surfaces at once, maintaining the proper angle and the proper distance between the top of the teeth and the top of the depth gauge (Fig. 13). The trick in sharpening

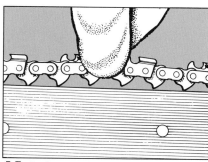

15 *The bottom of a properly adjusted chain should just clear the top edge of the bar. Always adjust the chain when it is cool.*

is to file all the teeth the same way. Start by finding any tooth that has a chip or nick and file until that fault is removed. Keep track of the number of file strokes required. Then proceed to file all the remaining teeth, using the same stroke and the same number of strokes. If your chain is in particularly rough shape, have it sharpened professionally or buy a new one to replace it.

Once the chain is sharp, readjust the chain tension to manufacturer's specifications (Figs. 14 and 15), lubricate the front chain sprocket on the guide bar (Fig. 16), and reinstall the spark plug. Fill the chain-oil reservoir, add the proper fuel mixture to the fuel tank, and give the cord a pull. Your chain saw should start right up without any hesitation.

If it doesn't, if it runs rough or if the chain moves even when the saw is idling, then you'll have to make adjustments to the carburetor. Because carburetor adjustments vary depending on the chain saw model, read your owner's manual carefully for specific instructions on what steps to take. As a general rule of thumb, you'll have to adjust both the low- and high-speed mixture needles first, followed by the idle screw once the saw is running.

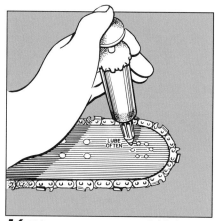

16 *Using a grease gun—available from your dealer—lubricate roller at nose of chain bar with automotive grease.*

212

SAFETY & TOOLS 6

How to work SAFELY

To accomplish do-it-yourself projects safely, follow a few simple guidelines.

Don't attempt to tackle a fire by yourself unless you discover it early—and then only with the proper equipment. Fire extinguishers are rated according to the types of fires they are designed to put out. Install Class ABC fire extinguishers in your home and workshop; they can be used to snuff out most small blazes.

Whether your project is a big one or a small one, the key to its success is planning and preparation. This is important not only because it helps save time, but also because it ensures that all work is done with the greatest attention to safety. By following a few simple, commonsense rules when working, you can fend off emergencies before they are allowed to happen.

When working with electricity, always shut off power to the circuit you are working on and check to make sure it has indeed been turned off. Plug power tools into circuits protected by ground-fault circuit interrupters (GFCIs).

Always keep a fully charged, appropriately rated fire extinguisher on hand if you are working with flammable materials. When in doubt about your ability to contain a fire, evacuate the house and call the fire department from a neighbor's telephone. In the event that you need medical help, have emergency telephone numbers posted near the telephone; program electronic phones with emergency numbers so that help can be summoned at the touch of a button.

Guard against home renovation products containing hazardous materials by wearing a respirator fitted with an appropriate vapor cartridge, a long-sleeve shirt, work gloves and eye protection.

When in doubt about your ability to carry out a repair safely, seek advice from a professional.

Shutting off electrical circuits

When working on house wiring and appliances, always make sure to shut off electricity at the main breaker panel or fuse box. For added safety, post a note on the panel informing others that you are working. Always use a voltage tester to make sure that the power is indeed off before proceeding with any electrical works. Follow the directions for using a voltage tester; they are outlined on Page 216.

Electrical safety features

Breakers or fuses also act as safety features in your home's electrical system. They keep temporary malfunctions from starting fires. A fuse can be blown or a breaker tripped when one of a few things happens. The most frequent cause of trouble is an overloaded circuit. When too many lights or appliances are plugged into a circuit, they call for more amperage than the circuit can deliver. This amperage overload causes the conductors or wires to heat up, which causes the fuses to blow. A short circuit will also cause a fuse to blow because of the greatly increased electrical charge it sends through the circuit. And finally, a fuse

will sometimes blow when it is loose in its socket.

Breakers have replaced fuses almost entirely in the last 30 years. Unlike a blown fuse, a tripped breaker does not have to be replaced every time it is tripped. When a short or overload trips a breaker, all you need to do is flip it back

on. Breakers differ in appearance and operation from one brand to the other. The main difference between the various types is that some breakers do not return to the off position when they are tripped. You will have to shut them all the way off before flipping them back on again.

Modern panels have renewable breakers. For increased safety, wear a rubber glove and use only one hand to shut off and reset breakers. Stand on a wooden board if area surrounding panel is wet.

Older panels use fuses to protect circuits. Blown fuses should always be replaced with identically rated ones. Follow the same safety advice for breakers; twist fuses counterclockwise to remove them.

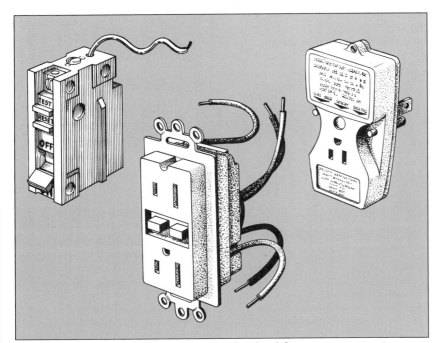

Install one of the GFCIs pictured above: A GFCI breaker (left) protects an entire circuit from inside the panel; a GFCI receptacle (center) protects the outlet it is in and all the outlets after it on a circuit; a plug-in GFCI (right) protects only the receptacle it is plugged into.

Installing GFCIs

If you touch an appliance or tool that has a loose positive wire, the resistance created there could send a shock through your body. When you are on wet ground or in a damp bathroom, your body improves as a conductor. Water allows you to conduct much more electricity. In damp situations, a ground fault can be fatal.

To protect yourself from possible electrical shock by power tools and appliances, install a ground-fault circuit interrupter (GFCI).

GFCIs work by monitoring the current in the black and white wires. As long as the current is equal in both wires, the circuit remains closed. As soon as an imbalance occurs, a GFCI shuts off power to the circuit or receptacle within $\frac{1}{40}$ of a second.

One of three devices will offer GFCI protection. The most versatile GFCI is contained in a breaker; everything on the circuit is protected. A second alternative is a GFCI receptacle. The third option is a GFCI receptacle adapter, which fits between the tool or appliance and the socket.

Testing for voltage

Safe electrical work depends on several things. First and foremost, all electrical work should be done with the power shut off. (Consult Page 215 for instructions on how to shut off electricity at a breaker panel or fuse box.) Next, test to make sure the power is indeed off.

Testing is accomplished with an inexpensive device called a voltage tester. It tells you if there is electricity in a cable, outlet or switch.

A voltage tester has no power of its own, but merely conducts voltage from one wire to another. As current passes through the wire, it lights a small neon bulb, which signals the presence—or absence—of electrical current.

Because a voltage tester can prevent you from accidentally touching a hot wire while you are working, you should buy one before you begin any project involving electricity. Voltage testers are also useful for checking proper grounding and for determining which wire in a cable is hot.

Guarding against electrical shock

Because testing for voltage is the preliminary step in arming yourself against accidental electrical shock, take extra care when handling outlets, ceiling fixtures and switches. After shutting off the power, carefully remove an electrical box, switch or fixture, taking care not to contact any wires in the process. Then, carefully unscrew the wire caps to expose the bare wire ends. Test for voltage, as described on this page. (If cutting off the circuit has left you in the dark, use a flashlight or attach a work light to an operating outlet with an extension cord.) Caution: When using a voltage tester, hold the tester's probes by their insulated ends to avoid contacting any metal. Once you've determined that the power is off, proceed with the project at hand.

In the unlikely event that someone should contact live electrical current, use a broomstick, chair, board or any poor conductor to push the victim away from the current. Do not attempt to free the person with your bare hands, as you may also get a severe electrical shock in the process. Once the victim has been freed, phone for medical assistance immediately; administer artificial respiration or cardiopulmonary resuscitation if you are trained to do so.

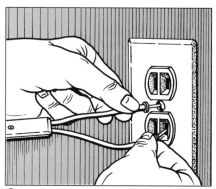

To determine if an outlet is hot, remove the cover plate, undo wire caps and touch one probe to the metal box or bare wire ground (inset). Then touch the other probe to each of the wire terminals. If the tester lights, switch off the correct circuit at the breaker panel or fuse box.

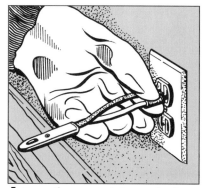

1 To see if a receptacle is energized, insert one probe of the tester into each plug slot. If the tester lights, the receptacle is energized. If not, power to the receptacle is off or the receptacle is defective. Also check for ground. To make sure power is off, test the other receptacles on the same circuit.

2 Next, check to see if the tester lights when you test between the hot (narrow) slot on the outlet and the cover plate grounding screw. Test between the wide slot and the screw. If the receptacle is a three-prong model, insert the ground probe into the U-shaped ground slot. If the tester lights, power to the circuit is reaching the outlet; shut off the power.

Dealing with hazardous products

Some products for home renovation and improvement projects pose special problems in terms of disposal and care. Triangular warning symbols are clues to how these products should be handled and stored. Pay particular attention to these symbols if children are present in your home. Should a child ingest a product, do not induce vomiting unless advised to do so by a qualified person. Immediately phone your local poison control center for advice on what steps to take in your situation; have the product's container with you when you call.

For maximum safety, store poisonous products in a locked cupboard out of the reach of children, and keep children away from the work site.

Some municipalities ban the disposal of household chemicals along with regular garbage. Consult your local authorities about toxic chemical pickup days and the regulations governing toxic waste disposal: You may have to take certain products to a special location. Never pour unused chemicals down a drain.

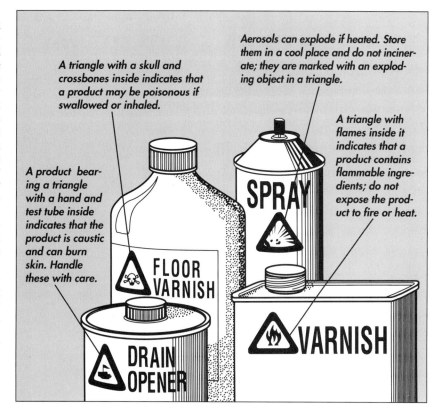

A triangle with a skull and crossbones inside indicates that a product may be poisonous if swallowed or inhaled.

Aerosols can explode if heated. Store them in a cool place and do not incinerate; they are marked with an exploding object in a triangle.

A triangle with flames inside it indicates that a product contains flammable ingredients; do not expose the product to fire or heat.

A product bearing a triangle with a hand and test tube inside indicates that the product is caustic and can burn skin. Handle these with care.

Protective equipment

Part of protecting oneself from the harmful by-products of home renovation and improvement involves wearing the appropriate protective gear and equipment. Whether the task at hand is stripping paint from woodwork, or sawing wood to rebuild a porch, it's important that fix-it-yourselfers take note of the dangers that go along with their projects. Label directions will advise of the hazards associated with a product's use, and users should heed this advice.

The degree of protection needed will depend on the job: Wear heavy work gloves and a long-sleeve shirt if you work with sharp sheet metal; a dust mask if you're working with plaster or other friable materials; and eye protection if you are working overhead. Take special precautions if you are using chemical paint strippers. In this case, you should fully protect yourself by wearing eye protection, a respirator equipped with chemical vapor cartridges, a long-sleeve shirt and rubber work gloves. Because paint strippers are extremely toxic, wearing all this gear is important.

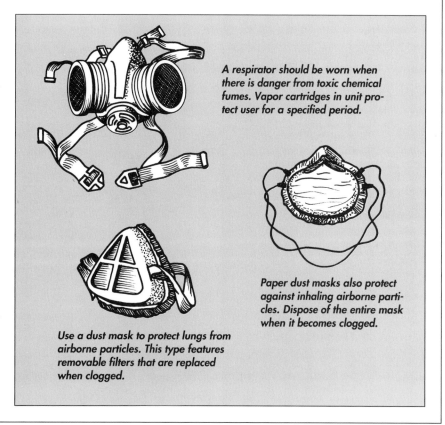

A respirator should be worn when there is danger from toxic chemical fumes. Vapor cartridges in unit protect user for a specified period.

Paper dust masks also protect against inhaling airborne particles. Dispose of the entire mask when it becomes clogged.

Use a dust mask to protect lungs from airborne particles. This type features removable filters that are replaced when clogged.

How to assemble
A BASIC TOOL KIT

Here is a list of some essential tools you'll want to purchase.

Moving into a new home may seem like a ticket to trouble-free living, but that's not always the case. A new home is like a new car, it sometimes takes a while to work the bugs out. And in the arena of the lowest bidder, even a custom home will harbor a few blemishes and oversights. Then too, neither you or your builder will foresee all the minor changes and upgrades you'll want after moving in. When the construction dust settles, chances are you'll still need a few tools.

With reasonable care most quality tools will last a lifetime. To ensure that this happens, follow a few simple guidelines when working:

Always use a tool for the job it was designed for, and never use a tool that you want to keep in good shape for a project that may bend, dull or otherwise impair its ability to work the way it should. When using tools around water, always dry them after the job is completed or at the end of the day. Apply a light coat of oil to metal tool parts with a rag. Remove any rust by rubbing the affected area with a piece of steel wool dipped in a solvent such as kerosene. Remove sawdust from motor vents on power tools.

You may not need or want all the tools we've compiled for the ideal home tool kit, but you'll probably find the need for most at one time or another. You might buy the basics now and add the specialty tools later when you need them. In any case, here's our selection, along with a few words on each tool's features and most likely uses.

(1) Claw hammer
A good finishing hammer will last a lifetime and help you through a wide variety of improvement and repair projects. A hammer with a steel or fiberglass handle will be the most durable, especially when pulling nails. We suggest one with a curved claw and a 1-lb. head. This combination will work well on rough carpentry as well as finish work. A quality hammer, in the $16 to $20 range, can mean the difference between driving nails and bending them.

(2) Handsaw
Next on your list will be a good crosscut saw. Handsaws cost a good deal less ($10

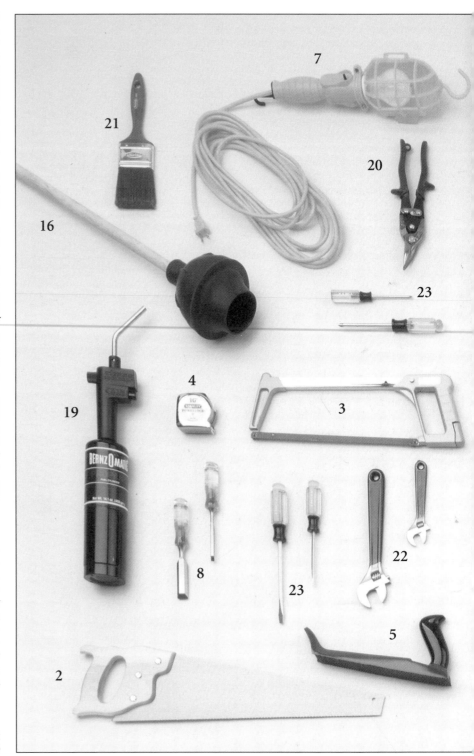

to $16) than powered saws and work just as well in limited-use situations. You'll also be able to reach into spaces too cramped for a circular saw. A 10-point crosscut saw, having ten teeth points per in., will serve you well around the house and yard. This saw will cut clean enough for most finish work and quickly enough for most rough work. If you'll be doing mostly rough carpentry, a 6- or 8-point saw will speed your work greatly.

(3) Hacksaw

There are many occasions when a hacksaw comes in handy, from cutting plumbing pipes to trimming downspouts and slicing through ceramic tile. The most important thing to look for is rigidity. A saw that flexes when used will bend or break the blade, or will simply refuse to cut straight. Most are adjustable and will accept 10- or 12-in. blades. Look for a brand that provides for two different blade installations, either straight or at a

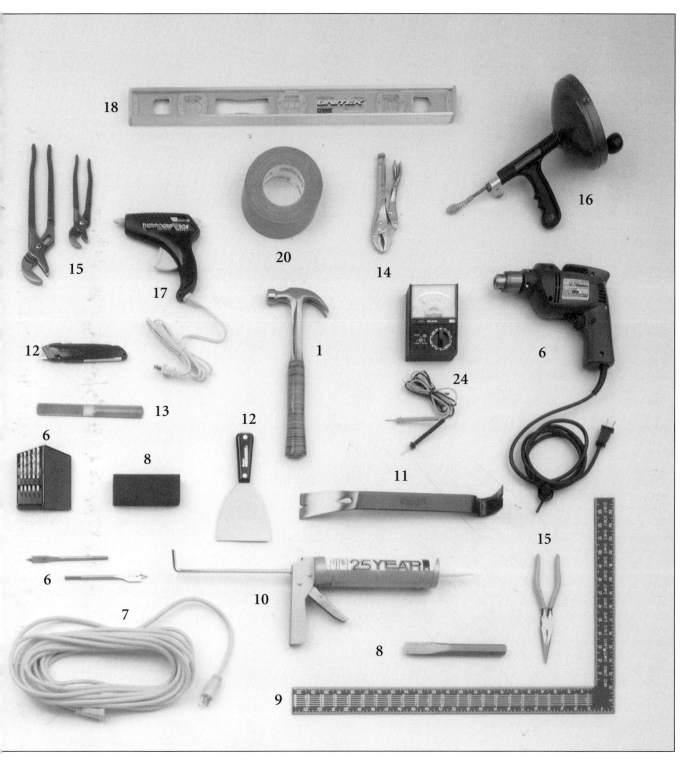

45° angle. A good quality hacksaw will cost between $12 and $16, a nominal fee for a very useful tool.

(4) Tape measure

The best advice we can give in selecting a tape measure is to avoid the short and narrow. For general household use, choose one that is at least ¾ in. wide and 15 ft. long, and clips to a belt or pocket. Beyond that, it's a matter of which style appeals to you most. And remember, a broken tape does not always mean a ruined tape measure. Replacement tapes are available for most brands. We chose a tape measure costing only $11, even though cheaper ones are available.

(5) Plane

For trimming marginal thicknesses of lumber, consider buying a plane. As planes require exact adjustment and dull easily when used by untrained hands, a Surform-type tool is a good household alternative. This type of plane has a replaceable, slotted blade that gouges out narrow ribbons of wood, plastic, vinyl and even aluminum, all without clogging. Unlike other planes, it will not yield the clean, hard-edged surface of a block plane, but it's a snap to use. We paid just under $12 for a 10-in. model.

(6) ⅜-inch drill

Another tool that will quickly earn its keep is a ⅜-in. drill. While cordless drills are ideal for the quick fix, a cord-type drill is more versatile. And because you won't be paying for a charger, you'll get more power per dollar invested. Look for one with a variable-speed, reversible motor capable of at least 2000 RPMs. The one we chose has 2.8 amps of power and offers an industry-standard 1-year warranty. We paid just under $70.

You'll also want a selection of drill bits and possibly a few specialty attachments. We chose a 13-piece, high-speed bit set with sizes graduating from ¹⁄₁₆- to ¼-in. Buying bits in a case makes selection easier and also reveals at a glance which sizes you'll need to replace.

In addition to the $16 set, we chose ½- and ¾-in. spade bits designed for boring larger holes in wood. Spade bits are reasonably priced, around $2.50 each, and are easily resharpened. A ⅜-in. drill also accepts a variety of bits and attachments such as a magnetized nut driver which drives self-tapping sheet-metal screws

(7) Extension cords and trouble lights

To keep your projects well powered and better lighted, you'll need a grounded extension cord and a trouble light. A drop cord in the 30- to 50-ft. category will serve most needs, but don't skimp on its wire size. A lightweight cord will allow too much voltage drop, which will in turn shorten the life of the tool or appliance it serves. Generally speaking, the longer the cord the heavier it will need to be.

We chose a grounded 30-ft. model with 16-gauge wire and a carrying capacity of 13 amps, which was priced at about $10.

As for trouble lights, look for the same features. If the light you fancy does not have a receptacle, an ungrounded cord will do. We paid just under $11 for a 25-ft. model with a plastic cage.

(8) Chisels and a sharpening stone

Every household should have a chisel or two for roughing out of wood or drywall that can't be reached with a larger, more precise tool. And as many of us can blunt the edges of chisels just by picking them up, you'll also want a double-sided (fine/course) sharpening stone. When used with honing oil, a sharpening stone will resharpen the edges of all but the most abused chisels and knives.

You'll need to decide which sizes best suit your purposes, but two will often do. We chose ¼- and ¾-in. chisels and a 5 x 2-in. combination stone. We paid $6 and $8 for the chisels and $12 for the sharpening stone.

And finally, you may want a cold chisel in your tool box for those materials not made of wood. A cold chisel can be used to chip concrete or split light-gauge metal. It's especially handy for cutting bricks, blocks and paving stones. We paid $6 for a hefty 1-in. model.

(9) Framing square

A framing square in the hands of a professional can work wonders, but even a beginner will find this a useful tool, if only as straight edge and angle finder. It can be used to check the squareness of a room before laying floor coverings or to ensure a square cut in plywood or dimensional lumber. You'll find them in steel and aluminum for around $10.

(10) Caulk gun

With everything from caulk and glue to grout and roofing tar packaged in tubes these days, a good caulk gun is a must. Expect to find two or three levels of quality in caulk guns. Go right past the bargain basket on your way to those in the $4- to $5-range. These mid-priced guns will accommodate all ¹⁄₁₀-gallon tubes and are sturdy enough for years of casual use.

(11) Pry bar

A pry bar is another useful tool, with more real-life uses than its manufacturers probably intended. A pry bar is designed to pry things apart, primarily pieces of wood. It is equipped with beveled nail claws at each end and has a curved shank ending in a sharp right-angle. When a block of wood is placed under one end, it makes a great lever and fulcrum. Invest $8 or $9 in one of these and you're just about guaranteed that you'll find a way to use it.

(12) Knives

Everyone is familiar with the uses of a putty knife, but when you head out to buy one, consider up-sizing to a 4-in. drywall knife for greater versatility. A flexible drywall knife can be used to apply spackling, scrape paint, strip furniture or press wallpaper into corners. Make sure that the model you choose has a chrome plated blade to resist corrosive drywall compounds. Beyond that, the choice is yours. We paid $8 for ours.

You'll also want a sturdy utility knife for cutting open cartons, trimming wallpaper and floor coverings, and for a dozen other chores. We suggest a knife with a retractable blade for easier and safer storage. You'll find plenty of good utility knives in the $5- to $7-category.

(13) Four-in-one rasp/file

You might also consider purchasing a combination wood rasp and file for your tool kit. With both a course and fine rasp, as well as a course and fine file on each tool, you'll be able to shape wood and sharpen garden tools whenever the need arises, and for under $9.

(14) Locking pliers

Locking pliers first became popular in shipyards during WWII. Before long they found their way into just about every mechanic's tool box and have lately turned up in a good many kitchen drawers as well. This tool is so popular because it can do so much. It's a plier, a makeshift wrench, a wire cutter and a sturdy clamp, which is about all you can ask of a tool costing between $10 and $12.

(15) Slip-jaw and needle-nose pliers

Slip-jaw pliers make a good choice because the jaws are able to expand to meet the job requirements. Their offset jaw configuration also provides a little more leverage than standard pliers. We decided on two sizes, a 6½- and a 10-in. model. The smaller pliers are good for small household projects, while the larger version will easily handle the chrome or plastic trap nuts on plumbing fixtures. With new home construction including almost all plastic pipes and fittings, this size makes a good substitute for a standard pipe wrench. We paid $9 for the smaller pliers and $11 for the larger ones. The 8-in. needle-nose pliers shown here have a long reach for getting into cramped spaces, which is where needle-nose pliers work best. This one also has a wire cutter built into the jaws. Expect good needle-nose pliers to cost between $8 and $9.

(16) Drain auger and plunger

There's a perverse physical law that has drains clogging only when plumbers and drain services are hard to reach, and if you are lucky enough to find one that will answer your call for help quickly, the job will likely be frightfully expensive. Drain clogs like holidays best.

For those times and others, plan ahead and invest in an inexpensive drain auger. The one shown here costs a mere $15, (roughly half that of a daytime service call) and will work in most situations. Avoid the simple, bare-cable type augers, they won't give enough cranking power in problem situations.

A plunger is the other half of the clogged drain solution. Most clogs can be broken free with a good plunger, almost to the complete exclusion of caustic chemicals. Look for one that has a large cup with a folding funnel. With the funnel folded in, this plunger will work well on sinks and tubs. Folded out, it's perfect for toilet clogs, and all for a mere $5. Avoid purchasing smaller plungers. While they're easy to store, you'll get little clog-busting force out of them.

In addition to these tools, you may also want to include a pipe wrench to round out your plumbing tool needs and forestall other difficulties later.

(17) Hot glue gun

Hot glue guns used to be hobby tools, but more and more of us are finding them useful around the house. They work especially well in repairing small fittings on toys and other household items, especially plastics. Best of all, hot glue sets as soon as it cools, which can speed things up substantially. You'll find inexpensive versions that are fed simply by pushing the glue stick through the gun. Others, such as the one shown here, feature a trigger-feed mechanism that offers better control when applying the glue. Expect to pay between $17 and $19 for a trigger-fed model.

(18) Level

A good 2-ft. level is another tool you'll find yourself using over and over again. It can level picture frames, start wallpaper, measure short items, level appliances and provide a straight edge for a knife or pencil. You'll find them made of steel, aluminum, plastic and wood. The metal

versions offer the most versatility and strength for the money, which in this case, was just under $14.

(19) Propane torch

When making plumbing improvements, a propane torch will put the most distance between you and a professional plumber. As a skill, soldering is largely overrated. But you will need a torch. You'll find two varieties in home centers. One will require that you light it with a striker or match. The other is self starting. We chose the substantially more expensive model simply because the self-starting feature is so handy. Just turn it on and pull the trigger for a clean blue flame. The price of this self starter was just under $28. Purchase a small tin of flux and a roll of lead-free solder along with the torch. (The EPA has prohibited the use of high-lead solders in plumbing since 1986). Many torches come with soldering instructions. Read the instructions and practice with a few fittings and some copper pipe. If you buy a self-cleaning flux, you won't even need to sand the pipe and fittings.

(20) Tin snips

Tin snips may seem at the outer edge of household tool selection, but when you need them there's no substitute. Try cutting an extra heat register in an unfinished basement without them. If the need arises, choose a pair designed to cut along a straight line. They can be made to cut wide, sweeping curves as well. Our selection cost $17.

While you're at it, buy a roll of quality duct tape. You may never need it for ductwork, but you'll find a use for it just about everywhere else. Expect to pay $5 to $6 for a 2-in. roll that is 60 yards long.

(21) Paintbrushes

When it comes to paintbrushes, don't skimp. Cheap throw-aways have a way of finding their own revenge. The material your brush is made from should be determined by your choice of paint. A brush with polyester or nylon bristles is suitable for latex or oil paint.

If you're going to buy one brush, make it polyester. Brushes made from hog bristle are best used with oil paints and get limp when used with latex paint. Good quality bristle brushes are expensive. Don't buy inexpensive bristle brushes, they lose their bristles. For a quick touch-up, use a small, inexpensive foam brush. Don't load it with too much paint; these brushes have a habit of dripping.

Consider brush shape when you're buying supplies. Brushes are available with tapered or straight bristles. The

straight-cuts work best on large areas, while the tapered versions work better as trim brushes. You may need both, but a straight bristle brush is a good start.

(22) Adjustable wrenches

We recommend two adjustable wrenches for projects around the house and garage. A 6-in. wrench will work well in tightening furniture bolts, toilet bolts, appliance leveling legs and the like. A 10-in. spanner will handle many plumbing repairs and do double duty in automotive work. Adjustable wrenches are available at several price levels. Avoid the low-end imports like the plague; mid-priced versions should serve you quite well for many years.

(23) Screwdrivers

Screwdrivers are typically the most abused tools going. As such, steer clear of bargain-priced screwdrivers. Look for handles that are large enough to be comfortable and shanks that are long enough to let you see your work. The better brands will have hardened steel tips and may be magnetized. We recommend two Phillips-head and two slotted-head screwdrivers in small and medium sizes. The combination will cost between $10 and $12.

(24) Ohmmeter

An ohmmeter is a good choice if you plan to handle your own electrical problems. With it, you'll be able to test for voltage, continuity and ohm levels. It can be used for checking out your home's electrical system, both wiring and devices, as well as the appliances within your home. An ohmmeter will tell you if a switch is defective (by checking continuity), or if the problem lies elsewhere. Simple ohmmeters start at around $25. (Consult Page 66 for instructions on how to use an ohmmeter to test appliances.)

In addition to an ohmmeter, you'll also want to have on hand several other tools when undertaking electrical work.

A voltage tester consists of two probes joined by a tiny neon light. It is commonly used to determine whether power is present in a set of wires or a receptacle. Also purchase a continuity tester, which will help you in testing if a switch or circuit is in operating condition. A continuity tester differs from a voltage tester in that it has a power source—a small battery. When the alligator clip at one end of the tester is touched to the probe at the other end, a circuit is completed and the light within the tester lights up in the handle. In like fashion, any device placed between the clip and probe will will complete the circuit if it is in operating order.

INDEX

SOURCES

You may want to contact one of the professional
associations or organizations listed below for information.
They may also be helpful in answering questions you might
have about standards and business practices.

American Home Lighting Institute
435 N. Michigan Ave., Suite 1717
Chicago, Ill. 60611
(312) 644-0828

American Institute of Architects
1735 New York Ave., N.W.
Washington, D.C. 20006
(202) 626-7300

American Society of Interior Designers
608 Massachusetts Ave., N.E.,
Washington, D.C. 20002
(202) 546-3480

Asbestos Information Association
1745 Jefferson Davis Hwy., Suite 509
Arlington, Va. 22202
(703) 979-1150

Association of Home
Appliance Manufacturers
20 N. Wacker Dr.
Chicago, Ill. 60606
(312) 984-5800

Floor Covering Installation Contractors
Association
P.O. Box 948
Dalton, Ga. 30720
(404) 226-5488

Independent Electrical Contractors
317 S. Patrick St.
Alexandria, Va. 22314
(703) 549-7351

International Association
of Lighting Designers
30 W. 22nd St., 4th Floor,
New York, N.Y. 10010
(212) 206-1281

National Association of Asbestos
Abatement Contractors
Box 477,
Lawrence, Kan. 66044
(913) 749-4032

National Association of Home Builders
15th and M Sts., N.W.
Washington, D.C. 20005
(202) 822-0200

National Association of Plumbing,
Heating & Cooling Contractors
P.O. Box 6808
180 S. Washington St.
Falls Church, Va. 22046
(703) 237-8100

National Association of the
Remodeling Industry
1901 N. Moore St., Suite 808
Arlington, Va. 22209
(703) 276-7600

Society of Certified Kitchen Designers
687 Willow Grove St.
Hackettstown, N.J. 07840
(201) 852-0033

The following persons assisted in the preparation of this book:

Dominique Gagné, Fiona Gilsenan, Christine M. Jacobs, Solange Laberge,
Julie Leger, Michael MacDonald, Gérard Mariscalchi, Heather Mills, Brian Parsons,
Jean-Luc Roy, Sandra Silbermintz, Michelle Turbide, Natalie Watanabe.

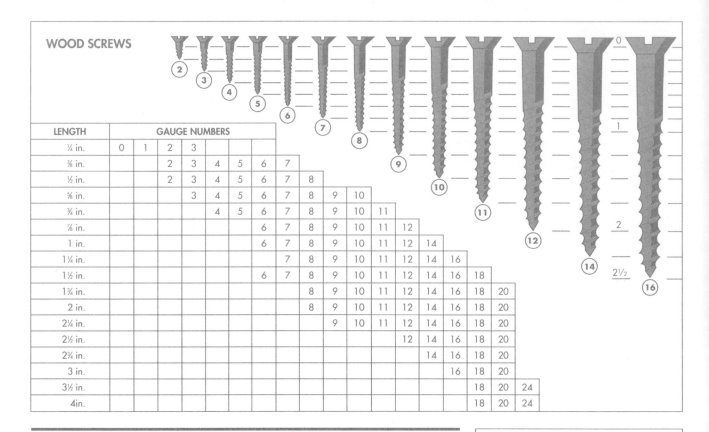

WOOD SCREWS

LENGTH	GAUGE NUMBERS																	
¼ in.	0	1	2	3														
⅜ in.			2	3	4	5	6	7										
½ in.			2	3	4	5	6	7	8									
⅝ in.				3	4	5	6	7	8	9	10							
¾ in.					4	5	6	7	8	9	10	11						
⅞ in.							6	7	8	9	10	11	12					
1 in.							6	7	8	9	10	11	12	14				
1¼ in.								7	8	9	10	11	12	14	16			
1½ in.							6	7	8	9	10	11	12	14	16	18		
1¾ in.									8	9	10	11	12	14	16	18	20	
2 in.									8	9	10	11	12	14	16	18	20	
2¼ in.										9	10	11	12	14	16	18	20	
2½ in.													12	14	16	18	20	
2¾ in.														14	16	18	20	
3 in.															16	18	20	
3½ in.																18	20	24
4in.																18	20	24

SOFTWOOD

NOMINAL (INCHES)	DRY	GREEN
1x2	¾x1½	25/32x1⁹/16
1x3	¾x2½	25/32x2⁹/16
1x4	¾x3½	25/32x3⁹/16
1x5	¾x4½	25/32x4⁹/16
1x6	¾x5½	25/32x5⁵/8
1x8	¾x7¼	25/32x7½
1x10	¾x9¼	25/32x9½
1x12	¾x11¼	25/32x11½
2x2	1½x1½	1⁹/16x1⁹/16
2x3	1½x2½	1⁹/16x2⁹/16
2x4	1½x3½	1⁹/16x3⁹/16
2x6	1½x5½	1⁹/16x5⁵/8
2x8	1½x7¼	1⁹/16x7½
2x10	1½x9¼	1⁹/16x9½
2x12	1½x11¼	1⁹/16x11½
3x4	2½x3½	2⁹/16x3⁹/16
4x4	3½x3 ½	3⁹/16x3⁹/16
4x6	3½x5½	3⁹/16x5⁵/8
6x6	5½x5½	5⁵/8x5⁵/8
8x8	7¼x7¼	7½x7½

SAW CUTS

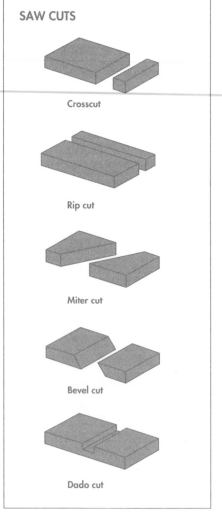

Crosscut

Rip cut

Miter cut

Bevel cut

Dado cut